THE EMERGENCE OF MAN

Books by John E. Pfeiffer

THE HUMAN BRAIN

CHANGING UNIVERSE

FROM GALAXIES TO MAN

THE THINKING MACHINE

THE SEARCH FOR EARLY MAN

THE CELL

THE EMERGENCE OF MAN

THE

EMERGENCE

OF MAN

SECOND EDITION

John E. Pfeiffer

Harper & Row, Publishers

New York, Evanston, San Francisco

London

to Naomi

Maps by Harry Scott
Diagrams by Rudolf Freund
Designed by Sidney Feinberg

Contents

"Taung baby"; evidence against the large-brain theory; the Pilt-down fraud; evolution and adjustment to change

Olduvai Gorge, one of the world's richest sources of knowledge about man's beginnings; the discovery of stone tools a million years "too soon"; the painstaking excavation and mapping of living floors; the study of living baboons as a guide to man's past; baboon troops and their responses to emergencies; early diseases

The discovery of Poor George in Africa and a relative, Lantian man, in China; discovery of Java man; Peking man on Dragon's Hill; the Vallonet and Escale caves; quantum evolution and increase in brain size, and its relation to meat eating

The unsolved problem of regular meat eating as part of the hominid way of life; scavenging and the shift from small to big game; the evolution of hunting tactics; the Torralba and Ambrona sites in Spain, and the mystery of the aligned elephant bones; Oldowan and Acheulian tool industries

Hunting as a factor in the evolution of larger brains; the relationship between larger brains and prolonged infant dependency; changes in male-female roles and increasing female dependency; female sexual receptivity and the prehistory of love; the male hunting society and homosexuality; incest taboos and the reduction of conflict; fire as a force for human change

Three lucky finds in Swanscombe village; a possible contemporary of Swanscombe man; the use of computers in investigating human origins; another gap in the record; the discovery of Neanderthal man and his rejection by outraged Victorians; the persistence of prejudice; the Le Moustier and Shanidar caves; burial and religious ritual

vals"; prolonged infant dependency and patterns of play; tool use among the wild apes; the roots of human restlessness; the need for long-term studies; taboo and hierarchy

Macaque monkeys raised as human infants; the laboratory study of infant monkeys and mother surrogates and the development of abnormal behavior; Washoe and her security blanket; an orangutan that makes stone tools; studies of Ceylon elephants, wild dogs and lions; electrode implantation as a research instrument

Exploitation of primitive men as subhuman; the rise in respect for the "uncivilized"; the study of the Australian aborigines, their work and hunting habits, their community, their songs and legends; their religious rituals; conservatism as a mode of adaptation

"Magic numbers" and social groups; recently vanished societies; living prehistory research among aboriginal hunting-gathering bands; study of living floors, fire sites, and bone deposits as indicators of hunting-gathering and cooking methods; food sharing; leisure; the rise of gambling; child dependency patterns; the religious dance and ritualistic trances

Participant observers' reenactment of prehistoric man's way of life; relearning of extinct skills in use of tools and survival techniques; necessary revision of old theories of hunting and farming; construction of artificial "prehistoric" sites for experimental and teaching purposes

The beginning of the "smile" before birth; the use of the eyes, then the social smile as a tracking, reaching, communicating method; its origins and prehistoric behavior; the evolutionary modification of the "grin" as cringing submissiveness; crying, maternal responsiveness and feeding schedules

The infant's discovery of language; his inherent sense of grammar; the nonverbal conversation of trained captive animals; tool using and children's play as steps toward prehistoric language, call systems and development of abstractions; invention of a "vocal" alphabet; the anatomy of learning

New studies of mothers and children, the significance of giving and the need for relaxing current tensions; play and art as sources of novelty; man's unique restlessness; crowding and intertroop conflicts among rhesus monkeys; war as the most human form of hunting; social interactions in cities; evolution and mental disease; Freud's concern with primate behavior and the irrational past

The probability that species outside the solar system confront problems like man's; the symbiosis between man and computer; computers as devices that speed the pace of evolution; the interaction of man and environment, an experiment in violence; an urban environment to meet the need for close human contact; the limited value of hierarchies in the modern world; conditions promoting aggression in young people; the future of home and family

Illustrations

DIAGRAMS

MAPS

Acknowledgments, Revised
and Enlarged Edition

Three years can be a very long time when things move as fast as
they have in the study of prehistory. The past three years have
seen a number of discoveries which are extending ideas about the
tensions that gave rise to modern man and affect him still. Beyond
that is an even more noteworthy change in approach, the increasingly successful introduction of evidence and hypothesis into
fields which have had more than their fair share of interminable
descriptions and pronouncements based on practically everything
but solid data.

The unfolding story of human evolution involves recent findings about the splitting up and drifting of continents, primates and
other new life forms spreading into new ecological niches, and
the appearance of men or near-men on African savannas a million
or more years earlier than we realized way back in 1970. More
advanced methods of studying flint tools and other artifacts
recovered from prehistoric sites are providing a clearer picture of
what our ancestors did and what they were incapable of doing.
An increasing respect for the abilities of all primates, nonhuman
as well as human, infants and children as well as adults, has come
from investigations of the behavior of living species.

These and other developments are all the more impressive
because they were achieved during a period of sharply reduced
support for scientific research. For the time being, at least, it

seems that the curtailment of learning has become a social necessity, a phenomenon of some evolutionary significance in itself. Nothing could point more forcefully to the need for a major change in what we consider important and unimportant.

Most of the investigators who helped with the first edition of this book deserve double thanks. I have seen them again, many on several occasions, in the course of trying to keep myself reasonably up to date on their results and plans. In addition I visited new sites and met for the first time with other investigators who have also helped me considerably by a generous sharing of their time and ideas. Specifically, I am indebted to Owen Aldis, Behavioral Science Research Fund, Menlo Park, California; Ofer Bar-Yosef, Hebrew University, Jerusalem; Charles Brain, Transvaal Museum, Pretoria, South Africa; Karl Butzer, University of Chicago; David Bygott, Cambridge University.

Also, Woodrow Denham, University of Washington; Patricia Draper, Harvard University; Eugene Giles, University of Illinois; Ian Glover, Institute of Archaeology, London; Annette Hamilton, University of Sydney; Henry Harpending, Yale University; June Helm, University of Iowa; Gordon Hewes, University of Colorado; Nancy Howell-Lee, Princeton University; Clifford Jolly, New York University; Rhys Jones, Australian National University, Canberra; Charles Keller, University of Illinois; Jack Kelso, University of Colorado; Melvin Konner, Harvard University; Ronald Lampert, Australian National University; Foss and Helen Leach, University of Otago, New Zealand; Richard Leakey, National Museums of Kenya; Vincent Maglio, Princeton University; Alan Mann, University of Pennsylvania; Robert Martin, University College, London; Patrick McGinnis, Cambridge University; John Mulvaney, Australian National University.

Also, Bryan Patterson, Harvard University; Nicolas Peterson, Australian National University; Anthony Pfeiffer, Rutgers University; Carmel Schrire, State University of New York, Binghamton; John Speth, Hunter College, New York; Alan Swedlund, Prescott College, Arizona; Alan Thorne, Australian National University; Robert Trivers, Harvard University; Peter White, University of Sydney; Edwin Wilmsen, University of Michigan; Martin Wobst, University of Massachusetts, Amherst; Richard Wrangham, Cambridge University; Richard Wright, University of Sydney; John Yellen, Harvard University.

Lisa Katz has contributed more than she realizes in handling, quietly and efficiently and with the soundest judgment throughout, a variety of editorial decisions. For continued support and coordination I am still, and again, grateful to Jeannette Hopkins.

Acknowledgments

A noteworthy sign of the times has been a growing interest in prehistory among people concerned predominantly with today's social and political problems, educators and social scientists as well as laymen. The success of efforts to modify human behavior depends on a fuller understanding of tensions and modes of thinking and acting which were established millions of years ago. The fact that much contemporary behavior has deep and ancient roots is not a cause for pessimism. It does not imply that change is impossible. But it does imply that changes had better be based on knowledge, on observation and analysis, rather than preconceived notions about human nature.

So the remote past takes on a wider scope and significance. More schools are offering fuller accounts of what happened in prehistory to more pupils and at an earlier age, often in the eighth and ninth grades, and high school and college students are exposed to knowledge once offered to graduate students only. Above all, many barriers are being broken down, notably the barriers which separate academic departments and which have done so much to frustrate the study of human evolution and human behavior. Findings about life in prehistoric times bear on problems in neurophysiology, psychology and psychiatry, animal behavior, and architecture—and research along these lines, in turn, bears on problems in archeology and anthropology.

In presenting and coordinating material from such diverse

sources, I have received help from many persons. I was fortunate in meeting Sherwood Washburn of the University of California, Berkeley, early in the preparation of this book. He indicated the nature of the work ahead in its full complexity, advised me in the planning of research and interviews, and has kept me posted on progress in his own research and in the research of his students and associates. Throughout the writing of the book Clark Howell of the University of Chicago has given most generously of his time, sharing his extensive knowledge and experience and evaluating controversial points in a field where controversies are common and evaluation is exceedingly tricky.

My debt to François Bordes, director of the Laboratory of Quaternary Geology and Prehistory of the University of Bordeaux, is particularly difficult to acknowledge. It is not only what I learned from him about excavating methods and the analysis of artifact assemblages of Neanderthal people, although that was considerable, but also what he conveyed simply by being himself—a feeling for the honesty, passion and imagination that go into creative research. For the sheer flow of stimulating ideas and a glimpse of future trends, I owe a great deal to Lewis Binford of the University of New Mexico, perhaps the most articulate and forceful representative of the new archeology, a discipline in which relatively sophisticated mathematical techniques will play a far larger role than they have in the past. At Harvard Hallam Movius contributed a great deal to the archeological sections of this book, conveying basic ideas as well as factual information.

I also received other kinds of help. A number of investigators contributed to my archeological education by permitting me to work with them on actual excavations, on the theory that first-hand experience is essential in writing about any area of research. My most extensive digging was done with François Bordes at Combe Grenal, André Leroi-Gourhan of the University of Paris at Arcy-sur-Cure in the Yonne Valley, and Cynthia Irwin-Williams of Eastern New Mexico University in the foothills of the Rockies near Denver. Mary Leakey and the late Louis Leakey of the Center for Prehistory and Archaeology in Nairobi, Kenya, served as my guides during a visit to the Olduvai Gorge.

Revil Mason and Phillip Tobias of the University of the Witwatersrand in Johannesburg, Ray Inskeep of the University of

Cape Town, and Ronald Singer of the University of Chicago showed me South African sites, including those of *Australopithecus* and several Bushman art caves. Desmond Clark, one of Washburn's colleagues at the University of California, led me through some formidable back country during a search for new sites in the Karonga district of northern Malawi; and J. Gonzales Echegaray and M. A. Garcia-Guinea of the Santander Museum of Prehistory and Archaeology conducted me through Altamira and other art caves in northern Spain. My observations of nonhuman primates in the wild included several weeks spent in East Africa with Irven DeVore of Harvard University following baboon troops in Nairobi Park and the Amboseli Game Reserve.

Checking for accuracy and proper emphasis is a major task in a book like this one which draws on so many areas of research. I am reasonably sure that most errors have been found and corrected, since every chapter has been read critically by four to eight persons. I take full responsibility, however, for any errors that remain. Bernard Campbell of Cambridge University and Clark Howell read the entire book, and their suggestions have done much to improve the text.

The following are among the other investigators who provided me with information during interviews, or read individual chapters or sections of chapters: Emiliano de Aguirre, Museo Nacional de Ciencias Naturales, Madrid; Mary Ainsworth, Johns Hopkins University; Anthony Ambrose, Behavior Development Research Unit, St. Mary's Hospital, London; Richard Andrew, Sussex University, Brighton, England; Alex Bavelas, University of British Columbia; Sally Binford, University of New Mexico; Joseph Birdsell, University of California at Los Angeles; John Bowlby, Tavistock Clinic, London; Robert Braidwood, University of Chicago; Harvey Bricker, Tulane University; Don Brothwell, British Museum of Natural History, London; John Calhoun, National Institute of Mental Health; Michael Chance, University of Birmingham, England; Glen Cole, Field Museum of Natural History, Chicago; Desmond Collins, University of London; Shirley Coryndon, British Museum of Natural History; Don Crabtree, Idaho State University Museum; Macdonald Critchley, National Hospital for Nervous Diseases, London; Raymond Dart, Institute for the Achievement of Human Potential, Philadelphia; John Eisenberg, National Zoological Park, Smithsonian Institution; Richard Estes, Harvard University; Brian Fagan, University of California, Santa Barbara; Willliam Farrand, University of Michigan; Kent Flannery, University of Michigan; Robin Fox, Rutgers University; Leslie Freeman, University of Chicago; Allen and Beatrice Gardner, University of Nevada; the late Dorothy Garrod, Villebois, Lavalette, France; Norman Geschwind, Harvard Medical School; Richard Gould, University of Hawaii.

Also David Hamburg, Stanford University Medical Center; Jack Harlan, University of Illinois; Richard Hay, University of California, Berkeley; Eric Higgs, Cambridge University, England; Robert Hinde, Cambridge University; Charles Hockett, Cornell University; Corinne and John Hutt, Park Hospital for Children, Oxford, England; Dell Hymes, University of Pennsylvania; Glynn Isaac, University of California, Berkeley; Arthur Jelinek, University of Arizona; Peter Jewell, University College, London; Nicholas Blurton Jones, Institute of Child Health, London; Sheldon Judson, Princeton University; William Kessen, Yale University; Richard Klein, University of Washington; Jane Lancaster, Rutgers University; Jane van Lawick-Goodall, Nairobi, Kenya; Richard Lee, University of Toronto; Eric Lenneberg, Cornell University Medical College, New York; Jerome Lettvin, Massachusetts Institute of Technology; Alvin Liberman, Haskins Laboratories, New York; William Longacre, University of Arizona; Henry de Lumley, University of Aix-Marseilles, France.

Also Paul MacLean, National Institute of Mental Health; Brian Maguire, University of the Witwatersrand, Johannesburg, South Africa; Peter Marler, Rockefeller University; John Mawby, Deep Springs College, California; Ernst Mayr, Harvard University; David McNeill, University of Chicago; George Miller, Rockefeller University; John Napier, Royal Free Hospital, London; Walle Nauta, Massachusetts Institute of Technology; Kenneth Oakley, British Museum of Natural History; Armand Oppenheimer, Columbia University; Jean Perrot, French Archaeological Mission, Jerusalem; David Pilbeam, Yale University; David Premack, University of California, Santa Barbara; Karl Pribram, Stanford University Medical Center; John Price, Maudsley Hospital, London; Vernon Reynolds, Oxford University, England; John Robinson, University of Wisconsin; Thelma Rowell,

Makerere University College, Kampala, Uganda; James Sackett, University of California at Los Angeles; George B. Schaller, New York Zoological Society; Ann and Gale Sieveking, British Museum; Elwyn Simons, Yale University; Philip Smith, University of Montreal; Ralph and Rose Solecki, Columbia University; Denise de Sonneville-Bordes, University of Bordeaux; Augustus Sordinas, Memphis State University; Axel Steensberg, University of Copenhagen; Theodor Strehlow, University of Adelaide, Australia; James Tanner, Institute of Child Health, London; Harold Thomas, Harvard University; Lionel Tiger, Rutgers University; Niko Tinbergen, Oxford University; Jorgen Troels-Smith, National Museum, Copenhagen; Peter Ucko, University College, London; John Waechter, Institute of Archaeology, London; Lawrence Wells, University of Cape Town, South Africa; John Witthoft, University of Pennsylvania; Henry Wright, University of Michigan; Vero Wynne-Edwards, University of Aberdeen, Scotland; J. Z. Young, University College, London; and Adrienne Zihlman, University of California, Santa Cruz.

The book would never have been completed without foundation support. I received travel grants from the Wenner-Gren Foundation for Anthropological Research for work in England and France, and from the National Institute of Mental Health for my first trip to Africa and the Olduvai Gorge. Special thanks are due to the Carnegie Corporation of New York for a "reflective year" grant which permitted me not only to make a second trip to Europe and Africa but also to take time out for organizing notes and writing.

Finally, I am most grateful to Jeannette Hopkins. She has improved the style and clarity of the writing, and I am fortunate to have had the benefit of her experience and creative editing. Susan Phelps helped considerably in suggesting, planning, and scheduling illustrations.

THE EMERGENCE OF MAN

■ The role of the savanna in prehistory; man's fifteen million years as a wild animal; the formation and persistence of archeological sites; the worldwide search for new sites; the element of chance and a lucky find; outline of the human story; the nature of human evolution; archeology and living prehistory

PROLOGUE

Techniques and Prospects
in the Search for Man

■ Parts of the past still endure in Africa, stretches of relic wilderness wide as inland seas. There is a hilltop in Kenya's Amboseli Game Reserve, for instance, where you look west across a savanna that extends bright and yellowish brown and bone-dry as far as the eye can see. This is usually an empty semidesert land with a few flat-topped fever trees and nothing abroad but dust devils, little whirlwinds which appear out of nowhere as brown spiral puffs and spin along for a distance and then vanish.

But a change takes place during certain dry-season days. The land becomes a great gathering place and the Amboseli hilltop becomes an observation post. It is a mass coming together of species, as if to a sanctuary or an Ark. Streams of animals move toward you, leading to a place not far from the foot of the hill, a large pool of stagnant green-gray water.

I remember watching the scene one glaring mid-July morning. A herd of zebras was already drinking at the edge of the pool and, not yet at the edge, wildebeests with curved horns and high shoulders moved slowly in a single file as if queuing up for their turn—and behind them more animals and still more until all I could make out were black specks in the far distance. Suddenly the zebras panicked, perhaps at a rustle in the low bushes growing nearby, and dashed from the pool. Then some of the wildebeests waded in and drank and left, and a herd of gazelles took

3

their place and left in another brief panic, and half a dozen ostriches and two troops of baboons and a lone giraffe, and on and on all day till sunset.

This is the part of Africa that is dying, the wild and primeval part, the Africa that once belonged to animals other than man. This Africa produces a strange sort of double vision or double perspective, a sense of being in two worlds. One world, of course, is completely alien. The savanna and all that is going on there are so different from anything the observer has known that it might just as well be happening on another planet. He is a spectator, uninvolved and uncommitted, trying to take it in.

The other world stirs an undercurrent of nostalgia, as a place known long ago and revisited. The observer responds to it for the same reason that he responds to all lonely places—during walks along beaches with no one in sight, camping out in a ravine in the desert, going off paved highways to dirt roads and tracks into the interior and then on into trackless areas, heading for lakes and canyons with waterfalls and no roads leading to them. Something is lost by going too long without such places. A feeling of belonging to the wilderness persists, and the feeling is strongest and most moving in Africa because that is the land of man's ancestors.

They lived on African savannas as animals among animals. They were once part of the great processions and approached water holes along ancient trails and waited their turn during times of thirst. They stepped aside unhurried and without looking up as wildebeests and zebras moved by, strode through herds of gazelles and chased the baboons, their closest relatives in the crowd. They came to drink and bolted in panic when there were sounds in the bushes. And sometimes near the edges of stagnant waters they became victims of lions and other predators.

Their way of life is not remote. "Hominids," or members of the family of man, have spent about 15 million years foraging on savannas and only a few thousand years living in cities. Man has been a wild animal for 15 million years and a domesticated animal, or rather a partly domesticated animal, for a fraction of one per cent of that span. In a basic sense, far from having arrived, he is just beginning to find his way, his place in the scheme of things.

This is the point of the statement that man is a missing link, the missing link between anthropoid apes and human beings. The assumption that he is already fully human is open to argument. It leads to questions which are difficult to answer, for example, the question of why he so frequently behaves in a fashion which he himself considers inhuman. Such contradictions emphasize the need for a shift in viewpoint. Man's sense of urgency about things to come demands a harder and longer look at the way things were. So he looks backward as well as forward.

In a time when the accent is more and more on what the future may bring, on visits to other planets and the problem of surviving and evolving on our own planet, research on the remote past is beginning to come into its own. Investigators are engaged in an expanding effort to look at man more realistically, and a major part of that effort is the search for fresh evidence about the origins of man. Everything suggests that the events of prehistoric times are as important in understanding the species as the events of infancy and early childhood are in understanding the individual.

The marks of early man may endure for long periods. Imagine a prehistoric twilight with hunters stopping by a stream, scooping a hollow place in the earth for a hearth, sharpening old flints and shaping new ones, eating meat by the fire and coming close for warmth and curling up at the edge of the fire to sleep. After a stay of a few days or a few weeks, the hunters abandon camp and the seasons go to work. Leaves and branches fall and form new earth; winds blow in dust and sand and volcanic ash. The area is flooded and a lake appears. Sediments drift down through the waters and settle and accumulate on the bottom.

Then the lake dries up, and another cycle starts. Decades pass and centuries and millennia, and something endures. The original occupation floor may be preserved like a flower pressed between the pages of a diary, or the fossil imprint of a fern on rock. There are discarded tools, charred bones, and the remains of fires that sputtered out long ago, traces of camps where men stayed a while and disturbed the earth and then moved on. There are sites where living patterns have persisted for as much as two to three million years.

A worldwide search is under way for new sites which will reveal more about the ways of creatures in the first throes of becoming human. Every lead is followed up, every tale of fields

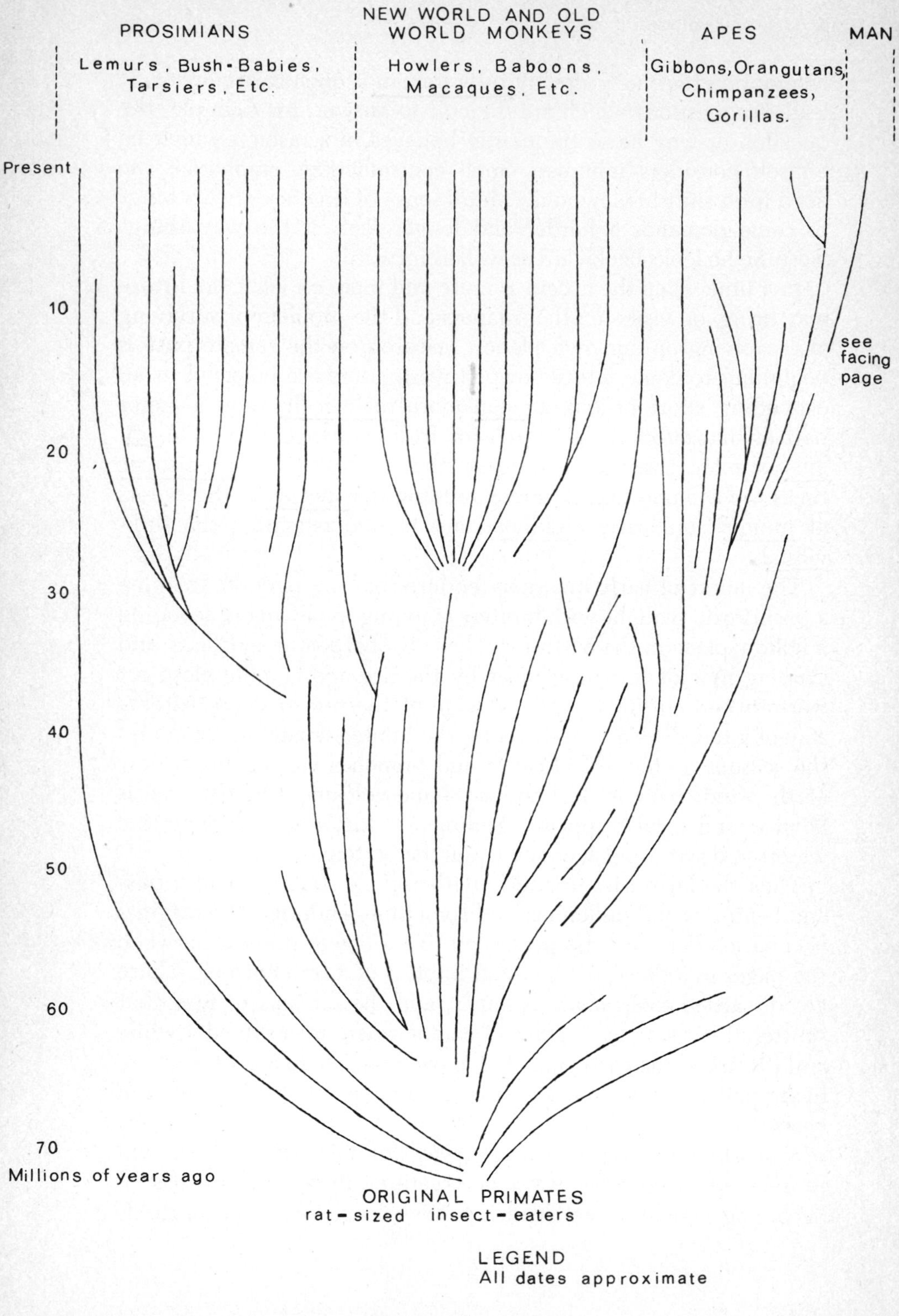

PROSIMIANS
Lemurs, Bush-Babies, Tarsiers, Etc.

NEW WORLD AND OLD WORLD MONKEYS
Howlers, Baboons, Macaques, Etc.

APES
Gibbons, Orangutans, Chimpanzees, Gorillas.

MAN

Present

10

see facing page

20

30

40

50

60

70
Millions of years ago

ORIGINAL PRIMATES
rat-sized insect-eaters

LEGEND
All dates approximate

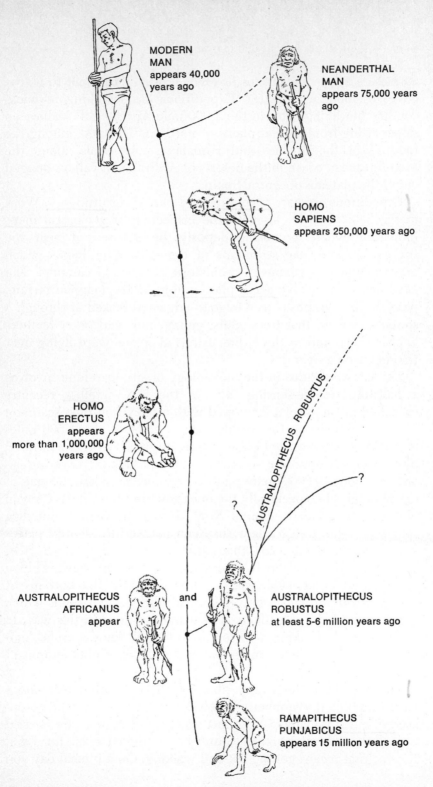

MODERN MAN
appears 40,000 years ago

NEANDERTHAL MAN
appears 75,000 years ago

HOMO SAPIENS
appears 250,000 years ago

AUSTRALOPITHECUS ROBUSTUS

HOMO ERECTUS
appears more than 1,000,000 years ago

?

?

AUSTRALOPITHECUS AFRICANUS
appear

and

AUSTRALOPITHECUS ROBUSTUS
at least 5-6 million years ago

RAMAPITHECUS PUNJABICUS
appears 15 million years ago

Evolution of man in Europe, Asia and Africa from about 70 million years ago to the present

and caves rich in ancient fossils (which usually turn out to be the bones of modern animals). Expeditions are searching in back-country bordering lakes in the 4,000-mile African Rift Valley, on slopes rising from the flat plains of northern Thailand, among the foothills of the Rockies and Himalayas and Urals, along the Mediterranean coast, in the deserts of Australia, in valleys gouged out of the plateaus of central Spain.

Expeditions are part adventure and part sheer drudgery. Work in the field often begins with the inspection of geological maps indicating where promising deposits lie exposed or near the surface, ancient lake sediments or dunes or river banks which may include the remains of prehistoric camps and campers. The next step may involve aerial photographs of the mapped terrain, pairs of photographs placed edge to edge and looked at through a stereo viewer so that trees, cliffs, gullies, hills and other features appear sharp and in three dimensions as if one were flying over the region on a clear day.

The latest advance in the technology of site-searching involves a half-ton, remote-sensing "eye in the sky" satellite recently launched in California. Equipped with a television-type scanning device, it is viewing the world from a height of about 500 miles and taking synchronized photographs in green, red, and infrared light every twenty-five seconds, each photograph covering an area of about 10,000 square miles (100 miles on a side). Some of the photographs, specifically the ones covering the Chaco Canyon National Monument region of New Mexico, are being studied in intensive detail to learn how they can be used to identify places where people lived many thousands of years ago—extinct river beds and lakes, soils rich in organic matter and clays, hidden springs and other water sources, fine debris at the bottoms of cliffs, stream and beach gravels and wind-deposited sands which may contain ancient artifacts. The insights gained in this way, in the course of checking a region already well known archeologi-cally, will be used to examine features of satellite photographs of less well known regions.

The real work starts after photography and other techniques have pinpointed a number of likely-looking areas for detailed on-the-ground surveying. Since most unexplored regions are located far off the beaten track in country too rugged even for Land Rovers, that means getting out and walking. On a typical day you wake at sunrise, tramp through brush and brambles, bending low to avoid the thorns, half-slide and half-fall down the steep sides of ravines, follow the courses of dried-out stream beds, and then try to find your way back before nightfall. You may walk fifteen miles or more in eight hours, with about forty minutes off to eat and rest, and that goes on day after day for as long as it takes to cover an area systematically.

Every search is a gamble, and many searches end with little or nothing to show for them. Under such conditions success, when it comes, is especially sweet. For example, an important site was discovered a number of years ago by Desmond Clark of the University of California in Berkeley just as he was on the verge of quitting. The setting is one of the wildest and most magnificent in Africa, near the southern end of Lake Tanganyika where the Kalambo River winds sluggishly through a high valley, moves faster as it nears the edge of a cliff, and plunges seven hundred feet into a dark tropical canyon. One morning Clark was walking back from the falls along the spillway gorge when, after nearly falling into a pit dug by natives to trap wild pigs, he happened to look down at a point where the river makes a sharp meander.

"I almost missed the place completely," he recalls. "The grass, which is normally about eight feet high and thick as your finger, had been burned off, revealing a sheer erosion cut in the river bank, and you look at practically every sheer cut. This one was touch and go, but I did look. I hung on to a couple of roots, lowered myself over the edge, and found some nice tools dating back to the Middle Stone Age of Africa about 25,000 to 30,000 years ago. Then I dropped to the bottom, where still older tools, hand axes and cleavers, were sticking out from the bank as well as pieces of carbonized wood. I could hardly believe that it was the real thing."

Clark came back three years later for a full-scale effort. Modern excavating techniques demand time and patience, thousands of tools, flakes and other objects being uncovered bit by bit with trowels and brushes. Furthermore, one never knows how long a dig will take, how much time one will need to pass through layer after layer until reaching bedrock. It required nearly twelve months of digging over several seasons to do the job at Kalambo, and many excavations take a great deal longer.

The general practice is not to excavate a site completely,

because of the peculiar nature of archeological evidence. In other sciences experiments can always be repeated and results checked. Astronomers can always make new observations of the sun and planets; biologists have an ample supply of organisms for continuing laboratory studies. Once an archeologist excavates a site, however, there can be no checking or retracing of steps. That particular arrangement of buried objects is unique. There is no other arrangement like it, and it can never be fully re-created again. Clues missed because of carelessness or ignorance are gone forever.

An appalling amount of information has been lost because of bad practices in the not-too-remote past. Profit-minded diggers have destroyed many fine sites simply to obtain a few beautifully worked flint and bone tools to sell to museums, tourists or private collectors, using rush tactics to complete in a few hours excavations which should have been carried out over periods of weeks. One notorious plunderer was caught in the act of trying to remove a section of the ceiling of a French rock shelter, a section containing a sculpted fish. The organized and semisanctioned looting of archeological sites has been an international scandal for some time, and legislation is at last being considered not only to prosecute the looters but also to prevent the purchase of looted material by some museum officials and other not overly scrupulous collectors whose desire for objects of art keeps the looters in business.

Even without such hazards, excavating is sufficiently difficult to tax the ingenuity and patience of legitimate workers. Even seasoned archeologists have unwittingly destroyed evidence, simply because they did not know it was there. For example, about fifty years ago Danish investigators developed the so-called flotation technique which makes it possible to collect fragments of organic material from excavated deposits—and takes advantage of the fact that materials of different densities may be separated by their tendencies to float or sink in different solutions. At successive stages flotation separates plant and bone from clay and stone particles, plants from bone, and different sizes of bone and plant material from one another.

The procedure has proved of considerable value to a number of investigators. For example, Stuart Struever of Northwestern University is conducting large-scale studies of Hopewell Indian communities in Illinois, and at one of his sites the technique helped provide a far more balanced picture of human activities than did conventional methods alone. The old picture, based on the excavation of large quantities of large animal bones and flint points, was of a community living predominantly by hunting. But plant remains hitherto discarded and now extracted by flotation included thousands of tiny fish bones, seed and nutshell and wood-charcoal fragments, and indicated a far more varied hunting-gathering way of life. The technique is used more widely than it was a few years ago, but a great deal of information is still being thrown away with the dirt discarded at many prehistoric sites.

Another increasingly useful technique is the analysis of fossil pollen, grains whose tough outer coatings have been preserved in such fine detail that grasses, shrubs, oak, holly, pine, juniper, palm and dozens of other plants can be identified under the microscope. It is painstaking work. Each grain is examined at magnifications of 400 to more than 1,500 times for size, shape, types and distribution of spiny and rodlike extensions, and a wide variety of surface features. Each grain has about 40 to 50 different features which are significant and must be noted; hundreds of grains may be analyzed daily, and a project may continue for weeks. The result is a powerful aid in reconstructing past climates and environments.

In New Zealand, at the University of Otago, Dunedin, Foss Leach and his associates are specialists in developing new ways of extracting more and more information from archeological deposits. One procedure depends on the observation that certain mollusks which prehistoric people ate in large quantities show shell growth patterns like tree rings. Since the rings tend to be formed at a regular rate and are about twenty times broader in summer than winter, microscopic studies of many excavated shells indicates when the mollusks were caught and eaten and, of course, when the particular site was occupied. Other experiments are based on examinations of fish scales, teeth, stonelike remains of prehistoric plants known as plant "opals," and other material. Contemporary diggers, knowing of such research, generally leave one-fourth to one-half of a site undug for future workers who will come with more advanced techniques and greater knowledge.

There are exceptions, of course. Sites may be excavated completely and in a hurry when they are scheduled to be destroyed for nonarcheological reasons, and that is happening more and more frequently as construction crews build new homes and highways for expanding populations. For example, work was recently halted for five months during the building of new apartments on the French Riviera, when bulldozers exposed tools and other signs of a prehistoric encampment. In this case, as in the case of Nile Valley sites flooded by the Aswan Dam in Egypt, the objective was to recover as much evidence as possible in a limited time.

Emotional involvement and feuding of various types, by no means unknown in other sciences, reach a strikingly high level among prehistorians, an occupational ailment which may have something to do with the sustained loneliness of digging and the difficulty of obtaining solid evidence. "I can't account for it," says an anthropologist who has been in the thick of a number of heated debates, "but there is something about exploring the past that affects you. It seems that every time a man finds a human bone he goes crazy on the spot." Traces of the remote past affect us strongly, for reasons which have yet to be determined.

The human story is known in broad outline. The hominids of some 15 million years ago were small, hairy, apelike creatures—considerably less than men, but something more than apes. They probably used tools such as digging sticks and clubs, and walked upright a good deal of the time as they carried their tools. Furthermore, although the odds are that monkeys and apes lived almost exclusively on plant foods in those days as they do now, the tool users were acquiring a strong taste for meat. In fact, the search for more abundant supplies of meat may have been the main reason for their venture into the open, for coming out of their ancestral forests where game was scarce and elusive, and invading savanna lands, the grazing grounds of herd animals.

They started slowly and remained small-time hunters for a long time. Their earliest known campsites date back two to three million years, and contain the remains of rodents and other small animals predominantly. But gradually they became bolder and more resourceful, competing increasingly with other savanna predators, a development indicated by the increasing proportion of large-animal fossils in later sites. Another significant change, taking place at the same time, was an expansion of the brain. The first big-game hunters appeared about a million to half a million years ago and had brains up to about 70 per cent larger than those of their predecessors, brains in the modern size range.

In the process of becoming more highly organized predators, man's ancestors also became more human. Previously the members of small bands lived together largely for purposes of defense. They were considerably safer in groups than as individuals when it came to discouraging the attacks of other predators, but they still operated as individuals in obtaining small game and other food. Going after large animals, however, demanded a new order of cooperation. Adult males, generally the least sociable members of groups, had to devise strategies and share their kills with one another and with nonhunters back at the home base.

The rise of *Homo sapiens* is intimately connected to the rise of increasingly complex social organizations and methods of obtaining food. He began to dominate the scene more than a hundred thousand years ago, and ever since then cultural evolution has been moving at an accelerating rate. The final phase of prehistory, the last twentieth or so of the long journey from the pre-men who were newcomers on the savanna to modern man, includes the oldest traces of religion and art. It also includes the high point in the development of the hunt, mass killing of herd animals on a many-band or tribal basis—and then the decline of the hunt as an activity essential to the community, a decline that began some ten thousand years ago with the invention of agriculture. The invention of writing about four or five millennia later may be taken as the official end of prehistory.

Something unprecedented happened during the course of these and subsequent events, something that acquires special meaning in the light of all that happened before the appearance of man. His position with respect to other animals involves two apparently contradictory truths, namely, that he has much in common with them (far more than is generally realized) and, at the same time, that he represents another order of being. Man is not merely a new species but the pioneer of a very recent and entirely new kind of evolution.

All previous species, some 500 million of them including extinct as well as surviving forms, evolved by mutation and natural selection. And all species, from whales and giant redwood trees to tadpole-shaped viruses so small that several billion of them would fit comfortably into a sphere no bigger across than the period at the end of this sentence, share certain basic similarities at the molecular level. They transmit their characteristics from generation to generation in the form of genes, discrete and highly organized molecules of hereditary materials known as nucleic acids, almost always the one known as DNA (short for deoxyribonucleic acid).

There are other similarities. The DNA generally comes in the form of a double helix, two long atomic chains interconnected and tightly coiled into a spiral-staircase structure, and including large numbers of the same four nitrogen-containing units or "bases": adenine (A), thymine (T), cytosine (C) and guanine (G). The order in which these units occur in the DNA of a particular species determines the nature of that species. The bases may be thought of as a kind of genetic alphabet, letters which spell out the specifications for organisms and control the manufacture of proteins that form living tissue. Imagine a series of DNA molecules, genes, uncoiled to produce long strings of bases attached to one another. A string starting "C-A-G-T-T-A . . ." might represent the instructions for the shaping of an amoeba, and strings starting "C-G-A-C-T-G . . ." and "A-C-C-T-A-G . . ." might represent a monkey and an elephant respectively.

A complete collection would consist of some 10 million such strings, one for each existing species. Furthermore, although there are some exceptions, the general rule is that the more complicated an organism, the longer the genetic message it transmits to its offspring, that is, the more instructions required for the building of future generations. The total length of all the DNA chains in some viruses is less than 1/25,000 of an inch, while it takes about five feet of DNA to make a man.

Living things are designed to maintain the integrity of the hereditary material. DNA molecules with their bases in proper order are duplicated over and over again in generations of sperm and egg cells, and the duplicating mechanisms may work with wonderful accuracy. They may turn out a million or more highly organized molecules in succession, each one made up of millions and millions of atoms and each one a faithful copy of the one before it, within close biological tolerances.

This process reflects a massive conservatism, a way developed over the ages to preserve things as they are, to maintain distinct and unchanging species. Powerful biological forces resist change. No other process is so nearly flawless; certainly no man-made machine can approach it. But sooner or later a slip-up or mutation occurs on the genetic assembly line. It may be a very small change, perhaps a missing base or two, or a "misspelling" in the form of a change of base order, say, from "A-T-C-G" to "A-G-C-T."

A DNA molecule departs in a small way from inherited genetic blueprints, and that makes all the difference. If there were no slip-ups, no mutations, the highest form of life today, assuming life could exist at all, might be a single-celled organism. Evolution, the "force like a hundred thousand wedges" which so impressed Darwin, exists simply because nothing is perfect, not even the chemical operations of heredity which represent the closest thing to perfection, to infallible reproduction, that we know of.

New species are formed in isolation, under conditions which permit a measure of independent evolution. In the vast majority of cases the first steps take place when geographic barriers, anything from a stream that cannot be crossed to an ocean or a range of mountains, divide parts of the ancestral species from one another. The separated subpopulations begin to undergo distinctive changes. Mutations which would formerly have spread throughout the ancestral population now accumulate on either side of the barrier. Furthermore, since no two environments are exactly alike, the adaptations called for on either side of the barrier will differ in certain respects.

After a sufficient number of generations, the net effect is two genetically incompatible subpopulations. The differences between them have become so great that even if the barrier is removed or crossed they can no longer interbreed to reproduce generations of viable offspring. At this point a new species is said to have arisen. Darwin studied such a case on the Galapagos Islands which lie in the Pacific Ocean about 600 miles from the nearest mainland, the coast of Ecuador. The islands included more than a dozen species of finches, all of them the descendants of a colony of finches presumably blown to the islands by high winds, and all of them sufficiently isolated from one another to develop different adaptations and species status.

The Galapagos finches provide a good model for the origin of species throughout the course of evolution, and new species are still being formed. For example, the Grand Canyon in northern Arizona separates two kinds of squirrel, one on the northern side of the canyon and the other on the southern side, which had a common ancestor centuries ago and have been diverging genetically ever since. It is a question whether the squirrels have yet become sufficiently different to be classified as different species, but they seem to be heading in that direction.

Man is subject to the same evolutionary forces that shaped and are shaping his fellow species. The geography of his speciation, the specific barriers that isolated hominid populations at various times in the past, is unknown. But there were barriers, and we are the result of them. Like all other creatures man arose by the process of mutation and natural selection, and he continues to depend on his genes. The big difference is that in them genetic evolution plays the major role, while in him cultural evolution has developed to an unprecedented degree.

The things other species need to survive, to escape and kill and adapt, are generally built in as part of their bodies. Their genes determine the growth of fur, horns, scales, claws, wings, and so on. Man learns and passes accumulating knowledge as well as genes from generation to generation; he makes a wide variety of shelters and weapons and, to an increasing extent, his own environments. It is culture that permits him, a single species, to spread throughout the world, to live and reproduce in high mountain valleys, semideserts, tropical rain forests, and subzero Arctic regions. Of course, genes continue to operate in him, just as learning may play an important role among other species. After all, he inherits his brain, and it, more than anything else, makes him human. But in his world learning and tradition have acquired a new order of importance.

This is a relatively recent trend. In the earliest hominid days on the savanna man's ancestors were still very much genetic creatures, in the sense that heredity played a far greater part in their activities than it does in ours. The way was prepared for new possibilities sometime during the development of social organization and hunting psychology and the accompanying expansion of the brain perhaps half a million years ago. It was still later, about a hundred millennia ago, that culture began overtaking genetics as the major determinant in human behavior.

The most important development of all, a kind of overgrowth or hypertrophy of culture, is even more recent. All other species are basically standpatters. They tend to live today very much the way they lived yesterday, assuming, of course, that the environment does not change. Given reasonably stable conditions, a favorable climate and plenty of food and no human beings in the area, even chimpanzees—the animals most like man—would continue living in the same way indefinitely. The point is that they adapt, and in the process of adapting, they do not change their forests. This is what we mean by saying they are in balance with nature.

The same cannot be said for man as he has evolved in our times. Stability is not for him. When he settles down, forests are felled and earth is moved and the world begins changing radically. He is the only species to produce major changes in the environment as he tries to adapt, which puts him in a difficult and unique situation. In effect, he creates an environment sufficiently altered so that he must adapt again and change his environment again and re-adapt and so on. Moreover, his tendency is not to minimize change but to seek it out and discover and invent it. Man has created in himself a new chronic restlessness, a process which continually works against equilibrium, antihomeostasis. At present it seems that his genes can barely keep up with the pace of cultural change.

Science offers no problem more complex than that of reconstructing the events and forces which have produced this condition, perhaps the outstanding characteristic of human evolution. This book is concerned with prehistory, with man as nomadic hunter and gatherer. It follows him in his evolution to the point when he is just beginning to settle down on farms. Subsequent events mark the coming of writing and records, the end of prehistory. The first part of the book deals chiefly with archeological evidence about extinct species, with artifacts and fossils and other material dug out of the earth. The second part, starting with Chapter XII, focuses on another important and closely related area of study, "living prehistory," which provides clues to the past as revealed by the behavior of existing species.

Much can be learned from other members of the order of primates which includes monkeys and apes as well as man. Recent investigations show that their behavior in their native forests and savannas may be surprisingly human. They have traditions, often rather sophisticated traditions, and leaders and hierarchies, and spend considerable time trying to maintain or improve their social status. When an opportunity arises, some of them will break their vegetarian diets and eat meat, even hunting upon occasion. Savanna-dwelling monkeys have evolved ways of defending themselves against predators which may well have been used by early hominids.

As wildernesses vanish, investigators are taking a last look at the last surviving bands of hunter-gatherers, people still living much as man's ancestors lived forty thousand or more years ago. They still endure without agriculture in desert places where they have been forced to live and where they fare much better than one might expect, thus demonstrating once again man's capacity for making his way under demanding conditions. And investigators are also studying people in cities and suburbs. New knowledge about such things as the bond between a mother and her infant, the nature of language and how children acquire it, and mass aggressiveness as a predominantly male characteristic inevitably deepens the understanding of the past because it is rooted in the past.

Contemporary research in living prehistory and archeology looks in both directions. It is relevant to the present and future as well as to the past. The study of prehistory presents modern times in wider perspective so that man sees himself more dispassionately in the light of remote origins, and above all so that he may rid himself of at least a few of the clichés and preconceptions that hold him down. We live with the past and always, to some extent, in it; we explore it to learn more about ourselves and what we may become.

■ From ground burrows to trees; the evolution of a thumb and fingers; three-dimensional color vision; a complex cortex; the development of insecurity and inhibition; the possibility of choice

CHAPTER I

Primate Origins

■ A number of summers ago two excavators made an important find on Purgatory Hill, not far from the Fort Peck Reservoir in northeastern Montana. Leigh Van Valen of the American Museum of Natural History and Robert Sloan of the University of Minnesota were working at a bone-dry and eroded site. Long ago a stream flowed there through abundant forests. Animals died near the banks. When the banks collapsed or heavy rains came, they were swept downstream to a place where a large slow eddy had formed. Their bodies swirled on the lee side of the eddy, sank, and settled on a bed of clams. Over the ages sediments filtered down to cover everything.

Today the site is a compacted rocky conglomerate of clam shells, minerals, and bits of fossil embedded in a silty matrix. Van Valen and Sloan tossed chunks into hundred-pound sacks and rolled the sacks down the steep hillside to a truck at a nearby reservoir. They poured the rock into fine-mesh screens, washing it in the lake until the matrix dissolved. The remainder went to a University of Minnesota laboratory to be dumped into a bathtub-sized vat of dilute acetic acid. The acid dissolved the clam shells, leaving a mixture which included, among other things, the fragmentary remains of extinct species.

Similar projects throughout the world are part of the continuing effort to reconstruct the past. The Montana project yielded important prehistoric remains after the scientists had removed more than 30,000 pounds of rock from Purgatory Hill

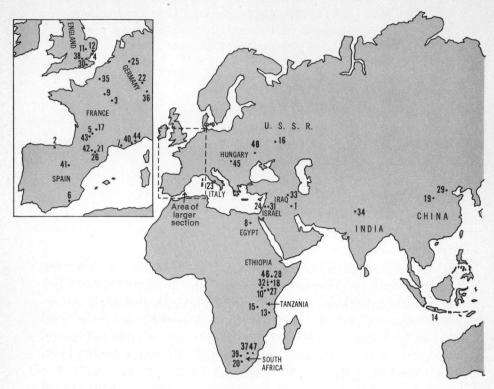

MAJOR PREHISTORIC SITES: EUROPE, AFRICA, AND ASIA

Time Code:
① 60,000,000 to 4,000,000 years ago
② 4,000,000 to 1,000,000 years ago
③ 1,000,000 to 200,000 years ago
④ 200,000 years ago to the present

Things Found:
A   art
B   bones of primates
F   fire
L   living floors
T   tools

Key to sites on map

1   Ali Kosh ④ L,T
2   Altamira ④ A,T
3   Arcy ④ B,F,L,T
4   Clacton-on-Sea ③ T
5   Combe Grenal ④ F,L,T
6   Cueva de Ambrosio ④ B,F,T
7   Escale cave ③ B,F,L,T
8   Fayum Depression ① B
9   Pincevent ④ A,F,L,T
10   Fort Ternan ① B
11   High Lodge ④ T
12   Hoxne ③ T
13   Isimila ④ F,L,T
14   Java site ③ B
15   Kalambo Falls ④ B,F,L,T
16   Kostenki ④ A,B,F,L,T

17   LaChapelle-aux-Saints ④ B,T
18   Lake Rudolf site ② B,T
19   Lantian site ③ B
20   Makapan ② B
21   Mas D'Azil ④ A,T
22   Mauer site ③ B
23   Monte Circeo ④ B,T
24   Mt. Carmel ④ B,F,T
25   Neanderthal ④ B
26   Niaux ④ A,T
27   Olduvai Gorge ② B,L,T
28   Omo ② B,T
29   Peking Man ③ B,F,T
30   Piltdown (discredited)
31   Qafzeh ④ B,F,T
32   Rusinga Island ① B

33   Shanidar cave ④ B,F,L,T
34   Siwalik Hills ① B
35   St. Acheul ③ T
36   Steinheim ④ B
37   Sterkfontein ② B,T
38   Swanscombe ④ B,T
39   Taung ② B
40   Terra Amata ④ F,L,T
41   Torralba-Ambrona ③ B,F,L,T
42   Tuc d'Audoubert ④ A,T
43   "Valley of Caves" ④ (p. 223)
44   Vallonet cave ② B,T
45   Verteszöllös ③ B,F,L,T
46   Lothagam ① B
47   Swartkrans ② B
48   Molodova ④ B,T,L,F

and sifted through the debris. The most striking find consisted of 65-million-year-old bits of bony fossil each about the size of the head of a paper book match, half a dozen molar and premolar teeth. They were traces of the earliest known primates, the order that includes monkeys and apes and men.

The coming of primates has its own prehistory. It was part of a much earlier sequence of events which includes the rise and fall of reptiles, the rise of mammals, and a global splitting up of continents. Reptiles dominated the earth some 225 million years ago, when the first dinosaurs appeared along with the first ancestors of mammals. At the time the world was literally one world. No separate continents existed, only a great single land mass or island in the midst of a great single ocean, a supercontinent known as Pangea.

But divisive stresses were already at work. Cracks or rifts were appearing deep in the earth, under the land mass and under the ocean, perhaps as a result of cosmic events still under way. According to one theory, as the universe expands and our Milky Way and other galaxies recede farther and farther from one another, the force of gravity is gradually decreasing everywhere. Since gravity compresses and holds matter together against explosive internal pressures, that implies a gradual "inflation" of all celestial bodies, the earth included.

Whether future research confirms this or some other theory, there is no doubt about what happened during the heyday of the reptiles. The earth started splitting at the seams, along flaw lines possibly built into the planet during its formation four to five billion years ago. The first piece to break away from the supercontinent of Pangea was India-Antarctica which formed a single block of land. By 200 million years ago there were three pieces, India and Antarctica having drifted apart, while South America-Africa was attached to North America-Europe-Asia at only one place, Gibraltar. In one of the most recent developments North America separated from Europe-Asia and attached itself to South America, which had previously separated from Africa. (The process is continuing. Within 10 million years or so parts of Somaliland-Kenya-Tanzania are scheduled to become an island off mainland Africa, and a piece of southern California including Los Angeles will have broken off and started drifting toward San Francisco.)

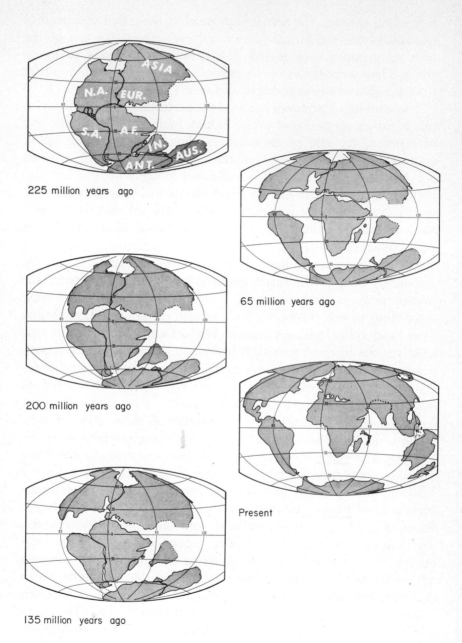

225 million years ago

200 million years ago

135 million years ago

65 million years ago

Present

Breakup of the universal continent, Pangea

These changes had a major impact on all subsequent evolution. The breaking up of Pangea produced an "island" effect, creating huge blocks of land and isolating large groups of species from one another—and isolation is one of the main factors promoting rapid and diverse evolution. Such conditions favor the appearance of new adaptations and new orders of creatures, since they have a chance to develop on their own in many different environments. Certainly the class of mammals spread widely and produced a rich variety of orders, more than thirty of them including the primates.

Mammals existed for more than 100 million years before they began dominating the earth some 70 million years ago. Beady-eyed and bewhiskered and long-snouted, they probably looked and behaved very much like rats. They scurried and snuffled through fallen leaves and undergrowth, for their food was chiefly insects, although the odds are that they also devoured practically anything else edible. Most seem to have been night feeders who spent the day huddled in nests and burrows. These remote ancestors of man were unimpressive and inconspicuous, and with good reason. They had to walk small, because giants were abroad.

Dinosaurs like *Triceratops*, a lumbering three-horned plant eater of about five tons with a seven-foot-long head. A number of years ago excavators recovered most of a *Triceratops* skeleton from the same Montana deposits that contained the newly found primate fossils. These and other reptiles were adapted to cold-blooded existence in warm stable climates. They lived essentially automatic lives, turned on and off in effect by rising and falling temperatures. Like present-day reptiles, they were almost complete slaves of prevailing climates. They stopped moving at night when their blood temperatures fell with the setting of the sun, and began stirring again some time after sunrise when the sun had warmed their blood. They could not endure too high a temperature. Contemporary crocodiles, too, die in the hot sun, and they undoubtedly idled at midday in shaded parts of swamplands.

The fact that most of the dominant species of the age of reptiles were daytime feeders and hunters, specifically sunshine feeders and hunters, had certain implications for the rise of primates and other mammals. For other forms of life nighttime was a relatively safe time, and offered a number of evolutionary opportunities which were exploited by many early mammals, including our primate predecessors. And in the process they achieved a new degree of adjustability, a new degree of independence. Warm-blooded species evolved physiological controls, built-in furnaces of a sort and circulating heat, which enabled them to survive and be active over a wider range of temperatures than reptiles, in the midday sun as well as during the night.

So in a sense the mammals were ready for conditions yet to come. The hundred million years preceding their rise were ideal for cold-blooded reptiles. The climate had been uniformly warm and mild. Much of what is dry land today was low and level, covered by calm and widespread shallow seas. Much of North America lay under water. A vast sea rolled over most of Europe and stretched across Iran and India, its waves lapping along shorelines in Spain to the west and in Burma and Malaya to the east.

But the earth was becoming restless about 70 million years ago. The reptiles found themselves obsolescent. Rumblings underground accompanied the continuing drifting of continents and heralded a period of cataclysm, the most violent earthquakes and volcanoes and mountain-building activity in more than half a billion years. The land was rising; retreating waters exposed larger and larger areas of earlier island continents. Within the next 5 million years or so, a brief time on the evolutionary scale, the dinosaurs and related species would become extinct.

Evolution is an intricate system of adjustments and readjustments. Many changes were too subtle to leave traces in the fossil record. The dinosaurs did not vanish in a sudden twilight-of-the-gods melodrama, inundated en masse in waves of white-hot lava or dying of thirst, as pictured in the fantasy-clichés of Hollywood and Disney and the comic strips. They disappeared gradually as climates became somewhat cooler and drier, and their swamp-lands dwindled. Incapable of changing with changing times, they produced fewer and fewer offspring in successive generations.

Disease may have speeded their departure. There had been an enormous expansion of grasses, ivies, broad-leafed shrubs and trees, and other flowering plants—and a corresponding expansion of fungi and insects including new varieties that might have spread major epidemics among vulnerable reptiles. It is also possible that early mammals, perhaps early primates, helped wipe out the dinosaurs by acquiring a taste for dinosaur eggs, often left in the open to be hatched by the heat of the sun (although many reptiles bury their eggs). In any case, mammals finally came into their own after a hundred million years in the shadows.

The earliest primates, small rodent-like creatures known as prosimians or premonkeys, quickly took to the trees. It was a time of rising temperatures and extensive forests. Today's dwindling forests, stretches or patches of woodland among cities and deserts and eroded regions and farms, are mere remnants of what used to be. A belt of almost continuous tropical and subtropical forests thousands of miles wide extended from Seattle and Vancouver to southern Argentina and Chile, from London to Cape Town, from Japan to southern Australia. In the Sahara, woodlands and savannas and lakes existed where desert is now. There were crocodiles, palm trees, and swamps in England, France, and the northwestern United States.

Prosimians had to adapt to a strange new world, a new dimension, among the dense foliage and branches and canopies of the forests, and how they did it is of direct concern to man. Humans are forest creatures to the extent that their basic structures, brain, sense organs, limbs, and reproductive system, evolved in the forests. Later developments generally called for modifications and elaborations of those structures rather than for totally new ones. Preadaptation, the evolution of features in one environment which also happens to be as appropriate or even more so in a future environment, has been important in the shaping of all species including man.

Life in the trees offered interesting evolutionary possibilities, largely because it was not a complete exploitation of the third dimension like the flight of birds. Flying, which puts a premium on lightness, produced small and highly specialized species. As in man-made flying machines, every fraction of an ounce of weight that could be dispensed with was. One result has been a brain incorporating within a small space circuitry far more compact than anything yet designed by engineers concerned with transistors and solid-state physics. It coordinates elaborate nesting and mating behavior, communications, keen eyesight, and swift maneuvers in space. It gained compactness at the price of some flexibility—bird behavior tends to have a set, stereotyped quality.

Life on the ground provided another range of opportunities. Proceeding at a different pace, it did not need to be as automatic. It permitted the development of big bodies and big brains and offered the possibility of flexible, adjustable behavior based to a greater degree on learning. There was time on the ground for watching, pausing, and a measure of preparation. Species could prowl about and lie in wait. Lying in wait demands control and the delay of reflexes and, at the same time, a readiness for swift responses. Inhibition achieved through regulatory centers in the nervous system serves the survival of animals that can bide their time. On the other hand, the challenge and complexity of general navigation, of hunting and escaping, was less on the ground than in free flight.

Life in the trees combined certain features of the earthbound and aerial modes of existence. Species could evolve with brains large enough for considerable learning as well as for the built-in circuitry to subserve advanced visual powers and sensory and muscular coordination. Even more significant, life in the trees introduced a unique feature, a new and chronic psychological insecurity or uncertainty. Air and ground do not suddenly change their properties. As a rule, the ground is reasonably broad and solid, and makes a dependable platform; the air is consistently insubstantial and must be coped with accordingly. The uncertainty in the trees amounts almost to unpredictable changes of state. The environment is full of discontinuities, surprises. Regarded from a ground dweller's point of view, it is roughly equivalent to moving too rapidly to stop through tall dense grasses without being able to see more than a few feet ahead. At any moment, one may suddenly come upon a deep hole directly in the path, too wide to step across. Such hazards may be numerous and scattered at random over the terrain. Frequent swift decisions are required about how far to jump and in what direction. To live in trees is to be confronted continually with analogous emergencies, analogous "holes" in the form of gaps between branches.

Branches are never absolutely reliable as launching or landing sites, or even as resting places. A branch may be as firm and solid

Water hole at Amboseli: early man lived on such savannas

as the ground itself, or it may sway and give or break because it is too small or brittle to bear weight. One of the most amazing recoveries from a serious and seemingly unavoidable accident has been described by Ray Carpenter of Pennsylvania State University, a pioneer observer of primate behavior.

One day in Thailand he saw a female gibbon swinging out on a limb and preparing for a take-off leap to another tree. At just that instant, the limb snapped off, leaving a stub about six inches long, and leaving the ape suspended in space for a split second: "As the limb broke and fell the gibbon recovered by turning almost in midair and catching the remaining stub of the branch. With extreme rapidity she swung around under and then on top of the [stub] . . . and then, with only a slight loss of time and momen-

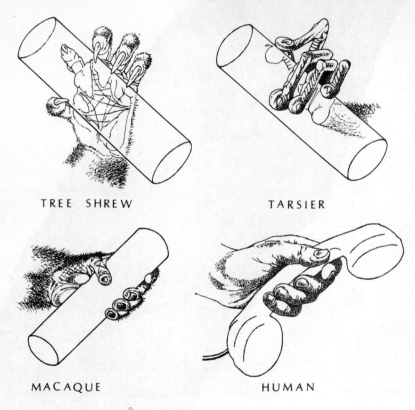

TREE SHREW   TARSIER

MACAQUE   HUMAN

Shrew and primate grips: from claws to human grip with fully opposable thumb

tum, jumped outward and downward thirty feet to an adjacent tree top."

This incident illustrates how a supreme trapeze artist, the product of hundreds of thousands of generations of evolution, managed to avoid trouble by a swift and superbly executed maneuver. But there was an ever-present possibility of falling

TREE SHREW

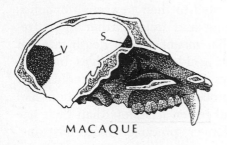

MACAQUE

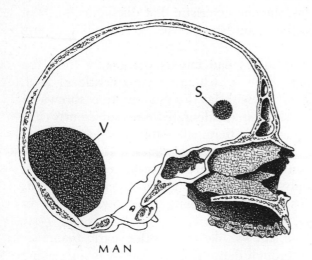

MAN

V - VISION
S - SMELL

Expansion of visual centers in primate evolution: relative decline of old "smell" brain

(Shrew brain included for comparison)

and severe injury. Gibbons, like all primates, occasionally mis-judge distances or the strength of a branch. Studies indicate that about one out of every four fully grown adults has broken at least one bone; some have as many as seven healed fractures. Evolution can increase the odds against but it cannot eliminate catastrophe.

Prosimians that took up life in the trees some 70 million years ago had only recently evolved from ground-dwelling insect eaters and were not yet thoroughly adapted to their new environments. They must have lost their footing and fallen rather more fre-quently than existing species. That meant a high death rate not only as a direct outcome of the accidents themselves but also from predators which are always ready to kill off handicapped individuals. The weeding-out process of natural selection had begun again. Individuals that had fewer accidents than their less fortunate contemporaries lived longer, produced more offspring, and eventually superseded them.

The most fundamental way of preventing falls is to hold on. It is no surprise, therefore, that the most highly evolved character-istic among prosimians, the characteristic that distinguishes them most sharply from their ancestors, was a refined grasping mechanism.

The odds are that primates had fingers practically from the beginning, rather than claws which are characteristic of such primitive species as the present-day long-tailed tree shrews of Southeast Asia. Tree shrews, incidentally, are sufficiently like both rodents and primates so that paleontologists have shifted them from one order to the other several times. (The latest, and probably final, decision is that they are not primates.) Some tree shrews go abroad only at night, and all of them are vicious fighters and voracious eaters, consuming their own weight or more of food each day.

The ancestors of tree shrews, like many other early mammals and reptiles, traveled through dense tropical forests mainly along branches too big around for grasping, and held on with claws adapted for digging into bark. The earliest primates, on the other hand, took advantage of a new niche. They moved along narrower motorways that had not been fully exploited, smaller and finer branches which could be grasped by fingers equipped with flat-tened nails and a thumb capable of moving opposite the other four digits to form a locking grip.

Other changes came with increasing exploitation of forest environments. In preprimate mammals the eyes tended to be small and were located on the sides of an extended and tapering snout. In prosimians the eyes became larger, perhaps as an adaptation to let in more light and improve nighttime vision. Furthermore, they moved forward like twin headlights as the snout retreated, which results in better depth perception, an enormous advantage related to the use of the hands and fingers and to close manipulative work. Although three-dimensional vision is limited to distances of about ten feet, it also helps improve accuracy and sure-footedness in leaping from bough to bough.

These and other developments were intimately connected with the development of more elaborate brains. In particular, moving about in a rich three-dimensional arboreal environment favored the expansion of the cerebral cortex or outer bark of the brain. This structure arose in response to an earlier adventure in evolution, appearing as a rudimentary pinhead-sized patch of cells on the brain surfaces of the first creatures that came out of the sea and took up life on land. But the cortex really began coming into its own with the rise of mammals, as an organ to coordinate highly complex behavior, to analyze messages flowing in from the sense organs, and to send messages of its own to the muscles.

The prosimian brain was still small, the size of a pea in a two-inch skull, but by this stage of evolution its cortex had spread like a gray tide over the brain's surface and consisted of a thin sheet of millions of nerve cells. One cortical area was located toward the front of the head. The most important part of the so-called smell brain, it had a long and respectable history dating back to creatures which guided themselves primarily with the sense of smell. The newer part of the cortex, located at the back of the brain, had expanded to deal with the increasing amount of visual information involved in the successful performance of arboreal acrobatics.

Improved grasping preceded improved "thinking," in line with an ancient evolutionary tradition. Muscle and the special senses such as sight and smell, movement and sensation, are primary—and nerves evolved to serve them. The predominance of the brain, of intelligence and language and discovery, is a very recent development.

A major turning point in the history of primates occurred about

35 million years ago. Prosimians had been highly successful for millions of years, multiplying and spreading widely and dominating the vast forests of the times. Then they began declining rapidly, probably because of intense competition from their own kind, from monkeys and apes. Geological changes that had begun long ago, and had helped accelerate the passing of the dinosaurs, were approaching a climax.

The weight of sediments accumulating on the floor of the great sea that stretched from Spain to Malaya caused a sagging in some places, an upward buckling in others, and the appearance of island ridges which were to become the Alps. Mountain-building processes elsewhere gave rise to precursors of the Himalayas, Rockies and Andes. The net effect was a further splitting up of the lands, continuing a process that dates back to the beginning of continental drift. New land masses came into being, creating new environments and zones for new species. A similar fragmenting affected parts of the forest belt; the trees dwindled in various localities, giving way to open grasslands which also offered zones for new species. All the changes offered new evolutionary opportunities. Elephants, deer, rhinoceroses and other modern mammals, as well as monkeys and apes, appeared.

An abundant region of this period lay on the Egyptian coast of the Mediterranean, part of the Spain-to-Malaya sea, extending some hundred miles farther inland to cover areas where Cairo and the Pyramids stand today. Coastal plains and savannas merged with thick and humid tropical forests, through which sluggish swamp-lined rivers moved to the shallow sea. The rivers carried the bodies of many animals, and their sands buried the bodies. In relatively recent times lava from the depths of the earth forced its way to the surface, and cracks in the crust formed steep cliffs and ridges.

The region called the Fayum Depression is a wasteland on the eastern edge of the Sahara, one of the world's richest fossil-primate sites. Between the turn of the century and 1960, collectors had found only seven pieces of primate remains in the Fayum, but since 1960 more than two hundred have been found in expeditions headed by Elwyn Simons of Yale University. Among the finds is part of a lower jaw which may represent the earliest-known ancestor of living monkeys, a diagnosis based

Fayum Depression, Egypt: searching for fossils

Fayum Depression, Egypt: fossil being prepared for removal

largely on tooth studies. It had thirty-two teeth, like most present-day monkeys, as compared with thirty-four teeth for most prosimians, and a special four-cusp pattern also typical of monkeys. It was probably about the size of a small cat, which is large enough for a prosimian (although not for a monkey) and accords with the general trend toward increasing size among primates.

Within 5 million years monkeys had spread throughout the forests and developed the basis for an entirely different kind of viewing and dealing with the world. Every change was part of a complex of interrelated changes, part of an emerging evolutionary pattern. The sense of smell declined in importance. A generation or two ago, investigators attributed this decline to the notion that it is impossible to make or to follow clear-cut scent trails in the trees, that arboreal primates could not use the sense of smell to detect sharply defined, coherent and directional patterns in the broken-up context of leaves and branches and gaps between them.

This turns out not to be the case. Primates and other arboreal species mark out clearly defined territories and trails by urinating at strategic spots; they can distinguish friend from foe by odors. But the sense of smell assumed a secondary position in comparison with sight. The olfactory nerve, which carries signals from nose to brain, decreases in diameter, a development indicated by comparative measurements of the holes in the nasal part of the skull through which the nerve passes. (The decline is recapitulated in human growth: some olfactory-nerve cells begin dying off even before birth, and about half of them have died by middle age.)

The hands acquired a considerably richer supply of nerve cells and fibers concerned with the sense of touch. Hands and sense organs evolved together, each development accelerating the other in an involved feedback relationship. Fingers became more and more mobile, capable not only of moving faster but also of assuming a far greater variety of positions. Devices designed originally for grasping and holding on were used increasingly to get food and, even more important, to pick up objects, bring them closer, and turn them around to examine from all angles. The ability to manipulate in this way was new in the history of terrestrial life, and reached a high point in the monkey family.

In fact, from one point of view the monkey's universe was the first to contain full-fledged objects. The very notion of objects, of an environment made up of separate and distinct things some of which could be moved for one's own purposes, came with the simian way of life, with a superbly developed visual sense and advanced manipulative powers. The world was "objectified," fragmented into things which stood out from the background, as it had never been before. Eyes placed at the sides of the head see landscapes as two-dimensional flat sheets and respond to motion across the sheets; they are poorly designed to detect what does not move or what moves slowly and directly toward rather than across the field of vision, such as a stalking tiger.

A more and more complete picture of reality, a revelation, came with the movement of the eyes from a side to an up-front position and, at least as important, with the coming of color vision, which developed to an advanced stage among monkeys. Imagine that you can see things in two dimensions only. You are standing on a plain looking toward a place where animals move among tall grasses and shrubs, and everything has a flat stage-set quality, some of the animals merging in part with the landscape and others well camouflaged and entirely invisible.

Then as you watch you acquire stereoscopic and color vision and the scene changes. The scene begins to take on depth, slowly at first and more rapidly later, as shapes and shadows seem to move forward and backward and assume their natural places. The animals and objects which were visible but not in full perspective begin to stand out more completely as distinct entities. The animals and objects which were invisible in two-dimensional black-and-white viewing become increasingly visible with the appearance of a richer and richer variety of colors, so that even at a distance you get the feeling of almost being among them.

Something like this happened gradually during primate evolution. Color vision helped in detecting predators and later, when primates themselves became increasingly predatory, potential prey. Also, Marcel Hladik and Georges Pariente at the National Museum of Natural History in Brunoy, France, are investigating the possibility that color vision played and plays a role in selecting food. Preliminary studies of monkeys sharing the same forest areas in Ceylon and Panama indicate that they tend to exploit foods of different colors, and that different species may be sensitive to these preferred colors.

Man's visual apparatus is a direct heritage from life in the trees. It has changed little since the days when monkeys were the earth's highest primates. The structure of the monkey brain reflected the increasing emphasis on vision. The cortex expanded considerably, perhaps about two to three times, burying most of the old smell-brain centers. Although a large part of the expansion involved the visual cortex at the back of the brain, other areas were affected, for example, certain areas concerned with the control of finger movements—a tiny strip of cortex on the right side of the brain controlling the fingers of the left hand, a corresponding left-side strip the right hand. The degree of detail on the map of the cortex depends on the evolutionary status of the species.

Judging by contemporary prosimians, ancestral forms must have operated their fingers en masse, in one gross movement. That is, they could not move fingers individually but moved them all together as a single mechanism. When they curved their hands to make a grip, nerve signals passed from the finger-control maps on the brain's surface to appropriate muscles in the hands, and the muscles contracted. Such generalized action did not require an elaborately organized map and consisted mainly of a "five-finger" area. But judging by observations of living species, monkeys evolving 30 million years or more ago moved their fingers far more freely and independently; among other things, they could bring thumb and forefinger together to pick up small objects such as insects and seeds. Their cortical maps evolved accordingly, including, instead of one five-finger area, five separate one-finger areas for more precise digital control.

Generally speaking, the finer the detail, the larger mapping area required, a principle which applies to the wrist, arm, foot, toes and other parts that became more mobile among monkeys. Furthermore, as the skin incorporated a richer supply of nerve cells registering the sense of touch, "touch" maps also became larger and more detailed. The expansion of the cortex was the net effect of the expansions of many kinds of maps. It also included larger association areas, areas devoted to the swift analysis of information flowing from many sense organs, those recording the state of affairs within as well as outside the body, and from non-cortical brain structures such as the cerebellum, attached to the brain stem at the back of the head, which coordinates balance and the tensions of more than 150 pairs of opposing muscles.

The brain, in short, was modified to serve the needs of a new kind of animal. It included structures designed to coordinate at extremely rapid rates the movements of muscles and sets of muscles involved in complex manipulations, climbing, leaping, chasing and being chased. These structures could take orders from the cortex. But they also had to be capable of automatic operations on their own, because monkeys are restless and agile

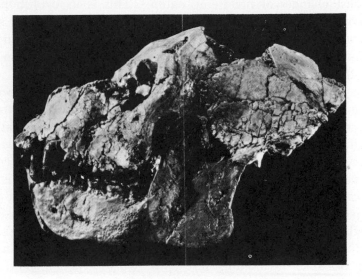

Aegyptopithecus: representative of earliest known apes

and lightweight, and often move so fast that there is no time for deliberation. Their entire behavior pattern represented and represents a special and highly dynamic adaptation to the forests.

There were other kinds of primates in the trees. The pressure is always on in evolution. Life does not stay put but tends always to become more diverse, to develop new forms adapted to new and varied conditions. Sometimes it is a matter of occupying new places, filling hitherto empty living zones—as, for example, when fish invaded the land more than 350 million years ago, or when prosimians and some rodents took to the trees. In other cases it may involve a new time zone, as when certain species of early mammals exploited the possibilities of nocturnal feeding. Another type of adaptation, another major variation of the primate theme, arose at about the same time monkeys appeared on the scene or perhaps somewhat later. The Fayum Depression has also yielded remains of the earliest-known members of the ape family, species which developed a different approach to the forest world and a different type of biological organization.

A large part of the difference involved ways of using branches to obtain food. Most of the food in trees hangs at the ends of branches where it is beyond the reach of many animals and has the best chances of not being eaten. (This is its evolution for survival.) But apes have an ingenious way of getting at such places. A characteristic posture of an ape in a tree is very roughly that of a monkey which has slipped and saved itself by hanging on with its hands.

But what represents an emergency for the monkey has become an important form of behavior for the ape. In the structure of their wrists, arms, elbows and shoulders they are adapted for hanging suspended full length under branches as well as for walking on top of them as monkeys generally do. In fact, feeding far out on slender branches is easier for apes than it is for monkeys; monkeys are lighter, but they must go on four feet. Sherwood Washburn of the University of California in Berkeley, a leading investigator of primate evolution and behavior, points out that an ape can distribute its weight strategically among three branches by holding fast with two feet and a hand and reaching out for a succulent piece of fruit with its free hand: "This is a distinctive behavior pattern of apes which can hang comfortably with one arm and do things with the other arm. Only an ape could have any possible reason for designing a bus or a subway train with straps."

But no ape is as good at swinging along through the trees as the gibbon. Using its powerful arm and shoulder muscles, it can propel itself thirty feet or more in one fluid movement, one of the most spectacular aerial maneuvers among nonflying animals. But in the course of evolving such talents, it had to stay small for the same reason that birds are small, to assure lightness and maximum mobility. (Gibbons are lighter than many monkeys, weighing only about ten to fifteen pounds.)

If all apes had gone the way of the gibbon, today's most advanced primates would be master aerialists rather than intellectuals. Some species followed another line of development, involving an evolutionary compromise between body weight and acrobatic skill. The most obvious advantage of being big was to discourage predators. The smallest prosimians and monkeys are fair game for the most abundant carnivores, small carnivores like snakes and eagles and jackals. (If they have any choice, large carnivores do not bother to eat such small game.) But only leopards, lions and other big cats take on orangutans and chimpanzees or the largest monkeys such as baboons. And nothing goes after gorillas but man, who goes after everything.

There may have been another reason for becoming bigger. The fossil record indicates that apes began spreading widely in Africa about 25 million years ago, reached a peak about 10 million years later with a record number of species, mostly relatively small forms—and then went into a sharp decline. The reasons for the decline are not at all clear. The number of species of arboreal monkeys seems to have increased enormously as the number of ape species decreased, which is somewhat surprising since apes had better brains. Apparently superior intelligence is not always enough.

Monkeys may have evolved more advanced social organizations than apes, perhaps because their troops tended to be larger and demanded more discipline and coordination. Another possibility, suggested by Robert Martin of University College, London, is based on observations of present-day species. Monkeys generally use food more efficiently than apes, grinding plant materials more thoroughly and thus permitting more complete digestion. Some species have compartments in their stomachs which are specialized to break down leafy foods; others, like the baboon, aid processes of digestion by softening food in cheek pouches before swallowing it. When competition for food is intense, as it might well have been 15 million years ago in African forests, any advantage in obtaining energy from food pays off handsomely in terms of survival.

So apes may have become bigger in self-defense, a point reinforced by the fact that in Asia, where arboreal monkeys are few, apes have remained relatively small. In Africa gorillas and their ancestors may have specialized in highland-mountain living, while chimpanzees foraged mainly in lower woodland-orchard regions. Big primates roamed more widely and spent more time on the ground as well as in the trees, partly because they had less to fear and partly because they needed more food and had to travel farther for it. (Most monkeys possess home ranges of a fraction of a square mile to three square miles or so; apes move over a territory of fifteen to twenty square miles, except for the little gibbon, whose range is at the low end of the monkey scale.) In other words, they encountered a wider and more varied environment.

Their evolving anatomy permitted a greater variety of movements. New nerve pathways developed in consequence—the cerebral expression of new possibilities. New cortical pathways appeared. The possible routes along which nerve signals may pass from sense organs to muscles increased enormously. The cortex is in part an organ of analysis, a dense feltwork of billions of nerve cells which lies between stimulus mechanisms and response mechanisms, between experience and action. Its complexity reflected the new complexity of the apes' world.

The ape brain responded to a new way of life and expanded with increased body size. As usual, the cortex expanded most. In early prosimians, as in most present-day prosimians, it tended to be a smooth gray sheet, since it lay almost entirely on the surface of the brain. But among apes it became wrinkled and folded primarily because the increasing variety of movement, the increasing role of hand-eye coordination, demanded more nerve pathways for the transmission and analysis of information. To meet this demand, natural selection favored the maximum cerebral tissue within the confines of a given skull capacity, so that the cortex spread down into crevices in the underlying white matter, a process already evident among monkeys. Perhaps 25 to 30 per cent of the ape cortex is buried in the crevices as compared with 7 per cent for monkeys.

The evolving cortex expressed another important trend, a greater and greater stress on inhibition, on the art of not doing things. This is implicit in the multiplicity of alternatives confronting advanced species. Choosing a course of action demands the ruling out of many possibilities. It also demands time, deliberation and delay. Life becomes less automatic and depends to a greater extent than ever before on learning, and learning is an inevitable consequence of complexity in evolution. It became increasingly important among higher species whose environments offered a wider and wider range of choices.

Many forces shaped primates during the period from 70 to 25 million years ago. Important parts of the record are still missing; for example, we do not know what happened during the transition time when prosimians evolved into monkeys and apes. The earliest-known species, represented by fossils in deposits of the Fayum, had obviously done considerable evolving before that.

But the record is clear on one point. Primates are evolution's most promising way of adapting mammals, inheritors of the earth after the decline of the dinosaurs, to the uncertainties and challenges of life in the trees. Something more happened in the process of adaptation. Some species were equipped not only for forest dwelling but also for a new and bold adventure, the invasion of open country which foreshadowed the coming of man.

■ The spread of savannas; the nature of prehuman apes; an ancestor near Lake Victoria; the significance of the small teeth of *Ramapithecus;* the advantages of bipedalism; tool use among pre-men and modern chimpanzees; new fossil finds

CHAPTER II

The First Members of the Family of Man

■ The ancestors of man arose 15 million years ago in the slowly changing subtropics of the Old World. The restlessness in the earth, a heritage from earlier periods, continued as the crust buckled and pushed up sediments thousands of feet thick that had accumulated on the floors of ancient seas. The buckling produced great mountain chains and intermontane valleys, including the great ranges of the Alps and Himalayas. Gases, ash and lava poured out of volcanic craters and increased rains produced intense erosion along the slopes of mountains and foothills. Worldwide annual temperatures fell, perhaps by as much as an average of five degrees Fahrenheit or so.

A broad forest extended from the west coast of Africa to the East Indies, but not the solid unbroken forest of former times. The savanna was on the move. Grasses spread in a slow tide among the trees, and there were dry plains wide as oceans, particularly on the lee side of newly formed highlands. Penetrating into the plains were dark peninsular stretches of gallery forest. In a sense nature was more natural then, the wilderness was wilder, than it has ever been since. It might have been an Eden of a sort except for, or perhaps because of, the fact that man had not yet put in an appearance.

But his coming, the shift into savanna lands, was imminent. Most primates spent most of their lives in the shade, leading enclosed lives inside "green caves" of leaves and vines. They

42

found pathways high in the forests, trails for leaping and swinging in the canopies of trees, familiar branches and footholds
among dense foliage. They avoided more exposed places like open
woodlands where trees were somewhat fewer and farther between. Most of all, they avoided the wide-open, bright, uneasy
places where savanna grasses rustled at the very edges of the
woodlands.

Of course, then as now a few individuals were always ready to
push their luck and investigate alien terrain. Such explorers have
long had a special influence on the course of mammalian evolution, a point emphasized by John Christian of the Albert Einstein
Medical Center in Philadelphia. He indicates that as a rule they
tend not to be high-ranking members of groups: "It seems that
the dominant core of a population or species is rarely primarily
involved in the evolutionary process." In other words, evolving is
a business for adventurers. More often than not the adventurers
are thwarted young males who have not found places for themselves in the ranks of established hierarchies, and who are driven
out of the group's central area and practically forced to investigate action at the edges of things.

So restless young prehominids, like their counterparts among
many other species, probably spent considerable time playing I-
dare-you games and trying out environments which primates had
not exploited. But it took more than that to bring about full-scale,
permanent changes. Something had to happen to make entire
populations move out of relatively safe forests into the favorite
hunting grounds of the big cats and other predators, and judging
by the sort of forces generally at work in evolution, it probably
involved the problem of getting enough food.

It could have been a matter of warmer and drier climates, less
rainfall and dwindling forests; or perhaps the forests were not
shrinking but primate populations were on the increase. Both
possibilities have been suggested, and the evidence is insufficient
to make out a solid case for either one of them. At any event, the
effect was the same—too many individuals for the available food
supply. The hominid story from this stage on seems to be an
increasing exploitation of increasingly open terrain.

The evidence indicates the sort of primate that gave rise to
man. For one thing, certain tests are based on comparisons of the

chemical nature of proteins taken from the blood of living primates. If certain proteins from two species each react to about the same degree with an appropriate antiserum, the implication is that they are closely related chemically, and that a close evolutionary relationship may exist between the two species. Proteins from two remotely related species, on the other hand, may react differently with the same antiserum, and the extent of the difference can be measured with some precision.

Such tests show not only that man is more closely related to apes than to monkeys but also that he is more closely related to the chimpanzee and gorilla than to the orangutan and gibbon, an observation which confirms the results of detailed anatomical studies. According to Morris Goodman of Wayne State University in Detroit, an authority on the comparative blood chemistry of primates, the kinship situation can be expressed even more strongly. He believes that as far as protein research is concerned, the chimpanzee and gorilla are closer to man than they are to other apes.

Tests involving heredity-transmitting chromosomes and other substances tend to support Goodman's findings. So do studies of primate parasites. Varieties of fleas, lice, and mites which live on man also live on chimpanzees and gorillas, but leave gibbons and orangutans alone. Similarly, species of organisms causing malaria in humans do not affect the gibbon and orang, although some of them may produce disease among chimpanzees and gorillas. It seems that certain parasites which infest man and chimpanzees and gorillas today had a common ancestor distinct from the common ancestors of gibbon and orang parasites, and the same sort of family tree applies to the primates themselves.

The first hominids, the first members of the family of man, were certainly different from any existing apes. According to David Pilbeam, who works closely with Simons at Yale, they may have looked most like the pygmy chimpanzee which lives south of the Congo River and has been described as a "slender animal with long, thin arms and legs, strongly suggestive of a tailless spider monkey." Pilbeam speculates that they weighed 45 to 60 pounds, stood some three and a half feet tall (about the height of a five-year-old child), and had a 250- to 300-cubic-centimeter brain, about one-fifth the size of the brain of modern man.

Pygmy chimps, mother and child: earliest hominids may have looked something like this

Our earliest ancestors were probably creatures like this who spent a good deal of time in trees and slept in trees at night. But during the day they came down to the ground increasingly, foraging for the most part for plant foods. That means they naturally moved away from denser parts of the forests, where plants were scarce because little sunlight penetrated the trees, to opener forest territory where sunlight and plants were more abundant, to woodlands and grassy areas near seasonally flooded lakes and rivers within the forests. At times they may have ventured away from the last stands of trees at forest fringes out into wide grassy savannas, foraged there for a while, and scampered back into the forests.

One result was a wider-ranging type of primate—since food tends to be more widely dispersed in open country—and significant changes in posture and walking. Apes used their feet not only as supports but also as grasping devices, for example, while eating fruit at the ends of slender branches. Furthermore, they naturally assumed a bent-forward posture, were capable of two-footed walking (but rarely and not for long periods), and usually moved along on their hands as well as on the soles of their feet. Their feet and hands were not fully specialized for support and grasping respectively.

A more complete division of labor was taking place among the first hominids. It was the beginning of the process which eventually resulted among other things in the human stride, a unique primate development involving a series of precisely controlled and timed operations. The stride starts with arch and toe acting as a lever, lifting the body gradually until it rises several inches above its standing height. Measurements show that at this point the average man remains in a delicate balance for about two-tenths of a second as his entire weight rests on the foot. Then a final push, which lasts less than half that time, propels him forward so that his other foot "glides" in for a smooth rather than a jarring landing.

The search continues for direct fossil evidence to document the evolution of the human stride and other hominid features. The ideal situation would be to have a record as ample as that which exists for the evolution of the horse, a series of fossils which shows the gradual change from a collie-sized creature with short chunky teeth and fourteen toes each with its own hoof to the modern long-toothed, four-hooved species. Unfortunately, the hominid record is still far less detailed, although recent years have seen some important new finds and new interpretations of old finds.

One development involves an|incredibly churned-up part of East Africa, the region around Fort Ternan in Kenya about forty miles east of Lake Victoria, where violent movements in the earth have formed a complex and heavily eroded system of hills and valleys.

In 1961 the late Louis Leakey, director of the National Museums' Center for Prehistory and Paleontology in Nairobi and perhaps the most successful searcher for hominid remains, started digging on the slope of one of the hills, at a site discovered by a local orange grower who was looking for mineral deposits and found fossils instead. The site is rich, having already yielded more than 10,000 bones in an area about the size of a large living room. Leakey believed that it may once have been a place where waters, and occasionally poisonous gases, rose up from fissures deep in the earth, and that the gases killed animals coming to drink. (He knew of several such places in the Congo.) During his first season of digging he found the remains of a pygmy giraffe, a pygmy elephant, numerous antelopes, and an unusual variety of primate.

Geologists at the University of California in Berkeley have dated the group of extinct species by dating samples of volcanic rock found with them.|Atoms of radioactive potassium in the rock break down spontaneously into the inert gas argon. The gas is trapped in rock crystals after the lava cools (there is no gas to start with) and accumulates at a steady rate which can be measured with the aid of devices capable of detecting fractions of a billionth of an ounce of material. According to this "radioactive clock" technique—which, incidentally, has also been used to date crystalline rocks brought back from the moon—the Fort Ternan fossils are about 14 million years old, give or take a few hundred thousand years.

Examination of the primate specimen, which includes part of an upper jawbone and several associated teeth, reveals certain distinctively human features. The proportions of the reconstructed jaw indicate a shortened face with a very much reduced snout; the curvature of the jaw suggests a widely arched dental arc rather than the narrow U-shaped arc typical of recent apes. These and other characteristics, such as the smallness of the teeth, can be interpreted in two ways. They are human characteristics in themselves, but that does not necessarily mean that this particular primate was a member of the family of man.

Many types of apes existed 14 million years ago, and this diversity implies a wide diversity and range of physical characteristics —long faces and intermediate-sized faces as well as shortened faces, differently shaped dental arcs, different-sized teeth, and so on. Thus certain primate species may have had a few hominid traits without being hominids in many other respects and thus, of course, without belonging to the human line. On the other hand, Leakey announced that the Fort Ternan specimen exhibits enough hominid features to qualify as an entirely new variety of primate, which helps fill "an enormous gap in the panorama of man's development," the gap between apes and creatures like ourselves.

The announcement proved of special interest to Elwyn Simons, whose digging in the Fayum region of Egypt is only part of a long and continuing investigation of primate evolution. He had spent considerable time studying hundreds of fossils from sites throughout the world in an effort to avoid the bad habit which affects paleontologists as well as others—overestimating the importance of one's own work. Since it is generally more satisfying to discover something new than to confirm someone else's discovery, paleontologists often make too much of their finds. The tendency is to interpret small differences in tooth size and other factors, differences that fall within the normal range of individual variation, as signs of a new genus or at least a new species. In an extreme case, North American grizzly bears, now recognized as members of a single species which also includes Old World varieties, were once divided into more than twenty species.

Aware of a similar tendency in primate studies, Simons recognized the Fort Ternan specimen as a hominid, a member of the family of man, but not as a new genus or even a new species. He pointed out that the collection at Yale's Peabody Museum included an upper-jaw fragment and four teeth of the same sort of creature which a native worker had found about three decades earlier in foothills of the Himalayas, in the Siwalik Hills of the Punjab Province of northern India. Furthermore, he had already reconstructed the jaw and estimated the size of a missing canine tooth by the size of the empty socket. This hypothetical tooth turned out to be an almost perfect match with a real canine found at the Kenya site.

Not long after the Fort Ternan announcement, Simons launched a more intensive survey of previously found material stored in museums, and gained as much fresh information as had been obtained during the previous search for new evidence in the field. For one thing, he "discovered" still another specimen of the same hominid species. That is, he reclassified an upper-jaw fragment which had also been found in the Punjab hills about half a century ago, kept in the Calcutta collection of the Geological Survey of India ever since, and identified mistakenly as belonging to an extinct ape.

At this point the reexamination of old finds took a new turn. The Yale investigator noted that the three specimens, one from East Africa and two from India, were all parts of upper jawbones, a curious observation because collectors generally find more lower jawbones, which are denser and more compact and hence more resistant to decomposition. He began to wonder whether some lower jawbones had actually been found and duly tucked away on museum shelves, but not recognized for what they were. As frequently happens in research, asking the right question is more than half the battle. No sooner had Simons decided on what to look for than he found it, and in his own museum.

The Yale collection included three specimens, all lower-jaw fragments with molar teeth, all found in India years ago, and all classified as remains of a special genus of fossil ape. But the fragments fitted neatly with corresponding upper-jaw fragments already identified tentatively as those of a creature on the direct line of human descent. If future studies confirm such conclusions, this phase of the work will eliminate an entire genus and several species from fossil records, a fitting climax to a survey which has helped clear away some of the debris of primate nomenclature and furnished for the first time a plausible reconstruction of the remote stages of human evolution.

One of man's earliest-known ancestors consisted of a single species with the official title _Ramapithecus punjabicus._ ("Rama" is the name of a hero in Hindu mythology, the incarnation of the deity Vishnu; "pithecus" is Greek for "ape"; and "punjabicus" signifies the part of India where typical material was first discovered.) Not many _Ramapithecus_ specimens have been recovered so far, a total of some fifteen jaw fragments and more than forty teeth, representing perhaps twelve to twenty individuals. But that is enough to serve as the basis for a number of interesting speculations. For example, fossil traces occur not only in Africa and India but also in the coal beds of Hunan Province in China, the Jura Mountains of southern Germany, and perhaps in north central Spain—and it is possible that members of this species moved about freely in the world's savannas and forests. If this assumption is correct, if widespread distribution is any criterion, they must have been highly adaptable and quite capable of dealing with a variety of circumstances.

Current thinking about the way _Ramapithecus_ lived is based in part on studies of his teeth, including his small canines, which have been used to support different theories. According to the oldest theory, small hominid canines are a sign of habitual tool use. Many primates have large canines and put them to good use for purposes indicated, for example, by the behavior of the type of baboon in the savannas of Kenya in Africa, another primate whose ancestors turned from tree dwelling to life on the ground. Under conditions of tension a male baboon in his prime will stop, face an opponent, open his mouth wide in a prodigious yawn, and flash a set of four huge and sharp canines. There is nothing particularly subtle about this gesture. It is a direct threat and warning. It says more clearly than words that the opponent is likely to be ripped if he does not get out of the way.

The flashing of canines serves as an effective symbol. More often than not trouble is avoided and the opponent does indeed get out of the way. When threats and warnings fail, however, these teeth may go into action. They are a baboon's most formidable weapons, and in the last analysis his position in the social order of the troop depends on how well he can fight. Apes as well as baboons, and for that matter carnivores such as lions and tigers, also use them in dismembering prey and shredding plant food. Gorillas have been seen ripping the tough outer layers off bamboo shoots to get at the pith inside, in a kind of banana-peeling operation.

But *Ramapithecus* was not equipped with such large, deep-rooted slashing and puncturing devices. His canines were small like ours and had smaller and more shallow roots, all of which has certain fundamental implications in the light of evolutionary theory. Since the survival of a species depends on vigorous offensive and defensive action, on eating and not being eaten, the body can include no superfluous structures, and generations of development ensure that every part of every individual is shaped for maximum efficiency. There must be a reason for every significant change. Bony armor does not become thinner or movement slower unless compensating factors come into play.

In this context the reduction of the canine teeth was interpreted to mean that *Ramapithecus* had other ways of taking care of himself. Darwin drew a similar conclusion a century ago: "The early male forefathers of man were . . . probably furnished with great canine teeth; but as they gradually acquired the habit of using stones, clubs, or other weapons for fighting with their enemies or rivals, they would use their jaws and teeth less and less." In other words, canines became smaller, because they were no longer needed for attack and defense.

Recent studies suggest a more plausible theory, which depends neither on the assumption of early and extensive hominid tool use nor on the notion of a tooth-and-claw struggle for existence. The theory involves original research by Clifford Jolly of New York University on fossil baboons, extinct relatives of so-called gelada baboons which today live on the high treeless plateaus of central Ethiopia. He notes, among other things, that the canines of males tended to become somewhat smaller and shorter in the course of their evolution than the canines of males belonging to a species of savanna-dwelling baboon.

Since these primates do not use weapons, some factor other than fighting must be at work, and Jolly believes the difference is primarily a matter of diet. Gelada baboons eat an unusually high proportion of grass seeds, stems and other tough plant tissues, and their extinct relatives probably consumed similar foods. Such material must be ground up and calls for a powerful chewing action. And that, in turn, poses a mechanical problem, since large canine teeth tend to interlock, making side-to-side jaw movements less efficient. This problem has put an evolutionary premium on those males with smaller and smaller canines, which reduce chances of interlocking and permit more complete grinding—and the same changes occurred in times past among early hominids who also had to cope with increasing quantities of tough plant foods as they foraged increasingly on the ground.

This argument does not rule out the possibility that early hominids used weapons. Indeed, if we can judge by the behavior of chimpanzees today, the odds are that they did—and that may have had an indirect bearing on canine reduction. The fact that our ancestors were quite capable of wielding weapons probably permitted the evolution of considerably smaller canine teeth without a great disadvantage in fighting and defense.

The main point about Jolly's theory is that it focuses on diet rather than fighting as the major factor in reducing canines. The theory is considerably broader than that, however, and helps account for a whole complex of further changes, dental and otherwise. For example, efficient grinding of tough foods also requires very large and closely packed cheek teeth, molars and premolars, a feature found in both gelada baboons and *Ramapithecus*.

Another feature of hominid behavior, and another major problem, concerns the development of an upright posture and walking in the human line. Many theories have been offered to explain why a two-footed gait should have developed in the first place. The value of this new form of primate locomotion is not at all self-evident. It is certainly not an inevitable consequence of coming down to earth from the trees, and the example of the baboon, among other species, shows that primates can live on the ground without walking upright. As a matter of fact, an upright posture has several important disadvantages. Animals balancing themselves on two feet are easier to knock over, more conspicuous, and less agile when it comes to dodging and feinting and other escape tactics.

So there must have been advantages. Furthermore, they must have been enormous advantages to overcome all the drawbacks, the illogic and awkwardness, of bipedalism. Certain theories turn out to be quite inadequate to account for so drastic a change in locomotion. For example, primates often stand erect for a time when circumstances demand it, say, when they want a better view of the surrounding terrain. This is a familiar sight in the Amboseli Game Reserve, where baboons, including infants no more than two or three months old, often stand up on their hind legs at the sound of a passing car or to keep track of the rest of the troop.

Such conduct is common among baboons and other ground-dwelling primates. In fact it has been cited in support of the "reconnaissance" theory of human bipedalism. The idea is that savanna-exploring hominids were frequently killed by lions and other predators lurking in tall grasses, that evolution put a premium on standing erect as a way of spotting predators at a distance and avoiding them—and that a by-product of standing erect was the release of the hands for use in coping with the environment. But this advantage is not big enough. The theory does not clarify the main problem. It presents a convincing argument for the benefits of occasional but not habitual bipedalism, without indicating what type of living conditions could have made reconnaissance so important that it brought about a radical departure from conventional patterns of primate locomotion.

There are better arguments for the notion that walking on two feet evolved as a way of carrying food more efficiently. There is plenty of evidence for such behavior among primates of all ages. Jane van Lawick-Goodall of the Gombe Stream Research Center on the shores of Lake Tanganyika, Africa, has spent more than ten years observing chimpanzees in the forests of northwest Tanzania, and has seen the apes "loading their arms with choice wild fruits, then walking erect for several yards to a spot of shade before sitting down to eat." Macaque monkeys on Kyushu Island, Japan, may walk more than sixty feet from forest to beach to wash dirt off handfuls of sweet potatoes (provided by scientists to entice the animals into open country where they can be observed).

These and many similar examples are sufficient to show that apes and monkeys can walk upright upon occasion just as we can go on all fours when the demand arises, as in clambering up a steep bank or moving along under low branches or crawling through low passages in caves. But food carrying is simply not a big enough advantage for them. They can do it perfectly well without full-time bipedalism and in environmental settings little different from those prevailing during the earliest days of hominid evolution.

The problem is to figure out what special forces and circumstances might have favored the major shift from part-time to full-time bipedalism. In this connection meat eating and sharing may be significant. (Individual plants are rarely big enough to share, and plant eaters are generally neither sharers nor carriers.) Killing even a small animal may provide a hunter with ten or fifteen pounds of meat, more than he can eat, and may be worth carrying back to a camp or home base. The record certainly indicates that meat eating inevitably led to greater sharing, and that meant carrying food over long distances—a development which could have contributed to the selection of populations made up of individuals who could walk several miles while carrying one or more small animals.

Another possibility is that more basic forces were at work even earlier. For one thing, the very fact that hominids foraged increasingly on the ground where food tends to be dispersed may have encouraged new forms of locomotion. Bipedalism happens to be a comfortable and convenient way of covering large areas, once it has been developed. It would also be promoted by the use of tools, a theory that differs from most other theories, which assume that erect posture came first and that the release of the hands was a secondary "bonus" effect. The notion that things also worked the other way around was originally suggested by Darwin, and has been reemphasized by Washburn.

Washburn points out that the factor which provided the primary selective pressure for the shift to full-time bipedalism was the enormous advantage of another highly developed human characteristic, the use of tools. Tools opened up many possibilities, not only in defense against predators but also in digging up and preparing food. So bands composed of individuals which could stand and walk upright more easily and for longer and longer periods, and hence had their hands free increasingly for tool use, flourished rapidly at the expense of bands less fitted to survive in the savanna.

Assuming that this is what happened, the problem is how tool use itself evolved. There are clues to a possible answer. Imagine an adventurous hominid or prehominid, a primitive *Ramapithecus* perhaps, looking for food in the savanna and wandering too far and suddenly being confronted by a predator directly in the escape route to the nearest trees. Such encounters could have been frequent in the beginning. They are by no means rare nowadays. One hardly ever observes actual attacks, which are generally carried out at night, but a leftover leg or some other fresh piece of primate carcass lying in the savanna dust the next morning indicates the failure of escape tactics. Also, examinations of the droppings of leopards and other big cats indicate that monkeys are well preyed on.

At one time our ancestors had no effective way of fighting back when brought to bay by large predators. But they may well have developed special forms of display, bluffing behavior, which helped them to delay attacks and even to get away in some cases. The trick among all animals in all such emergencies is to make themselves look more frightening, often by increasing apparent stature. Puffer fish double or triple their body size by inflating themselves into globes; birds may ruffle their feathers and puff out their chests and spread their wings wide; cats arch their backs and their fur stands on end.

All such reactions are "natural" in the sense that they tend to be automatic, hereditary, and that they consist essentially of mechanical and physiological changes in body structure. But it is possible that a new principle may have been at work in the displays of prehominids and that they began to reach out for something external, something not built in and not part of the body which would help them to appear bigger and more formidable. In other words, they may originally have put up a bluff by artificial means, using branches or clumps of tall grass or perhaps long bones to enlarge their body images.

The general tendency to pick up and wave things is common among contemporary apes. When chimpanzees and gorillas are aroused, they often grab a nearby stick or branch and swing it about in a vigorous, random flailing motion. Van Lawick-Goodall reports that on rare occasions playing with branches may take on a strange, ritualistic quality. A big male chimpanzee may become tremendously excited, break a branch off a tree, brandish it about, and rush down a mountain slope (often on two feet) dragging it behind him. Then he rushes up the slope and repeats the action several times. The significance of this behavior is not known, but sometimes other males will join the fun in a mass "branch-waving display . . . calling, tearing off and waving large branches, hurling themselves to the ground from the trees."

Branch-waving plays a less mysterious role when chimpanzees are frustrated or angry with one another, in which case shaking branches is part of displays that may include slapping or stamping on the ground and high-pitched screaming. They have been seen charging at one another with sticks in their hands, and although in general they simply threaten and do not strike, they sometimes use sticks to attack one another. The apes also show a special concern with branches when they climb into a tree where they expect to spend some time, either to build a nest for the night or to play with another chimpanzee. They move from limb to limb, breaking off dead branches and dropping them to the ground below, as if they were clearing away deadwood so that the tree would be a safe place for maneuvering.

Apes have an ample repertoire of basic branch-handling activities and manipulations which they use in different combinations and sequences under different circumstances. Although no one has ever reported seeing a real-life encounter between an armed ape and a predator, a Dutch zoologist produced an analogous situation experimentally about eight years ago in the Congo. Adriaan Kortlandt of the University of Amsterdam arranged things so that a stuffed dummy leopard could be pulled out of some shrubbery and into a meadow when a troop of wild chimpanzees was being observed.

Here is how he describes one such confrontation when the stuffed leopard appeared with a chimpanzee-doll "victim" in its claws: "There was a moment of silence first. Then hell broke loose. There was an uproar of yelling and barking, and most of the apes came forward and began to charge at the leopard. . . . Some charges were made bare-handed; in others the assailants broke off a small tree while they ran toward or past the leopard, or brandished a big stick or broken tree in their charge, or threw such a primitive weapon in the general direction of the enemy.

. . . Both when attacking and when looking at the leopard, the apes again and again uttered a special blood-curdling type of barking yell."

For all the sound and fury, however, it was more of a mobbing-type display calculated to harass the leopard and make it go away than a practiced and skillfully directed use of weapons. Clubs were brandished and hurled, but there were no actual hits. The interesting thing about all this is that the chimpanzees were forest dwellers, and attacks from leopards and other predators tend to be infrequent in forests.

In later studies Kortlandt reports far more direct action among wild chimpanzees living in the sort of open savanna country in Guinea, where predators are more common. There was no doubt about the chimpanzees' objectives under these conditions. They beat up the dummy leopard with repeated and well-aimed heavy blows using clubs up to six feet long. Van Lawick-Goodall has seen chimpanzees throwing stones at baboons, and although they seldom hit their targets, some individuals are more accurate than others. The implication is that early hominids may also have used clubs and missiles from time to time.

Some investigators have another explanation for the origins of tool use, an explanation which accents the search for food rather than defense. According to Leakey, evidence for the food hypothesis may already have been uncovered in the form of the broken shinbone of an oxlike animal found at Fort Ternan. The break is the depressed or indented kind which might have been produced by a rock, and suggests that perhaps a hungry *Ramapithecus* wielded the rock to make a meal of the bone marrow, although similar breaks have been found among bones in leopard lairs. The effort to check such possibilities indicates why analyzing fractured fossil bones is an important phase of present-day research.

Tools could have been used in gathering plant foods. During dry periods baboons may use their fingers to dig holes as much as fifteen inches deep and two feet across to get at succulent roots and tubers, but, as far as we know, they have not discovered that the job would be considerably easier with the aid of a sturdy stick or a sharp rock. On the other hand, hominids or prehominid apes might well have learned the trick, since they were probably rather skillful in working with tools.

They might also have learned to use probes, perhaps somewhat as wild chimpanzees do today. The observations of van Lawick-Goodall in Tanzania do much to weaken a notion supported over the years by many investigators from Benjamin Franklin and Friedrich Engels to modern anthropologists, namely, that although other animals may upon occasion use tools, man is the only regular maker of tools. Chimpanzees also make tools to obtain one of their favorite foods, termites. During most of the year termite hills are covered with a thick concretelike shell to protect them from birds, monkeys and other termite eaters. But in late October or early November, just before the onset of the rainy season, worker termites drill holes through the shell, destroying all but the outermost fraction of an inch—so that they can emerge quickly when the rains come, begin their nuptial flights, and found new colonies.

While the termite operates by instinct, the chimpanzee operates by insight. He has learned when a termite hill is ripe for exploitation and where the thinly covered holes are. Then he takes a bit of vine or a slender stick, trims it neatly and carefully by pulling off leaves and side shoots, breaks it off to a length of six to twelve inches, and approaches the hill. After licking the probe he pokes it through the shell and into one of the holes, and waits a moment or two. When he draws the probe out, termites are clinging to it and he licks them off as gleefully as a child with a lollipop. (Incidentally, van Lawick-Goodall has eaten termites and finds them "rather flavorless.")

In such foraging, chimpanzees may plan ahead. For example, they do not always find a promising termite hill and then proceed to make a probe. They may make the probe first, anticipating a meal of termites, although neither termites nor termite hills are in sight. One chimpanzee carried a suitably prepared stick in its mouth for half a mile, inspected eight hills without finding a good one, and then dropped the tool. So these apes seem to have the basic concept of a tool as something to be shaped for a situation that has not yet materialized, and there is reason to believe that *Ramapithecus* was at least as ingenious.

In any case, notice that the use of implements as accessories or extensions of the body bears a direct relationship to developments that had taken place beforehand in the trees. Part of the story, of course, concerns the sort of dexterity required to grasp and pull branches and to swing along from branch to branch. But the coming of stereoscopic color vision was an even more important factor. As already indicated, objects acquired a new meaning, a new reality, with the appearance of highly advanced visual

Prehuman tool user: chimpanzee probing for termites

mechanisms. They were viewed in full perspective and tended to "leap out" of the background more completely and vividly for primates than for other visually inferior animals. To put it another way, primates acquired richer and more detailed perceptions—and it is precisely this faculty which more than anything else created a heightened awareness of objects as distinct and clear-cut entities capable of serving as display elements and ultimately as tools.

It follows from Washburn's theory that once the new way of life caught on, once its advantages were proved in the field as it were, it achieved a new kind of momentum of its own. The relationship between tool use and bipedalism acquired a two-way self-reinforcing quality. It was not only that increased tool use brought about the selection of changes in body structure which made for more efficient bipedalism. More efficient bipedalism, in turn, freed the hands more and more for increased tool use and provided more time for acquiring new manipulative skills. In such a developing process it becomes increasingly difficult to distinguish cause and effect.

The process yielded further advantages as by-products. Walking erect resulted in a continuous and more panoramic view of the savanna, an increased ability to see things coming and to detect and anticipate danger. Looking ahead from an elevated position may also have extended the sense of the future. So there is something to the reconnaissance theory. There is also something to the food-carrying theory, although it may have been more important to carry infants than food, which is generally eaten on the spot. If bipedalism produced a foot designed above all for support and with greatly reduced grasping capacities, infants could no longer have clung as effectively to their mothers and would have had to be carried. In fact, the one case that I have seen of upright walking among baboons involved a mother who from time to time was forced to move a few steps on two feet so that she could support her infant.

Another indirect benefit of bipedalism may have been that it helped to discourage the most dangerous predators, the big cats. A predator knows its prey from repeated encounters, repeated successes and failures in the hunt, and part of that knowledge in early hominid times must have been a firmly ingrained image of its prey as a four-footed animal. George Schaller of the New York Zoological Society, who has observed tigers in India and lions in Tanzania as well as gorillas in the Congo, comments on this possibility: "Some big cats turn into man-eaters, a fact interesting chiefly because it is so rare. They hunt by lying in wait or approaching stealthily and bounding on the victim's back, and they bite at the neck. Man is bipedal and thus does not furnish a good target, a good horizontal plane for the cats to jump on.

Perhaps that is one thing that deters them today, and deterred them in the past."

These and other ideas lean heavily on speculation; they are neither proved nor universally accepted. On the other hand, they fit in with much of what we have learned to date from fossils, primate behavior and related studies. The inference is strong that *Ramapithecus* was among the first hominids, that he represents a widespread and successful breed. Also, he probably used tools and perhaps was somewhat better than present-day apes at walking about on two feet.

There is much to learn about the forerunners of *Ramapithecus*. Efforts have been made to trace the hominid line back further than the 14-million-year-old date at Fort Ternan. A date of 20 million years has been estimated for certain fossil primate specimens, including some found on Rusinga Island in Lake Victoria, long a favorite hunting ground of Leakey and his wife Mary, an accomplished investigator in her own right. But most qualified specialists feel that the specimens are the remains of an ape rather than a hominid.

Some doubt also exists about evidence from Egypt's Fayum which Simons has suggested may indicate that the first representatives of the human line appeared 25 million years ago. Other investigators favor a more recent date. Washburn, for example, cites biochemical studies of primate blood proteins conducted by Victor Sarich at the University of California as part of his argument that hominids and apes did not emerge as separate lines until 5 million to 10 million years ago. As of now, the tendency is to stick with *Ramapithecus* and an estimate of about 15 million years.

■ A 5-million-year gap in the record; dwindling seas and the spread of savannas; the African Rift Valley; Dart's discovery of the "Taung baby"; evidence against the large-brain theory; the Piltdown fraud; evolution and adjustment to change

CHAPTER III

"Southern Apes"—Links in the Evolution of Man

■ |*Ramapithecus* stands alone, isolated in time, a face or the shadow of a face seen in the distance. His successors, like his predecessors, are still elusive. Practically nothing is known about his development from about 10 million years ago, which represents roughly the most recent date for *Ramapithecus* as identified by Pilbeam and Simons, to about 5 million years ago, the biggest gap in the story of human evolution. We can expect to obtain new knowledge in the years ahead, because expeditions are under way or planned in East Africa, the Siwalik Hills, Saudi Arabia and other regions.

But we cannot expect too much. Conditions widely prevalent during that period could hardly have been less favorable for the preservation of fossils. Many places where hominids might have lived were undergoing a period of erosion marked by the wearing away of old deposits rather than the formation of new ones in which primate remains might have been preserved. In other places deposits were buried by lava, or they were too acid, hastening the decomposition of bone and other organic material. Furthermore, since most of the deposits do not contain important natural resources such as coal, they have been far less thoroughly explored than earlier and later deposits of greater commercial interest. (Some of the rare remains of the period have been found by workers in the diamond mines of southwest Africa.)

So the 5 million years after *Ramapithecus* are still an almost complete blank as far as hominid traces are concerned. The geological record, however, is highly articulate. Compared to the silence of the fossil record, it practically shouts at us. Human evolution proceeded in times and places of unprecedented unrest, and part of the change was the dwindling of seas and the spread of savannas and deserts and semideserts. The vast sea that stretched from Spain to Malaya 70 million years ago when the first primates appeared, the sea that was itself the remnant of an even more extensive earlier sea, continued to shrink toward its present-day dimensions, leaving the Mediterranean and three smaller "puddles," the Black, Caspian and Aral seas.

It was more of the same general sort of process that began with the fragmenting of the original supercontinent. New barriers were appearing, separating populations of primates and other animals from one another. *Ramapithecus* had ranged through widespread Africa-to-Asia open woodlands and grasslands, and now the wilderness was being split as rainfall declined in the Middle East, producing a desert too wide and too barren to cross. Conditions must have been different to the west and to the east of the barrier. The east presumably had greater unbroken regions of dense forest, because primate populations on the Asian side of the desert included the ancestors of present-day orangutans, which live almost exclusively in the trees.

Evolution took a different direction in Africa, in lands to the west of the desert which included the ancestors of chimpanzees and gorillas, and our ancestors. The red wind-blown sands of the Kalahari, which move back and forth with changing climates like the glaciers of Europe, were spreading from the Orange and Vaal rivers of the south to the Congo, leaving forest regions in East Africa and in a ring around the central Congo Basin.

This sort of terrain offered two main types of environment: island or residual forests in which specialized tree dwellers lived their entire lives, sometimes mainly in a single grove of trees—and savannas and semiarid plains where primates, four-footed and two-footed, spent a large proportion of their time on the ground. Chimpanzees and gorillas evolved in the island forests; men evolved in the open places. In the absence of fossil evidence we can only infer that the descendants of *Ramapithecus* adapted to the changing terrain, that they broke more of their ancestral ties with the forests, spent less and less of their time in wood-lands, and devoted more and more time to savannas rich in grasses, seeds and tender shoots. In the process they probably had increasing encounters with predators.

The arboreal life was not yet completely abandoned, however. At first they may have continued sleeping in trees among the woodlands where they returned every night. Later, when they no longer returned to the woodlands, they slept in groves out in the savanna. When trees were not available they most likely chose places where predators could not follow, perhaps spending their nights on the ledges of cliffs, facing the cliff wall as some baboons do in the twentieth century.

Baboons, like early man, keeping lookout over savanna

Exploiting grassy savannas and semiarid regions demands wider ranging. Early hominids presumably had to cover a rela-tively wide area on the principle that vegetation was sparse, and the sparser the vegetation the farther an individual must travel to obtain its quota of food. In fact, the energy spent ranging in search of food increased that quota. Our ancestors were probably on the move a good part of the day. They may have made increasing use of digging sticks and pointed rocks to get at water-containing tubers and other buried food. Incidentally, the rocks and digging sticks could also have served as weapons to ward off carnivores which were busy in their ways exploiting food sources to the utmost.

There was plenty of space and time for these and other developments. It has been estimated that the coming of deserts, the declining rainfall which separated the forests of Africa from those of India and the Far East, reduced the living space of *Ramaphithecus* and later hominids by some 5 million square miles, about half the area of North America. The decrease took place over a period of more than 10 million years, and at any one time 20 million hominids were at large in Africa, divided into perhaps 300,000 or more separate bands or troops.

Meanwhile, other changes were taking place besides the general increase in the extent of arid lands. Africa was about to experience one of the most spectacular series of upheavals in the history of the earth. The southernmost part of the continent remained quiet, geologically speaking, having had its period of fire and brimstone some 150 million years ago, when volcanoes erupted everywhere and buried it beneath more than 6,000 feet of lava. But trouble came in more northerly regions, where the earth's interior was rumbling and unstable, and where there were and still are marks of the continuing splitting up of continents.

Traces of what happened can be seen today in Kenya, less than an hour's drive out of Nairobi, from the edge of a cliff overlooking a valley fifty miles across. At the other side is another cliff and in between, on the valley floor fifteen hundred feet below, are signs of a time when the earth tossed like an angry sea. Here the waves and the churnings are frozen in solid rock—Mount Eburru, black and craggy and flat along the top, a volcano that may become active again; Mount Longonot, with its peak hidden in clouds and long sloping terraces formed by ancient lava flows; domes like the tops of bubbles about to burst and craters where bubbles burst ages ago; and Lake Naivasha, with no visible outlet, drained by deep fissures.

This part of the world was stirring some 35 million years ago about the time when modern varieties of monkeys and apes were evolving from prosimians. East Africa consisted mainly of a dry flat plain marked here and there by depressions, sagging places in the crust of the earth. Nearby volcanoes had thrust their cones a mile or two high, and air masses sweeping up the slopes expanded and became cooler. Rains fell on the windward sides of the mountains, producing lakes in the depressions, local "oases" and swamps in a broad setting of active volcanoes and arid lands. (Sediments accumulating in the lakes provided excellent conditions for the preservation of fossils, but unfortunately most of them are buried beyond recovery beneath lava and other deposits.)

The pace of change picked up ten or twelve million years ago particularly in the depressed areas, those forming the lake basins and many others as well. These areas marked lines of weakness in the crust, unstable zones in which tides of rock were welling up from deep underground and creating enormous tensions. Some of the stresses were relaxed as the earth let off steam in the escaping gases, waters and molten rock of numerous volcanoes and geysers and sulfurous blowholes. But the coming of new cataclysms was being prepared along the weak, depressed zones where stresses were still unrelieved.

Pressures which had been increasing for ages were released in a thousand places as the crust shifted in great jerking movements. Earthquakes shook and shattered the crust. Fracture lines appeared like giant cracks in glass, some slicing through hills and the eroded stubs of old mountains, and others ripping open the bottoms of lakes or tilting lake basins so that the waters poured off to form flash-flood gorges. New structures took shape along the fracture lines. Entire sections of the crust rose or dropped, creating escarpments or palisades and, in between, broad valleys like the one outside Nairobi.

This was no local affair, however, but an upheaval of continental dimensions, and part of the drifting apart of land masses all over the world. In Africa the result was a far-flung fracturing, the Great Rift Valley, extending about 4,000 miles from the Zambezi River area of Mozambique in the south, up through East Africa and Ethiopia, and north as far as the Valley of the Jordan in Israel. The Jordan River, the Dead and Red seas, Lakes Edward and Albert and Tanganyika and Malawi are some of the places where water has filled steep, parallel-sided valleys along the fracture lines of the Rift.

The violent rifting started between five and two million years ago, but the earth has not yet recovered and still trembles and heaves in response to forces deep in the earth. Steam still hisses from vents and fissures on the slopes of Mount Eburru, and local farmers use it to cook potatoes and, in condensed form, to water livestock. Some two thousand miles away, in the floor of the Red Sea offshore from Mecca more than a mile deep, are cracks out of which flows water at temperatures as high as 133 degrees Fahrenheit and ten times saltier than the sea water above it, cracks associated with continuing rift activity and the shaping of a new ocean where the Red Sea and the Gulf of Aden are now. In fact, in this area the Rift Valley is widening at a rate of about half an inch a year. The process is under way in the current formation of the island-to-be mentioned in Chapter I and consisting of parts of Somaliland, Kenya and Tanzania.

The Rift itself makes up only part of an even greater system, also connected with worldwide continental drift. There is an enormous widening crack in the crust that runs nearly twice around the earth and lies submerged beneath the world's oceans, a continuous range of mountains 40,000 miles long and split along most of its length by a canyon up to thirty miles wide and averaging more than a mile deep. This super-Rift has been traced from a point not far off the coast of Alaska, under the Pacific Ocean along the coast of Canada and southern California, into the Pacific, due west past New Zealand to the Indian Ocean, and then around Africa and north through the middle of the Atlantic Ocean toward the Arctic Circle. Almost the entire range is under water. But it comes up on dry land in several places, including the San Andreas Fault of the California coast, the central Icelandic graben or "ditch," and Africa's Rift Valley (a branch of the main system).

The effects of rifting in Africa on human evolution are more difficult to specify than the effects of the increase of deserts and semideserts. But the movements of hominids were certainly altered. Traditional migration routes had to be abandoned and new ones established. Before the rifting, Africa was essentially a broad plain created by the erosion of ancient mountain ranges, a plain rising gradually to heights of more than a mile. The top of the rise formed a continental divide running north and south, waters of the Congo Basin draining west off the slopes into the Atlantic Ocean and other waters draining east into the Indian Ocean. Rivers tended to separate hominid populations from one another, to restrict their movements to zones running east and west. (Apes are afraid of water when they cannot see bottom, and they will not cross a stream more than a foot deep and more than twenty feet or so wide.)

Rifting changed that pattern. Instead of flowing in a west-to-east direction from the divide to the Indian Ocean, rivers tended to flow north and south along Rift lines and drained internally in Rift Valleys. So hominid bands could also move more freely along new north-south migration routes, although the all-important question of timing remains to be answered. Did populations of advanced hominids evolve on the plains of southern Africa and spread to the north when the rivers shifted, or evolve in East Africa and spread south, or in both regions and mingle? Some investigators suspect that post-Rift migrations were from south to north, but the evidence is so sparse that no one really knows.

The picture becomes even more complicated when one considers that rifting closed certain routes while it opened others. In pre-Rift times a land bridge connected Asia and Africa, so that it was possible to move directly from Egypt or the Sudan or Ethiopia across Saudi Arabia into Iran and India. But that bridge was broken by the formation of the Red Sea. Furthermore, studies of closely related species of trees, mollusks and birds now separated by five hundred miles of hot, dry terrain suggest that the rising of Rift mountains cut West Africa from East Africa and isolated populations that once mingled freely.

Some 5 million years of geological change passed during the time between *Ramapithecus* and the next phase of the fossil record. Then the story picks up again, and it is a new story based on new evidence discovered in increasing quantities during the past two or three years. A different kind of human ancestor emerges. Imagine that you are in a helicopter flying high over an African savanna late one hot prehistoric afternoon. From that perspective things appear very much as they do today. You look down on a dry grassy plain, straw-colored except for scattered bushes and trees, dark green clumps near swamps and water holes, and the lone winding ribbon of green that marks the course of a large river where it empties into a lake.

Coming down for a closer view, hovering at the edge of the trees along a stretch of the river, you might at first sight see nothing unusual, nothing to indicate that you are not in the twentieth century. There are many familiar-looking birds, familiar-looking monkeys performing in the trees, hyenas and antelopes and giraffes, and a hippopotamus wallowing in the mud— all of them very much like today's varieties. Then you notice some strange animals: little three-toed horses grazing near the trees, and a herd of elephants with two tusks in their lower jaws and two in their upper jaws.

But the most surprising sight of all lies in another direction. You turn, the trees at your back, look out over the wide savanna, and see a troop of creatures heading for the forest. They have not yet come close, but even at a distance there is something familiar about them. They move like people. They walk fully upright, their arms swinging freely at their sides. A mother runs over to a group of scuffling children and scolds as she snatches her child away. The leader strides forward confidently with the alert no-nonsense attitude of a Western sheriff making sure the coast is clear.

Now you have a shock as he approaches and you see him clearly for the first time. Judging by his gait and posture and by the general feeling of humanness about the troop, you expect to confront a fellow human being. But he is surprisingly small, four feet tall, or about the size of a modern child of seven or eight. Even more surprising is his alien and disturbing face. His jaw and mouth are thrust forward with the trace of a muzzle. He has a low forehead and flattish nose and a remote half-wild look which is not human and yet somehow reminds you of humanity. The sun is setting as the troop reaches the water hole and begins climbing into the trees to prepare for the night.

The earliest known trace of these creatures exists in the form of an age-blackened bit of lower jawbone from Africa, announced in 1971 by Bryan Patterson of Harvard's Museum of Comparative Zoology. The specimen had been studied on and off for nearly four years, ever since it was found one scorching August afternoon lying on a sun-baked clay slope of Lothagam Hill in the Kenya badlands near the southwestern end of Lake Rudolf, which is part of the African Rift Valley.

The significance of the discovery was immediately evident to Patterson and his associates, who had been searching in the general region because of its promising fossil-bearing sediments. But their work had just begun. First of all, whenever an important fossil is found, efforts are redoubled to find further evidence on the spot, hopefully including other pieces of the same specimen. In this case, the Harvard investigators and a dozen workers recruited from a tribe of local nomads spent the better part of a month digging and sifting through tons of deposits, with only a lone unexciting monkey premolar tooth to show for their trouble.

So all the information had to come from the original specimen in detailed laboratory studies, and part of the job was to identify it as definitely as possible. Patterson went mainly by the shape of the jawbone, and the shape and wear patterns of the single tooth remaining in place, a molar. For example, the tooth's grinding surface was worn unevenly, included a number of deep pits, and showed extensive wear on the sides where the tooth had fitted against neighboring teeth. These characteristics and others are rare among apes, but typical of creatures far more like man than any other previous primate—members of the genus *Australopithecus* or "southern ape."

The Lothagam fossil yielded further information. The genus included two species: *Australopithecus africanus,* which was about four feet tall, and the somewhat taller and heavier *Australopithecus robustus.* A clue to distinguishing one species from the other involves the location of pits on the surfaces of lower molar teeth. In the *africanus* form the pits tend to be located on the tooth's outer edge, the edge nearest the cheek; in the *robustus* form, on the other hand, the pits generally lie on the inner edge. The single Lothagam tooth had the *africanus* pattern, and that, together with other features, served to identify the species. Finally, the smallish size of the jawbone hints that it may have been that of a female.

The most striking thing about the specimen turns out to be its age. Unfortunately, the deposits in which it was found contain no volcanic rock suitable for dating by the potassium-argon technique. But they do contain remains of elephants which were evolving swiftly during early *Australopithecus* days, and hence provide a relatively sensitive index to the passage of time. Vincent Maglio of Princeton University found a massive four-tusked variety of elephant in the Lothagam deposits, and nearby deposits bearing somewhat less primitive, somewhat more recent elephants had been dated by the potassium-argon radioactive clock. By conservative estimates, the jawbone is more than 5 million years old, which makes it at least a million years older than the oldest previously known *Australopithecus* specimen.

This find is only one of a series of recent finds which are providing a fuller picture of the near-men or pre-men of Africa. The new work confirms, vindicates, the insights of an investigator who recognized the importance of such fossils nearly half a century ago, about a generation before the time was ripe for acceptance of his ideas. *Australopithecus* remains were first discovered in the southern part of Africa by Raymond Dart, professor of anatomy at the Medical School of the University of the Witwatersrand in Johannesburg. One afternoon in 1924 he received two crates filled with fossil-bearing rocks collected by a miner at a limestone quarry in the village of Taung ("place of the lion" in Bantu) near the edge of the Kalahari Desert about two hundred miles away. He was expected at a wedding and wrestling with a stiff-winged collar at the time, but promptly tore it off and began examining the material.

The quarry had already yielded the skull of a baboon, among other things, and there was always the possibility of finding something more interesting, say, the remains of a more advanced primate. This is precisely what happened. Dart came across a large block which had been blasted out of a tunnel-like cave in a limestone cliff and which contained the cast of a large brain case and major parts of a skull and jaw. He speculated that "the face might be somewhere there in the block." He went to work with hammer and chisel and, for the most delicate work, one of his wife's knitting needles.

In a subsequent report he recalls the long process of separating the fossil bones from their matrix of sand and lime: "No diamond cutter ever worked more lovingly or with such care on a priceless jewel—nor, I am sure, with such inadequate tools. But on the seventy-third day, December 23, the rock parted. I could view the face from the front, although the right side was still imbedded. [The complete extraction process took more than four

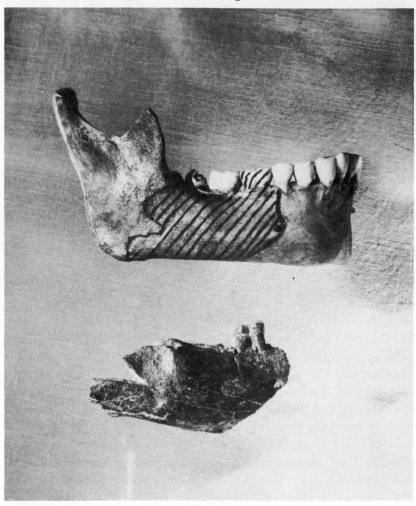

New fossil: bottom—*Australopithecus* jawbone fragment more than 5 million years old. Top—modern jawbone showing location of fragment

years.] The creature which had contained this massive brain was no giant anthropoid such as a gorilla. What emerged was a baby's face, an infant with a full set of milk teeth and its permanent molars just in the process of erupting. I doubt if there was any parent prouder of his offspring than I was of my Taung baby on that Christmas."

About five weeks later the South African anatomist announced his find in a paper published in the British journal *Nature*. The report noted that the canine teeth of the Taung specimen were small, and that this implied an upright posture and increasing use of the hands and the probable use of tools and weapons. It also noted the significance of the fact that the specimen had been found in a near-desert site where life must have been difficult and required "enhanced cerebral powers" for survival. Dart described the specimen as that of an "ultra-simian and prehuman stock," "a manlike ape," and officially christened it *Australopithecus africanus*, the first representative of a new species.

His report also made a strong case for Africa as the continent where man first appeared, a point first emphasized by Darwin. More specifically, it suggested that man must have arisen in dry and grassy savannas rather than in dense tropical forests, as many anthropologists believed. Food was so abundant in the forests and life so easy that apes faced no major challenges, and remained apes. "For the production of man a different apprenticeship was needed to sharpen the wits and quicken the higher manifestations of intellect—a more open veldt country where competition was keener between swiftness and stealth, and where adroitness of thinking and movement played a preponderating role in the preservation of the species."

It was a typical example of a report written too soon for contemporary thinking. Dart's general conclusions were right, but they came at the wrong time. *Ramapithecus* had not yet been identified, and it was widely assumed that walking on two feet and tool use could not be expected among apes, even among manlike apes. Most investigators, including his former teacher Elliot Smith at University College in London, regarded the "Taung baby" as an ape not on the line that led to man but more like the chimpanzee or gorilla. So they were less interested in discussing its nature than in the fact that it had been discovered so far south and in a near-desert region.

Furthermore, all eyes then were on Asia, where the earliest traces of man known at the time had been found. One of the major scientific projects of the times was a large-scale and lib-erally financed American expedition organized to look for human remains in Mongolia and the Gobi Desert, an expedition which in the words of one caustic commentator "promised man but delivered eggs," dinosaur eggs uncovered in the Gobi sands. (Very early human or prehuman remains have not yet been found in this region, but Polish workers, digging near the place where dinosaur eggs were collected during the 1920's, recently returned with many tons of fossils, including 125-million-year-old skulls of the earliest known mammals.)

So far as most anthropologists were concerned, Dart was working in the wrong part of the world. They also felt that he had found the wrong kind of human ancestor. *Australopithecus* had a small brain, weighing perhaps a pound, or about a third as much as the brain of modern man, and that did not fit in with prevailing theory. According to Elliot Smith and most of his colleagues, the brain was a kind of pacemaker in the evolution of man, and man had arisen from apelike species which had big brains to start with and then proceeded to take advantage of this favorable beginning by evolving to human status.

There was some evidence for this theory. In 1913, a British lawyer and part-time antiquarian, Charles Dawson, reported that he had discovered the remains of an individual with a human skull and an apelike jaw in a gravel pit in the village of Piltdown near the eastern coast of England. This material, together with skull fragments and apelike teeth which Dawson found later in a field two miles away, puzzled many investigators because the contrast between the humanness of the skull and the apishness of the jaw was so great. But since the remains tended to confirm the brain-as-pacemaker theory, they were more readily accepted at face value.

Dart had to wait until the time was ripe for his point of view, until the weight of accumulating evidence and the exposure of Piltdown man as a fraud forced other workers to recognize that his "southern apes" were actually full-fledged hominids. The first confirmation came a dozen years later from a site nearer home, thirty miles west of Johannesburg. It lies in the Transvaal with its wide, dry rolling plains, waist-high golden grasses, clumps of trees, and a dryness so prevalent that there is a joke about what to do when you fall into a South African river. You get up and brush yourself off.

The land here, as in many parts of Africa, is itself a prehistoric relic. It must have looked much the same in the time of *Australopithecus* and earlier, though the grasses are less hostile now, lions and other predators having been driven out and confined together with their prey to game reserves far from the city. One of the few wet waterways of the region, the Klip River, winds through a broad valley and rises from a swamp. Not far from the swamp, on a farm known as Sterkfontein, is a kopje or little hill with a long history.

The hill is a block of limestone formed some two billion years ago when Africa was submerged beneath a shallow sea, covered by more than six miles of sediments and lava, and then exposed by erosion. Waters seeped down through cracks in the rock and dissolved away calcium-containing deposits, producing small cavities at first and later a system of deep caves. One of the caves still exists; the others have crumbled away. Limestone quarrymen moved into its several hundred yards of underground passages more than sixty years ago. There they found fossils, many of which were sold to tourists on Sundays when the mine was open to the public. Also on sale was a guidebook which included an invitation: "Come to Sterkfontein and find the missing link."

One Sunday visitor took the invitation literally. Robert Broom, a Scottish-born physician and paleontologist who lived in South Africa, and was noted among other things for digging in all weather wearing a formal business suit complete with tie and high starched collar, had immediately recognized the significance of Dart's specimen. In 1936 he dropped in to have a look at Sterkfontein, where, as at Taung, baboon fossils had recently been discovered. (As fellow ground dwellers, the ancestors of man and baboons shared life on the savanna.) It was the start of a second career for the sixty-nine-year-old investigator. Within two weeks he found pieces of the skull of an adult *Australopithecus*, and he decided to concentrate on the search for early man.

During the succeeding years Broom and his young assistant John Robinson, now professor of anthropology at the University of Wisconsin, conducted excavations at Sterkfontein and two nearby sites. It was slow work. The fossil-containing deposits of sand, earth, bone and shattered rock were cemented together by lime salts and as hard as concrete. The only practical way to get at the material was to drill holes in it, blast it into chunks with sticks of dynamite, and, later in the laboratory, pick away at the chunks or treat them with mild acid.

This procedure yielded several dozen new specimens, including the remains of another kind of *Australopithecus* which also walked upright and had a somewhat larger brain but was considerably more rugged. It was heavier (weighing about 100 or more pounds as compared with perhaps 75 pounds for *Australopithecus africanus*), taller (about four and a half to five feet

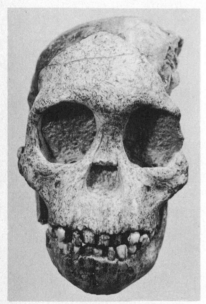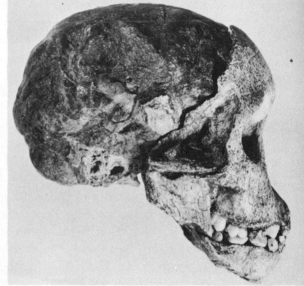

Dart's "Taung baby": the original *Australopithecus* discovery

against four feet), and had a more massive skull. This is the species that has been classified as *Australopithecus robustus*.

Meanwhile, Dart sent students to another rich site he had heard about during the 1920's, located about 150 miles away in the Makapan Valley. At one end were red cliffs and a waterfall, a "Lost World" valley as wild in appearance today as it was when man's ancestors wandered there more than 20,000 centuries ago. Makapan included a network of caves under a domed roof larger than a football field and some ten stories high.

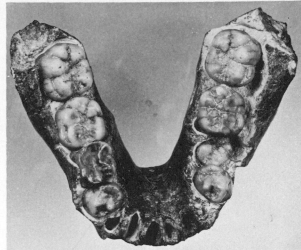

Australopithecus robustus: artist's conception of head (left); *Australopithecus robustus:* lower jawbone and teeth (right)

Man's ancestors, *Australopithecus,* as they may have looked five or six million years ago

A familiar pattern led Dart to the ruins of this huge cave system in 1945: a limestone quarry, abandoned long ago, and the finding of a fossil baboon. Two years later one of his students recovered the back part of an *Australopithecus* skull from the quarry dump. A year after that it was a lower jaw, and within another four months part of a face and several other pieces, parts of a skullcap and upper jaw and pelvis. The evidence was piling up, and none of it checked with the notion that men had a big brain from the beginning, or with the increasingly puzzling Piltdown remains.

Finally things reached a point where it had to occur to someone that the chances of the find's being genuine were somewhat less than the chances of its being a fake. The someone was Joseph Weiner, now at the London School of Hygiene and Tropical Medicine and then at Oxford University. Driving from work one afternoon in 1953 and mulling over the peculiar remains, he suddenly considered deception as a serious possibility, and special studies conducted at Oxford and the British Museum of Natural History removed all doubts. The Piltdown skull fragments belonged to a modern man, the jawbone and teeth to a modern ape. The material had been filed down, chemically treated and otherwise tampered with to make it appear ancient and authentic. Then someone had planted the doctored specimens in the gravel pit.

The job was done quite skillfully. But that is not what fooled the experts, who, like all scientists, had been trained to take the evidence as it came. They were taken in mainly because they had absolutely no reason to suspect a deliberate fraud. The truth became evident as soon as the possibility of fraud was seriously considered. The culprit has not been publicly identified, and his motive is a mystery. According to one theory, it all started as a joke, which was taken so seriously and went so far that the joker did not dare to reveal the truth. Another theory is that it was no joke at all, but an act of malice aforethought by a man who wanted to embarrass investigators and undermine the entire idea of human evolution.

In any case, because exposure of the skulduggery at Piltdown alerted anthropologists to the possibility of deception, the odds against their succumbing to another major hoax are enormous.

Furthermore, it helped discredit once and for all the theory that man was created big-brained and fully human, and cleared the way for a more plausible theory based on evidence from South Africa and elsewhere.

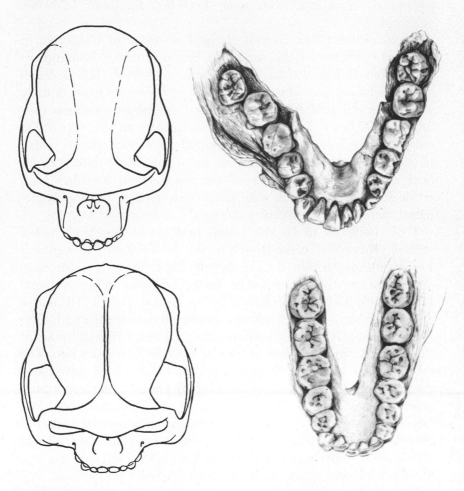

Australopithecus skulls, top view, and jaws: *africanus* (top) and *robustus* (bottom)

New evidence has been accumulating ever since. Besides the Lothagam Hill specimen, Patterson found part of a 4-million-year-old upper arm bone of *Australopithecus* at another site about forty miles away; its status, *robustus* or *africanus*, is still uncertain. In fact, hominid remains are turning up at an impressive rate in many parts of the Rift Valley region around Lake Rudolf. In Ethiopia's Omo River Valley French and American investigators have worked five seasons beginning in 1967, seeking material in geological formations from some 4,000,000 to about 1,700,000 years old.

According to Clark Howell of the University of California in Berkeley, director of the American group at Omo, hominid remains already found there include some 150 teeth, half a dozen lower jawbones, part of a skull, partial leg bones, an exceptionally well-preserved forearm bone (the first complete specimen ever found in Africa), and even fossil footprints. In all, expedition workers have found about 65 "hominid localities," places which have yielded *Australopithecus* remains, the oldest dating as far back as 3,500,000 years. There are also several localities with crude stone flakes which may have been used as cutting implements more than two million years ago.

Tools believed to be still older, perhaps as much as half a million years older, come from a region not far away, in northern Kenya on the east side of Lake Rudolf. Exploring this region is an expedition organized and led by Richard Leakey of the National Museums of Kenya (Louis and Mary Leakey's son). He and a group of specialists are working together to document and understand more fully what is perhaps one of Africa's richest areas for the period from about two to four or more million years ago. The tools include so-called choppers, cobblestones which have been given a rough cutting or bashing edge by knocking flakes off both sides. They were found among fragments of animal bone, and Glynn Isaac of the University of California believes that hominids may have lived in this spot. Another site, about three-quarters of a mile away, may have been used as a slaughtering place, since it also has tools and bones, perhaps from a single hippopotamus.

Some 50 hominid specimens have been found in the area. There are a complete *Australopithecus* skull, two other skull specimens, a massive lower jawbone with huge molar teeth, other jawbone fragments, and parts of a badly smashed skeleton which were collected by painstaking and extensive sifting. (According to Maglio, "we practically took a whole hill apart.") Richard Leakey has interpreted his material with cautious imagination. He believes it includes male and female members of *Australopithecus* and remains of a different hominid which may be a member of the genus *Homo*.

Work is going on at old as well as new sites. Present-day investigators have revisited the scenes of some of the most important discoveries of a generation ago, and have come up with new material and new interpretations of old material. To cite only one example, Charles Brain of the Transvaal Museum in Pretoria, South Africa, has done further excavating at a site previously excavated by Broom and Robinson—the Swartkrans Cave, which is located less than a mile from Sterkfontein and has yielded remains of at least 60 hominid individuals, more than any other site.

The cave is also rich in fossil animal bones, some 15,000 of them having been collected to date (3,000 by previous workers, 12,000 by Brain), representing the leftovers of meals eaten by some prehistoric carnivore. It has been suggested that the killer was *Australopithecus robustus,* whose remains have also been found in the cave. But Brain believes that this theory overrates our early ancestors, that they contributed very little to the total debris, mainly because only a small proportion of the bones are shattered to bits, the typical hominid practice.

A careful investigation of the habits of other carnivores convinces Brain that the actual culprits were leopards. He has even reconstructed the scene of the action. The Swartkrans Cave had a vertical shaft leading down into its underground chambers, the sort of location where trees often grow today. Combining this observation with the observation that contemporary leopards often drag their prey into trees where they can eat undisturbed by scavengers such as hyenas, Brain suggests that prehistoric leopards did the same and that the discarded bones fell into the chambers below.

He also has an explanation for the presence of most of the hominid remains among the cave's animal fossils. Our ancestors were hunted as well as hunters, victims of leopards along with antelopes, zebras, baboons and other species. As part of his proof, he offers a piece of the skull of a young *robustus* individual. The skull has two puncture holes in it, 33 millimeters or about an inch and a third apart, which is about the distance between the lower canine teeth of an adult leopard.

Who killed the Swartkrans ape-men?

There was another hominid in the cave. One July day Brain, Howell and Ronald Clarke of the Center for Prehistory and Palaeontology were in the Transvaal Museum examining a collection of Swartkrans fossils classified as *Australopithecus robustus* remains. Suddenly Clarke noticed that a number of skull fragments including an upper jawbone fragment and a cheekbone and part of an eye socket found more than 20 years ago did not seem to fit into the *robustus* category, and that led to a fruitful jigsaw-puzzle session.

The investigators managed to fit the fragments together to produce most of the left side of a skull. The result was a newly reconstructed face from the past—a hominid which seems to be more advanced than other Swartkrans *robustus* individuals, and in certain respects resembles Richard Leakey's suspected *Homo* specimen from the Lake Rudolf area. Incidentally, this work confirms the insights of one of the original Swartkrans investigators, John Robinson, who reached the same conclusion long ago and had difficulty convincing many of his colleagues.

It will take time to analyze all the new findings. A major problem, for instance, is to determine the relationship between *Australopithecus robustus* and *Australopithecus africanus*. To become distinct species they must have been separated by some sort of geographical barrier, a barrier which later must have changed and become less effective, because the two breeds eventually occupied the same general areas. The bigger species apparently stayed big, coexisting and possibly competing with its smaller relatives and vanishing between a million and half a million years ago without leaving direct descendants. According to one theory, the smaller species proved more successful, became bigger, and continued the human line.

The smaller species may have been a superior toolmaker and played an active role in the extinction of its fellow hominids, killing them off in the course of fighting for food and territory in the savanna. An appealing counter-idea is that *robustus* and *africanus* made love not war, that they represent one not two species, *robustus* being the male and *africanus* the female. But current evidence fails to encourage such thinking; for one thing, the differences in tooth size and shape seem to be too great to be accounted for on the basis of sex differences.

Perhaps the most impressive and challenging thing about the present situation is the variety of specimens being gathered. If this represents a corresponding variety in the forms and adaptations of early hominids, life in times long past was probably rather more complicated than anything yet contemplated in present-day theories. Certainly the facts confirm that in a fundamental sense our ancestors played a central role in making themselves more human. Starting with relatively small brains, they evolved together with their evolving purposes.

■ Olduvai Gorge, one of the world's richest sources of knowledge about man's beginnings; the discovery of stone tools a million years "too soon"; the painstaking excavation and mapping of living floors; the study of living baboons as a guide to man's past; baboon troops and their responses to emergencies; early diseases

CHAPTER IV

Fossils and Tools as Clues to Man's Beginnings

■ Creatures like *Australopithecus* left more than their bones and artifacts behind, more than the scattered remains of individuals preserved ages before the invention of burial and burial rites. Objects dug out of the ground are raw data, and what they can tell us is not always self-evident. In other words, analysis and the framing of hypotheses that can be checked help arrange data into patterns, information about life as it was lived in the remote past.

There are enduring living patterns—places where bands of primitive hominids came, settled down for a time in the open near trees and lakes and streams and then left forever to exploit new territory or never left and died where they were. But before passing on they rearranged things a bit to make themselves safer and more comfortable. They brought in stones from other places, shaped some of the stones into tools, put up barriers to keep animals away at night and left a variety of camping debris. They changed the environment sufficiently so that signs of the changes have endured for more than twenty thousand centuries.

These places are as impressive as the sites of tombs and temples built a few hundred or a few thousand years before the birth of Christ. One of the most important and spectacular of them, like the fossil-rich regions around Lake Rudolf, is also part of East Africa's Rift Valley and deserves special attention, because so much has been found there which bears on the social life of early hominids. It is located about 350 miles from Nairobi—past Mount Kilimanjaro, fever trees, herds of antelopes, giraffes and zebras; cliffs as high and steep as the Hudson River Palisades; past an extinct Rift Valley volcano, Ngorongoro, with a twelve-mile crater, the world's largest; and down the other side into the Serengeti Plain, one of Africa's great game reserves.

Buried deep beneath the Serengeti is another plain. Runoff streams flowing from mountains to the south and east fed a brackish lake five to eight miles across, whose fossil shorelines are visible today as rippled margins of black sand and whose central portion is marked by clays, transformed muds that are still soft. Many generations of hominids lived near the lake and the streams in a region which had already seen some spectacular geological displays. About half a million years before the coming of man's ancestors, the entire top of Ngorongoro, some two miles of mountain, had collapsed to form the present crater. Later, during hominid occupation times, a peak in the south, probably Mount Olmoti, became violent and expelled a *nuée ardente* or "glowing cloud," a huge mushroom of red-hot particles rising thousands of feet high. Then the particles started falling back to earth, rolled down the sides of the mountains at speeds of more than a mile a minute, and buried part of the lake and probably all the lakeside dwellers beneath fifteen feet of ash and molten fragments. (In 1902 a similar volcanic avalanche on Martinique Island killed 28,000 persons in the town of Saint-Pierre, the sole survivor being a prisoner locked in an underground dungeon.)

This was the first of a series of major events. Another glowing cloud burst out of the mountain, or perhaps a flow of hot volcanic mud. Then things became relatively peaceful for a time, only to stir up again with the onset of Rift movements in the region and a dramatic change in climate. Before the change the lake was ex-tensive, as indicated not only by the black-sand shorelines but also by the remains of crocodiles, which require an abundance of fish and deep waters. Afterward, after Rift-produced dislocations and cracks formed in the earth's crust, traces of the lake dis-appeared and twenty-foot deposits of wind-blown sand and vol-canic ash mark the prevalence of desert conditions. Then there were alternating wet times when the lake reappeared and dry dust-bowl times when sand dunes dominated the landscape and the lakes shrank or turned into a system of ponds and swamps or vanished entirely.

As a result of all this activity the original plain, thousands of square miles of "fossil" wilderness where populations of hominids lived and died, is inaccessible. It lies under some three hundred feet of volcanic ash and sand and lake sediments, except for one area in which nature has carried out a large-scale excavation. About fifty thousand years ago, rifting produced a series of cliffs over which swift rivers cascaded, gouging down through accumulated deposits and exposing part of the old plain. The torrents created a miniature Grand Canyon, the twenty-five-mile-long Olduvai Gorge, the world's richest source of information about the beginnings of man.

The information has been obtained largely through the efforts of Leakey, who was born in Kenya and grew up with his two sisters and brothers as the only white children in a Kikuyu village (his parents were English missionaries). Leakey devoted his life to the discovery and excavation of African sites. From the beginning he felt there was something special about Olduvai, even before it yielded anything extraordinary. Within a few hours after arriving there for the first time, he found stone tools on the slope of a side gully less than a hundred yards from his tent, and determined on the spot to start a continuing search for remains of the toolmakers.

That was in 1931, a generation after a German entomologist discovered Olduvai, when the trip from Nairobi took the better part of a week. Leakey returned again and again over the years, accompanied by his wife Mary. Season after season, they camped not far from the edge of the gorge, walked down into canyons to explore areas as much as ten miles away, and shared a water hole with rhinoceroses and other big game. ("We could never get rid of the taste of rhino urine," Leakey recalled "even after filtering the water through charcoal and boiling it and using it in tea with lemon.")

They found many concentrations of tools and animal bones, sites to be excavated some time in the future if sufficient funds and help became available, but few hominid fossils until one July morning in 1959 when the Leakeys were digging on borrowed time, having exhausted current research funds and drawn on the next year's budget. Prehistorians in the field never stop looking, and Mary happened to be walking along the same slope where her husband had first found tools nearly three decades before. Only this time a recent rock slide had exposed previously buried deposits. Mary noticed a bit of skull and, stuck firmly in the face of a nearby cliff, two very large and shining brown-black pre-molar teeth whose size and cusp pattern indicated a primate more advanced than a monkey or ape.

It took the Leakeys nineteen days to free the teeth and parts of a fossil palate from the soft rock, sift tons of rubble and dirt, and gather a total of more than four hundred bone fragments. Some months later at a scientific meeting, Leakey, whose flair for showmanship matched his flair for anthropology, invited a few privileged colleagues to an advance preview of a new find. He opened a black box and removed the beautifully reconstructed skull of an eighteen-year-old *Australopithecus*. Not long after-ward the National Geographic Society began supporting his work, providing funds for workers and equipment. During the next thirteen months about 7,000 tons of dirt and rock were moved, more than twice as much as had been moved during all the previous digging seasons.

Since then Olduvai has yielded a number of important and surprising discoveries, including the first absolute date for such early sites. The South African sites have not been dated because the only sufficiently accurate "radioactive clock" currently avail-able, the potassium-argon technique, depends on the analysis of volcanic minerals, and volcanoes were not erupting in South Africa during hominid times. But there are such minerals at Olduvai, and the deposits containing the 1959 skull turned out to be about 1,750,000 years old, nearly twice as old as had previ-ously been estimated on the basis of geological studies. The new date has done a great deal to increase respect for the hominids of the times, since their relatively advanced development appears more striking the earlier they lived. In an analogous way an adult may not be particularly impressed with a painting until he learns that the painter is a child.

So far, remains representing more than twenty individuals have been found in older and more recent deposits, including the remains of a more advanced hominid perhaps related to hominids found near Lake Rudolf and at Swartkrans. There were also a number of rarely preserved foot and hand bones. The feet of the Olduvai hominids are remarkable because they are so much like ours. They are smaller, the foot of one adult being about seven inches long, or about the foot size of an eight-year-old child today, and show a few other minor differences. But they show that *Australopithecus* and his contemporaries walked upright, a conclusion supported by studies of his pelvis, particularly the upper part of the hipbone blade, which is shortened and tilted toward the vertical position. As a rule, apes bend forward when they walk on two feet, because their hipbone blade is long and bent forward. Also they cannot stride as we do, because their main thigh and buttock muscles tend to flex the leg so that walking must be done in a weak, bent-kneed fashion.

Whether *Australopithecus* walked as well as we do is something else again. Adrienne Zihlman of the University of California in Santa Cruz has conducted intensive studies of walking patterns in chimpanzees and other nonhuman primates and modern man, as well as the relevant fossil material, and reaches the following conclusion: "*Australopithecus* would have required more muscle energy than modern man to perform the same actions. He probably walked with toes turned out and might have carried his weight more on the outside of the foot."

In other words, he was a creature in transition. Achieving an upright stance was only part of the story, although a most important part. Yet to come were further refinements of "internal rotation," more efficient hip-joint action which would reduce fatigue during long trips in search of food and new places to live. Zihlman emphasizes that these and related developments also favored the coordination and balance required to aim and throw accurately, and to stand still for long periods during the stalking of game.

A great deal more can be deduced from the structure of the foot—for example, the beginnings of a unique form of human dependence. Infant monkeys have gripping feet, half-hands with mobile and opposable big toes designed to bend around and cling to the mother's hair as she moves along with the troop. *Australopithecus* infants had feet already so specialized for walking that clinging was no longer possible. The inference is clear. The infants were more helpless than other primate infants. They had to be carried by their mothers, a fact of life which undoubtedly favored the evolution of a home, or home base, a strictly human invention. The notion of leaving a group of waiting individuals behind is totally foreign to monkeys and apes, whose troops generally move as single units. Only men among primates have places where women and children may stay in relative safety while other troop members go away to obtain food, and the foot structure of *Australopithecus* is one sign that he established similar bases.

His hands were less advanced than his feet. According to the anatomist John Napier of the Royal Free Hospital in London, their structure is "strangely nonhuman," chiefly because the fingers are robust and curved like those of a young gorilla rather than straight and slender as in the human hand. Furthermore, although most of the thumb is missing from the Olduvai specimen, indirect evidence shows that this important digit was apparently shorter and somewhat less mobile, indicating a hand less well developed for precision work than for sheer power. It had one distinctly human feature, however. In contrast to the narrow, rounded fingertips of apes, its tip was broad and flattish like ours. The fingertips provided not only good cushions for a firm grip but also room for a rich supply of nerve pathways to coordinate intricate hand-wrist-finger movements, and for special sense organs designed to respond to pressure, pain, temperature and textural differences. An estimated 5 million such sensory detectors are located in the skin of the body, about a third of them concentrated in the hands, mostly in the fingertips and palms.

There is another and more direct way of assessing the manual skills of the African hominids. Their stone tools discovered in recent excavations reveal as much as fossil remains. Findings indicate that they were not as backward or primitive as was once believed. For a long time no stone tools were announced from any of the South African sites, which was no surprise. Most investigators expected no tools. They assumed that toolmaking was beyond the capacities of such small-brained hominids, although tool use involving "readymade" unworked objects was considered a definite possibility. In fact, this notion was so taken for granted that when uncontrovertibly shaped tools were found at Sterk-fontein in 1956, they were immediately and widely attributed to more advanced creatures.

This position had to be abandoned four years later with the finding of the first skull at Olduvai and the Leakeys' increased pace of excavation. The evidence was about as clear-cut as evidence can be; shaped tools were found in the same layers that contained hominid remains. But the tenor of the times was still very reluctant, as if the objective at every stage of discovery was to concede as little as possible. Granted that the hominids actually made tools, the general opinion or expectation seemed to be that they must have been extremely crude tools, and at first only extremely crude tools were recognized and reported. As a matter of fact, the tools found were so crude that it would be impossible to identify anything much cruder as an artifact. Scientists as well as other committed persons often see what they believe, and their findings and interpretations tend to confirm their expectations.

The older sites of Olduvai, those located in deposits not far from the bottom of the gorge, have yielded interesting collections of stone materials. In the first place the great majority of pieces look like nothing in particular and would be gathered by specialists only. They may not be tools at all and are simply rubble, natural chunks of rock which have not been shaped or altered in any way. Yet even unworked material has something to tell us about prehistoric activities and purposes. The stones consist mainly of lava and quartz which do not come from the immediate vicinity of the site itself. They were carried in from places at least three miles away, perhaps to hurl at marauding animals or to hold down animal skins. If the hominids slept on the ground, as Leakey believed, stones could have been placed on damp surfaces under straw and grasses to make a dry bedding, or above the straw and grasses to keep the material from blowing away during the day.

One of the most common worked tools found among the rubble is the chopper, the sort of implement also found near Lake Rudolf. Such pieces must be studied on a statistical basis to be identified positively as artifacts. If they make up an appreciable proportion of the total stone assemblage, then one can be reasonably sure that they were made by human hands. But the finding of a few flaked stones that could be tools means nothing at all, because they could also have been produced by nature rather than man.

Desmond Clark has walked along English beaches at Dover and elsewhere, examining stones chipped and broken by pounding surf. Many stones showed the removal of a single flake from one side, and some had flakes removed from both sides or both ends. Revil Mason of the University of the Witwatersrand in Johannesburg once examined 20,000 stones collected at Makapan. A number of them looked as if they were worked tools, but after considering the assemblage as a whole he realized that there was no solid evidence for the presence of artifacts. Nature had done the shaping, such as it was. So categories grade off into one another, and at the most rudimentary level it is not easy to distinguish accidents from artifacts. The late Abbé Henri Breuil, one of France's foremost prehistorians, expressed the problem as follows: "Man made one, God made ten thousand—God help the man who tries to see the one in ten thousand."

Most of the choppers among the earliest Olduvai collections are about the size of a tennis ball or perhaps a bit smaller. But there is another kind of chopper, which I first saw in Napier's London office. He has two walnut-sized choppers made of greenish lava, and although the hand of the ape man was smaller than ours, it was not so small that such miniature tools would fit it comfortably. They must have been held with the thumb and ring and index fingers, and used for some purpose such as preparing small pieces of plant or animal food. Olduvai sites also include bone tools such as a flattened and highly polished rib of a zebra or some other horselike species, which was possibly rubbed against hides to make them smooth and pliable. A similar tool has been found at Sterkfontein.

The most unusual discoveries, however, have been made recently and show that the hominids were not only versatile tool-makers but that they engaged in fairly complex activities. For example, a site at the bottom of the gorge contains eleven different kinds of stone implements, such as engraving-gouging tools, quadrilateral "chisels," large and small scrapers, and other special-purpose tools generally made of difficult-to-work lavas and quartz. Incidentally, these materials have rough, irregular surfaces which are coarse-grained and do not show clearly where flakes and chips have been knocked off, one reason why the tools were not recognized immediately. The same kinds of tools were made by later generations of hominids that had access to finer-grained materials. Their work is easier to appreciate.

These tools seem highly individualistic in the sense that they cannot be classified readily and are not shaped according to a few standardized traditional patterns. But they are not crude. In fact, they represent a complete surprise to prehistorians who had previously found related tools only in sites a million years more recent. In this sense the tools come a million years too soon, and it is almost as if one opened up a musty vault in the Great Pyramid of Egypt and found vacuum cleaners and television sets. "At first the tools were a great shock to us," Mary Leakey comments, "and we had a hard time believing it. After this, it should be easy to believe anything."

The discovery of tool assemblages is only one of the results of excavations at Olduvai. Another major discovery is that at some sites tools and other objects exist in their original context, in practically the same positions they occupied when hominids lived near the ancient lake and streams. It is nothing new that evidence of this sort may be preserved at more recent sites representing the days of early civilizations with elaborate purposes and elaborate structures to match, palaces and courtyards and battlements. The ashes of Vesuvius which buried Pompeii only yesterday, A.D. 79, left houses and floors and furniture and bodies in place. But few investigators suspected that there were living patterns of any sort two million years before Pompeii, much less that they could possibly have survived ancient eruptions and subsequent geological changes.

Yet such patterns do exist. Objects covered gently by volcanic ash or fine lake sediments may be moved little or not at all, and such "living floors" survive almost in mint condition like intricate three-dimensional mosaics. Archeologists are always on the lookout for intact sites like the one Clark discovered at Kalambo Falls (see Prologue), places where erosion has laid bare the remains of prehistoric man. Or they may inspect miniature mesas, flat elevated areas surrounded by steep erosion gullies. If tools and fossils are abundant in the gullies, it is possible that the uneroded

Looking down 300 feet into Olduvai Gorge, where pre-men lived twenty thousand centuries ago

Louis and Mary Leakey examining early Olduvai living floor

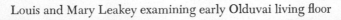

Remains of the oldest known structure, possibly a windbreak, uncovered at foot of Olduvai Gorge

Revil Mason, University of the Witwatersrand archeologist, trying to identify man-made tools among chipped and broken stones at Makapan *Australopithecus* site

Pebble tool and a chopper, first stone tools made by man's ancestors

highlands may include sealed-in layers containing undisturbed traces of the distant past.

Once a living-floor site has been found, the work really starts, and it is slow and demanding work. It calls for the application of new digging methods, or rather methods developed chiefly during the past seventy-five years by archeologists in Germany, Denmark, England and other countries at farm and village sites of the past four or five thousand years. A site is approached with almost surgical care and precision. First the outer cover of very recent rock and soil must be removed, taking pains to expose but not cut into underlying occupation layers. Then the job is to obtain as complete a picture as possible of the patterns in the layers.

Every item, every piece of bone and rock, worked or unworked, and chips and flakes as well as tools, must be exposed but not moved. Every object is part of the pattern of objects; it means nothing by itself. Its position is all important. The digging rate varies depending on how much material lies on the living floor. But in a reasonably good spot it may take one person an entire eight-hour day squatting in the dust under a hot sun to excavate two or three inches deep in an area about the size of a bridge-table top.

Much of the time is spent doing paperwork. Using a steel rule or a yardstick, you measure the position of every single one of several hundred pieces of material, its location on the living floor, and its depth beneath the surface of the site. One may also record the direction in which the piece is pointing because, among other things, that may help you check on whether or not the site has actually been disturbed. If a large proportion of the pieces are pointing in the same general direction, it may mean that they have been moved by flowing water; while unmoved pieces tend to be oriented at random. All this information is written in a notebook together with the number of each piece and its type, that is, whether it is a tool and if so what sort of tool. Later the pieces are washed and numbered for identification, using a fine pen and India ink.

As far as the nonspecialist is concerned, the older the site, the less interesting or impressive the objects uncovered. A classical site can yield pottery, necklaces of gold, teacups of iridescent glass, bronze statuettes. Figurines and animals carved out of ivory and delicate engravings on stone may date back 25,000 years or more, and beautifully worked tools of flint and obsidian come from sites many millennia older than that. But as a rule pieces collected at the Olduvai sites hardly look worth collecting to the layman. Every archeologist who has brought such material to show to his nonscientific friends is familiar with the disappointment they try to conceal by polite interest.

So at the root of discovery, in archeology as well as in every other branch of science, there is tedium—the painstaking and sometimes grim accumulation of data, often under the loneliest of conditions. Tedium is and must be the guts of scientific endeavor because nothing worth coming by comes easily. In a sense no one person sees anything as he excavates the earliest living floors, brushing the dirt off individual pieces and measuring their positions and marking them day after day. Each excavator is part of a group that moves thousands of tons of dirt and rock. The full story may not be revealed until months or even years later, when the data have been analyzed and all the maps and charts drawn.

At that stage, seeing the whole picture or a major part of the picture, the results may be spectacular. Reading a living-floor map is something like trying to decipher a code or translate a manuscript in a strange language, the symbols being patterns in the positions of the objects. For example, the site at the bottom of the gorge which yielded surprisingly varied tools also included another unexpected feature. The work called for the marking of many chunks of unworked and individually undistinguished stone, and only gradually did it become apparent that the stones were arranged in a definite pattern. The pattern shows up clearly in a map prepared by Mary Leakey, who learned precise digging techniques at a hill-fort site in Devon, England. It consists of piles of rock placed in a rough semicircle around a saucer-shaped area, perhaps a crude wall which may have served as a windbreak.

Incidentally, this site has been dated by the potassium-argon method and also by a new radioactive-clock method which depends on the analysis of bits of volcanic glass scattered over the area. The glass contains traces of U-238, the radioactive form of uranium used in early atomic weapons, whose atoms split at a regular rate and leave "fission tracks" in the glass. The tracks look like tiny grooves under the microscope, and can be counted to provide a measure of the time elapsed since the glass cooled. According to results reported by General Electric investigators, the stone semicircle is 2,030,000 years old, plus or minus 280,000 years, which makes it the oldest man-made structure known.

Mary Leakey has also drawn a large map of the 3,400-square-foot living floor where she and her husband found the *Australopithecus* skull in 1959. The map shows the precise positions of more than four thousand artifacts and fossils, and includes an area about fifteen feet in diameter which is thick with shattered pieces of rock and bone and choppers, where "everything is bash, bash, bash." Outside this area the concentration of material drops off sharply until one comes to another area off to one side, a few feet from the main concentration, a place containing larger bone fragments and unshattered bones.

This pattern has been interpreted as a "dining room" complex. The tools, chips, flakes and bone splinters mark a part of the site set aside for the job of smashing bones to get at the marrow. Practically every bone that could yield marrow has been smashed. The nearby concentration of bones, including jaws and skulls which do not contain marrow, is believed to be a kind of garbage heap. Between the heap and the main concentration is an almost bare arc-shaped area, which may have been a windbreak of branches because it lies directly in the path of prevailing winds in the region today. Another possibility is that the barrier helped protect hominids from predators, a strategy still used today not only by native tribes but in the Leakeys' camp itself. (Leopards, rhinoceroses and lions wander in from time to time and must be discouraged.)

The living floor as a whole confirms the fact hinted at by studies of the Olduvai foot bones, which indicate that infants could not cling to their mothers and hence required especially intensive care. The site is definitely a home base. Although we cannot tell how long it was occupied, the bones and other material must have accumulated over a period of years during which hominid bands left their lakeside camp and returned many times. They achieved a new kind of stability, a source of experiences and associations centered about one relatively small region, a place where traditions and techniques and taboos could be developed.

A great deal more can be learned in the future from living

floors. Different patterns, different systems of bone-and-stone concentrations and crude structures, can be compared to hieroglyphics whose meanings may become increasingly clear as they are repeated in different contexts. The patterns so far uncovered are so few that their interpretation relies to a large extent on clever guesswork. But the discovery of related patterns and new details will transform the guesswork into highly probable hypotheses. At Olduvai alone the Leakeys knew of some fifty sites which have not yet been excavated and represent enough work to keep excavators and prehistorians busy for another generation or two.

Studies of existing primates supplement deductions based on material recovered from the earth. Baboons supply clues to early life on dry, wide African savannas. For all the differences between them and early hominids, highly probable and striking similarities exist. The large monkeys have been studied intensively in the wild by Irven DeVore of Harvard, Stuart Altmann of the University of Chicago, Thelma Rowell of Makerere University College in Uganda, and John Crook and the late Ronald Hall of the University of Bristol, England. (Hall died in the summer of 1965, probably of a virus infection, after a laboratory monkey had bitten him on the hand.)

Baboons of Nairobi Park and the Amboseli Game Reserve move in diurnal cycles, locked in as it were to the clockwork rhythm of sunrises and sunsets. They sleep in the trees, halfway out on the branches, and begin to stir with the first light of day, generally around five in the morning, and often in a groggy half-trance state somewhat reminiscent of more advanced primates like ourselves. "They tend to awaken very sluggishly," according to DeVore, "and you get the impression that what they need most is a cup of coffee." The next two hours are spent in waking up and grooming one another, always near the sleeping tree or trees.

Then the time comes for leaving the trees, and it is at this point that one begins to feel the difference between forest and savanna. The forest offers many hiding places and escape routes and refuges in the trees, and life can be relatively relaxed. But there is more fear and danger in the open savanna. Tourists today are forbidden to get out of their cars, and investigators do so at their own risk and generally make a practice of coughing softly so that any predators in the vicinity may hear and not be surprised. (A startled predator is more likely to attack.)

The boldest troop members leave the trees first, adult males who are not at the top of the social hierarchy and juveniles corresponding roughly to older teen-agers in a human group. They move rapidly in a beeline as if they know exactly where they are going, and they do not look back. Other older juveniles and adult females follow: next comes the central nucleus of the troop—mothers with their infants and the youngest juveniles and the most dominant and generally the biggest and oldest males. The back part of the troop is a mirror image of the front with more older juveniles and adult females following the nucleus group and more adult males bringing up the rear.

A baboon troop on the move makes a formidable array and is attacked only rarely and only by lions. Its early-morning trek takes it a few hundred yards to a few miles to the day's main feeding place, where intensive eating may go on for as much as two or three hours after the area has been surveyed for possible predators. Often you come across a troop feeding together with a herd of impalas in a natural and effective association, since baboons have fine eyesight and impalas have a fine sense of smell. Between them they can detect practically any predator and give the alarm in the form of warning barks. As a rule, it seems that baboons recognize and respond to the alarm cries of many other species.

Sometimes, particularly during the dry season, it is amazing how much food they can obtain from apparently barren areas. They pull up everything in plain sight, and then scan the ground for withered stalks and other signs of succulent plant runners that extend like tiny pipes just beneath the surface. They can also detect almost invisible wisps, hairlike filaments which mark the location of deeper-lying tubers, bulbs and roots. At midday they rest, usually not far from the feeding place in a shady spot where grooming clusters form, juveniles and infants play, and adults may take a siesta or sit quietly and keep watch.

Later the baboons move in formation toward another feeding place, again after making sure the coast is clear. On one occasion Altmann and I observed a dramatic example of courage and caution in the Amboseli Game Reserve at the foot of Mount Kilimanjaro. Something had frightened a troop when it was about to move into the plains from the shade of a fever tree. The leader, a sleek husky male with a magnificent mane, was sitting on a rock looking ahead. Then, apparently deciding that it was safe to advance, he got up and started moving past a bush toward tall grasses.

Baboons moving in defense formation, adult males and older male juveniles guarding troop nucleus including mothers and infants. Early man probably moved in similar formations

All at once something we could neither see nor hear made him change his mind. He hesitated, turned his head, and retreated to the rock as the rest of the troop, which had started to follow, scampered back into the tree. He peered around once more in such a human fashion and so intensely that I expected him to shade his eyes with his hand like a lookout aboard ship. Finally he started again with a firm and confident this-is-it stride and led his troop out into the savanna.

After resting, the troop does not go any farther from the trees where it will spend the night. In fact, the second feeding place generally lies on the way back, because tensions rise as the afternoon wears on and the sun sinks. Several years ago DeVore observed an encounter between predators and a troop which was already within sight of its sleeping place in a shallow valley. One baboon stopped eating and turned to look in the direction of a clump of trees about a hundred yards away; gradually, over a

Baboons at leisure: mothers and infants resting and playing; male juveniles chasing one another while an adult male watches

period of a minute or so, every monkey was sitting and looking in the same direction, that is, all but two infants that started playing and were promptly slapped down.

Suddenly an old male baboon grunted twice and walked toward the trees. Almost immediately he was joined by about half a dozen other males, big adults and juveniles that advanced with him side by side in a tight line. At this stage DeVore first saw what was upsetting the baboons, the heads of two cheetahs sticking up out of the grass near the trees and only a hundred feet or so ahead of the line. The line advanced until it was only about sixty feet away, when several of the baboons broke out of formation and made a lunging charge directly at the cheetahs. The big cats turned and ran off, and the baboons behind the line started eating again.

Defensive tactics are not always so successful; lions do not run under similar circumstances. Baboons are safe or comparatively safe only when they have reached sleeping trees near rivers and permanent water holes, and even there they may occasionally fall prey to leopards. Shortly after sunset they are dozing off and the day has come full circle. The troop moves about three miles a day on the average, often returning to the same trees which it left early in the morning. Normally every member of this tightly organized little cluster of monkeys is constantly in sight of the other members, and many baboons spend their entire lives within a few miles of the places where they were born.

Man's ancestors may have lived comparable lives on similar savannas millions of years ago. They had little choice about it, since there are certain fundamental ways of dealing with such environments which would have to be used by practically any primate, or practically any mammal, for that matter. They had to face the same dangers, the same predators, and they had to evolve some type of social hierarchy. A high degree of organization is essential on the savanna. It is not that emergencies occasionally arise, but life is a continual emergency and the odds in favor of survival are greater if each individual knows what to do in case of trouble. Man's ancestors also took cues from the alarm cries of other creatures, and moved across open areas with rear guards and vanguards and "side riders" in the same basic formation used more recently in covered-wagon trains and naval convoys.

There were other dangers besides predators. The teeth of the eighteen-year-old *Australopithecus* found at Olduvai in 1959, for example, reveal that he was sickly as a child. The enamel of permanent teeth is built up layer by layer during a child's development, and periods of illness show up as tiny hollows resulting from retarded growth in the layers. An illness like measles or chicken pox which usually runs a brief course may leave shallow hollows. But the hollows in the teeth of this hominid are deep and suggest that he had a disease that lasted for many months, probably gastroenteritis due to malnutrition. Furthermore, he suffered three major attacks of the disease—at the ages of two, four, and four and a half.

In general, Olduvai hominids and their contemporaries harbored two types of disease-producing organisms, those shared with other primates and those restricted to members of the family of man. From a study of primate infections Aidan Cockburn of the Mayor's Committee for Human Resources Development in Detroit believes that among the diseases which may date back more than 25 million years to the ape ancestors of modern apes and man are amoebic dysentery, yellow fever, pinworm infections, malaria, and syphilis and yaws. Diseases which may have appeared and evolved with man include typhoid and leprosy. (Certain modern diseases, such as measles, mumps, cholera and the common cold, which require large concentrated populations to support them, probably could not for this reason have existed in prehistoric times.)

Early hominids, like their fellow primates, lived mainly exposed to the elements. Sometimes on stormy nights, however, they may have been driven to seek cover under overhanging cliffs, where they huddled together wet and cold in the dark in a world still dominated by other animals. Sometimes bad weather may even have driven them into caves. Early one morning in Southwest Africa during a very cold, harsh season, Hall saw a troop of baboons emerging from a cave high in a cliff overlooking a river bed, and on another occasion he took motion pictures of a troop leaving a cave by the edge of the sea.

But habitual cave dwelling came later. Caves were occupied by more efficient killers which had to be driven out and kept out, and that had to await the widespread use of fire. (There is no evidence that early African hominids used fire.) On the other hand, brief visits may have been common, a possibility suggested by the finding of hominid remains, and bones presumably shattered by hominids, at Swartkrans and other Transvaal caves. According to Kenneth Oakley of the British Museum of Natural History, hominids may have entered these caves in the daytime to obtain water or get out of the noonday sun rather than for extended periods of shelter.

Of course, emphasizing the similarities between baboons and hominids can take us just so far. There were also great differences just on the verge of making their impact and, more significant, a potential for even greater differences. *Australopithecus* was hunting regularly. Furthermore, he was already beginning to change nature in a new way, to "fight back" by refusing to take things as he found them and modifying things, however slightly, and evolving toward an increasing measure of independence. Signs of the trend may be seen in the existence of home bases and a crude wall-like structure which shows that, although he lived in the open, he may have been learning to protect himself from savanna winds.

His surprisingly advanced tools imply a variety of activities and purposes, a brain already capable of some sort of language, and the possibility of social organizations far more elaborate than those of lesser primates. Bernard Campbell of Cambridge University in England has recently suggested that the family originated during early *Australopithecus* times, on the theory that troops and bands tend to break into small groups when rainfall declines and the land turns to semidesert, and dwindling sources of food and water are few and widely dispersed.

Such conditions demand the dispersal of populations. Many individuals coming en masse upon one of these sources would soon exhaust it without satisfying their needs, and some might perish before reaching the nearest source perhaps miles away. Limited resources are best exploited by small groups consisting of a single male and one or more females and their children. Similar behavior occurs during dry seasons among primates today, among the Bushmen of the Kalahari as well as baboons. Campbell believes that the human family may have developed as an established institution during year-long periods of grave and extensive food and water shortages.

As more is learned about the hominids who appeared five or more million years ago, they seem less and less like apes and more and more like men. Some anthropologists believe that *Australopithecus* deserves to be promoted and may actually belong to the genus *Homo*. The matter is under debate and involves highly technical points, mainly because it is not always easy to distinguish primitive men from advanced near-men. But the trend is definitely toward assigning a higher status to *Australopithecus* and recognizing that the gap between him and subsequent species is not as great as we once believed.

■ The discovery of Poor George in Africa and a relative, Lantian man, in China; discovery of Java man; Peking man on Dragon's Hill; the Vallonet and Escale caves; quantum evolution and increase in brain size, and its relation to meat eating

CHAPTER V

Early Migrations of Man's Ancestors

■ A major surprise of the 1963 digging season at the Olduvai Gorge occurred one January morning when an African worker announced he was going to find a fossil man, and did precisely that—turning up some time later with a matchbox containing a few badly broken hominid teeth. He had picked them up in the middle of a track made by cattle belonging to local Masai tribesmen, which meant that a valuable specimen had probably been trampled to bits. In fact, hundreds of further fragments were recovered after some two months of scraping, sweeping and sifting mud.

One result of this episode was a top-level meeting of Masai elders, government officials, and the Leakeys, who agreed to build dams and establish watering places for the cattle, provided that the Masai would keep their herds out of the gorge. Another result was a specimen known unofficially as "Poor George" (or, at the suggestion of an anonymous punster, "Olduvai George"). I saw the specimen one Sunday at the Leakeys' home outside Nairobi. Mary removed it from a safe in her office and placed it, as carefully as an antique dealer with a fragile vase, on a folded blanket. It was a skull about the size of a softball, with prominent brow ridges, representing some two hundred fragments glued and plastered together by Mary "on odd Sundays" over a period of more than eight months.

Poor George in his prime was more of a man than *Australo-*

pithecus. Among other things, his brain was bigger; his teeth were smaller, more like ours. His remains were found just below the sterile wind-blown deposits, which indicates that he lived more than a million years ago. He or individuals very much like him may have made tools at one of Olduvai's most unusual sites, which was located near a deposit of flintlike stone, has vast amounts of waste flakes and chips, and is probably the oldest known quarry-workshop. And records dating back as much as a million or more years before that include traces of some of his probable ancestors, the advanced hominids reported from older Olduvai sites and from Lake Rudolf and Swartkrans.

The status of most of these specimens has not yet been settled once and for all. Identifications tend to be, or should be, tentative, and some doubt still exists whether certain specimens currently classified as *Australopithecus* are or are not men. This state of affairs is to be expected. Investigators are dealing with creatures in transition. Furthermore, the investigators themselves are in transition as far as their thinking goes. The more specimens they find, the more they take into account in attempting to put together a consistent picture, and they are finding more specimens all the time.

But there is little doubt about the evolutionary status of Poor George and his descendants. They represent true men, and belong to the widespread species known as *Homo erectus.* The species includes a number of highly publicized representatives which stirred up some debate during the early days of research in human evolution, and whose significance is just beginning to be appreciated in light of recent studies. A notable story, according to one anthropologist "the greatest story of serene confidence I have ever heard," concerns the first *erectus* remains to be discovered.

About seventy-five years ago Eugène Dubois, a young Dutch anatomist, performed the highly unlikely feat of deducing where hominid remains should be found, and then going out and finding them. His argument was that one should look in the tropics, specifically in the East Indies, where apes still lived and where no glaciers had come to disturb possible sites. By 1892 he had extracted part of the jaw, skull and other fossil bones of a "missing

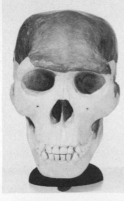

Homo erectus: reconstructed skull and artist's conception

link" from the bank of a river in central Java, a creature which he regarded as more advanced than an ape and not quite a man.

Dubois found a reasonably respectful audience for his ideas, especially considering the tradition of heated disbelief which still prevails among prehistorians. (For some reason, when investigators in this field disagree, they disagree rather more violently and bitterly than investigators in other branches of science.) Certainly the Java remains received far more support than Dart's Taung baby was to receive three decades or so later. But some anthropologists were skeptical and suggested that the remains might be those of a small-brained relatively modern man, perhaps a microcephalic idiot. Others believed it was a giant gibbon; still others refused to commit themselves.

The situation became clearer following excavations in China which started during the 1920's as the result of a strange series of events. For centuries expeditions had gone out into the remote mountain gorges and caves of Mongolia, China and Indonesia and brought back tons of fossils annually, but not in the name of science. The expeditions were led by traders supplying the enormous demand for "dragons' teeth" which, according to Far Eastern folklore, had potent medical effects. Chemists and apothecaries ground the bones into a fine sour-tasting powder and used it in a variety of elixirs and tonics probably no more ineffective than many over-the-counter preparations currently for sale in the drugstores of the western world.

Paleontologists aware of these practices had long been shopping for fossils at local apothecary stores and inquiring about the locations of promising sites. One such inquiry led from a human tooth purchased at a Peking store to a large debris-filled limestone cave in Dragon's Hill about thirty miles from the city, where excavations were carried out between 1923 and 1936. By the time digging stopped, workers had reached a depth of some 160 feet without hitting bedrock and had unearthed fourteen "Peking man" skulls, about 150 teeth and other remains representing more than forty individuals who resembled the Java individual.

Hearths and tools were found in the deposits, and also signs of a long struggle between Peking man and other cave dwellers. Some of the deepest and oldest layers contained animal bones only, large carnivores like sabertooth tigers and giant hyenas together with their prey. Other layers sandwiched between the animal layers contained only human remains, indicating that the carnivores had been driven out of the caves for a time. There were no animal layers in the uppermost deposits. Peking man seems eventually to have won in the struggle.

Artist's conception of *Homo erectus* foraging in wilderness of Java perhaps half a million years ago

These discoveries more than vindicated Dubois. In fact, they showed that he had been too conservative and that his Java find was not a pre-man but a full-fledged man. But by that time Dubois had become a secretive, conservative and eccentric old man. He went into virtual hiding, belittled the significance of the Chinese excavations, felt his colleagues were plotting against him, and buried his fossils in a chest in the ground beneath his dining-room floor. But he never lost confidence in his original discoveries. (The rumor that he retracted his ideas and decided that after all he had found only a big gibbon, a myth incorporated into practically all textbooks, was deliberately circulated by another paleontologist whose own finds had been challenged by Dubois.)

It happens that all the Peking man material, which had taken so long to find, was lost without trace during World War II. According to a recent version of what occurred, the remains had been packed in crates and were en route to the United States for the duration as part of the personal luggage of a young Marine doctor heading for home in 1941. Intercepted by the Japanese, he managed to leave the crates with Chinese friends and Swiss and French officials before being imprisoned until the end of the war. Now there is a chance the material may be traced, and perhaps recovered.

Fortunately, the record remains, and it includes fine plaster casts of the skulls, although the original specimens would be much more useful in continuing studies. During the past decade digging has resumed on Dragon's Hill. Workers have found tools, animal bones, and some further Peking man fragments in deeper levels of the large cave as well as in nearby caves. Digging has also resumed in Java, and two other skulls and skull fragments have recently been found in the central part of the island not far from the site where Dubois made his original discovery.

Java and Peking man may be more than 750,000 years old, and most other *Homo erectus* remains date back at least 400,000 to 500,000 years. The earliest specimen in Europe is a lower jawbone uncovered in 1907 in a sandpit near Heidelberg, Germany. In 1963, the year when Poor George was found, an expedition led by Woo Ju-kang of the Chinese Academy of Sciences discovered the lower jawbone of an individual named Lantian man after Lantian County in northwest China. The specimen was embedded deep in a hundred-foot deposit of red clay and, judging by its size, Lantian man was probably a woman. The following year Ju-kang and his associates unearthed the skull of another Lantian specimen, again, probably a woman more than thirty years old.

Other *erectus* traces have been found during the past decade, among other places near a Mohammedan cemetery on top of a sand dune in Algeria and on an ancient shoreline of Lake Chad in the Sahara. Further remains come from a Hungarian limestone quarry in the village of Vertesszöllös about thirty miles from Budapest. In a valley where a tributary of the Danube once flowed, investigators are excavating an important sealed-in site with hearths, burned bones and charcoal, many tools, and several teeth and part of a skull representing what is probably an advanced *erectus* individual.

So evidence accumulates to give a fuller picture of the rise and spread of the family of man throughout the Old World. Africa is man's homeland, the place where his oldest known remains and sites are located. It was in Africa that he established himself as a toolmaker and hunter and advanced social animal learning to live in millions of square miles of open country with no winters, among ocean-wide grasslands and herds among the grasses. But as time passed, his future involved the rest of the world to a greater and greater extent.

The oldest and only *Australopithecus* specimen yet recovered outside Africa may be a lower-jawbone fragment which comes from Java and dates back some two million years. But the earliest known works of man, traces of his camping sites and tools, do not turn up until about a million years later, more than 3,500 miles from the Olduvai Gorge, in southeastern France. They were collected in Vallonet cave, found some time ago by a young schoolgirl, among frost-shattered rocks and deposits sealed in by stalagmites. The cave extends deep into a 300-foot limestone promontory overlooking the Mediterranean. The evidence obtained to date is scanty but as clear-cut as the unearthing of an entire settlement. It consists of five pebbles chipped on one side, two of them choppers like those found at Olduvai; four flakes, two of which show use or working on the edges; and the fossil bones of rhinoceroses, elephants, horses and whales, including several bones which seem to have been broken deliberately. According to estimates based on animal remains and the geology of the site, this material may be more than a million years old.

Another site, the Escale cave, contains traces of about the same age or perhaps somewhat younger. In 1960, workers dynamiting a road through the valley of the Durance River not far from Marseilles exposed the back chambers of the buried cave and noted old bones among the limestone debris. Excavations conducted since then have furnished the earliest conclusive evidence for the use of fire, traces of charcoal and ash, fire-cracked stones, and five reddened hearth areas up to a yard in diameter. Escale is believed to include relatively undisturbed living floors; it promises to be one of the most important sites ever discovered in Europe.

Vallonet cave near Monte Carlo, oldest known campsite in Europe

An important question, and we have no answer for it, is why our ancestors left Africa at all and, given that fact, why specifically during this period—say, two million to one million years ago—and not sooner. After all, they had been around for at least four to five million years before that without, as far as currently available evidence goes, entering the vast Eurasian continent. A complete theory would take account of such problems, and might have a bearing on the sort of restlessness that moves people today.

Geological changes certainly affected the movements of hominids and other animals, and the last two million years or so mark not only the rise of man but also one of the most unstable climatic periods in the earth's history. As already indicated, large-scale northward migrations may have become possible for the first time after the formation of the African Rift Valley removed water barriers by shifting the courses of major rivers from a general east-west to a north-south direction.

The coming of glaciers also had at least an indirect effect on the timing and course of migrations from Africa into other continents. Prehistory features what Karl Butzer of the University of Chicago calls "one of the rare spasms of extensive and recurrent glaciation affecting the planet." Indeed, no human being has yet lived under conditions which, considering the prevailing climates of the past, can be regarded as normal. The previous spasm had come and gone more than 200 million years ago. The latest one was preceded by a relatively quiet period, a long calm before the storm.

More than 60 million years ago, in prosimian times long before the appearance of modern monkeys and apes, the earth consisted mainly of tropics. Vast forests and grasslands were widespread; alligators and other reptiles splashed about in streamy swamps as far north as Montana and Wyoming. The average year-round temperature of Central Europe was about 70 degrees Fahrenheit. Temperatures held fairly steady for about 30 million years and then started falling, probably as a result of mountain-building upheavals which created the Alps, Himalayas and Rockies and altered wind flows and general weather conditions over oceans and continents. Gradually the world became much cooler, average temperatures in Europe dropping some twenty degrees.

The stage was set for a spectacular phenomenon. About 10 million years ago climates started to "oscillate," temperatures falling to subfreezing levels and rising and falling again in a series of cold spasms. Snows in the north and on the highest mountains no longer melted away during summer thaws, but piled up layer by layer season after season to form great ice masses or glaciers. During cold periods ocean levels fell as more and more water was locked up in the glaciers which advanced from the poles and covered large portions of the earth. The process reversed during warmer periods, ocean levels rising again as the glaciers melted and retreated.

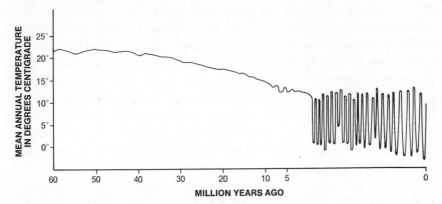

Schematic curve showing slow temperature decline and recent oscillations in Central Europe during past sixty million years. Time scale greatly exaggerated for the past five million years

We do not know why these oscillations occurred, but one of the most recent and plausible theories associates them with events in regions around the South Pole. The enormous pressure of growing glaciers on the Antarctic continent caused the ice at the bottom of the glaciers to melt, creating layers of water; melting may also have been produced by heat rising from radioactive minerals in the earth. The net effect was that the Antarctic glaciers tended to float on the layers of water, which acted as a kind of hydraulic jack, lifting the ice masses until parts broke off and slid into the sea. These segments were more than a mile high and hundreds of thousands of square miles in area, enough to cool the oceans and produce ice ages in the Northern Hemisphere.

According to the theory, this is a cyclical process. Fresh ice formed in Antarctica, broke off again, reaccumulated, and so on in periods of about 70,000 years. Each time new ice masses plunged into the seas worldwide ocean levels rose thirty to a hundred feet within a few decades. John Hollin of Princeton University has found some evidence for such effects in England's Thames Valley. If the theory is correct, sometime within the next

50,000 years or so the start of another ice age would be heralded by the sliding of millions of tons of glaciers into polar seas, an event which would flood New York, San Francisco, and coastal areas throughout the world.

Certainly some such process was at work in times past to bring about a series of glacial stages and warmer interglacial periods. Incidentally, the question of how many glacial stages there were is still wide open. The traditional number based on older observations is four, and is still cited in widely read books. But new research, most of it conducted within the past decade, has changed the picture entirely. Studies of fossil pollen, sea-floor sediments and sedimentation rates, and changing concentrations of oxygen isotopes in microscopic marine shells point toward many major advances and retreats of great ice sheets, more than twenty and perhaps as many as forty.

Africa was far from the steep fronts of mile-high ice masses that moved like giant bulldozers down from polar regions. But its highest mountains felt the cold, and during glacial times the snow line on the slopes of Mount Kenya extended some five thousand feet lower than it does today. More widespread effects are suggested by pollen studies which indicate that the Ice Age influenced climates all over the world, conditions being cooler and wetter in Africa when glaciation was most extensive in polar regions.

The new work draws attention to possible relationships between such changes and barriers to free migration. For example, increased rainfall during the first glacial stage may have created steppes and savannas and lakes in the Sahara and opened up routes across previously impassable desert. On the other hand, the Kalahari to the south may have advanced as the glaciers retreated in drier times during the subsequent interglacial stage, while at Olduvai layers containing early hominid remains and traces of a broad lake with deep waters are covered by deposits of wind-blown sand and ash. The deposits are more than forty feet thick, indicating a long stretch of extremely arid conditions, and "sterile" in the sense that they contain no trace of living things. So climate produced at the poles influenced the movements of our ancestors in and out of traditional living zones.

Social forces, critical changes in evolving human behavior

patterns, may have been at least as important as geological forces in early migrations from Africa. For example, there was the establishment of home bases where members of prehistoric bands could rest if necessary in comparative safety. As indicated in Chapter IV, such bases are unknown among lesser primates. All members of a baboon troop, for example, leave sleeping trees together in the morning and return together at night. Weak or sick or injured members must try to keep up, and if they cannot they are left behind. Within hours after the troop has gone and probably before its heart stops beating, the deserted baboon is devoured by a predator. (Lions and other carnivores prey primarily on incapacitated animals.)

Washburn emphasizes the importance of the home base: "The whole evolutionary impact of disease and accident on the human species was changed when it became possible for an individual to stay in one place and not have to take part in the daily round of the troop. Certainly one of the reasons why it has been possible for man to migrate without building immunity to local diseases is that his way of life allows him to be far sicker than a baboon and still recover. Injuries to the legs are common and are far more serious, of course, for a biped than for a quadruped. It is the home base that changes sprained ankles and fevers from fatal diseases to minor ailments."

If home bases helped make migrations possible, however, they do not explain why—or when—migrations actually occurred. Perhaps crowding or, since crowding can be a relative thing, as we are learning today, the feeling of being crowded has remote prehistoric origins. Perhaps groups of younger individuals felt an urge to live well away from the old folks at home, and moved on to the next valley. Or it could have been an urge to wander and explore, to go somewhere simply for the sake of going, and preferably to a place where no one had been before.

But why during a particular period, and not before or after? There is no shortage of possibilities or bright ideas; there rarely is. The problem remains to figure out what sort of evidence could prove or disprove a particular theory, and then to go out and find the evidence. In general, such work has not been done. So we continue to speculate about the forces which sent our ancestors across the Sahara and out of Africa. The *Australopithecus* wanderers who reached Java two million years ago presumably came by way of northeastern Africa, Israel, Iran and southern India and found tropical climates in the Far East.

But later emigrants who settled in places like the Vallonet and Escale caves had to deal with harsher conditions in glacial lands. Their probable route into Europe was also through northeastern Africa and Israel, and then perhaps across the Dardanelles in Turkey where there was either a land bridge or else very narrow straits with slow tides. The most direct route, across Gibraltar, had tremendous tides associated with a deep submarine canyon, and was a formidable barrier to early hominids. Based on estimates of prehistoric migration rates in more recent times, and the estimates are very rough, it might have taken them about three to four thousand years to spread from Olduvai to southeastern France, moving and settling down and moving again generation after generation at an average rate of about a mile a year.

Who made the crossing is not known for certain, since no hominid remains have been found in the earliest living sites such as those at Vallonet and Escale. It might have been *Australopithecus*, although the odds favor *Homo erectus*, who had an appreciably larger brain and presumably an enhanced ability to adapt to new environments. In fact, the expansion of the brain is one of the most spectacular developments in human prehistory.

It is a good example of what George Gaylord Simpson of Harvard calls "quantum evolution," an explosive burst of new adaptations. Of course, "explosive" is a relative term. Simpson warns that "considerable imagination must be used to conceive of an explosion that makes no noise and goes on for several million years," and a process which lasts that long is fast only on a time scale involving many hundreds of millions of years.

Quantum evolution occurred among horses some 25 million years ago. Horses had lived mainly on succulent leaves which are easy to chew up but their survival was threatened when forests became sparse, and they had to survive on a diet of tough, gritty grasses. Although many species failed to adapt to the new conditions, as their short teeth were worn away at an early age, populations that included a relatively high proportion of longer-toothed individuals proved more successful. The shift from browsing to grazing, which brought about changes in tooth shape to provide more efficient grinding surfaces and the appearance of a special tough cement as well as longer teeth, was extremely rapid in evolutionary terms, requiring about eight to ten million years.

More rapid changes took place among early hominids. There are a number of ways of looking at the phenomenon. According to one study, the average cranial capacity of *Australopithecus africanus*, dating back more than five million years, is 442 cubic centimeters. The cranial capacity of *Homo erectus*, which includes Java man and Peking man together with specimens discovered more recently and dating back less than half a million years ago, varied from 775 to nearly 1,300 cubic centimeters, with an average of 937.7 cubic centimeters. The upper part of that range overlaps the range for modern man, less than 1,000 to about 2,000 cubic centimeters. In other words, some members of *Homo erectus* had brains larger than many people living today. The brain had more than doubled in some five million years.

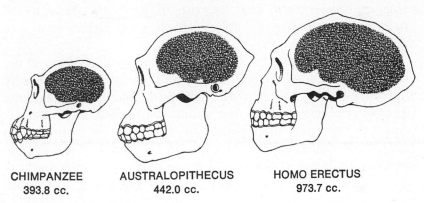

CHIMPANZEE	AUSTRALOPITHECUS	HOMO ERECTUS
393.8 cc.	442.0 cc.	973.7 cc.

Average cranial capacities, indicating more than doubling of brain size from *Australopithecus* to *Homo erectus* (chimpanzee cranial capacity included for comparison)

Another, somewhat broader, way of looking at the development involves body as well as brain changes. Although the following figures are averages and rough estimates, and different figures could be selected, the general trend can be regarded as a process in three stages:

1. From _Ramapithecus_ (15,000,000 years ago) to the first _Australo-pithecus_ (5,000,000 years ago), a 10,000,000-year span during which body weight increased from perhaps 50 to 75 pounds and cranial capacity increased from 300 to 450 cubic centimeters.
2. From the _first Australopithecus_ (5,000,000 years ago) to more advanced forms as found at Olduvai and elsewhere (2,000,000 years ago), a time span of 3,000,000 years, during which body weight increased from 75 to 100 pounds and cranial capacity increased from 450 to 700 cubic centimeters.
3. From _advanced forms_ (2,000,000 years ago) to full-fledged _Homo erectus_ (500,000 to 400,000 years ago), a time span of about 1,500,000 years during which body weight increased from 100 to 125 pounds and cranial capacity increased from 700 to 1,200 cubic centimeters.

The picture is one of _accelerating increase._ Something had happened to _step up_ the _pace_ of change, or to put it another way, something had interrupted the naturally slow course of evolution—and a shift in _dietary habits_ was one significant factor. The period which saw an increase in brain size from 700 to 1,200 cubic centimeters also saw the rise of _hunting,_ although the beginnings of hunting probably go back much further than two million years.

The remains of animals found at Taung in South Africa and the oldest Olduvai sites suggest that man's ancestors were hardly impressive hunters to start with. They undoubtedly killed and ate large species very early in the game, the earliest record so far being the presumed hippopotamus-butchering site found in the east Lake Rudolf area. But there is a predominance of small-game remains, the bones of ducks and geese and many other birds as well as lizards, rats, hares, tortoises and the young of various antelopes.

The pattern changes in more recent times. Moving upward from sites in the lowest levels of Olduvai to those below and above the wind-blown deposits, a number of things seem to be on the increase together. There were changes in species other than hominids. Apparently many previous species were scattered and wiped out during arid _desert times,_ and replaced by new forms, including an assortment of unusually _large breeds,_ particularly among the _plant eaters._

The coming of oversized animals may have been an indirect result of volcanic action. Lava and ash are known to contain traces of cobalt, copper and other elements which may affect the growth-stimulating pituitary gland, and perhaps rains resulting from glacial advances from polar regions washed these elements into the soil, where they were incorporated into plants. Another explanation is simply that times were good and animals generally tend to become larger when food supplies are abundant. In any case, man's ancestors lived among giants, a rhinoceros nearly twice the size of today's species, a pig about as big as a hippopotamus, a gorilla-sized baboon, and a sheeplike creature higher than a horse with horns measuring some ten feet from tip to tip. This represents a worldwide trend. In Australia, for example, there was a variety of giant forms including a kangaroo about ten feet high.

Man was among the predators of such species, and of species outside Africa. At Vertesszöllös the bones of large animals such as bears, bison and deer (broken and split, presumably for the marrow) tend to be concentrated in those deposits which also contain tools and other traces of man, while Peking man showed a marked preference for venison, nearly three-quarters of the remains found at the Dragon's Hill cave being those of two species of wild deer.

The basic problem is why man turned increasingly from small to big game and, before that, why he turned to meat eating in the first place. A tradition exists that meat eating is corrupt, something to be guilty about, a sign of how far we have fallen from an original state of innocence. A seventeenth-century theologian described "Those artless Ages, when Mortals lived by plain Nature. . . . Men were not carnivores . . . and did not feed upon Flesh, but only upon Fruit and Herbs." More recently William Golding in *The Inheritors*, a novel about prehistoric life, writes of the guilt which primitive man felt as he tore into a doe and of "the rich smell of meat and wickedness."

The origins of morals are always difficult to trace, but there was certainly a time when men's ancestors ate less meat than we do now. Most primates are vegetarians in the sense that they live chiefly on fruits, grasses, leaves and other plant foods. But probably many primates, and many mammals, for that matter, may become meat eaters under certain circumstances. For example, if a baboon happens to come across a nest of fledgling birds or newborn rodents, it may on rare occasions scoop up the contents casually, without breaking stride. In other words, meat eating may be an act performed in passing.

Carnivorous primate: baboon eating young gazelle

It may also be considerably more than that, however. A male baboon has been observed pursuing a hare in a zigzag dodging course for about seventy yards. The chase lasted more than a minute. It ended when the hare jumped over a log and "froze" motionless on the other side, only to be picked up and devoured by its pursuer. This tactic fools many predators with poor color vision, and baboons may use it themselves, but in general it plays into the hands of primates whose highly developed color vision helps them to detect motionless objects.

A more complex event took place a few years ago, when I spent several weeks in Kenya with Irven DeVore. One July afternoon we were driving through the Royal Nairobi National Park, looking for baboons as usual and heading for a ford across a shallow stream. Suddenly we saw directly ahead a large male baboon with a freshly killed hare in its mouth, a noteworthy event in itself since meat eating is rarely observed. But there was more to come. A whole troop was crossing the stream, and a few seconds later another large male passed with another hare, and not long after that a third male carrying the remains of a small antelope.

This was an unusual observation, the only recorded example of multiple killings among primates in the wild. But we had missed seeing, probably by only a few minutes, something even more unusual—how the killings had been carried out. Although further knowledge about predatory behavior is required to account for what happened, DeVore suggests a possible explanation: "The whole troop seemed excited, jittery. Since baboons eat small animals in a matter of minutes these animals must all have been killed recently and almost simultaneously. Perhaps one baboon came upon a hare lying in the grass and picked it up casually, and the sight of the act aroused other baboons to go after hares and other small game in the vicinity. In other words, it might have been a spontaneous flurry of activity, a kind of brief blood-lust episode."

The episode, of course, represented only one incident in the experience of one troop. It might never occur again in just that way. A casual killing in the future might arouse troop members as before, but the excitement could peter out quickly if other small animals did not happen to be nearby. On the other hand, if a similar experience did recur, the practice of killing could catch on and be passed along from generation to generation within the troop, and also to other troops occupying the same region. The practice might never become established in another region, either because favorable circumstances do not occur frequently enough or because there is ample plant food. DeVore emphasizes that meat eating among baboons may be a matter of group tradition, like the washing off and eating of sweet potatoes among Japanese monkeys (see Chapters II and XIII).

Similar influences may have been at work in determining the

evolutionary adaptations of early hominids. Man bears the marks of vegetarian origins in teeth not specialized for ripping and tearing like those of true carnivores and in the sort of long gut generally associated with a diet of plant food. Furthermore, man still seems to digest vegetable fats better than animal fats. Medical research indicates that an important factor in hardening of the arteries may be the formation of deposits of poorly digested fatty products on inner blood-vessel walls.

According to current thinking, *Australopithecus* adapted to life on the savanna and acquired a taste for red meat. In the beginning it may be that his ancestors ventured out of the forests mainly during times of temporary and relatively mild shortages of fruits and other preferred foods. Today in the Budongo Forest of Uganda, for example, intermittent periods of scarcity last for a total of about three months a year. It would be interesting to learn whether chimpanzees living there move into surrounding open woodlands or grasslands during such periods. The earliest hominids may have gone into the savanna in search of new food sources, and returned to an almost exclusive forest existence as soon as the shortages passed.

Later on during prolonged dry periods when *Australopithecus* and his forerunners came to stay, they had to find an evolutionary zone for themselves and exploit the natural resources of the savanna to the fullest possible extent. They began competing in earnest with other species—with herbivores and their fellow primates for plant foods and perhaps with other primates, including giant baboons, for sleeping trees. And perhaps the conflicts and occasional killings that resulted from competitive encounters had something to do with promoting an increased awareness of other species as potential prey.

Certainly meat might have been especially important in providing a well-balanced diet. As far as plant foods are concerned, grassy savanna lands may offer less protein to vegetarian primates than a forest or woodland environment, and in addition the work of foraging over wider areas in a less abundant environment could have contributed to an increased need for protein. Furthermore, there may have been an expanding need for more protein to nourish an expanding brain.

Running down small game was probably one of the early methods of obtaining meat. Many animals are swift runners, in relatively short spurts. But then they tend to slow down and stop as if they were going on the assumption that the spurts would be enough to shake off or discourage pursuers. Even larger animals like kangaroos and zebras and wildebeests can be run down by species that do not give up after the first dash but follow persistently, species like wolves and wild dogs and men.

One archeologist observed a chase of this sort a few years ago while he was looking for artifacts on a rock-covered hill in Zambia. An African was running at top speed over and around the rocks, chasing a young antelope about the size of a collie dog and losing ground as the antelope darted over a slope and disappeared. But the African kept running and came back a while later with the live animal in his arms. (He took it home to feed and kill later.)

Members of the Poka tribe on the Nyika Plateau of northern Malawi use similar tactics to catch elands and the francolin or spur fowl, a kind of partridge. This bird operates on a built-in almost automatic "schedule" consisting of three flights, each flight being shorter than the one before it. When first startled, the francolin flies away swiftly for a hundred yards or so before coming to earth; then if it is still pursued it soars off for perhaps half that distance. But a third approach will send it flying only a few yards away, and that is the final stage. At this point the bird is through escaping. It freezes, huddling close to the earth wherever it happens to land, in the grass or fully exposed on bare ground—an easy catch for anyone in the vicinity. *Australopithecus* may have been clever enough to figure all this out. At any rate, quantities of francolin bones are found among his leavings at Olduvai sites.

Leakey studied primitive hunting techniques and tried many of them himself in an effort to understand better and perhaps reconstruct prehistoric strategies. He actually learned an effective way of running down hares: "When you see a hare, it runs straight away and you run straight after it. It has its ears back as it goes, but not all the way back. The ears move all the way back when it's about to dodge, a sharp right or a sharp left.

"Now if you're right-handed you always dash to the right anticipating a dodge to the right. That means the odds are fifty-fifty, and you should catch half the hares you chase right off. If you've guessed correctly, the hare runs by instinct directly at you and you can scoop it up like fielding a fast grounder. Even if it happens to get past you, you haven't necessarily lost it. Stop and watch. It will probably dart under a bush and freeze there, assuming it has gotten rid of you. Then you can go over and simply pick it up."

Hares are among the animals that can be killed and dismembered in a few moments with teeth and bare hands. But this direct method will not work for other small game. The skins of young antelopes which must have been a significant source of meat, are so tough that they can be penetrated only with sharp cutting tools, and efforts to get at the meat may well have led to the regular use of such tools. *Australopithecus* probably first turned to naturally sharp rocks or rocks split as a consequence of bashing bones, or rocks that were hurled at escaping prey and missed and broke as they ricocheted off cliff walls.

The increasingly frequent use of deliberately shaped stone tools in preference to the ready-made variety, the imitation of accidental chipping and flaking, could have come about in a relatively straightforward manner. It could have been "discovered" several times before being accepted as a tradition to be passed along from generation to generation like meat eating itself. Certainly the result was a new and efficient pattern of behavior, as Leakey demonstrated on a number of occasions. One Christmas Eve at his Olduvai camp an audience of attentive Masai tribesmen watched him spend half a minute making a chopper out of a handy rock, and twenty minutes skinning and cutting up the carcass of a freshly killed antelope.

A widespread tendency among certain primates, the casual and episodic eating of meat, had been transformed into something habitual and part of a way of life. The transformation involved a complex combination of circumstances in the continuing transition from primitive ape-man forms to human beings—the use and shaping of stone tools, migrations out of Africa, the spread of savannas, the availability of prey and undoubtedly other factors. Going after small game represents an important early stage. It leads at an accelerating rate to full-scale hunting, which involves increased division of labor between the sexes, and to the full-scale development of evolution by culture and tradition.

■ The unsolved problem of regular meat eating as part of the hominid way of life; scavenging and the shift from small to big game; the evolution of hunting tactics; the Torralba and Ambrona sites in Spain, and the mystery of the aligned elephant bones; Oldowan and Acheulian tool industries

CHAPTER VI

The Rise of Big-Game Hunting
and the Psychology of the Hunt

■ An interesting site lies on top of the arid 3,000-foot plateau of Old Castile in north-central Spain, near the village of Torralba. It is at least 300,000 years old, and provides first-rate evidence of early man's effectiveness as a hunter of big game. By that time he had already become the most formidable of predators. He was killing elephants systematically, among other animals, and not even the big cats did that.

The site, like many prehistoric sites, was discovered by workers excavating for nonscientific reasons. In 1888 railroad workers were digging a trench for a water main and found fossil bones and stone tools. Starting in 1907, a Spanish nobleman and amateur archeologist spent about five years excavating not far from the now-abandoned railroad station. Although his findings indicated that the site was one of the most important in Europe, no one thought of digging there again until 1960, when Clark Howell spent a day at Torralba.

Howell located the overgrown trenches and back dirt of the old excavation, collected a few tools and bone fragments in adjoining fields, and decided that further digging was called for. More than half the site had been left unexcavated, so he and his associates and crew including some thirty local farmers, worked in the region for the next three summers, thirty-four weeks in all. They spent about $75,000; excavated a total of 20,000 square feet to an average depth of about eight feet; collected more than 500 pollen samples, 2,000 stone tools and waste pieces, and uncounted fossil bones; and mapped twenty-odd living-floor areas.

Although the evidence is still in the process of being analyzed, work has progressed far enough to indicate the overriding impact of big-game hunting as a factor in human evolution, and the effectiveness of modern excavating methods. The living-floor approach, measuring and mapping the position of every object to reveal patterns of prehistoric associations, and the cooperation of specialists in different fields have provided considerable new information. They have also provided some new and difficult problems, a sure sign of advancement in research.

No one knows when hominids began eating meat, predominantly small game, on a regular basis. The practice was well established two million years ago, and may have started several million years earlier. But if it had never amounted to anything more than that, the course of human evolution would probably have been rather less spectacular, more a matter of evolution by genetic than by cultural change. The most advanced primates existing today would probably be a breed of relatively small-brained, small-time makers of stone tools.

But circumstances dictated more elaborate developments. Given continuing dry conditions, the ever-intense search for food on the savanna, a species capable of making sharp tools, and being already accustomed to a diet including small game and vast quantities of big game on the hoof, the next step was almost inevitable. Within the boundaries of today's shrinking reserves there is some evidence of prehistoric abundances, such as the 1959 census which François Bourliere of the University of Paris conducted in part of the Albert National Park along the Uganda border.

An actual count of some 21,000 ungulates or hooved animals in a 230-square-mile area of short-grass savanna near the edge of a forest included more than 7,400 buffaloes, 4,800 hippopotamuses and 1,026 elephants, an estimated density of about 130,000 pounds of big game per square mile. Assuming that animals were as plentiful on all the plains of Africa in prehistoric times as they are now in a few areas, and they were probably rather more plentiful, early hominids lived within the sight and sound and smell of huge herds.

The big game was theirs for the taking, almost waiting to be exploited, and in due course it was exploited. They may have consumed carrion upon occasion, perhaps more in the beginning than later. As they rose with the first light of sunrise and scanned the horizon from their sleeping trees or from the top of a nearby kopje, they must have seen vultures circling in the distance and heard the alarm sounds of other birds. They had to move swiftly for the carrion to outrace the vultures, which, swarming like maggots over a carcass in a commotion of wings and darting beaks, can strip the good meat away in minutes.

This is exactly what human and nonhuman scavengers do today. In the Ngorongoro Crater of Tanzania, jackals and hyenas frequently go where the vultures are, and so do the Gond tribesmen of north-central India, who are always ready to scavenge off the prey of tigers. They watch for vultures, listen for the food calls of crows, and as soon as they detect signs of a kill race over to the spot. If the tiger is still there, they stand at a safe distance and shout and toss stones and wave sticks. Generally the killer leaves within a few minutes, and the tribesmen move in to devour every scrap of meat and break up every bone, leaving only the stomach contents.

Driving such predators away may or may not have worked as effectively in prehistoric times, depending largely on the question of when they learned to fear and avoid man. They could have learned very early the wisdom of retreating. As already indicated, an upright stance itself may have offered a difficult target for pouncing and helped to discourage them. If man's ancestors were accomplished missile throwers, that might have been a far more effective deterrent, on the theory that predators would have steered clear of the only animals capable of inflicting pain at a distance without actually making physical body-to-body contact.

There are arguments on the other side, one point being that rocks and branches could hardly have served as formidable weapons against lions and leopards and sabertoothed tigers. Such tactics may work today because big cats, having learned to associate man with weapons that make noise and do lethal damage from afar, will generally walk away from their kills when human scavengers or observers like George Schaller appear on the scene. Ever since the widespread use of guns in Africa, natural selection has been favoring predators that fear man and retreat discreetly at his approach, since they presumably live longer and have more offspring than less-cautious predators. For the protection of tourists visiting South Africa's Kruger Park, rangers make a policy during the off season of deliberately killing off lions which do not fear men. In times before the coming of guns, however, predators may have stood their ground more often than they do today, and early hominids may have had to wait for the big cats to eat their fill.

In any case, scavenging of some sort probably took place, putting early hominids in direct competition with other species. Plant food comes relatively easy in the forests where chimpanzees and gorillas live today, but it is, and was, a constant problem on the savanna. In turning increasingly to meat, *Australopithecus* would have been compelled to beat off other scavengers, including jackals and hyenas as well as vultures, and presumably to carry chunks of meat into trees or rock shelters high on the sides of rocky slopes where he could eat in peace. He clearly had many reasons to fear lions and other large predators, but, if he was indeed a successful scavenger, he also benefited from their prowess.

As time passed he did more and more of his own killing, and he probably had many opportunities. Judging by conditions on present-day African savannas, there were very likely lion kills and leopard kills (often left dangling in trees), as well as a large number of newborn, crippled and otherwise helpless individuals in great herds of wildebeests and other antelopes. Although archeological proof of such behavior is difficult to come by, there are other ways of approaching the problem. Investigators themselves have gone out into the savanna searching for meat, in an effort to learn at first hand something about the tactics of early hominids.

For one week in July, 1969, Schaller and Gordon Lowther of York University, Toronto, camped by a river bank in the woodlands of Tanzania's Serengeti Plain, about 70 miles west of the Olduvai Gorge. They covered an area of about 75 square miles around the camp, five days on foot and two days by car. The scavenging was reasonably good, yielding four freshly abandoned lion kills which were thoroughly devoured but would have provided prehistoric hunters with brains and bone marrow. One day, guided to a thicket by circling vultures, they found a bull buffalo that had died of disease or old age; the vultures and hyenas had been at work, but more than 500 pounds of meat and skin still remained. Another source of scavenged meat would have been the prey of wild dogs, highly effective hunters which were surprisingly easy to chase away from their kills.

As far as doing their own killing was concerned, the investigators counted it a "kill" if they could run down or stalk an animal and come close enough to hold on to its tail. This happened on two occasions. Once Schaller saw a zebra foal standing alone, gave chase, and after a brief sprint, caught up with it and grasped it firmly by mane and tail. Judging by its awkward gait while trying to escape, and by the fact that it had been abandoned, the foal was suffering from some disease; it was released,

Schaller on the Serengeti: zebra foal "kill"

but undoubtedly fell prey not long afterward to carnivores who were playing for keeps.

Later on the same day Schaller stalked a young giraffe until he was directly in front of it, looking into its eyes. It was blind, and dashed off after he grabbed its tail. During another meat-gathering experiment, this one carried out on the open grassy plains instead of in woodlands, a hare and a number of crouching gazelle fauns were encountered and could have been killed without much trouble. Dismembering any prey could readily have been accomplished with the aid of sharp-edged rocks conveniently lying about.

Notice that in all cases the animals were very young, small, sick, old or dead. Capturing a large, live, healthy individual presents an entirely different problem. On one occasion Schaller ran full speed at a group of wildebeests with a stick in his hand, and succeeded in cornering an adult male. It was a fleeting triumph. The animal promptly turned and lunged at Schaller, who wisely stopped in his tracks and decided to leave well enough alone. A hunter ready to risk his life, and perhaps working with a companion or two, might have outmaneuvered and eventually killed the angry bull, but then again he might not have.

As a result of these studies, Schaller and Lowther conclude: "The means by which scavenging and hunting hominids might fit into the ecological community without competing too extensively with other predators pose a number of questions. Their primate heritage suggests that they were diurnal, and selection pressure from their primate and carnivore way of life undoubtedly favored a social existence. The only other diurnal social carnivore is the wild dog, which hunts at dawn and dusk, and favors prey weighing 60 kilograms or less (about 130 pounds). An ecological opening exists for a social predator hunting large animals and scavenging during the day, an opening some early hominid may well have filled, assuming that none of the saber-toothed cats did so."

Other primate adaptations were taking place as hominids exploited hunting, since it seems likely that gorillas and chimpanzees and hominids arose from a common ancestor at about the same time. As mentioned in Chapter I, gorillas may have specialized in highland-mountain living, while chimpanzees and hominids originally competed in open woodlands—and later separated when the latter found their place increasingly in grassy savannas. But we know very little about the nature of the barriers which isolated these primate populations and permitted the origin of new species.

It was only a matter of time until our ancestors evolved fairly elaborate predatory techniques. There is an excitement and challenge about hunting, and furthermore, they must have learned to appreciate the logic and sound economics of going after big instead of small game. Although a man operating on his own can catch a small or weakened animal and kill it and devour it on the spot, taking on bigger and stronger animals equipped with nothing but stone weapons is no job for individuals, however rugged. It is a matter of efficiency, for five hunters working together can obtain appreciably more than five times as much meat as a lone small-game hunter.

Other animals practice hunting strategies. Schaller reports that if a herd of gazelles is grazing on the bank of a stream, lions may attempt a "pincer" movement, one lion circling around to the left, another circling to the right and perhaps two or three others advancing at a very slow pace frontally, that is, directly toward the stream and herd. Wolves and wild dogs also hunt in groups. Recent studies of African hunting dogs on the Serengeti Plain show, surprisingly, that gazelles have not yet learned to flee soon enough. They start running away only when a dog approaches within 600 to 800 yards, at which distance the dog can generally overtake them. A gazelle has a reasonably good chance of escaping from a single dog by zigzagging tactics, but it rarely escapes from a pack which can attack from several directions at once.

Packs have also evolved ways of hunting wildebeest calves. The objective is to separate a calf from the herd, which means first of all snarling and snapping and coming as close as possible to the edge of the herd until the bulls charge. The dogs avoid the charge of the large antelopes, and then dart in to harass the mothers and calves in the core of the herd. As long as the core group remains together, the pack can do nothing. But the instant a calf becomes panicky and breaks away, the entire pack goes after it. The mother may try to defend the calf for a while, but she soon runs off to join the stampeding herd.

Hunting is rarely reported among nonhuman primates, although it, or something quite like it, does occur. Van Lawick-Goodall has seen a group of chimpanzees stalking a young baboon that had wandered from its troop, but it ran off before anything happened. On another occasion she saw a successful maneuver: "The prey, a red colobus monkey, was sitting in a tree when an adolescent male chimpanzee climbed a neighboring tree and remained very still as the monkey looked toward it. A second adolescent male chimpanzee then climbed the tree in which the colobus was sitting, ran quickly along the branch, leapt at the colobus, and caught it . . . presumably breaking its neck, as it did not struggle or call out." The other chimpanzee, a confederate, then jumped into the tree to share the kill.

Such cooperative activities are not seen often. But they take place often enough to indicate not only that chimpanzees like meat, but also that they have the skill and intelligence to become regular hunters should the pressure become sufficiently strong— as it did among our hominid ancestors. In more than a decade of observing, van Lawick-Goodall has recorded about a hundred cases of meat eating and some thirty examples of hunting.

She notes what seem to be meat-eating "crazes," periods when hunting and killing are notably more frequent than usual. One incident may be enough to serve as a trigger. Perhaps there is a brief and bloody encounter with a bush pig or some other small animal, and other members of the troop see and become excited and increasingly aware of meat and potential victims, in a kind of blood-lust episode inferred by DeVore among Nairobi baboons (see Chapter V). A chimpanzee craze may last for a month or more, during which time dominant males generally get the lion's share of the meat, and then generally peters out until the next episode.

Among men and pre-men this tendency became an important life style. The details of what happened, of how different kinds of hunting and hunting tactics evolved, have yet to be worked out, which is one reason why Howell decided to carry out excavations at Torralba. The Spanish site, one of the earliest that provides evidence for big-game hunting, apparently served as a prehistoric abattoir, a place for butchering and meat processing.

Concentrated in a relatively small region are the remains of at least thirty elephants, twenty-five horses, twenty-five red deer, ten wild oxen, and half a dozen rhinoceroses. The remains lie where they were abandoned long ago. One 270-square-foot area contains much of the left side of a large adult elephant with tusks and bones unbroken and in place as if put together for an exhibit. The pelvis is missing and so is the skull, although the lower jaw was left intact. The area also contained four flake tools that might have been used for cutting. Another somewhat larger area nearby includes some of the bones of this same elephant; most of them have been shattered. There is a broken right leg bone, some vertebrae, and fragments of ribs, upper jaw and collar bone as well as two stone cleavers and more flakes.

This evidence suggests that the two areas were used for different purposes. What seems to have happened is that the elephant was killed and dismembered in the area containing its left side and the unbroken bones, and that large pieces of meat were carried to the nearby area for further butchering and processing. Two other areas include finer splinters and fragments, and occur together with a cleaver and a number of heavy side scrapers. It is more difficult to deduce what was going on here, but hunters may have been eating their share of the spoils—perhaps cleaning all the meat off the bones with the aid of the scrapers and then, like *Australopithecus* at Olduvai more than a million years previously, smashing the bones for the marrow inside.

A great deal more can be learned from this association of remains. What is the significance of the arrangement of the large elephant's left-side bones? At first the theory was that the animal had been caught in a swamp, struggled to pull itself out, and finally fallen on its left side. According to this notion, it sank so deeply that only its right side was exposed and accessible to butchery, so prehistoric hunters took what they could and did not try to get at the buried left side.

But the theory has not survived a more detailed analysis. The elephant may indeed have become stuck in the mud; its remains are preserved in clay-silt deposits, signs of a fossil swampland. The left-side bones, however, were not left in place. Leslie Freeman of the University of Chicago has prepared an extensive report on Torralba and points out, among other things, that the bones are not completely articulated, that is, they are not all fitted neatly joint in joint. Also, they have all been turned over. It seems that the animal was completely butchered, and after the butchering, someone took some of the big left bones and vertebrae and laid them down side by side to produce a partially

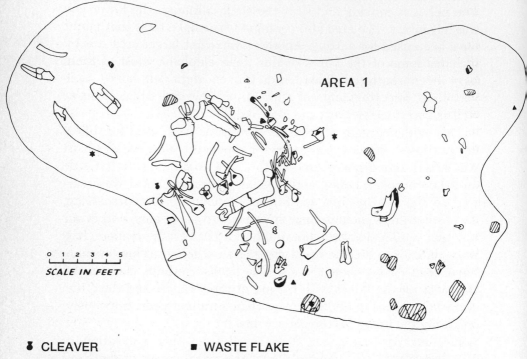

AREA 1

0 1 2 3 4 5
SCALE IN FEET

🦴 CLEAVER	■ WASTE FLAKE	
🔻 OTHER BIFACE	● RETOUCHED FLAKE	➤ WOOD
▼ SIDESCRAPER	✗ HAMMERSTONE	⊘ UNWORKED STONE
▲ FLAKE TOOL	✱ CORE	⊕ CHARCOAL

Living-floor map, showing location of objects unearthed at Torralba

reconstructed skeleton. Why anyone would have done this is another question. It may have been a game, joke or ritual, but there are no clues to support these or any other guesses.

The next question is how the elephant became bogged down in the first place. Torralba lies in a steep-sided little valley which includes the headwaters of a principal tributary of the Ebro River; even today, under generally dry conditions, places exist in the region where the water level rises to within a few inches of the surface and where a heavy animal would break through and sink. The terrain was wetter in the time of the elephant killers, perhaps representatives of *Homo erectus*. Fossil pollen gathered at the site indicates that there was a pine forest on the plateau, a sluggish meandering stream in the poorly drained valley, and seasonal swamplands with dense reeds and sedges.

Prehistoric man must have stood often on high ledges and slopes, and followed the leisurely movements of herds grazing in the valley below. Perhaps now and then a young and unwary elephant wandered away from the herd and suddenly found itself sinking in thick mud. If so, hunters would hardly have missed the chance to race down and close in for the kill; indeed, a surprisingly high proportion of the elephant bones unearthed at Torralba are those of juveniles. Perhaps the large adult, the elephant whose skeleton had been partially reassembled, had also wandered into a swamp and was promptly dispatched.

On the other hand, the hunters might have played a rather more active role. The elephants may not have simply blundered into the swamp, an explanation which after all implies that they were too stupid to avoid dangerous places during the course of their everyday movements, and which fails to account for the fact that many animals seem to have been driven to disaster, as indicated by certain items found in surrounding areas and carefully mapped, items that excavators of the past would not have considered worth charting.

In the area Howell collected many bits of charcoal and carbon which were distributed in an unusual fashion. Instead of being concentrated in a few spots, which would be the case if they represented hearths where fires burned over long periods of time, the materials are thinly and very widely scattered. Perhaps the charcoal represents the remains of hearths dispersed by the wind, but Howell suggests another possibility: "Whoever lit these fires was apparently burning grass and brush over large areas and for a definite purpose. My guess is that the purpose was to drive elephants along the valley into the swamps."

So the evidence, the burned material and the concentrated remains and the fossil bogs, tells a story of human activities more than three hundred millennia ago. It suggests that meat eaters were doing far more than waiting to take advantage of occasional accidents; that they had <u>observed herds</u> long and carefully, knew the habits of elephants, and were capable of a high degree of planning and cooperation. Other studies indicate that they generally lived in small bands of about thirty or so individuals, and a single band could not provide sufficient manpower for a large-scale, highly organized elephant drive. Several bands probably joined forces in the hunt at Torralba.

Howell discovered another major site in the region, or rather rediscovered a site where, according to old records, preliminary excavations had been carried out half a century ago. The records merely stated that the work was done "in Ambrona," a village in the same valley as Torralba and less than two miles away, but that was not enough information to locate the site. Then one day in 1962, when Howell asked his workers whether they knew of any places with fossil bones, a man answered: "Yes, in my field"— and it turned out to be the missing site. Subsequent investigations uncovered a kill and butchering site with deposits of about the same age as the Torralba deposits, remains of the same kinds of animals with elephants again predominant (perhaps forty to fifty individuals being represented), and a number of most important living floors.

One area included most of the skeleton of an enormous bull elephant, an old animal judging by his very worn molar teeth, together with a few isolated bones of an infant and a young female. The bones, left in place just as they were excavated, are now housed in a museum built on the spot. The area also contained bones of other elephants as well as horses and red deer and wild oxen, all in deposits which had once been deep swamplands; scattered clusters of charcoal and carbon, suggesting the deliberate use of fire; and cleavers and many other tools which served to dispatch and dismember the prey. The same techniques were used here as at Torralba, perhaps by the same hunters.

Some of the most intriguing and enigmatic patterns have been found on another Ambrona living floor. The main feature consists of three long elephant bones, two thigh bones and a large tusk, arranged in a line and forming a kind of boundary some twenty feet long. Other large bones lie perpendicular to the line, and one of them is the only complete elephant skull yet found during the entire excavation at Torralba and Ambrona. One of the mysteries at these sites is where the hunters took the heads of the elephants

Elephant remains, including large tusk (front) and boundary of long bones (rear), excavated at Ambrona

Excavators at Torralba hunting and butchering site

they killed; all but one of the heads is missing. Examination of the lone, almost-perfect Ambrona specimen shows one of the things they did with the heads. The top of the cranial vault has been smashed open, exposing the brain, which weighed ten pounds or so and was probably extracted and eaten.

One has a peculiar feeling while studying the living-floor diagram of the aligned bones and associated material—a feeling that pictured before one's eyes, in plain black and white, are patterns whose total meaning would be so clear if there were only a little more information. Not far away is another puzzling feature. For some unknown reason some prehistoric worker whittled a pencil-sharp point on the tip of an elephant tusk over four feet long.

Perhaps the tusk had something to do with the aligned bones. Specifically, it might have been driven into the ground and, together with other sharpened tusks, have served to support hides as part of a shelter. The hides might have been slung over the tusk-posts in a kind of tent formation, and anchored in place where they reached the ground by the line of large bones. Even a crude shelter would have provided at least some protection during cold nights, but whether or not it actually existed can be determined only by extensive excavations of living floors at other sites representing the same period of prehistory and comparable activities.

Clear-cut signs of more elaborate shelters, the oldest dwelling structures known, come from another site of the same general period. The hillside site is located in Nice on the French Riviera, on a dead-end street called Terra Amata overlooking the Mediterranean, and luxury apartments stand there today. But in 1966, when the apartments were being built, bulldozers uncovered some prehistoric tools, and work stopped for five months while Henry de Lumley of the University of Aix-Marseilles, his associates, other investigators, and student volunteers spent 40,000 man-hours excavating an area of about 1,100 square feet. The Mediterranean was higher several hundred thousand years ago, and eighty feet of water covered the site of today's boulevards and hotels and beaches. Surf broke high among the hills on the shores of other beaches, and people camped on one of them at Terra Amata, on a bay near the mouth of a small river where animals came to drink.

On the slopes of an ancient sand dune, de Lumley found remains of a number of oval huts twenty to fifty feet long and twelve to eighteen feet wide—postholes, hearths, a wall of stones probably to protect the hearths from prevailing northwest winds, and the bones of deer, elephants, wild boars and other animals. He believes that the huts were made of sturdy branches, bent so as to interlock at the top, with an entrance at one end and a hole at the center to let smoke escape. The branches were supported by posts and by large and small rocks placed against the posts. There are eleven fairly thin and undisturbed occupation layers near the dune, suggesting that hunters, probably the same group throughout, visited and revisited the site for perhaps only a few days during eleven consecutive seasons. We know that the hunters came in the spring because their "coproliths," fossilized feces, contain the pollen of plants which blossom in the late spring and early summer.

The huts may have housed ten to twenty persons. The areas closest to the firesides are clear of debris, indicating that the people slept there, a practice still observed today among the Australian aborigines. A number of domestic furnishings were also found. There are flat limestone blocks which may have provided convenient surfaces for sitting or breaking bones (similar blocks have been found at Torralba and Ambrona) as well as traces of the earliest container yet discovered, a wooden bowl with a rough bottom. In a corner near the bowl excavators found lumps of the natural pigment red ocher, lumps pointed like a pencil at one end and possibly used to color the body in preparation for some sort of ceremony.

Findings at Terra Amata supplement those at Torralba-Ambrona, specifically helping to reconstruct some details of life in early shelters. The Spanish sites have also yielded a rich and varied collection of tools, implying a correspondingly rich and varied range of activities. Cleavers, wedge-shaped objects which have a straight cutting edge at one end, were generally made by knocking flakes off both sides of a flattish piece of quartzite or flint or limestone, and served for heavy-duty chopping and hacking. Similar techniques went into the making of so-called hand axes, almond- or egg-shaped implements with thick heavy butts at one end, points at the other end and cutting edges along the sides.

Reconstructions of Terra Amata: (top) actual hearth as excavated; (top right) reconstruction of the hearth being used 300,000 years ago; (bottom right) reconstruction of the hut exterior, showing chimney and entrance

They were widely used over a period of more than half a million years, but, despite their name, probably for skinning and slicing meat and perhaps for woodworking rather than for chopping.

In addition to these tools Howell and Freeman collected many others which, because they are smaller and often less obviously worked, tended to be discarded along with the back dirt of past excavations. There are borers, scrapers, backed blades, burins or engravers, pointed flakes, and various kinds of notched tools. The important and exciting thing about such tools is that, like the tools found by Mary Leakey in the Olduvai Gorge, they appear far earlier in the record than anyone had expected—and signify

the very early appearance of relatively advanced purposes and the tools needed to carry them out.

At the same time the tools do not seem to have changed much over exceedingly long periods. Crude choppers occupied a prominent place in prehistoric tool kits for more than two million years, hand axes may have lasted a million years or more, and Neanderthal man was using notched and toothed tools nearly two million years after their first appearance in Olduvai deposits. To be sure, the passage of time brought some significant refinements, notably the use of bone, hardwood or antler to put the finishing touches on tools already roughed out with hammerstones. (The softer materials "give" more, produce thin flakes, and permit more controlled and delicate shaping.) But the basic ideas, the basic tool types, were there from the beginning. Such evidence implies a degree of stability or conservatism inconceivable to modern man.

We measure tradition in lesser terms, a few decades or a few centuries, and for us the good old days are not really so old. There are people who remember when and how things were different. But in a world without remembrances of different times where life and myths have remained much the same for thousands upon thousands of years, innovation would be bizarre and alien and dangerous, something to be resisted as a matter of sheer instinct. In times past changes came, often far-reaching changes, but they seem to have come almost despite the nature of man. Chronic change as a policy—the rising tradition of modern man—is something new.

There are tools of bone as well as stone at Torralba. This is one of the very few sites at which an appreciable number of undoubted bone tools have been found in living-floor contexts. (Olduvai is another such site.) Some of the more than one hundred implements appear to be versions of familiar stone types—scrapers, blades, cleavers and hand axes often made from specially split elephant tusks. Others were used to finish stone tools, to trim and retouch edges; still others, including "scoops" and spatula-like objects, have no known stone counterparts and serve as-yet-undetermined purposes.

Perhaps the most unique items found at Torralba are pieces of waterlogged wood which have somehow survived through the ages in clayey, boggy deposits. Marks of use and working have also survived, polishing, whittling and cutting scars, and hollowed-out sections. A few of the pieces may be parts of spears, which would make them the oldest known examples of a weapon that must have been invented early in the prehistory of hunting, although the oldest definite evidence currently is a fifteen-inch yew spear point found at Clacton-on-Sea, a site located on the eastern coast of England and believed to be at least 250,000 years old. But such remains are so rare and so fragmentary that unless very rich sources of preserved wood turn up, a remote possibility, we cannot expect to learn precisely how this material was used.

Another problem is the location of the home sites of the Torralba-Ambrona hunters. The sites we know them by are temporary only, places where they gathered for perhaps a few days and nights to kill and butcher their prey. Most of the excavated bones are the debris of meals eaten on the spot, and the hunters must have carried off the biggest, meatiest chunks. They must have had established camps in the valley, home bases not very far from the swamplands and the sluggish stream and protected from the bitter cold, for these were glacial times. Howell has not found any such camps, although he and his associates explored the entire valley for tools and other traces of man.

Living floors at a permanent campsite would not only add greatly to knowledge about early hunting life, but might also yield an important type of still-missing evidence, remains of the hunters themselves. As previously indicated, they may have been members of the species *Homo erectus*, relatives of Peking man. But this is only a guess, and direct evidence would be far more satisfactory.

Finally, the high proportion of elephant remains at the Spanish sites raises certain questions. Assuming that Howell's interpretation is correct and the animals were deliberately stampeded to their death, why did the hunters do it? The answer is not obvious. Land with sufficient plant foods to support elephants can generally support ample herds of other animals as well. Indeed buffaloes, horses, wild cattle and various species of antelope are likely to be several hundred times more numerous than elephants. So concentrating on elephants may have been more than a straightforward matter of getting meat. Perhaps something ritualistic was involved in the sense that hunters killed the large animals mainly to prove their courage and skill.

Whatever the motives, findings at other sites also suggest cooperative hunting. A site in the Olduvai Gorge, a clay bed once part of a swamp, contains signs of an organized drive that may have taken place more than half a million years ago—the fossilized bones of a number of large animals, including the horse-sized, sheeplike creature mentioned in Chapter V. Some sort of roundup or surrounding maneuver may account for the shattered remains of more than sixty giant baboons concentrated at a Rift Valley site outside Nairobi.

Analysis of tools found at various early hunting sites reveals some intriguing patterns. Comparing the Torralba-Ambrona tool assemblages as a whole with assemblages from other sites poses some new and subtle problems. There seem to have been two broad types of tools: the "Oldowan," named after sites in the Olduvai Gorge, where it was first identified, and the "Acheulian," which also exists at Olduvai but is named after the French site of Saint-Acheul in the Somme Valley where it was originally found. The Spanish sites fit into the latter category.

Oldowan tools trace back nearly two million years ago to the earliest sites at the bottom of the gorge, for example, the living-floor site which includes what may be a crude wall or windbreak. It includes the kind of chopper described in Chapter III, a heavy tool generally made on a cobblestone or oblong block, as well as lighter tools such as scrapers, engravers, notched implements and so on. This basic tool kit is found at Olduvai in higher and more recent deposits up to the bottom of the thick layer of wind-blown sand and ash, a time span of about a million years.

No traces of man and his works appear in this sterile layer. But above the layer, after an interval of many thousands of years, the Oldowan assemblage is found again with some additions. It not only includes choppers and other familiar tools found at earlier sites but also some new or rarely found items, the most characteristic of which are rough and battered spheroidal tools, purpose unknown. Presumably people had abandoned Olduvai during arid times, and their descendants had returned, bringing with them implements invented and refined elsewhere.

But there is an intriguing complication. Another tool kit, the

Acheulian, appears for the first time just above the sterile sand-ash layers at sites contemporary with those containing Oldowan assemblages. Together with some choppers and other older items, the tool kit contains the earliest unmistakable hand axes reported to date, hand axes perhaps 700,000 or more years old. It does not contain battered spheroids and other items more characteristic of the Oldowan industry.

The big question is what the two assemblages mean, what can be deduced from the fact that two different tool kits were being used at the same time in the same general region. It may have had something to do with where people settled. Olduvai Gorge camps containing Oldowan tools were located on flatlands next to lakes, at the mouths of streams fed by runoff from nearby mountains. On the other hand, African camps containing early Acheulian tools tend to be found away from lake shores along seasonal streams.

These upstream sites have an abundance of large stones washed down from the mountainsides and tools, notably hand axes and cleavers, made from correspondingly large flakes are common in Acheulian assemblages. Such stones are rarer at lakeside sites, however, and Oldowan assemblages rarely include tools made from large flakes. In other words, people tended to use what they had in the neighborhood to do their hunting and food processing. At this level the difference between the two kinds of tool kit is to some extent a matter of different kinds of local resources.

There is certainly more to the problem. A common view is that two "traditions" are involved, two different groups of people or tribes each with their own customs and way of life, that there are Oldowan and Acheulian cultures. The problem widens when other sites are considered. Oldowan tool kits, tool kits featuring a variety of choppers and lacking cleavers as well as hand axes, predominate in the eastern part of the Old World—in northwest India, Burma, China and Southeast Asia—until about a hundred thousand years ago. On the other hand, Acheulian tool kits, including those uncovered at Torralba and Ambrona, predominate throughout the rest of the Old World, in Africa, Europe, the Near East and peninsular India. They lasted until about 75,000 years ago.

Such facts suggest a number of possible explanations. For example, man may have <u>migrated</u> from <u>Africa</u> to <u>Europe</u> more than a million years ago, before the development of Acheulian tool kits. If so, he may not have done very well. His traces exist at only two sites, the Vertesszöllös limestone quarry in Hungary and Clacton in England, both of which have tool kits clearly derived from the Oldowan. The two oldest known European sites, the Vallonet and Escale caves of southern France, have not yet been thoroughly excavated; but if this theory is correct, they should also contain Oldowan tool assemblages. A <u>second migration</u> out of <u>Africa</u> may have come three or four hundred thousand years

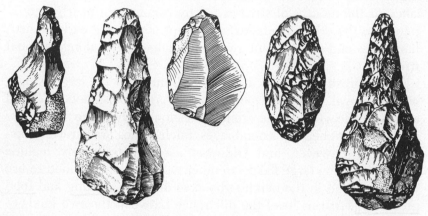

Acheulian tool kit showing flake tool (middle) and various forms of hand ax

later when people with <u>Acheulian tools</u> entered Europe and took over the vast majority of available sites, including the Torralba-Ambrona sites. These people may have settled in the west and either wiped out or assimilated the descendants of earlier immigrants from Africa, or else driven them east.

The theory will stand or fall on the basis of findings yet to be made. But it does seem that the "Oldowan" people who turned up in China and Java and other parts of Southeast Asia evolved little if at all while important changes were under way among "Acheulian" peoples in the West. Hallam Movius of Harvard University has pioneered in studies of Southeast Asia, and concludes: "It seems very unlikely that this vast area could ever have played a vital and dynamic role in early human evolution, although very

GLACIATED AREA

 Acheulian assemblages (hand ax tools)

Oldowan assemblages (chopping tools)

LOCATION OF OLDOWAN AND ACHEULIAN ASSEMBLAGES: AFRICA AND EURASIA

primitive forms of early man apparently persisted there long after types at a comparable stage of physical evolution became extinct elsewhere."

｜One possible reason for the relatively slow pace of change in the East is that forests tended to be more widespread and denser there and, since huge herds are not found in forests, big game was far less abundant than in the savannas and open woodlands of the West. In a sense, Movius' conclusion lends further support to the notion that big-game hunting represented a challenge, a major challenge which perhaps more than any other single factor accounts for man's uniqueness. It also emphasizes the importance of Southeast Asia as a rich and largely untapped source of information about the nature of our early ancestors, and about the role of environment in shaping human evolution.

■ Hunting as a factor in the evolution of larger brains; the relationship between larger brains and prolonged infant dependency; changes in male-female roles and increasing female dependency; female sexual receptivity and the prehistory of love; the male hunting society and homosexuality; incest taboos and the reduction of conflict; fire as a force for human change

CHAPTER VII

The Impact of Big-Game Hunting on Human Evolution

■ At this stage man has almost completed his journey through time. He stands only a brief span, a mere half-million years out of some fifteen million years of hominid development, away from the twentieth century, the equivalent of the last fifteen minutes or so of a jet flight from New York to Paris. His brain, the brain of *Homo erectus,* is already well within the size range of modern man.

But his way of life is far from modern. The future has hardly begun. The wonderfully complex process of human evolution has been accelerated and is building on tendencies rooted in times long past, before the coming of man, before *Ramapithecus.* The process started with a need for more meat, led to an increasing emphasis on hunting, and is culminating in an explosion of differences—or rather an extension and elaboration of differences already built into the scheme of things—differences between man and his fellow species, between men and women, between older and younger men, and so on.

A major trend in primate evolution has been a widening of horizons, an increase in range which may have originally been connected with the increase in body size discussed in Chapter I. Since big monkeys and apes need more food than smaller primates and are generally safer from predators, they can and do cover wider territories. To take extreme cases, some small

151

monkeys may spend a large part of their lives in half a square mile of forest, while gorillas have a range of fifteen to twenty square miles.

Our ancestors were no gorillas in stature, but they were hunters, and the search for game sent them roaming more widely than any other primate. In fact, judging by the extent of their range, they were more like wolves and wild dogs. Wolf packs may

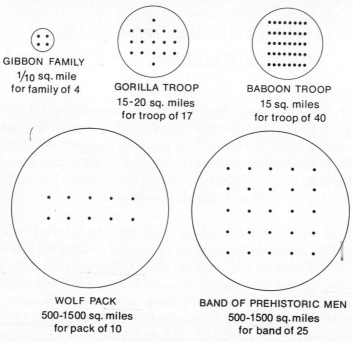

GIBBON FAMILY
1/10 sq. mile
for family of 4

GORILLA TROOP
15-20 sq. miles
for troop of 17

BABOON TROOP
15 sq. miles
for troop of 40

WOLF PACK
500-1500 sq. miles
for pack of 10

BAND OF PREHISTORIC MEN
500-1500 sq. miles
for band of 25

Primate home ranges

cover from some 500 to 1,500 square miles, and rough estimates based on the recent practices of primitive tribes suggest that early man may have had hunting territories of comparable size. According to Washburn, "the most minor hunting expedition covers an area larger than most nonhuman primates cover in a lifetime." Wider roving exposed man to a wider variety of experiences, thus increasing his chances of encountering novelty throughout life. In effect, that extended his youth with respect to nonhuman primates whose chances of encountering novelty, of being surprised, presumably decreased much faster after child-hood because of their restricted ranges.

Man had every incentive to know his wider world, and to know it well. When getting food is the most important thing in life, hunters cannot afford to miss anything. The Bushmen of southern Africa, for example, are intimately acquainted with the way of life of more than fifty animals. They can follow a herd of antelope even over hard dry ground which holds only the very faintest impressions of hoof prints, and can detect the almost invisible hoofprint pattern that distinguishes a wounded animal from its fellows in the herd. Furthermore, they know the great unmarked areas of their home territories in far greater detail than a postman knows the streets and houses of the village he has lived in all his life.

Elizabeth Marshall Thomas, who has spent much time with Bushmen, points out that in an area of hundreds of square miles they know "every bush and stone, every convolution of the ground, and have usually named every place in it where a certain kind of veld food may be even if that place is only a few yards in diameter, or where there is only a patch of tall arrow grass or a bee tree." They do not read or write, but they learn and remem-ber. If all their knowledge about their land and its resources were recorded and published, it would make up a library of thousands of volumes. Such knowledge was as essential to early man as it is to these people.

With the rise of hunting, early man became increasingly alien-ated from the rest of the animal kingdom. Once he had lived among other species, with considerably more than mutual toler-ance. As already indicated, baboons and impalas often feed to-gether on African savannas, enjoying the protection of a doubly effective early-warning system. The baboons' visual powers sup-plement the impalas' acute sense of smell. Each species is alert on its own, but together they are almost invulnerable to the attacks of lions and other big cats.

The remote ancestors of man probably once lived on similar terms with the ancestors of present-day antelopes in a symbiotic if not always idyllic relationship. Hunting widened the gap be-tween man and other species, in effect creating two worlds where one world had existed before. If there was ever a loss of innocence in man's past, a feeling of original sin or guilt about killing and eating creatures that had once been his equals or superiors, it would have dated back to the transition times when early hominids were developing their taste for meat.

Of course, there is very little likelihood that any species, prehuman or otherwise, has ever felt qualms about the process of adapting for survival. Prehistoric hunters learned predation so well that they probably helped kill off a number of species, perhaps including one of their most formidable competitors, the sabertoothed tiger. Man, in short, was beginning to live more against than with other animals.

Other differences were becoming sharper, for example, the differences between the sexes. Body structure was affected, as an indirect result of the rise of hunting which helped bring about larger brains. That, in turn, posed a fundamental problem in the design of the female body, specifically a problem involving the optimum dimensions of the female pelvis. From a strictly engineering point of view, the obvious way of allowing for the delivery of bigger-brained infants is to enlarge the pelvic opening and widen the hips, and evolutionary pressures were at work which favored this solution. The difficulty is that individuals with wider hips and related modifications lose a measure of mobility. As far as speed is concerned, the ideal pelvis is a male pelvis. Women cannot generally run as fast as men, a disadvantage in prehistoric times when flight was called for frequently.

Another theoretical way of meeting the problem is to go to the other extreme and avoid the necessity for widening the hips. If the infant is born sufficiently early in its development so that its brain is still small, delivery difficulties can be minimized or eliminated. The limitation in this direction, however, concerns the danger of being brought too immature into the world; the earlier an infant is born, the smaller its chances for survival. The death rates for premature infants, infants weighing 5.5 pounds or less, are about three times higher than for full-term infants.

Confronted with these alternatives, nature in effect did a little bit of both, achieving a not altogether happy compromise. Natural selection arrived at a solution in which the hips were indeed widened sufficiently to permit delivery of an infant with a somewhat larger brain, a brain sufficiently developed to ensure a reasonable chance of survival. On the other hand, the brain was by no means fully developed. It was still immature and small enough so that the hip widening did not reduce the mother's mobility to a dangerous extent. So the brain had to do most of its growing after birth. A rhesus monkey is born with a brain that has already reached nearly three-quarters of its adult size, but the brain of a newborn *Homo erectus* infant had probably completed only about a third of its growth.

Delayed maturity, of course, means extending the state of infancy, and that had crucial repercussions. Most mammals are ready to fend for themselves only a few months after birth, but a unique type of growth was established among primates and accelerated by big-game hunting. Monkeys remain helpless for about a year, apes for two to three years; *Homo erectus* was in a similar condition for perhaps four to five years (as compared with six to eight years for modern man). Indeed, the first human infants were not only helpless longer than the infants of other primates but they were also more helpless since they could not cling to their mothers.

Another trend in primate evolution is away from large litters and toward single births, or at least litters consisting of no more than two or three offspring. This development, like the development of stereoscopic vision and other features, is mainly a consequence of life in the trees, where it is considerably more difficult to care for infants than on the ground or in dens and burrows. One result is that prenatal growth can proceed at a more leisurely pace. Among species with large litters there is competition for nourishment and space within the uterus, a condition favoring relatively rapid growth and a short gestation period. Since higher primates typically give birth to only one infant, however, such competition does not exist and a slower rate of growth is possible.

The focus has been increasingly on the infant as an individual, in a way that can never be the case among species with large litters. A single birth is more special, and can receive more care and attention. Campbell points out that in the final analysis it is a matter of quality instead of quantity: "Evolution has selected in man a reproductive process that enables him to maintain his numbers in a hostile environment, not by mass production but by prenatal protection and postnatal care."

Perfect solutions are rare in evolution. Prolonged infant dependency certainly increased the chances of suffering early psychic traumas, a fact which psychoanalysts have interpreted as highly significant, even regarding dependency itself as an inevitable and therefore universal trauma. But elementary biological considerations suggest that this may possibly have been a price worth paying, that in us as in other species something of value was gained as well as lost. It is at least arguable that selection was taking place for something rather more directly advantageous to the species than an increased susceptibility to neurosis.

Prolonged infancy is only part of an evolutionary process which has brought prolonged childhood, prolonged adolescence, and prolonged life, part of the slower pacing of things in a species which relies more than any other species on learning. It is difficult to imagine the young of a rapidly maturing species learning to behave appropriately in a highly organized hunting band. A male that could run, fight, and feed itself within six months or less after birth would probably not excel at the art of learning complex and flexible social responses. It would find itself too busy being a vigorous animal. The human type of growing up demands a delay in such activities. It is well served by early immobility and dependency which permit observations and listening, contemplation of a sort, before full-time commitment to active doing. For example, although the circumstances under which language arose are unknown, it was probably evolving in important ways during the increasing emphasis on the hunting of big game—and a connection may have existed between slow maturation and the ability to acquire new linguistic skills. A docile infant and an experienced adult must have made an effective combination for the establishment of social communications, at least in prehistoric times.

Evidence is accumulating to indicate that culture was already of some importance in *Australopithecus*, a notion originally proposed by Dart more than a generation ago. In a key investigation of molar-tooth development Alan Mann of the University of Pennsylvania points out that the first, second, and third permanent molars erupt at about six, twelve, and eighteen years respectively—in both *Australopithecus* and modern man. On the basis of this observation, he suggests: "The growth stages of *Australopithecus* are comparable to those of *Homo sapiens* and . . .

childhood development is similar in both groups." The implication is clear that hominids have long depended on "a large complex of learned behavior, or culture."

One effect of prolonged infant dependency was to increase further the differences between the sexes. The widening of the hips to permit the delivery of infants with larger brains helped decrease female mobility in the sense that running became more awkward and slower. But another kind of decreased mobility was far more significant. The longer and more intensely an infant needs its mother, the longer and more intensely the mother needs a reliable adult male. In other words, female dependency increased markedly with increasing infant dependency.

At the same time other forces were fostering new and closer and more enduring bonds among males, a point stressed by Lionel Tiger of Rutgers University. As men cooperated in going after a wider variety of game, the emphasis was more and more on planning, selecting places for hunting and appropriate hunting strategies, developing more sophisticated ways of communicating, learning and sharing skills. Men on the hunt in wildernesses went away in groups, ranged widely and stayed away perhaps all night and perhaps on occasion for several nights. They began forming the all-male associations which more recently have led to such things as clubs, lodges, athletic competition, secret initiations, and an assortment of stag institutions. Women were in the process of becoming the "other" sex in a sense that is true for no other primate, the first females to be left behind and to fear being abandoned.

Differences intensified within the male community itself, stresses between younger and older males. This was nothing new among primates. Van Lawick-Goodall observes that among chimpanzees the young male has hard lessons to learn. Early in adolescence, which starts between the ages of seven and eight, he becomes independent of his mother and increasingly capable of dominating females, who used to dominate him. But this is also the time when larger, dominant males become increasingly aggressive toward him, and tend to keep him away from females. His frustration may be expressed by charging through the troop dragging branches and throwing rocks, but even here he must learn to be careful because all the hubbub may get on the nerves of the dominant males. Or he may wander off alone into the forest.

Making it, getting into the club of dominant males, was as important to hominid as to chimpanzee adolescents, only rather more complicated. The institution of hunting probably provided new ways for an adolescent to take out his frustrations—to prove himself. It was one further step in the accelerating development of symbols, as hunting and the eating of meat acquired new values and meanings. This aspect of prehistory is reenacted daily in restaurants catering chiefly to men and specializing in thick steaks and roast beef, rare, while "female" restaurants generally feature vegetables, fruits and salads.

Such changes dramatize man's very special position among species. He provides an example of evolution in the process of being put to its most severe test. All species survive by adapting, but his adaptations are far more elaborate and tend to become increasingly so. The past is only in part a story of divisive forces, forces which tended to create new and conflicting groups within groups. Society is possible because the conflicts served to accelerate the building up of powerful counterforces, in a continuing interplay of tension and the relaxation of tension.

Hunting had major unifying as well as divisive effects. It increased cooperation among all members of the group, not only among certain males. Man became the only primate to kill regularly for his living, and the only primate to share regularly on a day-to-day basis involving the entire group. All other primates are supremely self-centered when it comes to feeding; they forage strictly for themselves. Even more important, as Isaac emphasizes, another unique development came with the hunting—a division of labor between the sexes, with the males concentrating on obtaining animal foods and females concentrating on plant foods.

Intricate networks of causes and effects are involved in such major changes of life style. One cause-effect sequence begins with the question of what favored a male-female division of labor in obtaining food. The first answer is that infants were dependent longer, so that females were themselves more dependent, had less time for prolonged hunts and specialized in plant foods which could generally be gathered in the vicinity of the home base.

Tracing the sequence back one more step, infant dependency was prolonged because of the expansion of the brain, because limitations in widening the female pelvis demanded infants designed for considerable brain growth after birth. The major reason for bigger brains, in turn, was the rise of hunting.

This is where "positive feedback" comes in, that is, a process which favors its own acceleration. The division of labor in subsistence activities, a result of hunting, itself favored more effective hunting. Hunting is often a risky business, since hunters may return with no meat at all or with too little to feed the entire group. In other words, it could be conducted on a limited basis only, as long as there was no other source of food to count on. Females provided such a dependable source by collecting plant foods, an activity which made regular hunting possible in areas where the probability of coming back empty-handed was high. Note that increased hunting selected further for intelligence and cooperation and for further expansion of the brain.

So evolution worked to establish a secure, stable, social framework in a milieu of potentially disruptive forces. The new framework had to be strong and flexible enough to include male-male as well as male-female associations. The problem has not yet been solved to the complete satisfaction of either sex, but early steps toward a solution included changes in patterns of sexual behavior, changes designed to reduce other new tensions and anxieties.

The typical pattern among mammals involves regular bursts of sexual frenzy which take precedence over all other activities. At every ovulation or immediately after, all nonhuman females, including occasional nursing females, come into estrus or "heat." Sexual activity is so concentrated and intense during such periods that it tends to interrupt the care of the young and all other forms of behavior. This sort of all-inclusive estrus ensures effective reproduction among most mammals which have rapidly maturing offspring, but not among primates. If all the females in a primate troop were subject to three days of sexual mania every month or so, it would probably be to the detriment of their slow-maturing infants. Natural selection brought about a modification in monkeys and apes, to the extent that estrus ceases during the later part of pregnancy and the early part of nursing.

A modified form of estrus is fully compatible with the primate way of life, that is, with the way of life of nonhuman primates. Man is the only mammal in which estrus has disappeared entirely. Ralph Holloway of Columbia University suggests that this development may have started with the appearance of *Australopithecus,* which occurred more than five million years ago. It was certainly established among the hunting bands of *Homo erectus.* Estrus cycles may simply have made less and less sense in a species with single births spaced further and further apart as the period of infant dependency lengthened. A new reproductive rhythm was being established; estrus no longer served an evolutionary purpose and went by default, as it were.

More positive forces may have been at work to speed the departure of estrus. The female of the species became sexually receptive at practically any time rather than during estrus only, eliminating periods during which male competition and aggressiveness reached a peak and contributing further to the stability of life. Extended sexual receptivity on the part of females served also to extend the period of their attractiveness to males and may have helped counterbalance the new appeal of male-male associations. The changing pattern of female behavior helped to tie the male more securely into the mother-offspring group, the beginning of the family.

The extension of the possibility of choice in timing of sexual relations led to what Campbell calls "the individualization of sexual relations." Estrus, even as modified among nonhuman primates, is essentially beyond the individual's control. Its presence and absence are determined by the automatic turning on and turning off of sex-hormone secretions, presumably by a kind of biological clock in the brain which keeps track of the passage of time and periodically triggers the activity of centers concerned with the arousal of sexual urges. Under such conditions the sex act among early hominids, as among contemporary monkeys and apes, tended to be relatively impersonal and mechanical.

When sexual urges came under a measure of voluntary control, it became possible to select the time and place for intercourse and, in a way, the mate. Personal preference became meaningful for the first time, and male-female relationships became more enduring. These were the opening phases in the prehistory of love, at least love in the human sense. Homosexual love may have arisen at about the same time as heterosexual love as a by-product of the male-male associations of hunting bands—and, of course, as a by-product of the replacement of automatic hormonal control of sexual behavior by a measure of free selection of partners.

Changing sexual patterns brought new orders of social complexity, new things to be learned and remembered, new inhibitions and prohibitions. Early man might have developed incest taboos, for example, partly for economic reasons, as a method of population control. The fact that human males mature sexually years before they mature socially probably created as many problems in prehistoric times as it does today. Contemporary hunting and gathering groups have devised a variety of marriage customs and rituals to ensure that the production of children is delayed until the male has learned the ways of hunting and is fully prepared to provide for a family—and incest, like premarital sexual intercourse, is incompatible with these objectives.

Incest taboos may have helped reduce conflict, jealousies and rivalries, within hunter families or protofamilies. Such restrictions might also have reduced rivalries among families, counteracting any tendency of the group to break up into competing family units—just as exogamy counteracted any tendency of the tribe to break up into competing bands. The effect would be to produce a more integrated group, a wider and more inclusive system of communal bonds and the basis for formal kinship relations. Gregory Bateson of the University of Hawaii has pointed out that when the objective is just the opposite, when it is desired to create an exclusive rather than an inclusive situation, incest may be permitted and even enforced. Thus brother-sister marriages were the rule among the royal families of dynastic Egypt.

Other factors favored even wider, more "outgoing" sexual relationships. A great deal has been written during the past few years about the fact that fish, birds, rats and other species will fight to the death if necessary to defend their home grounds against invading members of their own species. Under certain circumstances this is also true of man.

There is an equally true and equally important side of the story which has generally been less widely publicized, because it does not fit in so neatly with old melodramatic tooth-and-claw clichés about evolution.

Man has unique capacities for cooperation as well as conflict, one reason why inference from the behavior of other species may be dangerous. Nonhuman primates may be highly organized, but the organization is in the main internal, within the troop; social systems are generally closed, most matings taking place among established troop members. Their foreign affairs, however, are rather less well ordered than their domestic affairs. Troops tend to ignore one another, or fight. Man alone attempts to form organizations of organizations, tribal unions, and confederations.

Mating among members of different groups, a characteristic of primitive tribes, may have arisen in prehistoric times when a number of hunting-gathering bands occupied the same region. "The exclusive control of a hunting territory can be efficiently maintained only with the mutual consent of neighboring bands," Washburn notes. "Excessive fighting over territorial borders both disturbs game and dissipates the energy of the hunters. The exchange of mates between neighboring groups helps to insure friendly relations . . . because it disperses persons with close emotional ties among many groups and over a large area."

Establishing social systems based on such exchanges, such alliances, became a matter of survival. Again, hunting emerged as a force favoring new kinds of cooperation as well as new kinds of conflict. There were new rules for playing the game, rules that required a greater flexibility of behavior. The control of mating within the group continued, but on appropriate occasions additional rules were followed involving the control of out-group mating, out-marriage or exogamy.

Natural selection also put a premium on the development of a moral sense. A hominid who at the approach of a predator cries out to warn the other members of his group may draw attention to himself and run the risk of being killed. But a mathematical analysis of such bevavior shows that he may actually thereby increase his reproductive success if close relatives are aided or if the individuals he has benefited return the favor. In other words, he acts so as to preserve and pass on his genes to succeeding generations, and so do other members of the group.

This is one result of an important study by Robert Trivers of Harvard. The system of course depends on doing unto others as they did unto you, on reciprocal altruism, and Trivers shows that such behavior is likely to be favored among groups of relatively long-lived individuals who live together over long periods and depend on one another for food and defense, precisely the sort of groups formed by early hominids. He indicates that selection favors a capacity for gratitude, sympathy, friendship and other qualities useful in playing the game of reciprocal altruism. Selection also favors such feelings as guilt, shame and moral indignation which tend to discourage individuals from "cheating" at the game by giving less than they receive or dodging their responsibilities entirely.

The basic phenomenon underlying all these changes is an enormous increase in complexity. Individuals were observing more, doing more different things, learning more, developing a wider range of emotions, participating in more and more complex social systems. The hominids' view of the world was expanding at an unprecedented rate—and so was the hominid brain.

The brain expresses in its actual tissue, its biological structure, the state of the world outside. Somehow it includes in the interconnections among its billions of nerve cells a small-scale model of the world and its processes, of reality as it appears to the species at a particular stage of evolution. As our ancestors roamed more widely in search of game, followed and anticipated the movements of their prey, and learned sharing and caring and other rules of evolving social systems, they had more to remember and analyze—all of which put a premium on a large brain with a larger memory capacity.

So there was a multiplication of memory units, and research like that conducted by John Young at University College London indicates the possible nature of such units. A memory unit or "mnemon" can be thought of as a small cerebral circuit consisting of perhaps half a dozen interconnected nerve cells. Its main component is a classifying cell which receives nerve impulses from a sense organ and has two extending fibers which transmit messages to appropriate muscles. Impulses transmitted along one "advance" fiber cause the animal to approach, while the other "retreat" fiber carries avoidance messages only.

We are designed to expect the best, at least to start with. In general the mnemon has a built-in positive bias, so that an object seen for the first time is apt to be attractive and stimulate the sending of signals along the advance fiber of the classifying cell to the muscles. If the object turns out to be dangerous or forbidden, however, the advance fiber is blocked chemically and all subsequent signals from the classifying cell pass along the retreat fiber. Actual behavior is based on the interplay of many mnemons, but generally this seems to be how we learn that discretion is the better part of valor.

So evolution added more mnemons, more nerve cells, and the brain grew like a benign tumor at the head end of the spinal cord. Of course, it was far more than a mere increase in gross size. Subtle changes were taking place in internal organization—especially in the nerve circuitry required to inhibit, to control the not-doing of things, continuing a long-established trend in primate evolution (Chapter I). The mnemon with its advance fiber and retreat fiber is the anatomical expression of an elementary choice, an alternative; depending on experience one of the two fibers will be blocked. The multiplication of mnemons is the anatomical expression of the increasing complexity of hominid society, the multiplication of alternative behavior patterns.

Restraint did not come automatically. Every choice, every course of action selected for the future benefit of the group rather than for the immediate satisfaction of the individual, had to be learned and remembered. Events weeded out those with an inferior capacity for learning and remembering. The hunt demanded patience and waiting—waiting for prey at water holes or salt licks, waiting for an animal to look away as you stalk it, and waiting after the kill so that you do not devour all the meat on the spot but save most of it for others waiting at the home base.

There was also waiting for the fulfillment of sexual urges. Younger males who could bide their time and control themselves in the presence of aggressive dominant males outlived those who could not. In anatomical terms, selection favored a "rewiring" of the brain so that increasing numbers of inhibitory, retreat fibers ran from the highest control center, the cerebral cortex, to subcortical centers which released sex hormones and aroused sexual urges. The controls did not work perfectly. Robin Fox, a colleague of Tiger at Rutgers University, indicates that the flare-up of sexual urges during adolescence demanded intensive initiation ceremonies and other social controls. Inhibition is also at the root of incest taboos and reciprocal altruism.

The entire process of human evolution was complicated and enriched by the greatest technological advance of the times, the use of fire. The first force of nature to be domesticated, fire gave early man a new degree of independence. By bringing fire to the places where he lived, he created zones of warmth and light in the darkness, halo spaces or "caves" of light. The wide wilderness became a little less wild and less lonely. He achieved a way of keeping the night and nighttime prowlers at bay, and the freedom to explore new lands with harsh climates.

Judging by the evidence at hand, still largely negative, man's ancestors first put fire to work on a regular basis to keep themselves warm somewhere along the route out of Africa across the Sahara and into Europe. Hominids must have been familiar with fire in Africa. They lived with it, and perhaps died by it, during volcanic upheavals associated with the formation of the African Rift Valley. They probably moved away when volcanoes were active and returned when the earth became quiet again, being no less persistent than people today who keep returning to areas devastated by floods, earthquakes and other natural disasters.

But no early hominid hearths have yet been found in Africa. Of course, most African sites may have been located in the open rather than in caves, and ashes and charcoal may have been scattered by winds blowing across savannas. On the other hand, early men presumably had no great need for fire in generally mild subtropical climates. In any case, ample evidence for fire exists in colder times and colder places, and as pointed out in Chapter V, the earliest known hearths burned some million years ago in the Escale cave of southeastern France. Man had wandered about as far north as he could at the time without starving and freezing to death. He was living where no normal primate should be, nearly within the shadows of alpine glaciers.

Man probably first obtained fire ready-made from natural sources. (The first sign of artificial firemaking, an iron-pyrites ball with a deep groove produced by repeated striking to create tinder-igniting sparks, comes from a Belgian site only about 15,000 years old.) The notion that Prometheus stole fire for man from the heights of Mount Olympus is not as widely believed as it once was. But Prometheus has a certain relevance if, as seems likely, volcanoes were a major source of fire in early prehistory. According to Kenneth Oakley of the British Museum of Natural History, other sources were available in less turbulent areas: "Man could also have relied on accidental fires started by lightning in dry brush or grassland or where there were seepages of mineral oil and gas. Occasionally in damp environments coal or shale-oil deposits might be ignited by spontaneous combustion and during the last century one such fire burned for four years in Dorset."

Perhaps hunters camped near fire, a natural resource like game and water and shelter. They may sometimes have left otherwise favorable areas when fires began petering out. If so, they had to take it with them when they moved away. It had to be kept burning like the Olympic flame, fed and nursed like a newborn infant. Each band may have had a fire bearer, perhaps one of its older members, who was responsible for carrying and guarding embers in a cup of clay covered with green leaves, and who breathed the embers into flame when the band found a new place to live.

Fire provided more than warmth. It soon became another factor in setting man apart from other species. With it he could move more freely, and instead of having to avoid other predators, they got out of his way. Fire must have kept predators as well as the cold at a safe distance. On icy wilderness nights big cats and other predators, attracted by the smell of meat and the light, stayed outside the protective circle of the fireside. Perhaps man observed that on occasion the animals scrambled even further away when sparks flew at them out of the flames, and he may have learned to produce the same effect by hurling glowing pieces of wood at their heads. In any case, he eventually began using fire more aggressively, in a shift from defense to offense.

With fire also he could drive predators from the caves he sought for his home. His earliest known hearths were located in caves, originally occupied by stronger and longer-established killers. Before fire he often had to be content with second-best sites, rock shelters, and overhangs with their less effective protection. Fire, however, could help him drive other killers out. Bears and hyenas and many other cave-dwelling animals shared the Durance Valley with early man, but they stayed out of his caves.

Fire probably enabled Peking man to take permanent possession of the Dragon's Hill cave. It is no coincidence that the first layers which provide evidence that man had moved into the cave also happen to be the layers which contain charcoal fragments, burned bones, and other traces of fire. Only after he had learned to tame fire could man become a regular cave dweller whenever conditions demanded it.

He also used fire to become a more and more effective predator himself, to stampede animals as he did in the Torralba Valley, and to produce more effective spears. The Australian aborigines charred the tips of their digging sticks lightly, a treatment which hardens the core of the wood and makes the outer part more crumbly and easier to sharpen. Man was acquainted with this technique at least 80,000 years ago, as indicated by a yew spear with a fire-hardened point found at a site in north Germany. Some investigators feel that equally advanced treatments had been developed as far back as the days of Peking man.

Cooking is also believed to date back to these times, mainly on the basis of indirect but convincing evidence involving teeth, sensitive indicators of evolutionary change. As described in Chapter II, one argument for dietary changes among the earliest hominids is that they had small canine teeth instead of the large canines characteristic of many other primates. But molar teeth, which serve chiefly for grinding and heavy-duty chewing, tended to remain large until *Homo erectus* times, when they began to become smaller, perhaps because he was eating softer cooked foods.

Regular cooking may have helped reshape the contours of the human face, in a kind of chain-reaction process. According to one theory, softer foods put less of a strain on the jaws and jaw muscles, which became smaller along with the molar teeth. This in turn had an effect on the design of the rest of the skull. Massive overhanging brow ridges and other thick bony protuberances had evolved largely as structures to which powerful jaw muscles could be attached, and they were reduced as the muscles dwindled in size. Furthermore, the skull itself became thinner, perhaps one of the changes involved in expanding the cranium to house a bigger brain.

As for the origin of cooking, no one has yet been able to improve on the basic point of Charles Lamb's story about the suckling pig that was done to a turn when a house burned down. There were no houses half a million years ago, but a forest fire could have done the job just as effectively. Or perhaps a careless hunter dropped his share of the day's kill into a blazing fire and relished the meat when it was recovered. Such accidents must have happened many times before man finally made a practice of roasting tough foods.

There were psychological as well as physical changes. Cooking played a part in promoting more restraint. With the advent of cookery men tended to spend less time devouring freshly killed game on the spot and more time back at the cave eating with the rest of the band around a hearth. The domestication of fire was one more step in human domestication. Inhibition is as much a mark of evolutionary advance as action itself.

And above all, fire was light. It increased the length of the day, creating a new kind of day independent of the movements of the sun. Life became less routine. Man no longer rose and slept with the rising and setting of the sun. As he had become independent of one great natural rhythm, the internal rhythm of estrus, so now he was independent of the external rhythm of day and night. The hours after dark were hours of relative leisure which he could use to plan activities more and more complex (often because of the new uses of fire, as during the Torralba elephant hunt, which may have required the cooperation of several bands).

The existence of elaborate plans implies the evolution of more sophisticated ways of communicating. Language, the most human form of human behavior, must have taken a tremendous spurt when hunting was on the rise and hearths burned brightly past sunset. There was so much to share: details of past successes in the hunt, tall tales about the big ones that got away, strategies for future hunts, rules about hunting territories and the division of kills, and a growing store of myths and legends and beliefs.

The fireside became an institution, a cohesive force bringing members of the band closer together, old as well as young. Other primates also had their patriarchs and matriarchs, but now old age acquired a new importance. Now individuals too old to fight or carry heavy things or hunt became important because they remembered things beyond the memories of others—particularly things that happened rarely, such as floods and other catastrophes, and things that required special knowledge, such as the settling of territorial disputes and the treatment of illnesses. The elders took their places at the fireside and were consulted and listened to.

Finally, fire presumably played a role in man's earliest religious experiences. A tendency to engage in rituals can be seen in our closest living primate relatives. Van Lawick-Goodall has observed chimpanzees engaging in elaborate "rain dances" during tropical storms. On one occasion seven adult males performed before an audience of appreciative females and juveniles that climbed into the trees to watch. The males moved to the top of a grassy slope, divided themselves into two groups of three and four members, and took turns making sudden charges down the slope—springing into a tree, tearing off branches, hurtling themselves to the ground, and dragging the branches along, barking and hooting.

They were responding to the elements. The entire ceremony, which lasted about half an hour, was carried out in the midst of a heavy rain to the accompaniment of thunderclaps and bolts of lightning. According to the British observer, "against the green grass they looked black and very large, like primitive men displaying their strength." It requires no great stretch of the imagination to think of early hominids responding with their own varieties of ritual to the forces of nature.

We know that prehistoric hunters carrying torches and lamps penetrated deep into the remotest chambers of caves, covered the walls with paintings and engravings of animals, and met by firelight to practice rituals whose purposes we can only speculate about. These underground meetings took place during the past 30,000 years or so. But many investigators are convinced that man engaged in similar activities hundreds of thousands of years before the coming of art, and that he used fire to serve a double purpose, to arouse excitement as well as provide light.

Such effects may have very ancient origins. Oakley emphasizes "the deep subconscious or sensual appeal" of fire, noting that the appeal may be traced back to the earliest days of primate evolution: "The fact that the Philippine tarsier has been named *Tarsius carbonarius* on account of its propensity for picking up hot embers from camp-fire sites suggested to me that man's prehuman ancestors may have been attracted to natural fires and toyed with burning matter." Fire may be a stimulant as potent as drugs in arousing visions and previsions, and as such would have served the purposes of priests and priestesses, the cultural descendants of the fire bearers of *Homo erectus* times.

Fire, like tools, had a double impact. It kept predators and the cold away, and at the same time drew people closer together. It served material needs, and at the same time helped create a new way of life and a new kind of evolution. Tracing cause-and-effect patterns in such a context becomes exceedingly difficult. Though we make inferences which go beyond the evidence, the effort is always to speculate along lines compatible with the evidence.

Many factors went into the shaping of *Homo erectus*—big-game hunting, fire, selection for bigger brains, prolonged infant and female dependency, loss of estrus, the coming of the family and taboos and traditions. Each factor contributed in an important way to his development. But the fundamental problem is to see things as a whole and not as "factors," as parts of the web or network of increasingly complex interrelationships which is human evolution.

■ Three lucky finds in Swanscombe village; a possible contemporary of Swanscombe man; the use of computers in investigating human origins; another gap in the record; the discovery of Neanderthal man and his rejection by outraged Victorians; the persistence of prejudice; the Le Moustier and Shanidar caves; burial and religious ritual

CHAPTER VIII

The Search for Remains of the Earliest Modern-Type Men

■ The rise of big-game hunting and all the changes which came with it brought our ancestors a long way toward modern man. Now for the first time we can describe them in words which do not really apply to other animals, which make sense only in a human context. Many of the institutions we live with today had already evolved in rudimentary forms, and the double-edged quality of the human condition had already become evident. Practically everything which contributed to the solution of problems important to the survival of the species created new problems, new sources of tension and discord. New conflicts as well as new affections arose in the family circle; and if in a sense love came with the passing of estrus, so did hate. Laws implied penalties for the breaking of laws. Hunting involved not only cooperation and sharing but also new subtleties in the art of killing.

Such complexities indicated a shift of emphasis in human development. It was no longer a matter of dealing only with the outside world, with climates and other species and prey and predators. An entirely new class of problems had come into being, uniquely human problems which seem to be chronically associated with cultural as contrasted to genetic or organic evolution. Dealing with the full impact of this sort of evolution demanded a new breed of men, our immediate ancestors and the direct descendants of people like the hunters who camped at Torralba and Ambrona.

Human populations and living conditions varied widely in those days, although not as widely perhaps as they do today. According to one estimate, some 40,000 bands of hunter-gatherers occupied as many home bases scattered like outposts through the wildernesses of Africa and Asia and Europe, which averages to about a million acres per band. The earth was hardly a crowded place, but crowding can be a relative thing, and certain regions were far more densely populated than others. So then as now some environments must have been especially favorable for hunting and for the elaboration of social systems.

The population centers of *Homo erectus* times were the richest grasslands, which attracted the largest herds and the greatest number of predators, including man. Hunting bands on the track of game crossed paths from time to time and exchanged wary glances or silent greetings as they proceeded on their ways. Planned as well as unplanned meetings probably took place, not only the joining of forces for group hunts and stampedes as at Torralba but also seasonal get-togethers involving several hundred individuals, the foreshadowings of county fairs. Some people may have found things too crowded for comfort and moved on to get away from it all.

There were also isolated "backwood" regions where the land and the living were less abundant. A band of hunter-gatherers could have wandered for years or a lifetime in these wildernesses without coming across another band or even the traces of another band—a burned-out hearth, worked flints and flint debris, a hollow sheltered place where people had slept, an almost overgrown trail leading from the fireside to the edge of the nearest stream or lake. In many cases members of such inbred, marginal bands subsisted on foods inferior to those exploited by bands in richer territories, and lived less interesting and less healthy and shorter lives.

Populations varied in many other ways. Some individuals may have had brains nearly twice as large as their smallest-brained contemporaries, as is the case today. Equally striking differences existed in the degree of sloping of the forehead, tooth size and cusp patterns, chin structure, the size of overhanging brow ridges, and so on. *Homo erectus* consisted of a number of sub-species or races. One of these, perhaps a subspecies, with a larger than average brain, living in a territory where life was neither so easy that it posed no major challenges nor so harsh as to crush initiative, developed into *Homo sapiens*.

We do not know where or when the transition took place, but a gravel pit in the English village of Swanscombe not far from London has yielded important fossil clues, as usual through a combination of searching and luck, in this case luck triply com-pounded. The Thames Valley site is a well-known collectors' paradise, possibly a place where hunters camped to kill big game coming to drink from the river. Several hundred thousand stone tools must have been found there during the past century or so. But no human remains had appeared until one Saturday noon in June, 1935, when local cement workers who had stopped digging for the day noticed a piece of bone protruding from a gravel bank. It turned out to be part of the skull of a prehistoric man who had died in his early twenties.

A second lucky find occurred the following March near the original find, another bone fragment which was not only human but also happened to be part of the same skull. The two pieces fitted neatly. The last discovery represents something of an an-thropological miracle. One moonlit evening during World War II a fleet of trucks came to the Swanscombe pit and removed hundreds of tons of gravel as part of the top-secret "Mulberry" harbor project to make concrete caissons or floating docks for the Allied invasion of Normandy. How many prehistoric remains were ground up for the concrete will never be known, but at least one important object was left behind and found after the war in 1955—a third skull fragment. This specimen turned up about seventy-five feet from the original find and, by remarkable coinci-dence, belongs to the same individual as the other two specimens; furthermore, it fits together with them to form the entire back half of a skull.

The relative age of these remains has been fairly well estab-lished. As pointed out in Chapter V, after some 60 million years of comparatively mild and stable climates, Europe experienced a number of climatic "oscillations" when mean annual temperatures varied from 50 degrees Fahrenheit to below-freezing levels. Geological studies show that the gravels which contained the Swanscombe remains were laid down during a period of glacial retreat, a so-called interglacial stage which dates back perhaps 250,000 years.

|Swanscombe man enjoyed a comfortable climate. In fact, as far as the weather is concerned, that was the time to be in England. Elephants and rhinoceroses which had come from Africa over the Dardanelles land bridge browsed in warm Thames Valley forests along with wild boar, deer and other woodland species. But cooler times were on the way. A decrease of these species and an increase of open-grassland species like giant oxen and horses indicate that the forests were beginning to recede, a prelude to the coming of another glaciation.

|Swanscombe man represents a distinct advance over his fossil predecessors, although the extent of the advance has been debated. Examination of the three fragments and reconstructions based on them indicate that he had a large brain; his cranial capacity is estimated at about 1,300 cubic centimeters, which, as pointed out in Chapter V, lies well within the modern range. Furthermore, there is a general suggestion of rounded and expanded skull contours somewhat like modern man's. These features have been interpreted as evidence for an apparent evolutionary leap, the sudden appearance of a man who was nearly fully modern. On the other hand, the relatively low brain case and certain other characteristics suggest that the specimen may be a less advanced form intermediate between *Homo erectus* and modern man.

Supporting the latter viewpoint is another fossil skull found in 1933 in another gravel pit near the village of Steinheim in western Germany. This specimen includes the face and upper jaw, which are lacking in the English specimen, and it may have something to tell us about Swanscombe man, assuming, of course, that the two were contemporaries (both skulls were found in interglacial deposits) and members of the same species or subspecies. In any case, Steinheim man was modern in back but not in front. He had a sloping forehead and very large brow ridges; it was argued that Swanscombe man may have been at the same stage of development.

These impressions have been put to the test by Campbell and

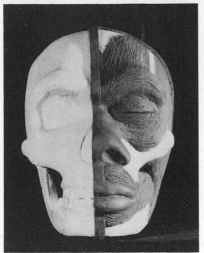

Stages in reconstruction of Steinheim man, one version of early *Homo sapiens*, front view: (top) skull in plaster; (center) building up muscles and skin with clay; (bottom) completed bust

Weiner, the man who exploded the Piltdown hoax. They turned to statistical techniques which depend on carefully selected measurements of corresponding areas and curvatures of different skulls. For example, one problem was to ascertain as precisely as possible the area of the neck region at the back of the skull, an area which tends to become smaller and smoother during the course of human evolution, reflecting the expansion of the brain and a decrease in the size of face and jaws.

In all, seventeen measurements were made between points on the Swanscombe skull. For purposes of comparison similar measurements were made of some 500 male and female skulls excavated from a 4,000-year-old communal tomb in southern Israel, about sixty skulls of contemporary races, and ten fossil specimens representing finds from 250,000 years ago (the Steinheim specimen) to 35,000 years ago. This information was used to calculate the so-called distance functions, numbers which indicate how closely different fossil skulls are related to modern skulls. The task required millions of calculations and would have taken years using desk-type adding machines. But it took only a few minutes of the time of an electronic computer at Oxford University.

Judging by the results, Swanscombe man meets the general specifications for a transitional species, a species which is on its way but has not yet arrived. Like Steinheim man he is definitely *Homo sapiens,* but very early *Homo sapiens,* embodying certain relatively primitive as well as modern features. In short, he is just about right for his time, the product of a gradual and continuing process rather than a sudden spurt. This is by no means a new notion; some investigators had already arrived at it without benefit of statistics. But the main point is that other investigators had arrived at quite different interpretations on the basis of the identical evidence, that the study provides a relatively objective evaluation of the evidence.

Even more important, the study establishes an approach which reduces personal bias to a minimum. It can be applied whenever experts disagree, and experts disagree with impressive frequency and intensity in the study of prehistory. For example, it showed that a big-toe bone found at Olduvai resembled the big-toe bone of modern man much more closely than it resembled that of the gorilla or chimpanzee, indicating that the individual walked with a human-type gait. A similar approach has also demonstrated the modern features of the *Australopithecus* upper-arm bone found near Lake Rudolf, and may be used to help determine the status of important specimens from Olduvai and other sites which may represent transitional forms between *Australopithecus* and *Homo erectus*. Advanced statistical methods will probably be used increasingly as anthropology becomes more and more quantitative, and as high-speed computers become available to take care of the prodigious number of calculations involved.

Statistics alone cannot solve all problems. More needs to be known about the origin of our species, for example, than the Weiner-Campbell analysis can possibly reveal. It concerns early but not earliest *Homo sapiens*. It indicates that he existed at least 250,000 years ago, but leaves open the question of when the first members of the species arose. They may have appeared fifty, a hundred, or several hundred millennia before Swanscombe-Steinheim times, depending on which current point of view strikes one as most plausible.

But the answer, if it is ever found, will come at excavations of sites yet to be discovered, and the same thing holds for the question of where our species arose. In certain respects the simplest and most direct theory is that it happened in Europe; that the men of Swanscombe and Steinheim were descendants of hunters who, judging by the remains at the Hungarian site of Vertesszöllös, may have been well on the way toward attaining *Homo sapiens* status as much as 400,000 or 500,000 years ago. According to another theory, however, they were immigrants rather than native Europeans and evolved either in the Far East, perhaps from an ancestral stock like Peking man, or else in Central Asia.

Wherever they came from, the early forerunners of modern man probably lived pretty much as late representatives of *Homo erectus* had lived. At least, stone tools and other excavated materials suggest no obvious differences. Although his workmanship was somewhat superior, Swanscombe man was no radical innovator and made the same basic Acheulian-type tools that had been made for hundreds of thousands of years: hand axes, notched and saw-toothed implements, scrapers, engravers, and so on. There are characteristics, however, which might represent differences in behavior if we only knew enough to interpret them.

Why did his tool kit include nearly twice as many hand axes as the tool kits of his Torralba-Ambrona predecessors? Why did he use an unusually high proportion of hand axes with a wide base, tapered to a point at the apex, and an unusually low proportion of ovate or egg-shaped hand axes?

Another English site at Hoxne, about sixty-five miles northeast of Swanscombe, and of about the same age or slightly more recent, provides further evidence. It contains rich deposits of clay which mark the place where a huge mass of ice broke off a retreating glacier perhaps 300,000 years ago and melted slowly to form a small lake. (At another site near Birmingham, England, a block of ice about fifty feet across took more than 30,000 years to melt.) Ever since the eighteenth century the clays have been used to make bricks and terra-cotta pipes. In 1797 the English antiquarian John Frere visited the site and made a remarkable observation.

People do not see what they are not prepared to see; and since the notion of a remote prehistoric past simply did not exist in those days, a variety of involved theories were invented to explain away traces of this past. Flint tools, some of them beautifully shaped, were considered natural accidents like shapes seen in drifting clouds or in the gnarled branches of trees—things that had been formed either by thunder in the clouds and then fallen to earth or by lightning as it struck and shattered flint lying on the ground. Frere knew better. He found hand axes and other tools in the Hoxne clay deposits and recognized them as man-made implements dating back "to a very remote period indeed, even beyond that of the present world." (Frere, by the way, has the added distinction of being Mary Leakey's great-great-grand-father.)

Modern excavations at the site reveal a Swanscombe-type Acheulian tool kit, including the same unexplained high proportion of pointed hand axes with wide bases. Another finding emerges from fossil-pollen studies conducted by Richard West of the University of Cambridge. Pollens recovered from gray clays and muds deposited before the coming of man show that thick oak-elm forests surrounded the lake. But signs of a different environment are found in overlying brown-green clay layers which contain tools and other human traces. A decline of oak-elm pollens and a sharp rise of grass pollens indicates that open grass-lands replaced the forests.

Geological research rules out the most obvious explanation for this change, a change in climate, for the climate was generally mild throughout. Another possibility exists, however. Charcoal has been found in the occupation layers, suggesting that the deforestation was caused by fires which were originally set during a dry summer, perhaps to stampede animals as in the valley of Torralba, and then raged out of control. In any case the forests returned soon after man left, first temperate oak-elm forests and later forests of dwarf willows and other trees found in arctic environments. Another major glaciation had begun.

Little evidence exists for the course of human evolution during the period, which lasted more than 150,000 years. This is a par-ticularly tantalizing state of affairs, since other information, such as the fact that surprising anatomical changes appeared later following the retreat of the glaciers, suggests that important developments were taking place. A number of French sites pro-vide evidence of human activity. One workshop area in the archeologically rich Somme Valley region near Amiens is no larger than a living room but has yielded thousands of flint tools and associated pieces, including various types of hand axes and cleavers as well as an assortment of scrapers and knives.

There is another interesting site in England at High Lodge not far from Cambridge, where people camped by a lake during a time of temporary relief from arctic conditions. (The climate was not stable in glacial periods, fluctuating from very cold below-zero temperatures to cooler conditions rather like those en-countered in mild winters today.) Many of the tools recovered from clay deposits marking the location of the lake are remark-ably similar to tools found at the Somme Valley site.

Until recently, however, practically nothing was known about the evolutionary status of the people who made the tools. The only human remains recovered were a few bits of skull too frag-mentary for reliable reconstructions. Now prospects are some-what brighter because of new material excavated last summer by de Lumley at a cave in the eastern Pyrenees region of France. The main find is the front half of a human face, the most com-plete skull specimen yet obtained for this glacial stage and the oldest-known Frenchman. His precise relationship to *Homo erectus* and *Homo sapiens* has yet to be determined.

The next glimpse of man comes from the following interglacial stage in Europe, the period from about 100,000 to 75,000 years ago. England and Ireland were part of the Continent then. Broad valleys existed where the English Channel and Irish Sea and North Sea are now, and great rivers flowed through the valleys, rivers which included the Seine, Thames and Rhine as tributaries.

The men living among lions, hyenas, elephants, and other European animals of the times were not what one might expect of modern man's evolving ancestors. They were definitely *Homo sapiens*, but they belonged to a new subspecies or race, and in certain respects a strikingly more primitive subspecies. Although their brains were about as large as the brain of Swanscombe-Steinheim man, their massive receding jaws and faces seem to have been throwbacks, and were actually closer to *Homo erectus* than to *Homo sapiens*. Their remains have been found in a limestone crevice in central Germany, in deposits on the left bank of a tributary of the Tiber near Rome, and at several other sites in Europe, the Soviet Union and Palestine.

Even stranger breeds of men arose later. The bands hunting in Western Europe during most of the subsequent cold period, the next-to-last glaciation, were made up of individuals anatomically more remote from modern men than were their predecessors who lived some six or seven thousand generations before them. They had appreciably larger brains, one of the features by which they are ranked as *Homo sapiens*. But their "primitive" features included lower cranial vaults which tended to be flat at the top and bulged at the sides, heavier bone ridges over the eyes and at the back of the neck, and more sharply receding chins. Their bodies were stocky, short, and heavy-limbed.

These were the classic Neanderthal people, the people who come to mind whenever cave men are mentioned and who almost invariably serve as models for artists depicting early man. They have become such symbols for good reason. As the first fossil men to be discovered, they made a powerful impression on a world that was not ready to accept the notion of evolution or its implications. The discovery and the reaction to it mark one of the most significant and extraordinary episodes in the annals of science.

This was the beginning of the study of prehistory. The field arose in an atmosphere of bitter debate and intense emotional involvement which bordered at times on hysteria and from which it has not yet completely recovered.

In 1856, when human bones were found in a small limestone-quarry cave in the Neanderthal, a valley near Düsseldorf, Germany, practically everything discussed in this book was unknown and the rest was ignored. Some investigators recognized the importance of the remains from the beginning, but they were a very small minority. The predominant opinion, the opinion which people were ready to accept, was that the bones represented not an extinct breed of man but a modern, freakish and sick individual. A prominent anatomist reported that the fossils were those of an idiot who had suffered from rickets and other bone diseases and had a violent disposition. The flat forehead and heavy brows, he explained, had been caused by blows on the head.

According to other authorities, the bones were those of a Cossack who had perished during Napoleon's retreat from Moscow, a victim of water on the brain, "an old Dutchman," "a member of the Celtic race." Everyone wanted to disown this human specimen. An English scholar was responsible for one of the most melodramatic diagnoses: "It may have been one of those wild men, half-crazed, half-idiotic, cruel and strong, who are always more or less to be found living on the outskirts of barbarous tribes, and who now and then appear in civilized communities to be consigned perhaps to the penitentiary or the gallows, when their murderous propensities manifest themselves."

These and other reactions amounted above all to a violent rejection of Neanderthal man as a legitimate human ancestor and, at a more basic level, a violent rejection of the notion that we have arisen from less-human species. Evolution, biological change, was an alien and heretical concept. It had long been taken for granted that species were immutable, that all living things had been created in their final perfect form in the beginning, and that nothing important had happened since. In the sixteenth century, for example, this belief was so firmly established that people simply refused to concede the existence of fossils of any sort.

Fossils implied extinctions, and extinctions, in turn, implied that the creator had designed species so poorly that they failed to endure. So the general attitude was to regard the objects which kept turning up, objects that looked very much like skulls and teeth and vertebrae and the imprints of ferns and seashells, as mere illusions produced by the action of thunder and other forces. In other words, fossils like flint tools were believed to be natural accidents. A less widely supported and slightly more realistic theory allowed that fossil bones were actually the remains of dead animals. On the other hand, the animals were not believed to be extinct; they still lived in unexplored parts of the world or in mammoth caverns deep beneath the earth's surface.

The theories had changed somewhat by the mid-nineteenth century. Extinction was recognized as a fact of nature, but the notion of perfect and unchanging species was preserved. According to prevailing ideas, fossils were the remains of creatures wiped out during the Flood (not having been passengers on the Ark) and not related to existing forms. Indeed, the whole past was a Biblical past. Genesis, Eden, the Flood, were not myths but familiar historical events, and very recent events at that. Different interpretations of the Scriptures gave different dates for the creation of the earth, 3700 or 4004 or 5199 B.C., but authorities generally agreed on a past so brief as to allow little time for evolution of any sort.

Furthermore, the world was in many ways a simpler and cozier place than it is today. There were no eons then, no vast stretches of geological time to make the past remote and evoke a feeling of infinity and other worlds. The past was close at hand and had a special aura to it, a glow like a long-lost childhood. Although there were vague notions of barbarian times, the emphasis was on golden ages and knights and chivalry. The living seemed shoddy by comparison.

In such times and against such a background of beliefs, the discovery of Neanderthal man came as a terrible shock. It might have created less of a scandal if other discoveries had been made in the proper evolutionary sequence, if the way had been prepared during preceding generations by the finding first of *Ramapithecus* and then *Australopithecus* and finally *Homo erectus*. The discoveries came in precisely the reverse order, however, which was partly to be expected by the nature of things. The laws of chance favored the possibility that fossil man would be found first in Western Europe, where population densities were highest and quarries most numerous, and that the first man found would be a Neanderthal because Neanderthal remains seem to outnumber all other human-fossil remains in this region.

Neanderthal man came into the world of the Victorians like a naked savage into a ladies' sewing circle. In their eyes he was a beast, which suggested not only that the past may have been less golden than the Scriptures implied but also that disturbing forces were at work in the present. He reminded people of their Jekyll-and-Hyde qualities, of the animal side of human nature. We, who live with our knowledge of fire bombs and Hiroshima and gas chambers and napalm, can afford to be tolerant of the Victorians' horrified response to the sort of self-understanding evolution offers. We are much closer to them than we like to think.

Attitudes began changing somewhat not long after the original 1856 discovery. The publication of Darwin's *On the Origin of Species* three years later provided a biological basis for evolution in general, and the discovery of more fossils provided new evidence for the evolution of man. Between 1866 and 1910, half a dozen sites in France and Belgium yielded Neanderthal remains associated with flint tools and the remains of woolly rhinoceroses, mammoths, cave bears, and other extinct species. There was no longer good reason to regard Neanderthal man as a mad or diseased modern. It was widely agreed that he had vanished tens of thousands of years ago.

But most investigators were slower to recognize his status as an advanced human being, much less as a fellow *Homo sapiens*, than they were to recognize his fossil status. As recently as the 1920's he was considered far more remote from modern man and far closer to the anthropoid apes than a reasonably sophisticated analysis of the evidence could possibly justify, a kind of half-monster, ungainly and ugly and brutish. This picture was based to a large extent on a highly respected and highly misleading study of a skeleton found in 1908 near the village of La Chapelle-aux-Saints in southern France.

The study is one of the most amazing phenomena in the history of man's efforts to downgrade his ancestors. On the basis of casts of the inner surface of the skull, it concluded that the convolutions of the brain had been simple and "coarse" and resembled the convolutions of the "great anthropoid apes or microencephalic man" more closely than those of modern man. Furthermore, it presented an outlandish view of Neanderthal man's posture and gait. It not only pointed to a supposed "simian arrangement" of certain spinal vertebrae and stated that he walked slumped over and with bent knees, but suggested that his feet may have been grasping organs like the feet of gorillas and chimpanzees.

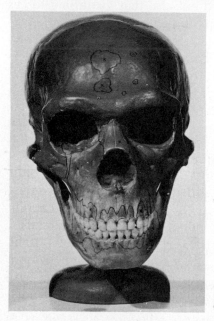

Reconstruction of skull
of Neanderthal man

As recently as 1957 this study was still being cited as a major source of information about the nature of Neanderthal man. In that year, however, the La Chapelle-aux-Saints skeleton was reexamined by William Straus of Johns Hopkins University and Alec Cave of St. Bartholomew's Hospital Medical College in London. They found that it was hardly typical, belonging to an "old" man between forty and fifty suffering from arthritis of the jaws, spine and perhaps lower limbs, and concluded with the following somewhat ambiguous statement: "There is thus no valid reason for the assumption that the posture of Neanderthal man . . . differed significantly from that of present-day man.

. . . If he could be reincarnated and placed in a New York subway—provided that he were bathed, shaved and dressed in modern clothing—it is doubtful whether he would attract any more attention than some of its other denizens."

Anatomical evidence does not support the stereotype of Neanderthal man as a semihuman brute. The trouble is that myths die hard, especially myths in the area of human origins, and it may take decades before his popular image coincides with his

Artist's conception of Neanderthal man: close-up

scientific image. The latest edition of a standard text on fossil men still presents certain major conclusions of the La Chapelle-aux-Saints study as if they had never been discredited. Apparently some anthropologists still accept these conclusions. It is little wonder that the old prejudices and clichés also persist among laymen.

Not all questions about Neanderthal man have been answered. He was one of the subspecies of *Homo sapiens* which lived in the Old World from about 70,000 to 35,000 years ago, and it should be no surprise that he walked fully erect. After all, his ancestors had been walking that way for several million years before him. Furthermore, it should be no surprise that he and other subspecies of the times differed widely in physical characteristics, since this was the case for *Homo erectus* as it is for us and other species. What calls for an explanation, however, is that his distinctive set of characteristics should reappear in the sense that it was reminiscent of earlier human forms, and that he seems to have confined himself largely if not entirely to Western Europe.

One possibility is that he was cut off from his contemporaries. The longer and more completely breeding populations of a single species are separated from one another, the more widely they differ. Brief and partial isolation, such as that imposed by the institution of royal families, may produce such characteristics as the well-known protruding lower lip of the Hapsburgs which, of course, are not sufficient to create new races. Longer periods of isolation, occasioned perhaps by geographical as well as social factors, may eventually produce differences so great that the result is distinct species such as *Australopithecus africanus* and *Australopithecus robustus*.

The conditions which gave rise to the Neanderthal subspecies were somewhere between these extremes. He may have been caught in a kind of "ice trap" in Western Europe, a glacial pincers movement. During the coldest periods glaciers crept southwest from the great Scandinavian Ice Sheet into central Poland, and at the same time glaciers from the Alps moved northeast toward the Carpathians and the Danube. It was by no means a complete trap. The ice masses never met, and there was always a corridor several hundred miles wide between them. But routes through the corridor may have been few and hazardous enough during periods of severe cold to isolate many Neanderthal populations and bring about the appearance of a new subspecies.

Moreover, there are traps more effective than the geographical variety. Neanderthal man was fully adapted to his environment, which may be reflected in the very shape of his body, since there is physiological evidence that people with short stocky builds conserve body heat better than lean and lanky individuals and hence are better suited to survive in arctic and sub-arctic climates. His massive jaw may have evolved as an adaptation to a diet of tough meat, raw or lightly cooked meat. He probably felt no greater urge to pack up and leave than Eskimo tribes feel today. People still tend to remain in their homelands, even in homelands where it is an unending struggle merely to keep alive, and bonds at least as strong may have formed among prehistoric hunters.

One can only wonder at the ability of the Neanderthals to endure the intense cold of Western Europe during the next-to-last glaciation. Their loneliness, for example, is something difficult to

Artist's conception of Neanderthal man: home base, limestone shelter, at beginning of rhinoceros hunt

imagine. In today's densely populated world news travels fast and there are always rescue parties on the way. But there were no rescues in that world, and every band was alone and on its own. Moving through the snow must have been a major problem, since the people probably had to get along without snowshoes and sleds. And no one moved during blizzards and when the snows were highest.

Survival would have been impossible without reserves of food and fuel. The chief hunting grounds must have been snow meadows, wide flat areas swept by icy prevailing winds, where the snow may be only a foot deep and edible grasses grow under it. Today in Canadian sub-Arctic regions such places are a major source of food for herds of caribou and for caribou hunters, and similar regions helped feed reindeer and Neanderthal reindeer hunters some 50,000 years ago. Small game also provided meat; many traps must have been set along snow trails, the habitual routes of animals on the move.

But winter hunting could never have provided enough food by itself. According to one estimate, it takes about 800 to 900 pounds of lean meat to feed ten people for a month, and Neanderthal winters may have lasted four to five months. Such conditions demanded stockpiling, and extensive stockpiling. The people may have used underground cellars—pits hacked out of permanently frozen ground known as permafrost, as Eskimos do today—or "blue ice caves," ice-cliff formations that could serve as deep-freeze lockers.

Natural refrigerators of this sort have not yet been found, although a study of where Eskimo hunters locate their storage places today might furnish clues to archeologists in search of evidence for prehistoric practices. The record suggests that at least one family had a special larder for its winter food. A pit in a Neanderthal cave on the island of Jersey off the western coast of France apparently contained a liberal supply of large chunks of meat ready for cooking. It had been dug through deposits next to a cave wall, and included three rhinoceros skulls and the remains of at least five mammoths.

Fuel was another problem, to collect as well as to store. When wood was scarce, the Neanderthals burned bones, and they may even have learned to use fat. They and earlier people also had ways of promoting efficient burning. Soviet investigators have discovered "tailed" hearths, basins each with a narrow trench or furrow extending out from one side. Actual tests indicate the reason for the trench. Apparently it provided a kind of flue or draft through which air was drawn to produce more complete burning.

Archeological excavations rarely provide direct information about the feelings of our remote ancestors; usually we are reduced to guesses, shrewd or otherwise. But now and then the past leaves patterns whose significance cannot be mistaken. During the early 1900's such evidence was uncovered at Le Moustier

about thirty miles west of La Chapelle-aux-Saints; it shows that
these people had developed a new way of thinking, a new attitude toward life and death..

A boy about fifteen or sixteen years old had been buried in a
cave. He had been lowered into a trench, placed on his right side
with knees slightly drawn and head resting on his forearm in a
sleeping position. A pile of flints lay under his head to form a sort
of stone pillow, and near his hand was a beautifully worked stone
ax. Around the remains were wild-cattle bones, many of them
charred, the remnants of roasted meat which may have been
provided to serve as sustenance in the world of the dead. (The
old man of La Chapelle-aux-Saints was also buried in a trench
and surrounded by stone tools.)

Not far from the Le Moustier site is a cave which was discovered by a road-building crew and probably served as a family
cemetery. The number of people buried there is unknown. Some
twenty-one mounds and pits have been found in the cave, but
only six of them contained skeletons representing four children
and two adults. The other fifteen may also have contained skeletons which were looted or disintegrated over the years. Or they
may have held meat and other perishable material for the use of
the dead in other worlds. One mound, one of a pattern of nine
neatly arranged mounds, included the skeleton of a very small
infant, perhaps a stillborn infant, and three flint tools. A nearby
pit was covered by a triangular limestone slab and included the
bones of a six-year-old child and, again, three flint tools.

The record is rich in symbols which we cannot decipher. Near
Monte Circeo, on the Mediterranean coast between Rome and
Naples, is a deep cave whose innermost chamber contained a
circle of stones, at the center of the circle a human skull with a
hole bored into it. There are also signs that animal rituals were
practiced along with burials. A cave in a steep ravine in the
mountains of Uzbek in Central Asia held the shallow grave of a
young boy, and half a dozen pairs of ibex horns were stuck in the
earth around the head end of the grave, indicating that an ibex
cult existed here among Neanderthals more than 50,000 years
ago, as it does today among people living in the same region.

Other rituals involved cave bears, which often had to be driven
out of caves before people could move in, and were killed by the

Artist's conception of Neanderthal burial at Le Moustier

Multiple Neanderthal burial, possibly a family cemetery
(Numbers indicate places where skeletons were found)

hundreds. They were respected and worshiped as well as eaten. A mountain cave in eastern Austria contained a rectangular vault holding seven bear skulls all facing the cave's entrance; while material excavated from Regourdou, another site in southern France, represents perhaps the most elaborate bear-cult burial known. It included a skeleton complete except for the skull (which had probably been taken by an amateur collector), stone drains, a rectangular pit covered by a flat stone slab weighing almost a ton, and the remains of more than twenty cave bears.

One of the most revealing of recent discoveries comes from a site in the Near East, the Shanidar Cave in the Zagros Mountain highlands of Iraq about 250 miles due north of Baghdad. Kurdish goatherds still live here, as they have for generations, in brush huts under a vaulting roof which encloses an area about the size of four tennis courts, making fire with steel and flint. The site was excavated by Ralph Solecki of Columbia University. He hit bedrock at a depth of forty-five feet, which represents deposits up to 100,000 years old. Seven Neanderthal skeletons were found, three of them the remains of people crushed to death by falling rocks. One of the three was apparently recovering from a spear or knife wound in the ribs.

At least one of the individuals, a man with a badly crushed skull, was buried deep in the cave with special ceremony. One spring day about 60,000 years ago members of his family went out into the hills, picked masses of wild flowers, and made a bed of them on the ground, a resting place for the deceased. Other flowers were probably laid on top of his grave; still others seem to have been woven together with the branches of a pinelike shrub to form a wreath. Traces of that offering endure in the form of fossil pollen collected from the burial site, the remains of the ancestors of present-day grape hyacinths, bachelor's buttons, hollyhocks, and yellow-flowering groundsels.

These findings, the graves and the patterns around them, mark a great change in human evolution. Death, and presumably life, had become something special. No comparable evidence appears in earlier records, and as far as we know, men and the ancestors of men had always died like other animals before Neanderthal times, being abandoned when they were too weak to keep up with the band or wandering off to wait alone for the end to come.

Find at Shanidar: ribs and pelvic region of a Neanderthal man of about forty years who lived at least 44,000 years ago (top); skull, as unearthed, of same individual, probably killed in a rock fall (bottom)

Burial implies a new kind of concern for the individual and, according to one theory, it arose as part of a response to bitter glacial conditions when people needed one another even more than in less demanding times and formed more intimate ties and cared more intensely when death came.

Severe climates may have had something to do with the new spirit. Certainly considerable evidence exists in our own times to suggest that people living under the most depressing circumstances often have the highest hopes for the future, in another world if not in this one. But there had been hard times before, and death must always have been a mysterious phenomenon. The new element was the evolution of a brain capable of framing questions, arriving at answers, and establishing rituals which by the very fact that they were practiced regularly reinforced the validity of the answers. Ritual expresses the belief or hope that a connection exists between repetition and truth, the notion that if a possibility is stated often enough it becomes a certainty.

There may have been another reason for an emphasis on ritual. Perhaps the Neanderthals, like many hunter-gatherers in recent times, believed in ghosts and the haunting of places where people have died—and preferred to move away or dispose of their dead at some distance. If so, these practices might not have been possible during glacial winters. They could not move far through deep snows, and besides, their home bases probably included large stockpiles of food and fuel. So perhaps they had to stay put, bury their dead nearby or even inside their caves, and devise special ceremonies to speed the departure of ancestral spirits.

Neanderthal man invented, or at least formalized, illusion when he invented burial. The belief in an afterlife says in effect that death is not what it seems; that it represents an apparent ending only, an ending only as far as the evidence of the senses is concerned; and that in this case, the crude evidence of the senses is wrong. Reality involves not observed and observable "facts" but an abstraction, the idea that death is actually a passage from one world to another. In this respect the burial ceremonies of prehistoric hunters expressed the kind of thinking used today to develop theories about the structure of the atomic nucleus or the expanding universe.

Another new phenomenon, another aspect of the new way of

thinking, makes an appearance during Neanderthal times. Traces of violence, in the sense of man killing man, become more common. Some sort of mayhem took place in a sandstone rock shelter overlooking a river in northern Yugoslavia, where at the turn of the century investigators recovered more than five hundred bones and bone fragments representing at least a dozen individuals. A number of the bones are charred, suggesting that cannibalism may have been practiced, while other bones show definite signs of having been cut.

Unfortunately, excavators did not work as painstakingly then as they do now, and no living-floor patterns were reported. But the mass killings hint at organized fighting among neighboring bands, a possibility strengthened by findings at other Old World sites—a flint projectile point in a rib cage, a pelvis with a spear hole in it, and skulls bashed and penetrated in various ways. Is this another sign of the *Homo sapiens* status of the Neanderthals? They not only believed in an afterlife, but they may also have taken the initiative in evolving effective ways of speeding the departure of their fellow men to the other world. They may have invented warfare as well as religion.

■ Les Eyzies, a center of prehistory in France; a decade of digging at the Neanderthal site of Combe Grenal; an empty burial pit and a posthole; tool kits as signs of tribes or traditions; statistics, controversy, and tool kits as signs of different activities; sites in China, the Soviet Union, Greece and Africa; national styles of digging

CHAPTER IX

Developments in the Scientific Study of Neanderthal Man

■ One of the most beautiful parts of France is the region surrounding the village of Les Eyzies more than three hundred miles southwest of Paris. Rivers have gouged the countryside out of a great limestone plateau. There are remote gorges and side valleys, wide-open valleys bounded by steep cliffs several hundred feet high, in the cliffs scooped-out places under massive overhangs—and caves, many small ones and others that extend deep into the rock.

This is an ideal land to live in, and has been for a long time. Much of the local activity takes place near the cliffs which dominate the landscape. Farmers plow to the edges of the cliffs, and some of their farmhouses are fitted so snugly into the hollows of overhangs that they seem to be growing out of the limestone. Indeed, cliff dwelling is an old tradition in these parts. In medieval times the nobility built castles on and into the cliffs, using natural caves for arsenals and storehouses and wine cellars. Roman legions came before the farmers and the feudal lords; remnants of the walls they made have been found underneath ruined stables and towers.

But the Les Eyzies area is primarily a center of prehistory. For all that has happened since, for all the conquests and pageantry, its richest records and deepest mysteries involve people who flourished a thousand centuries before the Romans, Neanderthal

Le Moustier cave, Les Eyzies region, early burial site

Les Eyzies, center of prehistory

man and his ancestors and descendants. Walking where they walked, one feels their presence everywhere, like ghosts. In good weather they camped and lived outdoors; their flints can be picked up by the dozen in plowed fields near rivers and in the shadows of the cliffs and on the plateaus above the cliffs. Traces of hearths as well as flints are found in the mouths of caves and under the overhangs used for homes in glacial climates.

The record in this region demonstrates man's extraordinary ability to adapt, to live practically anywhere. Here he probably encountered glacial climates more rigorous and demanding than his ancestors had ever encountered before, and yet he managed to cope with icy temperatures and blizzards and accumulating snows. Certainly he could never have endured without making the most of natural resources, and the land around Les Eyzies offered a unique combination of advantages.

Shelter, of course, was provided by the cliffs, eroded structures formed by the lime-containing remains of tiny animals deposited and consolidated more than a hundred million years ago in the warm shallow sea that covered most of Europe. The cliffs provided raw material as well as shelter. Embedded in the limestone were large quantities of fine-grained flint in the form of nodules which, like the limestone, consist of the remains of microorganisms (in this case, colonies of single-cell animals with silica-containing shells). Water was also available, runoff from mountains in the Massif Central, where the Dordogne and Vézère rivers rose and joined a few miles below Les Eyzies and passed through on their way to the Bay of Biscay, as they do today.

Above all, there was an abundance of game during the coldest times, chiefly reindeer, which seem to have been created in large measure for the nourishment of man and other large carnivores. Wild horses, for example, will not stay long in areas where they are being heavily hunted. But reindeer such as the caribou of the Canadian Arctic are creatures of habit, and vast herds tend to return to the same places year after year along the same well-rutted trails, across the same mountain passes, lakes, fords, rivers, and high gravel ridges. Judging by the quantities of reindeer bones found at numerous sites in the Les Eyzies region, prehistoric reindeer were equally predictable and equally vulnerable. Groups of Neanderthal hunters, working together rather like wolf packs, must have waited at strategic crossing points and stalked and killed individual animals.

So man found many resources he could use in the glacial climates of southern France. He must also have had a feeling for the beauty of the land and for the hard-won security of standing with a solid wall at his back and looking out over a river valley. Some two hundred prehistoric sites have been reported within a radius of about twenty miles of Les Eyzies, including Le Moustier and Regourdou and other burial sites mentioned in the last chapter. Many more sites are known but unreported, since every investigator familiar with the area has a private list of places he hopes to excavate some day.

Most archeologists feel reasonably certain that several hundred undiscovered sites exist in the area. The great majority of reported caves, rock shelters and open-air locations with prehistoric remains have been found within a mile or two of well-traveled routes, modern roads which often follow the original courses of old carriage roads. No one really knows what lies beyond. From the tops of the highest cliffs one looks into the distance and sees inviting backcountry valleys and other cliffs which have not yet been thoroughly explored and which almost surely contain the living places of prehistoric man.

A relatively straightforward approach would very likely lead to the discovery of further sites. The plan would be to start with a large-scale map of the region and detailed aerial photographs, concentrating first on valleys where no sites have been reported to date—and marking all cliffs and other uncovered limestone deposits which, like most presently known sites, have southern or western exposures. Archeologists believe that a trip into these valleys would reveal that an appreciable proportion of the locations had served as the occupation sites of prehistoric people. The only difficulty is that there has been little support for such a search because enough sites are known already to keep excavators busy for four to five decades.

One exceptionally interesting cave site lies in the little valley of Combe Grenal, about fourteen miles from Les Eyzies, on the side of a hill not far from the Dordogne River. A dirt road leads there, or rather a pair of ruts marking the remains of a dirt road—and off to the left, along a rising path hidden by trees and bushes, lies the site, a gouged-out place resembling an abandoned quarry. Higher up on the cliff and within sight of the excavations is a mine which provided flint in prehistoric times. Medieval stone workers also came there to obtain huge flint slabs for millstones.

François Bordes, director of the Laboratory of Quaternary Geology and Prehistory of the University of Bordeaux and archeologist in charge of all investigations in the Les Eyzies region, began digging at the Combe Grenal cave in June, 1953. He expected to complete the project in short order, probably by the end of the summer, because a colleague told him that since bedrock had already been reached, only a small area remained to be exposed. But it soon turned out that the bedrock sloped sharply downhill, and he and his associates followed the dipping rock line deeper and deeper season after season without hitting bottom in the form of a level floor. When the work finally came to an end in 1964, they had made a huge hole in the ground, digging to a maximum depth of some forty feet and uncovering sixty-four separate layers of geological and archeological deposits.

The oldest and deepest layers can be dated approximately by geological methods. They include a clayey red soil, the clay representing muds formed during thaws of the next-to-last glaciation. (The red color is "rust" resulting from chemical reactions between iron-containing minerals and oxygen, reactions which are limited in cold climates and took place during the subsequent interglacial stage.) These deposits are estimated to have been laid down 125,000 to 150,000 years ago, about the time when prehistoric pioneers explored the area, looked over the cave and decided to move in.

The first occupants left no fossil remains. But they may have been people rather like those represented by the skull fragments found at the Swanscombe and Steinheim sites, people definitely on the way to modern man. They had Acheulian-type tools like some of those unearthed at Swanscombe, including hand axes designed according to the same basic pattern used by their remote Olduvai ancestors hundreds of thousands of years before. Judging by the fact that about 80 per cent of the bones found among their tools were reindeer bones, their diet included ample supplies of venison.

Combe Grenal's richest and most important deposits lie directly above the red Acheulian deposits, furnishing an almost continuous record of Neanderthal occupation from about 90,000 to 40,000 years ago. There are a few sterile layers, layers without artifacts or any traces of man, when the climate may have become too severe even for the Neanderthals and chunks of rock from the roof remained where they fell since no one was around to clear away the debris. In at least one case people abandoned the site during favorable climatic conditions possibly to follow game other than reindeer, animals with sufficient good sense to move out when hunters moved in. One or two layers contain very little material, indicating that hunters had a home base elsewhere and used the cave only occasionally for brief stopovers.

Combe Grenal was a center of activity most of the time, however. Groups consisting of up to about thirty-five to forty individuals at any one time lived and died there over periods of many generations. The site includes an empty grave, extending through several of the deepest Neanderthal layers. Experienced excavators are continually observing changes in the soil, changes in color and texture and consistency, and one day Bordes noticed a small area of fine soil in a section consisting mainly of coarser material, the sort of pattern produced when earth has been loosened.

Removal of the fine material revealed a typical basin-shaped burial pit so small that it must have contained a very young child. The absence of fossil remains is difficult to explain. The grave had not been disturbed either by looters or scavenging animals. Most probably the skeleton was destroyed by the bone-dissolving action of waters seeping through layers containing sand and ashes and rock; also, young bones are not fully calcified and may tend to disintegrate faster than adult bones. Three smaller ceremonial pits near the grave may have held meat and clothing for the dead child, and they are also empty.

Another unusual feature was exposed in a higher, more recent layer. One of Bordes' co-workers noticed a dark circular patch of fine soil in an ashy layer; scooped out the soil, taking care to leave the ashy material intact; and ended with a hole about two inches in diameter and eight inches deep. Then he poured plaster into the hole, obtaining a cast which resembled the pointed end of a stake. This may have been one of several postholes at the mouth

Plaster cast of posthole, Combe Grenal

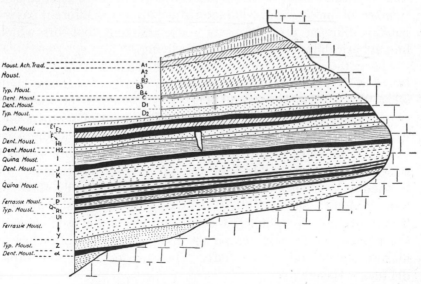

Cross section at Combe Grenal: location of posthole

of the cave, where stakes were driven into the ground to support skins or woven branches and provide shelter from wind, rain and snow. Or, as will be indicated later, it may have supported a meat-drying rack.

But Combe Grenal is especially important for the richness of its tool assemblages and for the analysis of those assemblages by a statistical approach which Bordes himself pioneered. Since excavating his first site at the age of fourteen in a valley not far from Les Eyzies, he has examined more than a million tools, most of them made by Neanderthal man. This experience is the basis for his widely used system of classifying tools. He has published a list of tool types, each type being identified clearly and objectively enough so that other investigators can make the same identifications on their own. The list includes a total of more than sixty different kinds of points, scrapers, knives, burins, and so on.

The variety of tool types itself is enough to indicate what may be deduced from other evidence such as the burial practices of the Neanderthals and their ability to live in rigorous climates, namely, that they were advanced and complicated human beings. But further analysis reveals another sort of variety, and more about the people. In the process of identifying and counting the tools in Neanderthal layers, Bordes discovered the existence of a number of unique and characteristic patterns. Different layers contain different proportions of tools, different tool kits which hint at basic differences in prehistoric living.

The patterns occur among the 19,000 Neanderthal tools collected at Combe Grenal. One of them is represented in the layer where the posthole was found. The layer contained 766 tools and a great many tool types, including an assortment of scrapers and even three hand axes. But nearly 600 items in the assemblage belong to a single broad class, flints with one or more notches struck on the edges. Most of the pieces are "denticulate" or toothed tools having several notches in a row, usually three or four, forming a set of teeth and looking much like saw blades. There are also single-notch tools which might be used, among other purposes, to help scrape the bark off narrow branches in making stakes and spear shafts. The site includes nine other denticulate layers.

A second kind of tool kit is found in fourteen other layers. It also includes a variety of different tools and, again, one class of tool predominates. Nearly two out of every three pieces is a scraper, a high proportion being so-called Quina scrapers, named after a site where they have been found in quantity, the La Quina shelter about seventy miles northwest of Combe Grenal. The large thick tools are often delicately chipped along their curved working edges to produce a characteristic overlapping "fish scale" appearance; they may have served as heavy-duty implements to clean hides for clothing.

The discovery of these and two other tool kits has changed ways of looking at tool assemblages everywhere. Tools uncovered in Neanderthal layers generally fit into one of Bordes' four categories wherever the layers are found—not only at Combe Grenal and in the Les Eyzies region but also in Spain, Syria, Germany, Israel and other countries. The problem is what to make of such widespread and persistent patterns. Apparently they have little to do with evolution among the Neanderthals, since the tool kits do not appear in any regular sequence from the oldest to the most recent layers at various sites, and there is no conclusive evidence of simple seasonal or climatic influences.

Bordes believes that the four tool kits belong to four tribes or traditions. Different Neanderthal groups had different ways of doing things, customs handed down from much earlier times and represented by the tool kits they left behind. For example, the Quina Neanderthals may be traced to a tradition that existed nearly a hundred thousand years before them at the High Lodge site in England, where people were using similar tools, including finely worked Quina-type scrapers. Another Neanderthal tool kit may stem from Acheulian industries which first appeared more than 600,000 years ago (see Chapter VI), a line passing through intermediate stages such as those observed in the remains at Torralba and Ambrona and, more recently, in the lowest layers at Combe Grenal itself.

The stress is on enduring elements in a world where cultural evolution proceeded very slowly compared to its current pace. Bordes believes that contacts among Neanderthal bands with different traditions were few and far between: "A man may well have lived all his life without more than a rare meeting with anyone from another tribe . . . and it is very possible that these contacts, when they did take place, were not always peaceful and fruitful." After all, it was a relatively empty world, the entire population of France probably numbering less than 20,000 persons.

Combe Grenal provides a record of successive wanderings in and out of the little Dordogne Valley by people who had developed different ways of doing things, different habits and beliefs. Groups settled in the cave, eventually died out or left in search of better living conditions or new hunting grounds or simply because they wanted a change of scene (there were always more than enough caves and shelters to go around), and were replaced by other groups in a series of occupations that took place over a period of some five hundred centuries.

The approach upon which Bordes' ideas are based, the statistical approach, has opened the way for still more extensive and more refined studies in the years ahead. Already some of his conclusions are being challenged as a direct result of work stimulated by his own research. The challenge calls for a major shift of emphasis, a different way of looking at and analyzing Neanderthal tool kits. Instead of interpreting them as the products of different tribes or traditions, they can be interpreted as signs that different sorts of activity were going on.

According to this viewpoint, different tool kits do not represent people with different traditions doing essentially the same things, such as hunting, gathering, preparing foods, making tools and fires, and so on. They represent people who shared many important cultural characteristics and were simply doing different things at different times and places. For example, the existence of Quina-type and denticulate tool kits might simply indicate that one group was engaged chiefly in scraping hides, while the other group was concentrating on woodworking. In other words, people were using Combe Grenal for different purposes. The focus is less on things that prehistoric man did because his forefathers did them, and more on things he did as part of the practical day-to-day business of staying alive.

The most articulate and influential spokesman for the so-called "functional" point of view is Lewis Binford of the University of New Mexico, who evolved his approach and philosophy during the course of work on American Indian sites. His increasing

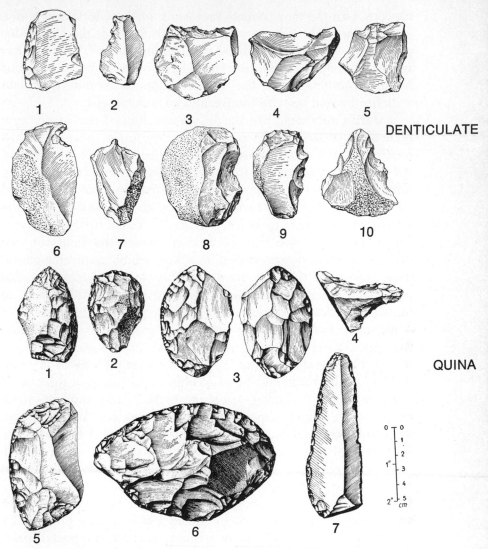

DENTICULATE

QUINA

1. side scraper
2, 3. denticulate tools
4, 5, 6. notched tools
7. borer
8. notched tool
9, 10. denticulate tools

1. side scraper
2. end scraper
3. bifacial scraper
4. nosed end scraper
5. side scraper
6. transverse scraper
7. retouched blade

Two Neanderthal tool kits: denticulate (top) and Quina (bottom)

concern with the more remote prehistory of the Old World is due in large part to his former wife Sally, a graduate of the University of Chicago who has specialized in Neanderthal problems and has worked closely with Bordes. There have been some friendly but heated arguments over the interpretation of Neanderthal data with Bordes and his wife Denise, also an archeologist.

Binford's approach, like Bordes', is a statistical one involving a refinement of the tool-kit concept. Any group of people, prehistoric or primitive or modern, has a large set of tools for carrying out all of its activities. Investigators interested in comparing different cultures may obtain some information from an unsorted collection of items representing the entire assemblage. But the information is likely to be very limited without further analysis. There must be some way of isolating, from the total set, the subsets of tools or specialized tool kits which naturally go together because they are used together in performing specific activities. These subsets and activities must be identified to understand in detail the lives of prehistoric people.

An individual completely ignorant of modern life would confront such a problem in trying to analyze an unsorted collection of the implements we use. The collection might consist of more than a hundred different types of objects, including a mixture of items used in grooming, cooking, writing and sewing: razor blades, pots, paper clips, thimbles, hair curlers, bread knives, ballpoint pens, safety pins, combs, frying pans, letter openers, needles, nail files, funnels, paperweights, and scissors. The task would be to find out which tools were used together and for what tasks.

Analogous problems arise in the study of prehistoric man. A single collection from a single living place means nothing by itself. The search for subsets of artifacts as clues to repeated practices, living habits, requires a sufficiently large and representative sample of collections—and Binford and his students have introduced a special statistical technique for the analysis of such samples. The technique, known as factor analysis, developed out of research conducted during the early 1900's by American psychologists concerned with discovering sets of questions to serve as effective measures of intelligence. It has been widely used in studies of executive morale, weather trends, accident-proneness, urban development, the voting behavior of Supreme Court justices, and many other projects.

An early application of factor analysis to research on prehistoric tool kits involves evidence obtained from a site in Israel near the Sea of Galilee. The area has been shaped by ancient volcanoes and earthquakes. It marks the northernmost part of the Great Rift Valley system, the huge split in the earth's crust which extends 4,000 miles down through East Africa and past the Olduvai Gorge and ends somewhere in Mozambique. It includes many caves where Neanderthal people lived in times when a now-extinct river flowed through the area to the Dead Sea.

In 1962 Sally Binford excavated one of the caves, a large two-chamber affair located in a steep limestone cliff more than a hundred feet above the floor or a river canyon. It was a difficult dig, not only because of the early-morning climb up the cliffside but also because most artifacts and other remains were buried deep in narrow crevices or embedded in hardened sand-limestone deposits. The site yielded a sample of eight tool collections from as many different deposits in the cave area, collections suitable for analysis, including a total of about 2,000 tools. Sally Binford identified the tools according to Bordes' list of types and under his supervision.

The size of the sample was increased by the addition of eight other tool collections, seven from levels in a shelter near Damascus in Syria and one from a French open-air site near Rouen. The collections were made up of about 2,000 more tools closely related to those found at the Israeli site and presumably manufactured during the same period of prehistory. Moreover, all the tools had been typed by Bordes, which ensured consistency of classification.

[Factor analysis calls for a detailed investigation of variations among the items of a sample. In this case the first step was to take one of the tool types, compare it with a second type for each of the sixteen collections, and then evaluate the result. A rating of +1 would indicate that the two types varied in exactly the same way—that both types increased by, say, 10 per cent from collection A to collection B, decreased by 25 per cent from B to C, maintained the same proportions in D, and so on. A −1 rating would indicate that the two tool types were exactly out of phase, varying in exactly the opposite way, while 0 would indicate no relationship at all. Intermediate values on the scale from +1 to −1 represented different degrees of correlation or association.

The process was repeated over and over again in the Neanderthal study. Each tool type was compared successively to every one of the other thirty-nine tool types (this particular sample including forty of the sixty-odd types listed by Bordes), and every one of the relationships was evaluated. These and many subsequent steps required a prodigious amount of arithmetic. With a high-speed electronic computer, it took about two minutes.

The final analysis produced five "factors," five sets of tools that varied together as independent clusters with high degrees of correlation. The following is a list of the specialized tool kits together with some suggestions as to how they might have been used:

1. Tool kit I, 12 tool types including two kinds of borer, a beak-shaped engraver or "bec," and other tools which may have been used to make objects out of wood and bone—perhaps shafts, handles or hafts, tent pegs, and cordage from hides. Maintenance activities.
2. Tool kit II, 10 tool types including three kinds of spear point as well as many kinds of scraper. Killing and butchering.
3. Tool kit III, 7 tool types including three kinds of knife for heavy cutting and three kinds of flake for delicate cutting. Food processing, mainly prepared meat.
4. Tool kit IV, 4 tool types including denticulates for sawing and shredding, and two special types of scraper for fine work. Shredding and cutting, perhaps of wood and other plant materials.
5. Tool kit V, 6 tool types including points, simple scrapers, and the rabot or push plane. Killing and butchering, but perhaps involving activities more specialized than those requiring tool kit II.

The main tool kits at the Israeli site turn out to be I, II, and III. Tool kit I predominates, which indicates that the cave was used chiefly for maintenance work, for repairing old tools and weapons and making new ones, the sort of tasks most likely to be carried out at a base camp. Tool kit III suggests food processing, another "domestic" activity, while the presence of tool kit II indicates that a small amount of killing and butchering may have been done at the site. The base-camp notion is supported by the fact that the cave is a large one enclosing a naturally lighted area of about 2,700 square feet, representing enough floor space for twenty-five to thirty individuals (on the basis of studies indicating a requirement in such settlements of at least a hundred square feet per person).

The analysis permits further deductions about how the cave was used. Most of the deposits contain tool assemblages that are remarkably alike in the number of tools and tool types and their proportions. This observation fits in with the notion, hinted at by other evidence, that the same group of people used the cave intensively to perform the same general tasks for a relatively short period, say, a few years. Their cooking area may have been located just outside the cave entrance. It is marked by a deposit that includes three small fire layers and an unusually high proportion of tool kit III knives and flakes, tools which could do an effective job of meat carving.

A different living pattern existed at the Syrian site, a shelter containing only about 1,600 square feet of floor space. Tool kits II and V, the killing and butchering factors, tend to predominate here. There is also evidence suggesting that tool kit V may represent the hunting of a type of game which demands that the hunters spend relatively long periods away from the base camp. The general impression is that the site served as a temporary work camp, where hunters stopped to do their butchering and perhaps to make plans for the next day's activities. Only one of its occupation levels contains traces of fire and, as at the Israeli site, this is also the only place where food-processing tool kit III is represented.

After completing the Near Eastern studies the Binfords carried out a more extensive analysis of evidence from Combe Grenal with its fifty-odd Neanderthal layers, 19,000 Neanderthal tools, abundant bone and pollen remains, and a 50,000-year record of Neanderthal occupations. In the Near Eastern study both hunting items (spear points) and scrapers were included in a single one of the five tool kits, II. But in the Combe Grenal analysis this unit breaks into its major components and becomes two distinct tool kits. The same effect was noted for maintenance and food processing, each being represented by several different tool kits. In all, the analysis yielded some fourteen different tool kits, believed to be fairly close to a complete listing for the Neanderthals, although future studies may reveal two or three more.

These statistically determined factors or clusters are elements of a most important kind. They can be compared to the small pieces of glass and stone used in making mosaics, and they may be used in re-creating a human pattern, the Neanderthal way of life. Some major features of the pattern have already been discovered.

Combe Grenal has fifty-five Neanderthal occupation layers, forty of them containing enough tools for statistical analysis. Twenty-five of the analyzed layers include one or more of the three kinds of tool kit associated with maintenance activities, and are probably camps—implying that they were either home bases for all members of the groups or else places away from the home site and reserved primarily for intensive activities associated with hunting or food processing. The rest of the layers did not contain maintenance tool kits and are interpreted as stations representing temporary occupations for more specialized activities. A few of these layers do not fit in with this preliminary hypothesis since they include abundant traces of fire, generally characteristic of intensive settlements rather than temporary stations.

Other associations stimulate new ideas about what was being done and by whom. One of the Binfords' arguments leads from a consideration of the kinds of flint used for different types of tools to new interpretations of some old and puzzling observations. They asked themselves what sort of archeological evidence might help indicate which tasks were done by women, and speculated that since women generally stay near the group's camp or station to care for the children, they might tend to make their tools out of readily available raw material near the site.

This notion immediately raised a simple question which had never been asked before: What sort of tools were made of local materials? The most readily available sources of flint available to the Neanderthals at Combe Grenal were dull grayish or blackish nodules embedded in the walls of their own cave, and the Binfords spent many hours at Bordes' laboratory in Bordeaux going through drawer after drawer jammed with tools, classifying every item by tool type and material and the layer in which it was found. They found that tools made of Combe Grenal flint are likely to be primarily denticulate or notched tools, items commonly associated with the processing of foods—which might well have been predominantly woman's work as it is in primitive hunting tribes today.

Reinforcing and complementing the theory is evidence bearing on man's work. Tools which may be made of any one of several different raw materials, generally from remote sources—for example, opalescent white flint from a site more than a mile away on the plateau above Combe Grenal, or brown flint from Dordogne River gravels—are most often those used in hunting, including spear points and certain types of scraper. One implication is that the variety of materials represents a mark of the hunting life, of men away from their base camp and ready to use whatever suitable material happened to be at hand.

Hunting tools seem to be associated with a special way of working flint, the purpose of which has never been fully clear. The so-called "Levallois" technique (named after a site in Levallois-Perret, a suburb of Paris) appeared in Africa and Western Europe some 150,000 years ago and required a high order of finesse, the careful preparation of a flint nodule by trimming the top and edges before striking off a flake for shaping into a finished tool. There has been a great deal of speculating about the significance of such flaking since, for no obvious reasons, it is common at some sites and rare or absent at others.

For many years the technique was believed to be a cultural trait, a matter mainly of tradition and style. Later, Bordes and others emphasized the fact that it generally occurred at sites where flint was plentiful and easily accessible. Now it may have a new significance, an advantage relevant specifically to the hunt. Hunting tools often require large and relatively standardized flakes (in contrast to denticulate tools, which are generally on the small side and made of flakes of widely varying shapes, the important thing apparently having been the cutting edge) and, as had been noted for some time, the Levallois technique permits the manufacture of such flakes.

Broader and more complex problems remain to be discovered and solved in the Combe Grenal data, problems involving the further application of factor analysis and the relationship of tool

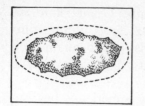
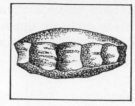

edges of nodule trimmed

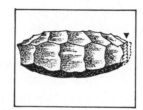

top surface trimmed

striking platform made

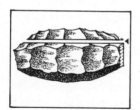
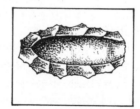

flake struck from nucleus

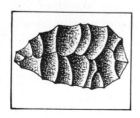
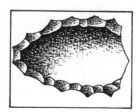

finished tool

Stages in making Levallois flakes, top and side views

assemblages to other traces of the past. Bordes collected fossil pollens from many layers at the site, and the Binfords have also subjected this material to statistical study, again with the aid of a high-speed computer. The result is eight clusters of pollen types which tend to occur together and tell a story of prevailing climates in the area.

One cluster includes oak, poplar, alder, elm, ivy, ferns and other plants characteristic of low, damp, shaded places such as are found in the upland meadows of the Dordogne region today. Other clusters suggest a typical very dry, very warm forest-margin terrain (blackberry, raspberry, roses, nettles), steppe grasslands (cool-climate grasses and sedges), and cold, seasonally wet conditions (hazel, willow, Queen Anne's lace). As might be expected, a clear-cut relationship exists between climate and activities as indicated by tool kits. In general the pattern of activities under way does not change much as long as the climate remains relatively stable.

There are also six animal clusters. Ibex, wolf and a northern species of horse are typical of cold steppes; deer, Irish elk and an extinct species of rhinoceros indicate open forest; and so on. The greatest variety of animal remains is usually found together with tool kits characteristic of base-camp layers, which suggests that the people chose to settle here precisely because the area contained many kinds of game. On the other hand, the last variety of fewest species are found at more temporary and specialized stations.

Combe Grenal includes three types of so-called shredding station, settlements characterized among other things by a high proportion of denticulates and other notched tools. The animal remains associated with one of the station types consist predominantly of horse and reindeer, and Lewis Binford has a hunch about what was going on. The saw-tooth tools may have been used by the Neanderthals to cut chunks of already butchered meat into little strips that could be hung on racks to dry in the sun or over fires. American Indians used this technique for preserving meat. French traders used to sell them special metal shredders for the cutting operations, tools designed along the same lines as small denticulate flints.

If this technique was practiced by the Neanderthals, one might expect to find clues in appropriate layers, such as the remains of smoke fires, postholes or even pieces of preserved wood from the drying racks. Unless a speculation suggests what excavators could possibly find by way of evidence, unless it suggests specific procedures for its own proof or disproof, it has very little value in stimulating new studies. Some confirmatory evidence exists at Combe Grenal; one of the denticulate layers, for example, contains the posthole as well as traces of fire.

Continuing analysis reveals patterns or fragments of patterns which are beginning to fit together. Small tools such as engravers, borers and endscrapers tend to be found together with the remains of salmon, marmots (a bushy-tailed rodent somewhat resembling a woodchuck), mountain sheep and other rarely killed animals. The association makes sense when you realize that these tools are used for maintenance activities like woodworking and preparing hides, activities generally carried out at base camps occupied for relatively long periods—and the longer the occupation, the greater the chances of finding some rare animals.

These and a great many other associations, the output of high-speed computers, are statistical patterns which provide clues to patterns of inferred behavior among prehistoric people. Another source of clues to the past is the actual behavior of people who still live primarily by hunting. Primitive people are by no means living in a pristine, untouched state; their world has been changed irrevocably by waves of foreign explorers and settlers. Yet even allowing for all that, certain practices endure, and some striking parallels exist between the present and the remote past.

Chapters XV and XVI consider such observations in some detail, but one example indicates a direct application to the understanding of Neanderthal times. As part of an effort to learn more about what happened at Combe Grenal and elsewhere, Binford is conducting a series of intensive studies among Eskimos living in the Brooks Range region of north-central Alaska, about 250 miles from Fairbanks. In one of his "recent archeology" projects, he excavated the site of a house occupied by Eskimos eighty to ninety years ago.

Among other things, he found caribou lower jawbones, all of which had been cracked open, a practice explained to him by Eskimos who remembered what their fathers and grandfathers had done. The jawbones contained "patik," a fibrous tissue eaten as a starvation food in times of near-famine. The Neanderthal hunters apparently faced similar emergencies, since all but one of several hundred reindeer, horse and ox-cattle jawbones found in Combe Grenal layers were also cracked open. Furthermore, it seems that Eskimos and Neanderthals shared related superstitions. The Alaskan hunters had a taboo against eating material from the jawbones of bears, foxes, wolves and other meat-eating animals—and not a single one of the two dozen or so bear, wolf, cave lion and hyena jawbones found at Combe Grenal had been shattered.

So observations of contemporary hunters enrich the understanding of prehistory, mainly by suggesting things to look for during archeological excavations, and providing evidence relevant to the question of whether different tool kits represent different traditions or different activities. Further support for the latter viewpoint comes from new work conducted during the last few years. Leslie Freeman, digging Neanderthal layers in the Morin Cave in northern Spain, has found separate concentrations of three different tool kits on the same living floors, indicating a functional rather than a traditional context. People were simply doing different things in different parts of the cave.

Freeman has also carried out a factor analysis for a pre-Neanderthal site, Torralba. The analysis is based on material from ten living floors and reveals a number of significant associations. For example, pointed tools known as perforators tend to be found together with fragments of elephant skulls, and elephant skulls have irregular surfaces with many hollows and narrow cavities which contain meat that might have to be pried out.

Desmond Clark, who has long suspected that different tool kits found at different places reflect different activities, reports a number of persisting patterns which turn up at a variety of sites occupied during the past two million years or so. One pattern is the general predominance of small tools, mainly cutting flakes and scrapers, at sites where one animal or only a few animals had been butchered. Another pattern involves the presence of large numbers of large cutting tools, hand axes and cleavers, at sites containing very little bone and no signs of butchering.

Clark's observations are confirmed and extended in a recent factor-analysis study by Binford, who makes a number of further inferences. For one thing, he suggests that the large cutting tools may not have been used in hunting at all. They may have been used primarily to dig for and process plant foods, and their prominence at a site may indicate a heavy reliance on such foods, a state of affairs which prevails among primitive people currently living in southern Africa and other warm regions.

This possibility has some provocative implications. It may help in understanding the unexplained east-west division of Oldowan and Acheulian industries, as described in Chapter VI. The idea is that Acheulian hand-ax industries—concentrated in Africa, Europe, the Near East and peninsular India—may reflect an emphasis on plant foods, while the Oldowan industries of southeastern Asia which include chopping and lighter flake tools represent the tool kits of people consuming higher proportions of meat. An intriguing question is the possible connection between this notion and the notion, proposed by some prehistorians, that modern-type men and large-scale cooperative hunting first appeared in Asia.

Such studies will have to be extended considerably to arrive at truly scientific theories about the lives of our prehistoric ancestors. A staggering amount of material has already been collected, including skeletal remains of more than 150 Neanderthal individuals from about seventy sites throughout the world. An important site is located in northeast China near the Great Wall. Soviet investigators have dug extensively at rich Neanderthal sites along river banks in the Crimea and elsewhere, and have found traces of elaborate burials and semipermanent dwellings. One of the dwelling sites, Molodova in the eastern Soviet Union more than 250 miles from Kiev, includes a large ring of mammoth tusks, perhaps used for supporting posts; inside the ring are bones of horses, rhinoceroses, bison and brown bears and 29,000 pieces of flint and fifteen hearths.

There has even been increased activity in Greece and Italy, where archeological interest has hitherto focused almost exclusively on classical sites. Eric Higgs of Cambridge University has located more than fifty prehistoric sites in red erosion gullies among the mountains of northwest Greece (as compared to less than half a dozen such sites reported previously for the entire country). His work at one site yielded a number of living floors as well as some unusual remains such as tool assemblages with a high proportion of "microliths" or miniature implements.

Other sites have been excavated in Africa, where, in certain regions at least, the pace of evolution seems to have been slower than in Europe, perhaps because life was so abundant and things came so easily that survival represented far less of a challenge. The world's richest hunting grounds existed in Africa throughout prehistory, and most of the world's hunters lived there. According to one study, during Neanderthal times there may have been two to four times more people in southern Africa alone than in all of Europe.

Evidence for a possible evolutionary lag comes from Isimila, a rich site where thousands of stone tools lie exposed for about three-quarters of a mile along a seasonal stream in the highlands of southern Tanzania. Excavated by Charles Keller of the University of Illinois and Clark Howell, the site includes a typical Acheulian hand-ax-cleaver industry which existed about 75,000 years ago when people at Combe Grenal and elsewhere were using a wider variety of tools. At Desmond Clark's Kalambo Falls site in Zambia, on the other hand, denticulate and notched tools appeared in high proportions not long before the Neanderthals and their tool kits began to disappear in Europe.

Factor analysis and other statistical techniques will be required increasingly for comparative studies of material from many sites. A new approach is being developed, a new way of looking at things. Results are not yet completely consistent and cannot serve as the basis for hard-and-fast conclusions. On the other hand, there is no choice but to use analytical techniques. The data must be organized, and that does not happen automatically. One of the most futile pursuits in research is to accumulate facts and keep accumulating them in the hope that sooner or later they will make sense and the truth will out.

Bare facts are neither particularly interesting nor particularly informative. They do not speak for themselves in archeology or in any other branch of science. But they will speak if they are treated properly, if they are marshaled and organized. That means using statistics to help get the most out of the evidence, a process which generally requires the aid of a high-speed computer. The relationships involved are too complicated for even the most imaginative investigators to deal with on their own.

Imagination comes into its own most effectively, most powerfully, after the analysis. Computers simply present information organized according to the instructions prepared for them. They indicate that certain types of tools tend to vary together and form statistical clusters, but they say nothing about the uses of individual tools or the activities represented by individual tool kits. It is up to the investigator to frame hypotheses that can be checked, like the notion that the Neanderthals may have used Levallois flakes to hunt large open-plain animals such as horses and wild cattle. And imagination and intuition will have to lead the way in interpreting tendencies involving subtler things than activities, things such as attitudes and beliefs.

Bordes has definite feelings about the men and women whose artifacts he is uncovering. They are still alive for him. As he digs in a rich Quina layer and finds one beautifully worked scraper after another, he is impressed not only with the craftsmanship but also with the fact that the craftsmen were working in an almost automatic fashion, as if they had perfected their techniques and had stopped inventing: "They made beautiful things stupidly. Digging Quina layers can be very boring. For the first week you are impressed with the tools, but after that you see scrapers and more scrapers and still more scrapers until you are sick of them!"

There is another observation about these people. They seem to have done most of the burying of the dead. At least, most Neanderthal graves in France are associated with Quina-type tool kits, a finding suggesting that ritual may have played a particularly important part in their lives. So one may ask whether a relationship exists between this quality and the stereotyped, repetitive aspect of their flint technology—and, if so, what special stresses and fears might have fostered the intensive development of their rituals.

One clue is that they lived chiefly during hard winters when death rates must have been high, which supports a possibility discussed in Chapter VIII. Furthermore, sites where Quina-type tools are found tend to be rock shelters located in small river valleys, suggesting that the people lived in small, isolated family groups. The loss of an individual would have had a special impact among people depending directly upon one another for survival, and if the individual was an adult male, his death could have meant the death of the group. Perhaps burial rites developed under the stress of such conditions.

The "feel" of layers related to earlier Acheulian industries hints at an entirely different attitude toward the world. These layers include some hand axes and a relatively high proportion of knives, especially backed knives blunted on one side for a firm and comfortable grip. Bordes believes that Neanderthals using such tools were far more inventive than those using Quina-type tools: "They had some imagination. They made all sorts of backed blades and offbeat tools which you can't classify, including some combination tools, prehistoric versions of today's Swiss pocket knives with scissors and screwdrivers and nail files as well as regular blades. They experimented a great deal, and their experiments worked."

The continuing cooperation between Bordes and Binford shows how productive results can be achieved by investigators whose basic viewpoints differ. The problems at issue demand both the "tribal" or cultural and the functional approaches. Archeologists concerned primarily with cultural factors tend to dig deep, to go back as far as possible into time and obtain a long record of successive changes. Functionally minded archeologists, on the other hand, tend to dig wide, to excavate broad areas at sites which cover more space and can reveal more about the organization of camping places and the variety of activities under way.

This difference of emphasis itself may express a cultural difference. After all, it is natural for Bordes and other investigators of Old World nations with long histories and established traditions to approach prehistory in cultural terms—and for the Binfords, as members of a nation whose history is brief, and whose pioneers and prehistory are recent, to stress the practical aspects of how things are done and for what purposes. Prehistory is sufficiently complex to benefit from both approaches. The best excavations are both deep and wide.

■ The mystery of the passing of the Neanderthals; new methods of big-game hunting in the Near East and the shaping of new men; the discovery of Cro-Magnon man; what may have happened when Cro-Magnon and Neanderthal peoples met; new tools and toolmaking techniques, new ways of life; a possible relationship between an early population explosion and the retreat of the glaciers; man enters Australia and the New World

CHAPTER X

The Disappearance of Neanderthal Man, the Appearance of Modern Man

■ One summer evening several years ago François Bordes played a recording for me in an old farmhouse not far from Combe Grenal, his home during the excavating season. He called the recording "The Song of the Neanderthals." It was a New Caledonian war chant sung loud and deep and half-shouted to the beating of drums, sung with feeling but strangely without pattern. There was no sustained rhythm, only occasional and random intervals of rhythm which came like interruptions. For a few moments the chanters sang in unison and their voices and the drumbeating seemed to gain in power and purpose, and then the rhythm broke again.

The song, with its flashes of harmony and style, symbolizes the situation of the Neanderthals before they and their works vanished from the archeological record 35,000 to 40,000 years ago. Something new was stirring, another series of changes whose nature investigators are still trying to figure out. But whatever the changes were, they resulted in the shaping of a new breed of man, closely related to the Neanderthals, but nevertheless quite different.

Fossil evidence for the transition is sparse in Europe, but exists at a number of sites in the Near East. For example, there is a cave in Israel, on the slopes of Mount Carmel overlooking the Mediterranean near Haifa, where excavators have found the skeleton of a

220

short, stocky individual with heavy limbs and bony brow ridges, definitely a Neanderthal but not the kind that was living in Western Europe. The brow ridges were less massive, the skull somewhat more rounded. Furthermore, near the cave is a rock shelter which served as a cemetery for people who lived in the region several thousand years later, and who were even closer to modern man. The ten skeletons recovered there had longer and straighter limbs than the Neanderthals, more prominent chins, and smaller faces.

Why did such changes occur at that particular time, 40,000 to 50,000 years ago, and why in the Near East? A basic reason, then as throughout the course of human evolution, probably had something to do with obtaining food. There are signs of a new development in hunting, a more intensive, continuous and highly organized exploitation of big game. The increasing emphasis on big game which started perhaps 2 million years before had an enormous effect on man, nearly doubling the size of his brain and transforming an advanced form of *Australopithecus* into *Homo erectus.*

For all its importance, however, this effect was simply a prelude. A revolution is often regarded as finished when it has just begun. Although we are in the throes of a continuing Industrial Revolution today, history books describe it as something that happened between 1750 and 1850, and a similar tendency exists in considering prehistoric events. It took a long time to spell out the implications of big-game hunting. In the beginning the practice called for cooperation on a small-band basis, for strategies involving no more than half a dozen individuals. Probably several bands joined forces upon occasion, as they may have at Torralba, but the associations were not permanent and did not grow into full-scale hunting communities.

The general practice during Neanderthal times seems to have been the killing of single animals by single bands, the killing of one animal at a time. The idea was to stalk a herd and go after a particular individual, often an individual weakened by injury or disease or advanced age. Lions, wild dogs and other carnivores use similar tactics to good advantage. Men and herds had long moved together, locked together in a natural rhythm set by the seasons, the herds moving instinctively along familiar trails, the men following and learning and preparing increasingly sophisticated ambushes. But for a long time there had been very small groups of hunters and very large groups of animals, and that part of the pattern changed with the evolution of modern man.

Man was being shaped more intensively by the creatures he hunted. To kill herd animals more efficiently, he himself became a herd animal in a new sense. With all the space in the world to live in, he formed more densely settled communities. He invented crowds to become a better predator. The change was reflected in the evolution of a new brain, no larger than that of the Neanderthals but incorporating, within a more rounded cranium, whatever nerve circuitry is required to increase the likelihood that we will establish rules and abide by them.

Conditions were ripe for such developments in the Near East. More specifically, conditions were ripe within a particular region which includes the cave on Mount Carmel as well as a number of other sites. The full-scale hunting of big game may have originated in lands along the coastline of what is now Israel, Lebanon and Syria—in the corridor formed by the Mediterranean to the west, and to the east by the Lebanon Mountains and other ranges running parallel to the coast and walling the corridor off from the Syrian and Arabian deserts. This is the central idea of a study by Sally Binford, a synthesis of information from many sources, which suggests a new "model" or hypothesis to explain why the Near Eastern corridor became an evolutionary focal area.

Many factors helped bring large groups of people together in this area. Wild cattle, fallow deer and other herd animals grazed in green wooded valleys which rose from the coastal plains and extended into the foothills of the mountains. When leaves and grasses became scarce they moved on, in the spring to pasturelands on the plains and in the fall to highland meadows tucked away in the foothills. Small bands of hunters naturally concentrated where the game was, in the valleys and the narrowest places along seasonal migration routes, and a number of further circumstances encouraged increasing cooperation among them.

For one thing, pollen analysis and other studies indicate that a shift to somewhat drier climates occurred about 40,000 to 45,000 years ago, and that probably helped step up the pace of evolution. It may have intensified the search for food among men and animals. Herds became larger and their movements through the valleys became more and more mass movements. For the hunters, risks increased as well as opportunities. A single band could go after wild cattle, for example. But it was a dangerous business, more suitable for a number of cooperating bands. These extinct animals should not be pictured as the docile cud-chewers of today's farmyards. They were fierce, fast on their feet, big (some of the bulls measuring six and a half feet high at the shoulder), and quite capable of fighting back.

Certain basic observations support the notion that major changes were under way in the Mediterranean corridor. The richest and deepest sites have been found where vegetation and game were most abundant, in the valleys on the western slopes of the coastal ranges. The Mount Carmel cave and rock shelter lie in such a valley, and so do other important sites. For example, farther inland, about fifty miles from Haifa and located not far from Nazareth at the narrowest part of a pass to the mountains of Lebanon, is the enormous Qafzeh Cave where the remains of at least seven individuals were found more than thirty years ago, transitional people resembling those found at the Mount Carmel shelter.

Investigators recently revisited this site, which had been blown up by British troops as a suspected Israeli ammunition depot. After spending about six weeks removing the debris of the explosion, tons of fallen rock, they found two beautifully preserved skeletons, enclosed them in blocks of plaster, and flew them back to Jerusalem by helicopter. Since then about half a dozen more individuals have been recovered. Although a full report has yet to be published, the skeletons have already been identified as the remains of people who were very closely related to modern-type man—and were still using Neanderthal tools.

Western valley sites have deposits up to about seventy-five feet deep. There are layers containing Neanderthal tool kits and, in most cases, layers above them containing later tool kits which include high proportions of blades, tool kits characteristic of modern-type people and representing long periods of occupation. There are also signs that wild cattle were hunted intensively. At two sites, the Mount Carmel shelter and a shelter located in a bluff north of Beirut in Lebanon, quantities of cattle bones increase sharply in late Neanderthal levels. One level at the Lebanese shelter contains the bones of only about a dozen individual animals, while the level immediately above it contains more than 500 individuals.

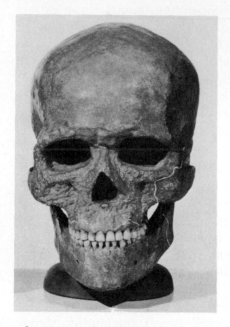

Reconstructed skull of Cro-Magnon man

These and other observations make a good case for the evolution of modern-type man in the Near East. As far as his appearance in Europe and elsewhere is concerned, there are two theories. The migration theory states that modern man arose in the Near East, moved northwest as well as in other directions, and dominated and eventually replaced the Neanderthals who had not evolved sufficiently to hold on to their ancestral lands. Perhaps they had adapted too well to glacial conditions, in the sense that when their world changed they could not change with it. This is hardly an unusual state of affairs. Groups exist today, such as the Bushmen and Afrikaaners of South Africa, which face extinction because they find it difficult to adjust to a changing world.

People like ourselves were first recognized at the famous Cro-Magnon shelter located in the limestone cliffs of Les Eyzies. In 1868 workers building a railroad through the Vézère Valley discovered five skeletons deep in the rock at the back of the shelter, the remains of individuals with small faces, high foreheads, protruding chins and other physical features typical of today's populations. (Incidentally, the cliff that includes the site is still inhabited and provides a ready-made rear wall for one of the village's most popular tourist hotels.)

According to the migration theory, Cro-Magnon man came from the Near East and appeared in Europe more than 35,000 years ago during a period of relatively mild, moist climates. They brought a new way of life with them. The change can be observed in their artifacts, among other things. They had mastered the art of shaping flints to a degree difficult to appreciate unless you actually try it yourself. Many archeologists are skillful flint workers, and Bordes is one of the best. The most beautiful hand ax in my own collection is one he made for me in a few minutes during a luncheon break at the Combe Grenal dig. But generally it takes several attempts to make one good tool, and the odds are that Cro-Magnon man achieved better results.

He developed a special technique to obtain the blades or long slender flakes out of which most of his tools were made. The first step was to prepare a roughly cylindrical flint core or nucleus perhaps four to six inches long, rest a bone or antler punch on the top of the core near the edge, and then strike the punch sharply with a hammerstone. The blow chipped a narrow sliver off the side of the core, and many more slivers were detached by successive blows along the edge in an inward-spiraling path. This "peeling" operation was very efficient. A single flint core weighing some two pounds could yield forty to fifty good blades for an estimated total of up to seventy-five feet of cutting edge, while only six feet would have resulted if the same core had been worked by earlier methods. Incidentally, full-scale cooperative hunting probably favored the development of this technique, stressing the need for cutting tools which could be manufactured rapidly and in large quantities.

New tools and new varieties of old tools were developed during the period from about 35,000 to 13,000 years ago—large selections of burins to make differently shaped grooves and slots, composite tools consisting of several barbs or other flint elements set into grooved hafts, spear throwers, harpoons, lamps, and so

Punched blade technique: bone punch, as probably used in Cro-Magnon times

Stages in making punched blade tool

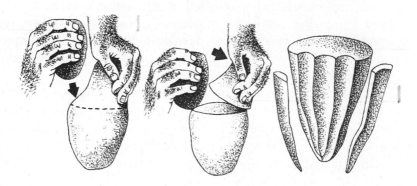

on. Tools made of bone and antler and ivory as well as flint turn up in increasing proportions in excavated tool collections. The first man-made material was invented, clay mixed with powdered bone as a binder and molded into female figurines and other items. People engaged in such specialized activities as reindeer hunting and mammoth hunting and fishing.

Cro-Magnon man brought with him social structures which may have evolved earlier during the course of big-game hunts in valleys of the Near East. He still lived in bands consisting of several families, from about thirty to as many as a hundred intermarrying persons. But the band was on the way out. He had taken the first major steps toward the full-fledged tribe, an association of many bands held together not only by marriage but also by shared traditions and shared problems, including large-scale cooperative hunting and perhaps warfare. He developed rituals for coming together and remaining together, accentuating traditions that may have arisen in the remote past, incest taboos and kinship rules which created more intricate and cohesive relationships among larger numbers of individuals.

Together with the rituals he developed art, perhaps his most impressive achievement. For the first time paintings and engravings appear on the walls of caves, often deep inside and far from natural light, in places that suggest secrecies and ceremonies, the nature of which can only be guessed at. Critics can be as obscure about the significance of the world's earliest art as about today's works and meanings. We do know that cave art, to be discussed in the next chapter, was produced by powerful, confident and imaginative people.

The Neanderthals of Western Europe had no chance against these people and these institutions. In any competition for the best living places and hunting grounds, and competitions must have occurred on many occasions, they came out second best. All fossil traces of the heavy-browed, heavy-limbed "natives" vanish from the record together with their toolmaking techniques and tool kits and most of their characteristic tools. Bordes reports signs of cultural decline in some of the upper layers at Combe Grenal, fewer tools made crudely out of poorly prepared flint nodules, and the end seems to have come with dramatic abruptness at certain sites where layers containing Cro-Magnon tools lie directly above Neanderthal layers.

Impressed by such evidence, a number of investigators have suggested that the Neanderthals were wiped out in a relatively short time, almost as if by plan. It is doubtful that the capacity for systematic mass extermination evolved so early, however, and other evidence suggests a more gradual and complicated process. Conflicts and catastrophes probably took place here and there. Some of the new men may have regarded their less advanced contemporaries as some early American settlers regarded the Indians, as creatures so brutish and inferior that they could be hunted and killed for the fun of it.

But things happened somewhat more gradually in other places. One cave in the Les Eyzies area includes a layer that is probably Neanderthal but contains a tool kit with a relatively high proportion of knives, some of them made on long narrow flakes in a manner closely resembling later techniques developed to an advanced stage by Cro-Magnon flint workers. As a matter of fact, the resemblance is so close that at one time the layer was believed to represent a Cro-Magnon rather than a Neanderthal occupation. Perhaps Neanderthal man, having already experimented with new toolmaking techniques, learned quickly from the newcomers and joined their tribes in certain localities and eventually became assimilated. All of us probably have some Neanderthal genes.

In still other places Neanderthal bands may have retreated and hidden themselves in a last effort to endure. In fact, some prehistorians believe that they may not have died out yet, and several Soviet-led expeditions are reported to have gone into the Himalayas to check the theory that the "Abominable Snowman" is a surviving Neanderthal. Although this very slender possibility is not widely entertained, some evidence exists for less extreme theories. The last surviving wild Indian in North America, a member of a tribe of northern California, died in 1916 after having spent years living undetected with a few of his fellow tribesmen in forests and canyons near densely settled areas, and pockets of Neanderthals may have survived for centuries before the breed died out entirely.

This is the story of what happened, according to the migration theory. Investigators who do not go along with the theory agree that Neanderthal man was replaced by Cro-Magnon man, but they doubt that Cro-Magnon man came from the Near East. Their argument rests on the notion of independent origins, the notion that evolution can proceed along parallel lines in different parts of the world. The transition from Neanderthal to modern-type man took place in the Near East, to be sure, but not only in the Near East. It may also have taken place in a number of other places during the same general period.

Among other places, it might have happened in Europe. For example, consider the Les Eyzies cave containing the layer made up of Neanderthal as well as Cro-Magnon tools. That can be interpreted as indicating that the Neanderthals learned from and joined the visitors from the Near East. It can also be interpreted as a sign that the Neanderthals were developing on their own, and that in the process of developing they evolved into modern-type man. Judging by similar evidence, as well as studies of fossil remains, some investigators believe that the same development probably occurred some 4,000 miles away in South Africa.

There are hints that the transition may have occurred independently in the Far East. A mixed tool kit has also been found at the Chinese site mentioned in the last chapter, the one near the Great Wall. The site includes a high proportion of denticulates and other typical Neanderthal tools—but nearly a third of the tools are the sort found predominantly in Cro-Magnon sites. It is clearly a transitional type of tool kit, and may have been used by a transitional type of man.

We do not know enough to choose between the two theories. The migration theory finds strong support in the fact that as far as the fossil record is concerned, the best evidence for men in transition comes from the Near East. Certainly the change might also have taken place elsewhere, but in general, direct fossil evidence is limited. Furthermore, the notion of independent origins sometimes seems to lean too heavily on coincidence, on accepting that people in different places can make the same sort of tools without communicating with one another. There is something more direct and appealing about the idea of technologies spreading out from central regions of origin.

On the other hand, considering that people are far more alike than they are different and that they faced very similar problems in the prehistoric past, it should hardly be surprising that they generally arrived at very similar solutions. Then as now, people may well have developed inventions independently in different places. Also, the very appeal of the migration theory and a central region is something to be wary of. It has the attraction of any Garden of Eden theory, and the danger—namely, that it tends to oversimplify a highly complex situation.

In any case, the Neanderthals were definitely on the way out. They had learned to cope with glacial conditions, and their ability to endure is all the more impressive considering that as far as we know they had neither snowshoes nor sleds for getting about during long hard winters. But from about 35,000 years ago on all the action, all the new ideas and new inventions, would be the work of modern man, and for the next 25,000 years or so we know him best from the record he left in France, especially in the Les Eyzies area. The record includes four major types of tool kit dated by a method which, like the potassium-argon clock, depends on the steady rate of decay of a radioactive element, in this case a radioactive form of carbon known as carbon 14. The technique involves chemical analyses of charcoal samples, working best for material less than 40,000 years old. It has provided the following approximate durations for the following tool kits which for reasons to be discussed later are generally believed to reflect cultural differences and new levels of cultural development:

Perigordian, named after the region which includes Les Eyzies. More than 35,000 to about 23,000 years ago.
Aurignacian, named after the Aurignac site in the Pyrenees. About 35,000 to 20,000 years ago.
Solutrean, named after the extensive open-air site near the village of Solutré in east central France. 20,000 to about 17,000 years ago.
Magdalenian, named after the La Madeleine shelter about three miles from Les Eyzies. 17,000 to 12,000 years ago.

Recent investigations emphasize the complexity that lies behind this deceptively straightforward sequence. An interesting early Perigordian occupation layer has been found in a cave in the village of Arcy-sur-Cure about a hundred miles southeast of Paris, one of the few caves which happens to have been discovered by design rather than by accident. About twenty years

ago, André Leroi-Gourhan of the University of Paris was surveying the village for prehistoric camping places and noticed, high
on a hillside, a little shelter formed by a peculiarly curved section
of rock.

He suspected that the shelter might be the top of a buried cave,
a possibility reinforced by two further clues. Badgers in the area
are good cave locaters. They seem to sense the location of hidden
chambers that will make cozy nests, and, sure enough, there was
a badger hole in the hillside with some flint tools in it. Also, a
large oak tree was growing in the rich loosened soil near the foot
of the hill, another local mark of caved-in places. The first season
of digging revealed a thick layer of red earth rich in prehistoric
remains, and excavating has been going on at the site, off and on,
ever since.

The layer, which lies above Neanderthal layers, contains an
early Perigordian tool kit, including characteristic knives with a
curved back blunted by the removal of tiny parallel flakes as well
as denticulates and other tools commonly found in Neanderthal
deposits. A tentlike structure apparently existed inside the cave
entrance. There are a dozen postholes arranged in a semicircle
around several hearths; the posts were probably mammoth tusks.
One of the holes contained an intact tusk with a piece of limestone wedged against it for support. Leroi-Gourhan estimates that
a family unit of no more than fifteen persons lived here about
32,000 years ago.

Indications of how their descendants lived some 10,000 years
later come from a site just off the main street of Les Eyzies, the
Abri Pataud. (Abri is French for "shelter" and Pataud is the
family name of the farmers who owned the site in the nineteenth
century.) The site lies directly against the limestone cliff that
dominates the town, a few minutes' walk from the hotel built into
the old Cro-Magnon shelter. It has been excavated by Hallam
Movius of Harvard University. Bedrock was reached at a depth of
more than thirty feet after six seasons of digging which uncovered
fourteen occupation layers. In all, more than 50,000 worked
pieces of flint have been cataloged.

The third layer from the top contains a tool kit typical of those
generally found at more recent sites representing the last stages
of the culture, the evolved or final Perigordian of about 23,000

years ago. Its outstanding feature is a row of hearths more than thirty feet long under the rocky overhang of the shelter. Lying around the hearths are smooth river pebbles, most of them broken and colored red or black by the action of heat. These stones were very probably "pot boilers" that had been heated in a fire and then dropped into water to bring it to a boil for cooking. American Indians used the technique not long ago, and Basque shepherds in the Cantabrian Mountains of northern Spain still use it occasionally to boil milk and water.

Movius has tested this hypothesis by direct experiment. He heated some river pebbles, tossed them into a pail, and observed that they boiled water effectively. He also observed that after being used three or four times the stones split in two, and split into smaller and smaller pieces during subsequent plunges. When the pieces reached a certain size they no longer split but burst into fragments, a phenomenon which undoubtedly startled prehistoric man as much as it did Movius. This experiment produced shattered stones and fragments closely resembling debris in the Perigordian layer. Notice that it implies the existence of skin containers of some kind or, more probably, wooden vessels.

The row of hearths is only part of a large complex. In front of the row and also roughly parallel to the rear of the shelter is a row of large limestone blocks, some weighing half a ton or more. They form a solid barrier, except for a gap at one end which may have served as the "doorway" into a long house built for a community of several families. The entire arrangement as well as the tool assemblage found with it suggests that the people who lived here, huddled around their fires during glacial winters, organized themselves into larger groups and engaged in a wider variety of activities than the Perigordians of earlier times.

The Aurignacian tradition is quite distinct from the Perigordian. It includes the first known cave art. There are also special kinds of scrapers and burins, and a variety of elaborate bone tools such as points with split bases for firm hafting, presumably at the ends of spear or javelin shafts. Apparently the Aurignacians came from some area outside Western Europe, and they came with an established way of life, generally involving large all-year-round camps with a number of "satellite" sites nearby for special activities.

The deepest nine Abri Pataud layers, ending at bedrock and covering a period of about 4,000 to 5,000 years, contain Aurignacian tool kits. Signs of change during that period include sharp reductions in the proportions of some bone and flint tools and the appearance of new types, notably new bone points. Also, while later Aurignacians burned wood in their hearths, earlier generations of perhaps 33,000 or more years ago burned bone predominantly, probably because they lived under cold and relatively barren conditions when wood was scarce. Bone must have served as a last-resort fuel then as it did in even earlier times, the practice having been observed at a number of Neanderthal sites, for example, at Combe Grenal.

Movius found an unusual pattern in one of the early Aurignacian layers, a complex made up of two shallow pits and seven hearths. The pits are located near the front of the shelter, measure four to five feet across, and served some purpose which is still obscure. One possibility is that they may represent the floors of small conical huts made of hides supported by a central pole, something like American Indian tepees. (Pits of this sort have been found at Indian sites.) Eskimos make similar huts in the Canadian Arctic today, using large stones at the base to hold the hides down, and large stones were placed around the Abri Pataud pits.

Another noteworthy site is the Morin Cave in northern Spain, which was probably occupied on and off over a span of some 50,000 years and includes, besides the Neanderthal layers mentioned in the preceding chapter, a number of Aurignacian living floors. One of them is of special interest since it has yielded evidence of intensive occupation and a unique burial complex. Freeman's reconstruction of the past begins about 30,000 years ago when a family of about half a dozen members moved in, cleared off and leveled the floor, and proceeded to make themselves at home for ten to twenty-five years.

They dug a roughly rectangular depression about fifteen feet from the cave mouth, built stone walls, and set up a row of posts to support a windbreak or roof. Five postholes were detected because the soil filling them was softer and darker than the surrounding soil, and finer in texture. Also, in two cases the dark circular area included a still darker central area, suggesting that a post had rotted away and been replaced. Careful excavating even uncovered marks made by a digging stick when the posts were being replaced, curved grooves whose shape and location indicate that they were made by a right-handed person kneeling as he dug. The result of this construction was a shelter within a shelter, a semisubterranean hut inside the cave.

The most striking find came from a deeper part of the cave. More than forty feet from the entrance were two burial mounds, and one of them contained a remarkable object—a kind of natural earth-model, a rounded three-dimensional mold of a person and associated grave goods. What had happened over the years was that as the body decomposed, the soft parts were replaced by fine sediments which filled the cavities and ultimately produced a replica of the body, a so-called pseudomorph.

A study of the mold reveals that the buried person was more than six feet tall, and had been decapitated and laid on his side with arms flexed in front of his face. The mold also shows traces of what may be thongs or rope used to bind the arms, as well as another pseudomorph representing a small animal, perhaps a kid or deer, which had been placed over the dead person's head. Freeman spent more than a month digging in this area and preparing the earth around the burial so that it could be removed, with the aid of winches and a home-built railroad, as a solid two-ton clay block. A model of the Aurignacian pseudomorph is on exhibit at the Smithsonian Institution in Washington.

The more that is learned about such early settlement patterns, the more we realize how much remains to be learned. Research in all fields of science leads to the discovery of new problems, new surprises. If that is regarded as a measure of success, research in prehistory has certainly been successful. The very coexistence of the Perigordians and Aurignacians in France raises some questions that cannot be answered at present. They apparently hunted in the same regions under the same conditions during the same general period, living as contemporaries for thousands of years. Yet they seem not to have influenced one another appreciably, a surprising state of affairs considering man's capacity for minding his neighbor's business.

A clue may be found in their ways of life. Denise Bordes, who has specialized in studies of the prehistoric cultures of modern

Freeman Aurignacian "pseudomorph" model on exhibit at Smithsonian Institution

man, points out that as a rule the Perigordians are represented by relatively thin layers which suggest brief or intermittent occupations. Also, their sites are generally scattered throughout the Les Eyzies region and located in different kinds of terrain. The Aurignacians, on the other hand, tended to concentrate in narrow valleys or against cliff walls which contain clusters of neighboring shelters. Their layers are usually on the thick side, implying more people or longer occupations or both.

|The Solutrean tradition, which appeared about 20,000 years ago with the passing of the Perigordian and Aurignacian, arose during a period of intense cold. In fact, conditions were probably colder then than at any previous time during the past million years or more. The Scandinavian Ice Sheet covered Scotland and most of Ireland and, together with other glacial systems, held so much water that sea levels fell sharply. As in previous glacial periods, there was no English Channel and North Sea; a plain connected England and France, and the Baltic Sea was a vast fresh-water lake. People living in southern France had to contend with severe climates, with winters which may have lasted nine months and brought average temperatures as low as 10 degrees Fahrenheit below zero.

Philip Smith of the University of Montreal, who has made the most recent extensive study of the Solutreans, suggests that they may have originated in the southeast corner of France—in the lower valley of the Rhone River, not far from the edges of the Alpine glaciers. Occupation layers at a number of sites in this region include tools closely resembling those found in early Solutrean tool kits. The same layers also include Neanderthal tools such as thick Quina-type scrapers which, as far as we know, had disappeared from Europe and from the rest of the Old World some ten thousand years before.

|The possibility exists that the ancestors of the Solutreans were Neanderthals living past their time in a kind of "lost world" environment, or at least people who had learned Neanderthal toolmaking techniques. The discovery of skeletal remains in precisely dated deposits might help confirm this possibility. But the terrain would certainly have made a good retreat. The lower Rhone valley is a rugged mountainous land, a backwater with caves and shelters located in remote canyons and ravines. In such

a region people might not only have preserved old toolmaking traditions but also have developed unusual techniques.

The Solutreans did not endure for long, only about two or three thousand years. But during that relatively brief span they introduced significant changes, and some of the changes may be inferred from the nature of their flintworking. Along with scrapers and burins and quantities of other ordinary items, their tool kits included some of the most beautifully shaped tools ever made. To cite only one example, they produced so-called "laurel leaf" blades, slender symmetrical pieces flat and tapering to a point, and produced dozens of different kinds, long blades and short blades, thin and thick ones, all variations on the same basic theme. Some sites contained so many laurel leaves and other finely shaped tools that they may have been special workshops organized for a flourishing export trade.

In its extreme form such craftsmanship is the earliest sign of the can-you-top-this quality of human nature, the tendency to exhaust the possibilities of a technique or idea, to drive it into the ground. The same spirit that impels modern man to race engines to the breaking point or engrave as many Lord's Prayers as possible on the head of a pin or create the most elaborate op-art effects was working at full force in Solutrean man. Like most virtuosos, he was upon occasion carried away by his own abilities.

Many laurel leaves, for instance, are far too delicate for any practical purpose. The longest one known to date was found in 1873, part of a cache of blades uncovered at a site near the Loire River in southeastern France. It was nearly fourteen inches long, about four inches across at its widest point, and only about a quarter of an inch thick. The blade could never have been applied with any force. It would have snapped in two if someone had tried to cut meat with it or use it as a spear point.

Tools like this one represent a new stage in the development of abstract thinking. Hunters had spent extra time producing finely worked hand axes and other implements long before, 200,000 or more years before, but not with such skill and in such large quantities. As far as the archeological record reveals, the Solutreans were the first people to engage on a regular basis in the making of tools to serve as symbols. They doubtless used the tools for some special function, perhaps in rituals or simply as showpieces, a form of art for art's sake. Or the delicate laurel leaves may have served a more practical purpose, combining art and utility. They may have been items for trading, a kind of prehistoric money.

The Solutreans introduced other advances. They probably had —and may have invented—the bow and arrow. Not long ago Eduardo Ripoll-Perello of Barcelona University dug in a cave in the mountains of southeast Spain, the Cueva de Ambrosio, and found an assortment of points closely resembling arrowheads found by the thousands at American Indian sites. Indeed, if the same points had been uncovered at one of these sites, they would have been identified without question as arrowheads. Similar points have been found in other Spanish caves, and they provide the earliest indirect evidence for the invention of the bow and arrow. (The earliest direct evidence, from a 10,000-year-old open site in Denmark, consists of two arrow shafts preserved in water-logged deposits with tanged arrowheads still in place.)

Smith notes that the Solutreans usually lived near streams in foothill country. They may have preferred to do their big-game hunting along trails which avoided mountain regions as well as soggy lowland terrain, in relatively dry country which was suffi-ciently open to permit the easy spotting and pursuit of large animals, and yet contained enough trees and brush for fuel and cover. They vanished abruptly, "like the puffing-out of a candle flame," according to one investigator. There are many problems awaiting further research, research involving the use of modern techniques at certain well-known but not well-excavated sites (notably at the rich type site of Solutré).

At this point the stage was set for perhaps the most spectacular development of the period, the rise and rapid expansion of the Magdalenian tradition. Part of the record has been found at the site for which the tradition was named. It lies on the banks of the Vézère River, in the hollow of a massive limestone-cliff overhang. To reach it one climbs up one side of a ridge rising above the river valley, passes a ruined medieval abbey at the top, and then goes down the other side of the ridge along the long face of a cliff to a place surrounded by a high wire fence and marked "Abri de la Madeleine—Fouilles Interdites" (digging prohibited).

The setting is remote now, hidden in the trees on a hairpin loop of the river with water rushing past and meadows nearby. But things hummed here during prehistoric times, perhaps 13,000 to 14,000 years ago. This was predominantly reindeer country, and there were also herds of bison and wild horses in the valley and salmon in the rapids of the river. Collections from this site feature tools made of bone and antler and ivory and often decorated with engravings of reindeer, horses, bison, mammoths, abstract spiral designs, fish and stylized fish motifs, and, more rarely, crude human figures.

Magdalenian tool kits include shaft straighteners, spear points, "wands" of unknown purpose and, above all, the first harpoons—a rich variety of harpoons, long and short, with single and double rows of differently shaped barbs. There are also bone needles, first seen in Solutrean deposits but now developed and used in quantity, generally containing eyes which must have required piercing with tiny flint awls. The needles imply the wearing on a large scale of fitted clothing made of hides sewn together, presumably with sinews.

Another prominent item is the spear thrower, a device designed essentially to amplify muscle power, and still used today by the Australian aborigines. In its contemporary form it consists of a thin flat piece of wood about two or three feet long with a barb at one end that hooks into a hole in the end of a spear shaft. Held over the shoulder with shaft in place, the thrower is snapped forward by a sharp twist of the wrist in a motion that propels the spear several times faster and farther than would be possible with the unaided hand. Prehistoric hunters probably also had wooden spear throwers, although the only surviving specimens are made of antler or ivory. These devices disappear toward the end of Magdalenian times in France, perhaps because bows and arrows were beginning to be used on a widespread basis.

Excavations have been resumed at the La Madeleine shelter after years of archeological inactivity, except for the efforts of enthusiastic amateurs digging for discarded flints in the back dirt outside the wire fence. Jean-Marc Bouvier, one of Bordes' associates, has found large numbers of artifacts including narrow little blades which are less than half an inch long and were made as cutting elements to be hafted in composite tools. His main objective is to obtain a clearer picture of the origin and evolution of the toolmakers, and so far he has dug to a depth of more than twelve feet and identified several Magdalenian layers representing different stages of development.

The shelter itself is only part of a larger living complex. It marks the first in a line of prehistoric "row houses," occupied shelters strung out side by side for several hundred feet along the cliff. About twenty miles farther downstream along a two-mile stretch of the Dordogne River is another row of shelters which housed an estimated 400 to 600 persons. This sort of housing pattern is often associated with the Magdalenians, particularly during their later stages. They tended increasingly to establish large concentrated settlements along low-lying river banks.

Such settlements were not confined to shelters and cliff edges. Rich and thick occupation layers, as yet unexcavated, extend out to the Vézère River at La Madeleine, and it seems that the people lived and worked in the open here and elsewhere, perhaps using the shelters only in the worst weather. As archeologists became more and more aware of this tendency, they began paying serious attention to reports of extensive open-air sites in areas containing no caves or shelters. Flints kept turning up during the plowing season on highland farms on the plateaus above the cliffs.

Most digging has been done in caves and shelters, which contained deep protected deposits with many occupation layers and offered the opportunity to go far back in time and reconstruct cultural changes. Current interest in sites on the open plains is in line with the renewed emphasis on wide excavations and the search for evidence of what people did, their full range of activities. A number of sites, known for some time in a broad area extending from Western Europe to Siberia, were home bases for hunters of the woolly mammoth. (These are the creatures which in recent times have been found deep-frozen and almost perfectly preserved in Arctic ice crevasses where they fell millennia ago.)

For example, extensive traces of the hunters and their prey have been uncovered along the Don River in the southwestern Soviet Union. A cluster of rich sites is located near Kostenki, Russian for "bone village," where mammoth fossils were found in medieval times and regarded as the remains of half-human giants who lived in underground caverns. This area includes a row of eight hearths in which bone was burned, almost certainly because wood was scarce on the plains; the hearths may have been

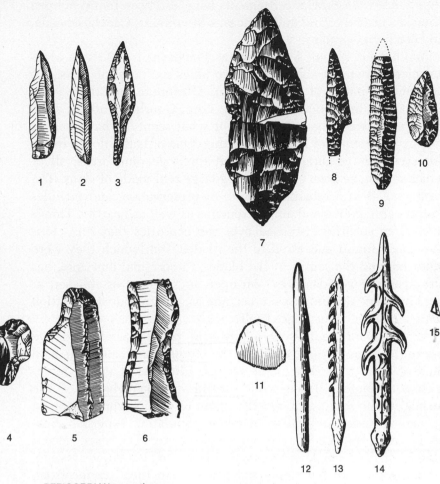

PERIGORDIAN: more than
35,000 to 23,000 years ago

1, 2, 3. typical Perigordian
points

AURIGNACIAN: about 35,000 to
20,000 years ago

4. nosed scraper
5. nosed scraper
6. blade

SOLUTREAN: About 20,000 to
17,000 years ago

7. laurel leaf

8. shouldered point
9. willow leaf
10. unifacial point (worked on
one side only)

MAGDALENIAN: 17,000 to
12,000 years ago

11. scraper
12, 13. harpoon with single
row of barbs
14. harpoon with double row
of barbs
15. triangle

Major tool kits of modern-type prehistoric men in Europe

located inside a long house with a gabled wooden roof and clay-supported walls. Similar settlements have also been found in open stretches near the Ural and Caucasus Mountains, Czechoslovakia, and northern Germany.

Another interesting site known as Pincevent is a 25-acre Magdalenian settlement about thirty-five miles southeast of Paris, not far from the palace of Fontainebleau. After more than three years and 300,000 man-hours of digging, Leroi-Gourhan and his associates uncovered about five acres of what seems to have been a summer-fall camp for reindeer hunting. One of half a dozen living floors consists of three hearths and three sleeping areas, all of which may have been enclosed by a large tent made of skins. The entire site is in a remarkable state of preservation, and includes considerable pollen and animal remains as well as hearths. Things have been so little disturbed over the centuries that tiny chips have been found and fitted to the blades from which they were removed, and the source of the blades, the original flint core, has also been recovered nearby. An open-air museum established at the Pincevent site promises to become as great a tourist attraction as the Fontainebleau palace itself.

All the evidence tells of a powerful people who could live where they wanted to live, where the big herd animals were. And there is more than that in the record. Life was changing in response to factors beyond the control and knowledge of the people, as the result of a complex chain of events which involved geological forces and caused a major population explosion. Surviving signs of the change are everywhere. The most recent Magdalenians, people who lived 14,000 to 12,000 years ago, occupied three to four times more sites than their predecessors, and occupied a large number of sites that had never been used before.

The change can also be seen at individual sites. At La Madeleine, for example, most occupation layers extended out from the cliffside toward the river. But the most recent layers happened to be by far the most extensive. They are also the widest and thickest and richest, including the most tools and the greatest variety of tools. The same pattern emerges at other sites, and it has been estimated that the total population of France alone increased from 15,000 to 50,000 during this period (in a world containing perhaps 10 million persons).

Artist's conception of camouflaged Magdalenian hunters stalking reindeer

Artist's conception of Cro-Magnon home, showing tents in rock shelter

New studies, particularly those of Lewis Binford, indicate that the population explosion may have been one result of widespread geographical and biological changes accompanying the retreat of the Scandinavian Ice Sheet and other glaciers. The changes depended on the shape of the ocean basins, on the contours of lands beneath the sea. In general the bottom does not dip sharply from the shoreline on out. There is a long gradual slope, amounting to a very gentle downhill grade and forming the so-called continental shelf, which may extend as much as 800 miles (off the Siberian coast in the Arctic Ocean). The shelf ends rather abruptly, with a precipitous drop at the edge to ocean floors more than two miles deep.

If sea levels started dropping today, and dropped at a steady rate of a foot per day, the slope of the continental shelf is such that in ten days the waves of the earth's oceans would recede about a mile on the average, adding that much dry land to national coasts. In a year or so sea levels would fall enough to expose some 11,500,000 square miles of land that had once been submerged, a total area about the size of Africa. Most of the great harbors of the world would become lesser inland cities with a wide coastal plain separating them from the sea. New York City, for example, would lie stranded more than a hundred miles from the Atlantic Ocean.

This is the way things stood about 20,000 years ago during early Solutrean times when the glaciers had completed one of their major advances. Masses of ice more than a mile high covered vast areas and captured enough water from the oceans to lower sea levels by 250 to 500 feet, exposing most of the continental shelf throughout the world.

Other changes affected the course of evolution. The coasts were more turbulent places than they are now and considerably less hospitable to life, human and otherwise. Since the land generally extended to the steep edge of the continental shelf, the waters along the shores were deep and cold. They contained relatively small quantities of plankton and other species, which provide food for schools of larger fish. Furthermore, most major rivers tended to flow swiftly into the seas, often cascading with a roar over the edge of the shelf—and such conditions are not particularly attractive to organisms which prefer quieter environments. According to Binford, only a few species of mollusk, mussel-like organisms, clung in clusters to rocks near the cascades, as compared to more than forty species found in the sluggish flat delta regions of today's rivers.

More abundant times came with the melting and retreat of the glaciers. Ocean levels rose and waters crept back across the plains of the exposed continental shelf, covering them with a wide sunlit and sun-warmed shallow sea, a natural marine farmland where many forms of life flourished. And the cascades vanished, as rivers instead of spilling over the edge of the shelf flowed into the shallows and merged less violently with the seas. The sheer bulk of marine life along the world's seacoasts is estimated to have increased more than a hundred times during the period from 20,000 to 16,000 years ago, and it is no coincidence that man seems to have begun eating seafood on a large scale during this period.

Life changed in the interior as well as along the coasts. Salmon and other fish that migrate upstream to spawn could not negotiate high coastal cascades; but when the cascades disappeared, they began using the rivers increasingly as waterways. And they turned up in southern France, among other places, in the Dordogne River and its tributaries and in the waters rushing past the fields and trees outside the La Madeleine shelter. The region was also a stopping place for flocks of migratory birds on their way to new breeding grounds created by the retreating glaciers.

The development of harpoons was part of the new technology created to take advantage of these food sources. The existence of other equipment made of less durable material can only be inferred. American Indians living on the northwest coast of the Pacific camp at salmon runs, suspend basket traps in the falls, and remove the heads of the fish on the spot before bringing their catch back to the village for drying. Prehistoric people were capable of developing similar techniques. Sites exist along the Dordogne River, near rapids, where the banks are practically solid with fish scales, and salmon vertebrae are found in many sites occupied by the Magdalenians.

But their population explosion was not simply due to a larger food supply and the development of large-scale food preservation and storage. The chief difference was a more steady and reliable supply. Migratory fish and birds came at a most convenient season, during the spring when food yields from reindeer and other migratory animals declined because herds dispersed to take care of their young. Binford suggests that one result may have been an increased trend toward all-year-round settlements, reducing the need to pack up and move on to new hunting grounds, and permitting an adjustment of primitive birth-control measures. As long as mothers had to keep on the move, they were limited to one child every three or four years, because that was all they could carry. Nomadic tribes have always been forced to rely on abortion, infanticide, and taboos against becoming pregnant during lactation, and these practices could be relaxed in more settled times, with fish and fowl to supplement basic supplies of reindeer meat.

According to this reconstruction of times past, all the conditions favoring expansion and population explosions had existed before, during former glacial retreats—that is, all but one. More ancient times had seen floodings of the great coastal plain and the vanishing of cascades beneath rising waters and migrations of previous generations of fish and birds. The new ingredient this time was a breed of man with the technology and capacity for social organization required to exploit the changing environment.

The record is rich in Western Europe, not only because the region was densely occupied in prehistoric times, but also because so many archeologists have lived and excavated there. But man was evolving all over the world, multiplying and expanding into a great many other regions. For example, hunters reached Australia at about the time when Aurignacian families were settling down in the Abri Pataud and Morin Cave, an outstanding achievement considering that the crossing required some island-hopping and boats seaworthy enough to negotiate perhaps 50 to more than 100 miles of open water. Finds in Australia include the world's oldest ground stone axes, reliably dated back at least 18,000 years, which is so much earlier than anything comparable found in Europe or the Near East that one British investigator came, saw, and simply refused to accept the evidence.

People entered the New World somewhat later, perhaps 15,000 to 20,000 years ago, and apparently did not have to make a water crossing. The glaciers had begun to melt, but sea levels were still

Mass slaughter site: fossil bison remains from Olsen Chubbuck site, eastern Colorado

low and men followed mammoths, mastodons, bison and other immigrants over a plain more than a thousand miles wide connecting northern Asia and Alaska. North America has a number of spectacular mass-slaughter sites, generally located in marshy areas or stream beds, and often at sharp bends or meanders which form deep-cut natural walls and keep animals from escaping. The remains of about 200 bison have been found at one such site in Colorado. But it should be pointed out that although killing big game has always been a glamorous thing, most bands subsisted on a day-to-day diet also including ample quantities of small game as well as plant foods.

Changes were under way at an accelerating rate and on a worldwide basis, social and psychological changes some of which can be inferred from studies of flint artifacts. If assemblages of Neanderthal tools from two widely separated sites in Western Europe were thoroughly mixed, even an expert would find it extremely difficult to sort them out again. But in a similar experiment involving two tool kits from the period that started only a few millennia later, say two Solutrean tool kits, the job of unmixing would be much easier.

The difference represents a change in outlook. Neanderthal groups did not make tools according to strictly controlled and distinctive regional patterns. But later as populations increased and people lived closer to one another geographically, they unconsciously developed ways of increasing what Edwin Wilmsen of the University of Michigan calls their "social distance." They developed a new quality of self-awareness and group-awareness, a way of making themselves distinct from "the others," an enhanced sense of style which is reflected in the making of their artifacts. And with all this came a new breed of human being and modern races and a new brain, essentially the same brain which shapes man's activities today.

■ Death rituals and personal adornment as factors in the origin of art; the earliest known art "galleries" discovered in caves of France and Spain; ridicule of the Spanish nobleman who first recognized the cave paintings as the works of prehistoric man; speculations about the role of caves and cave art in prehistoric times; the relationship between retreating glaciers and the decline of cave art in Europe; the invention of agriculture and the end of prehistory

CHAPTER XI

The Golden Age of Prehistory

■ |Religion and art appear in the archeological record with the appearance of *Homo sapiens*, religion with Neanderthal man, and art with Cro-Magnon or modern-type man. The oldest known paintings have been found in association with occupation layers deposited more than 30,000 years ago, at least 40,000 years after the earliest known burial ceremonies. It seems that some forty millennia of evolution were required before descendants of the first "philosophers," the first men to think about death and an afterlife, found reasons to portray things that were important to them.

Art came with a burst in the sense that from the very beginning the record includes works performed in a mature and established style. This does not mean that art actually appeared full-blown, only that there is a major gap in our knowledge. The earliest hint of an esthetic sense in the forerunners of man comes from the Olduvai Gorge. Near the bottom of the gorge, in places where *Australopithecus* foraged more than 1,500,000 years ago, are lumps of translucent pale pink quartzite, all of them unworked and obtained from a single mineral deposit—and all apparently picked up and carried around.

Later during Acheulian times there were crude designs engraved on bone and occasional hand axes shaped far more beautifully than required for strictly utilitarian purposes. Such pieces may represent pride of craftsmanship more than art, but they

249

show that man was expressing feelings for proportion and symmetry several hundred thousand years ago. Many factors were undoubtedly involved in the origin of art itself, for example, the use of symbols connected with death rituals. The notion that death is an apparent ending only, that part of a man lives on, demands external signs of some sort—something that will remain intact after the rituals are done.

The earliest symbols known from excavations are the stones and ibex horns and cave-bear skulls which Neanderthal man arranged in patterns around his graves. Judging by an unusual piece of bone found in the Morin Cave, a piece with a vaguely defined animal-like form engraved on it, there were images he wanted to preserve. It would be most surprising if he had not produced other patterns as well, less enduring symbols of permanence, possibly designs and figures which vanished long ago.

Personal adornment was another precursor of art. There was a time before people cared enough about themselves, before they were sufficiently aware of themselves, to want to appear more attractive or add to themselves. Then something happened to bring an increasing self-consciousness, perhaps the presence of more people in larger groups, and the threat of a loss of identity. Part of the response was to color their faces and bodies, to use the personal pronoun more, and say in effect: "I am an individual; look at me. Pay attention to me. I am different, something special."

The earliest sign of the change comes from the Neanderthals, an interesting fact considering that style does not show up in their artifacts, or at least we have not learned to see style in their artifacts. There are the flowers at the grave in Shanidar, for instance. Also, Neanderthal sites commonly include natural pigments, probably to serve as cosmetics for the dead in "viewings" and burial ceremonies as well as for the living, lumps of black manganese and red ocher, some sharpened like pencils and others scratched presumably to make powder.

The new spirit flowered among Cro-Magnon people. They not only used cosmetics, but made the earliest known jewelry. They wore clothes decorated with rows of colored beads, ivory bracelets, necklaces of pierced teeth and fish vertebrae. Their more elaborate decorations were related to a general increase in the complexity of communal living, to the rise of more advanced mass-hunting methods. Jewelry may have done more than beautify. It may have helped to identify the clan or the status of people associating in groups too large for individuals to know one another by sight or name. At the same time, more complex rituals served to teach and sanctify more complex rules of behavior. This is the framework, the social context, in which art had its beginnings.

The world's first great art "movement" lasted more than 20,000 years, from Aurignacian to Magdalenian times. Some of its most spectacular products are found in underground galleries, away from natural light in the passages and chambers and niches of limestone caves, and indicate in a most vivid fashion how completely hunting dominated the attention and imagination of prehistoric man. He rarely drew people, and never anything that would be recognized as a landscape, although there are a wide variety of signs which have no obvious meaning to us. His overwhelming concern was with game animals seen as individuals, clearly defined and detached, and isolated from their natural settings.

It is difficult to conceive of a reason why most of this art should have been produced in parts of the Old World which are still centers of artistic endeavor in modern times. But such happens to be the case; the great majority of art caves are located in France and Spain. According to one count, France has sixty-five sites and Spain thirty. About half of all known sites are concentrated in three regions: along a ninety-mile stretch of the northern coast of Spain, in the French Pyrenees fifty miles south of Toulouse, and in the countryside around Les Eyzies.

The Les Eyzies region includes the largest cluster of art sites as well as the most striking of the lot, the famous Lascaux cave located in the woods on a plateau above the valley of the Vézère. Four boys and a dog discovered it during a walk early one September afternoon in 1940, the dog disappearing down a hole half-concealed by roots and moss and the boys scrambling after. (Boys are officially credited with the discovery of about a dozen art caves, but the unofficial count would be considerably higher, since archeologists often receive sole credit for caves they originally learned about from boys in the neighborhood.)

What they were the first to see by the wavering light of a

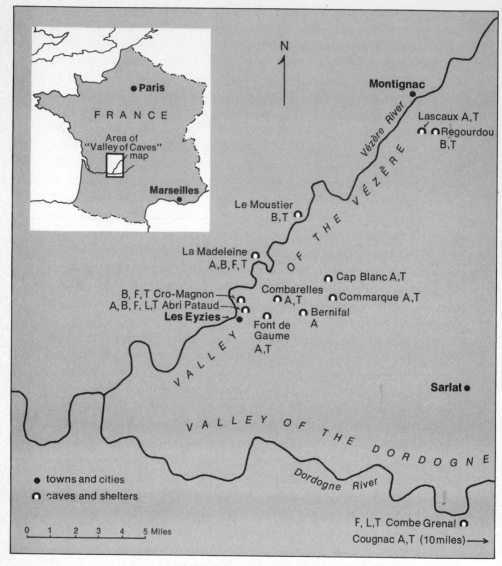

"VALLEY OF CAVES"

Homo sapiens Sites, in Les Eyzies Region, France

Things Found:

A art
B bones of primates
F fire

L living floors
T tools

homemade oil lamp thousands of visitors, tourists as well as archeologists and artists, have seen many times since. There is no prelude to the splendor of this gallery.|The entrance leads down a short flight of stairs directly into the main hall, into a world of huge horned animals painted red and black. In a way, the first moment is the high point of the visit. You stand silent in the dark and lights are turned on and images appear as if projected on a screen, in a kind of three-dimensional panorama since the wall curves in front of you and around at the sides. For that moment, almost before the eye has a chance to look and before the ideas and questions start flowing, you take it all in at once.

Then the experience breaks into parts. The animals become individuals in a frieze along the upper wall of the hall, along an overhanging ledge formed by the scooping-out action of an ancient river. Four bulls in black outline with black curving horns dominate the assemblage; one of them, the largest cave painting yet discovered, measures eighteen feet long. Two of the bulls face one another, and five red stags fill the space between them. The frieze also includes six black horses, a large red horse, three cows, a so-called "unicorn" which is actually a two-horned creature resembling no known species, and a number of other animals which are difficult to distinguish because they are partly covered by more recently painted figures.

|Below the frieze two dark holes mark passages which branch off from the main hall and lead to places underground which have not yet been thoroughly explored. The left-hand passage slopes downhill far into the rock. It contains more than forty pictures, among them a group of six large horses and three cows covering part of the wall and the entire ceiling near the entrance, a menacing black bull with head and horns lowered, and a brown horse falling over backward at the end of the passage, that is, the end of the easily navigable part of the passage. From here on it narrows to a twisting tunnel which runs still deeper into as yet uninvestigated parts of the cave.

The other passage is even more intriguing. A small chamber, which looks like a rather uninteresting dead end until one comes closer, lies off to the side. One must step carefully at this point because there is a pit here under a domed ceiling covered with a tangle of engraved lines and crisscross patterns and unidentifiable

Lascaux cave: ceiling paintings in one of galleries leading off main hall

Lascaux cave: close-up of
head of largest bull, about
18 feet, in main hall

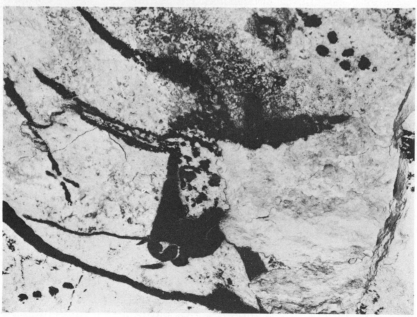

remnants of some red and black paintings. The edge of the hole is worn smooth as if many persons had lowered themselves to the bottom in times past, perhaps by rope. (A fragment of three-ply rope has been found in the cave.)

Today an iron ladder extends into the pit. It leads to a ledge and a work unique in the records of cave art—a buffalo disemboweled by a spear through its hindquarters, a stick-figure man with a bird's head falling backward directly in front of the buffalo, a pole with a bird on it below the man, and to the left behind the man a two-horned rhinoceros. This enigmatic scene has been often and variously interpreted. François Bordes has one

Lascaux Cave: Enigmatic scene in the Shaft of the Dead Man

version which he will impart if pressed, and if you do not take him too seriously: "Let me tell you my story of this painting, a science-fiction story. Once upon a time a hunter who belonged to the bird totem was killed by a bison. One of his companions, a member of the rhinoceros totem, came into the cave and drew the scene of his friend's death—and of his revenge. The bison has spears or arrows in it and is disemboweled, probably by the horn of the rhinoceros. This is how it was."

The most remote part of the cave lies more than two hundred feet past the pit, known as the Shaft of the Dead Man. The way in becomes lower and lower until one must crawl along, winding past little alcoves containing engravings of lions and other animals. Then it crosses a shallow pit, and ends at a cleft blocked with clay.

Lascaux has been closed to the public ever since 1963, and most prehistorians believe it should never have been opened in the first place. The more popular a cave, the faster its art deteriorates, mainly because exhaled carbon dioxide reacts with limestone and accelerates the erosion of rock surfaces and the formation of calcium films that obscure paintings. This happened at Lascaux. In addition, little patches of green, colonies of green algae, began spreading over the walls. Things have now been brought under a measure of control. For one thing, *le mal vert* has been conquered with the aid of an antibiotic spray including penicillin and streptomycin, and there has been some talk about a grand reopening, perhaps with a built-in glass tunnel which would help protect the art from the effects of exhaled air. But since the risk of renewed deterioration is still great, the cave will probably remain closed indefinitely to tourists, although a limited number of anthropologists and other investigators may obtain special permits.

Two major art caves are located some fifteen miles downriver from Lascaux in Les Eyzies: Font-de-Gaume and Les Combarelles. Font-de-Gaume has about two hundred paintings and engravings, many of which have also deteriorated, but after several visits one learns to follow the sweep of the visible lines, imagine the missing lines and re-create paintings which in their original condition may have surpassed those of Lascaux. After the closing of Lascaux, tourists turned to Font-de-Gaume in increasing numbers, causing the paintings there to fade faster than ever. At one time it seemed this cave would also have to be closed, but that has not yet been necessary. The walls received a careful washing, and some of the paintings are brighter and clearer than they have been for years.

Les Combarelles consists of a long narrow passage containing more than 300 engravings, many of which cannot be seen unless they are lighted from the side and at just the right angle. The region includes many other sites—the Cap Blanc shelter with a frieze of six sculptured horses; Bernifal and its engraved mammoths, one of them hidden in a narrow fissure; and the Cougnac cave, supposedly found by divining-rod methods, which includes a large elk in black outline and, drawn inside the elk just above its foreleg, a human figure with three spears or darts stuck in it.

There is also the little cave of Commarque, at the foot of a cliff under a ruined medieval castle. Commarque is noted for a magnificent horse's head which has been engraved at about eye level in a narrow side gallery and may be extremely difficult to find. One cannot see the engraving, which is about two feet long, unless the light of his lamp strikes the limestone surface at just the right angle. Some people have searched for several hours without finding it, while others find it after only a few minutes. (I explored the cave with three other searchers, and it took us about forty-five minutes to locate the engraving.)

The art of prehistoric man has inspired some strange and wonderful responses in us, his latter-day descendants. In the beginning, perhaps inevitably, the main response was violent disbelief and ridicule; as usual, the main reason was the traditional tendency to underrate people who lived so long ago. The tendency is understandable. After all, it seems reasonable to suppose that the lower their status, the higher our own would appear by comparison. But it does not work out that way, because modern man is so close to them that efforts to belittle the past always belittle the present as well.

The first man to present a good case for the antiquity of cave art was laughed out of court. In 1875 Don Marcelino de Sautuola, a nobleman and amateur archeologist, started investigating a cave called Altamira discovered near his estate, in the village of Santillana del Mar on the northern coast of Spain—again, as at Lascaux, after a dog had disappeared down a hole in the earth. He worked on and off for four years, often with his young daughter Maria for company, collecting bones and artifacts not far from the mouth of the cave and not far from a side chamber with a very low ceiling. He had gone into this chamber a number of times on his hands and knees, always looking down in an unsuccessful search for a place to dig.

One day Maria, who was twelve years old at the time and did not have to crawl, wandered into the chamber and looked up and saw paintings by candlelight. It must have been a breathtaking sight, as if one were viewing Font-de-Gaume fresh and in its original state. Even today, after appreciable fading, it is perhaps the most impressive cave-art exhibit, now that Lascaux is closed to the public. The ceiling looks something like an upside-down relief map of low hilly country, and animals up to seven feet long have been engraved and painted on its bulges and hollows to give an almost sculptured sense of three dimensions. About twenty of the paintings are in good condition, including some fifteen bison drawn in red and yellow and black with delicate line and shading.

The events which followed that day at Altamira demonstrate that given the right set of prevailing beliefs, one can avoid discovering practically anything. Caves have always been exciting places. Surprises and dangers are to be found underground, shapes high in the rocks and colors and moving shadows, miles of winding galleries in which to get lost, water dripping into pools so black they seem solid, chambers so large that lamps do not reveal the ceilings and winds rush past as on a mountainside. The urge to explore this unexpected world runs as deep in us as it did in our prehistoric ancestors.

Local people and tourists had been going into art caves for generations, and often saw the paintings and engravings. But the experience simply did not register; only the mildest sort of curiosity was aroused. During the early 1800's a guide to the Niaux cave in the French Pyrenees, which contains many beautifully executed pictures, told museum officials in the area about the art and, as far as we know, nothing ever came of it. In 1864 an archeologist visited the cave and entered the following comment in his diary: "There are some paintings on the wall. What on earth can they be?" And nothing came of that either.

De Sautuola had no trouble answering this question. He was convinced on the spot. The figures on the ceiling at Altamira were very much like those he had seen the year before at the Paris World's Fair, figures engraved on pieces of bone and antler and already identified as the work of prehistoric man. (One engraving found at La Madeleine not only depicted an extinct animal, a woolly mammoth, but was done on a fragment of mammoth tusk which had been fresh at the time it was worked.)

Most authorities found this line of reasoning too direct. They were ready to accept engravings on bone, but not engravings or paintings on cave walls. They balked at the notion that people who wore skins and used stone tools went deep into underground places equipped with pigments, brushes, lamps and other artist's supplies—and with the purposes and imagination required to create fine polychrome paintings. A Spanish artist offered the following argument to prove that such work must have been done by one of his contemporaries:

There are perhaps twenty figures, some life size, in profile on the vault of the roof, attempting to imitate antediluvian quadrupeds. Their execution shows no sign of primitive art. . . . By their composition, strength of line and proportions they show that their author was not uneducated. And though he was not a Raphael he must have studied Nature at least in pictures or well-made drawings. As is seen by the abandoned mannerism of their execution, such paintings have none of the character of either Stone Age, Archaic, Assyrian or Phoenician art. They are simply the expression of a mediocre student of the modern school.

Within a year of the Altamira find prehistorians attending an international congress in Lisbon challenged the claims of de Sautuola for a number of reasons, most of them quite plausible. The paintings seemed far too sophisticated to jibe with current ideas about the sophistication of Cro-Magnon man; the pigments were amazingly fresh; the limestone crumbled so readily that it was difficult to understand how the painted surfaces had remained intact; and so on. A Spanish professor administered the finishing touch by dismissing the paintings as forgeries and revealing to his assembled colleagues the identity of the presumed forger, an artist who had been living at de Sautuola's estate for a number of years.

That dampened official interest in cave art until just before the turn of the century, when resistance began to crumble under the pressure of new evidence. In 1895 a local archeologist reported paintings and engravings in a Les Eyzies cave, and although the find was greeted with the old cry of forgery, it encouraged another archeologist to report the existence in a cave near Bordeaux of art he had first seen more than ten years before. This news in turn attracted the attention of one of de Sautuola's bitterest opponents, who changed his mind after visiting the French caves and unearthing one painting himself.

Soon reports were coming from many quarters. In 1901 a group of prehistorians guided by a local farmer found pictures at Les Combarelles and, a week later, at Font-de-Gaume. One of the group, the young priest Henri Breuil, was to spend the next six decades reproducing and studying cave art. In 1902, fourteen years following the death of de Sautuola, he visited Altamira and helped establish the authenticity of its paintings. Not long afterward half a dozen further art caves were found within a few miles of Altamira.

About 120 art caves have been discovered to date, and the list is growing at a rate of about one new cave every year or two. Among recent finds are a cave overlooking the Lot River in southwestern France containing more than seventy engravings, several caves in Italy, and a cave in Brittany which has not yet been fully investigated. Another new cave in northern Spain is entered by rope ladders, has a river running through it—and includes a large wall panel with a dozen reindeer and horses and, half a mile deeper through muddy passages to a dead end, a number of abstract designs. The general practice is not to divulge the locations of new sites so that visitors will keep away until thorough studies are completed. Further discoveries can be expected. For instance, one archeologist hopes to reopen a French cave sealed off by a road-construction crew a number of years ago, because there is good reason to believe that it contains important paintings.

Any attempt to interpret prehistoric art must take account of the fact that artists had more immediate and wider responsibilities in earlier times than they do today. Human evolution requires learning, teaching, passing ideas on from generation to generation. For such things modern man has the written word. Prehistoric man had only memory and symbols, including spoken words and the only symbols that have left traces, the items we call art. He evolved and preserved traditions without writing, an example of adaptation on a par with living in glacial climates without snowshoes or sleds—and in the absence of writing, art carried an extra heavy cultural load.

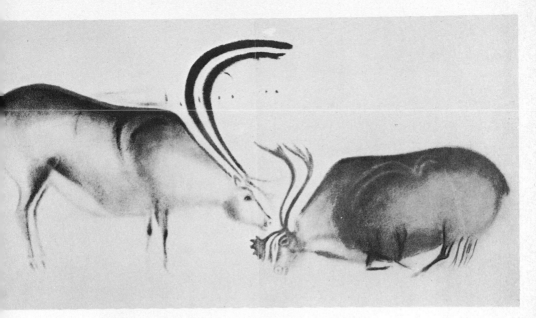

Font-de-Gaume cave: facing male and female reindeer

Altamira: curled female bison

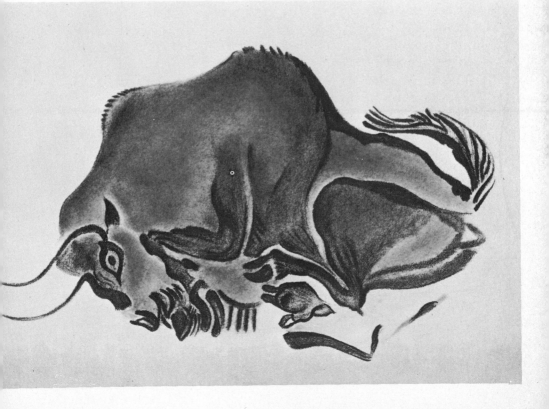

Cast of Venus figurine found at Willendorf, Austria

Prehistoric art served a number of purposes, perhaps the least complicated being to bring color and form into the home. Most paintings and engravings in living spaces at cave mouths or in rock shelters have disintegrated because they were exposed to the weather. Some complete figures survive, however, and remnants often turn up during excavations. Among debris found in occupation layers at Abri Pataud are fragments of rock colored red and black which broke off nearby walls and were once part of large paintings, while at another site Bordes has seen a painted foot on a large piece of fallen rock.

Les Trois Frères cave, French Pyrenees: the "sorcerer," one of the most famous expressions of prehistoric art

In a recent analysis of cave art, the first really critical analysis, Peter Ucko and André Rosenfeld of University College of London and the British Museum, respectively, consider it likely that such work "was intended to enliven and brighten domestic activities." There was also "furniture" art, pieces which could be moved in to make Cro-Magnon chambers more attractive, sculpted and painted limestone blocks probably propped up against convenient walls. Small statues of women, so-called Venus figurines, most commonly found in southern Russia and other Eastern European sites, may have had some special family significance since they tend to be associated with houses such as those constructed at Kostenki, often placed in special storage pits under the floor.

Other purposes are more elusive and involve a shift from open living quarters to hidden chambers and passages, from light to darkness. Most cave art is located deep underground, and some works are extremely difficult to get at. In Arcy-sur-Cure, Leroi-Gourhan once guided me through a small cave which extends only about a hundred yards into a cliffside, but it was a long hundred yards. The entrance was a "torpedo tube," a horizontal tunnel just about big enough for a man to squeeze into. He went in headfirst, wriggling along salamander-fashion and pushing a lamp in front of him over the muddy floor, and I followed.

Crawling is hard work with solid rock all around and one's face usually an inch or so above the mud and sometimes in it. At one point the tunnel becomes even more constricted, and I had to hunch my shoulders and inhale deeply to force myself through. (I learned later that Breuil became stuck in this part of the tunnel at the age of sixty-nine, and had to be pulled and shoved through; it was one of the last caves he ever explored.) Further hazards existed on the way to a chamber with engravings in it, including a place where one had to skirt the slippery edge of a pit leading to still deeper passages.

Even after negotiating such passages, additional problems may be encountered in finding the art. For motives which remain obscure but which certainly involved the deliberate creation and overcoming of obstacles, the artists often chose surfaces difficult of access where they would have to work in cramped and awkward positions—in crawl spaces and alcoves, close to the floor, crammed into corners, above and at the bottom of pits like the Shaft of the Dead Man at Lascaux. Near the end of the main gallery at Font-de-Gaume is a narrow damp place where the rock has split. You climb a ladder built into the fissure for the convenience of visitors, lean backward and twist your head sharply to the left, and see engraved at eye level ten feet or so above the floor a group of horses and a lion nearby, apparently ready to pounce.

There are many such places, and also many exceptions. Some art-cave entrances are wide enough to house factories, and were used to house factories during World War II. The majority of paintings and engravings are located so that they can be seen readily by lamplight, provided, of course, that one knows where to look. But the significant element in practically all cases is the trip underground, often by long and tortuous routes, to out-of-the-way but not necessarily secret or private places, and accounting for this phenomenon is one of the most challenging long-range problems in the study of prehistory.

An important clue involves Cro-Magnon man's concern with his effectiveness as a provider. Half the battle in hunting and fighting is confidence; and if he was anything like modern man, he used ritual on numerous occasions to help replenish and increase his powers. Perhaps he cast spells on his prey. Certain places in the depths of caves are covered with superimposed figures, figures drawn one on top of the other and overlapping as if the artists paid little attention to the work of their predecessors but considerable attention to where the art was located. They also represented some animals with darts or spears sticking into their sides, for example, the bison in the Shaft of the Dead Man, which may have been killed ritually in revenge for the death of a hunter.

Similar practices have been observed in modern times. As recently as a decade or two ago, for example, aborigines living in the stony tablelands and mountains of northern Australia prepared themselves for a successful hunt by painting animals they wanted to kill on sacred spots in rock shelters and ravines. The prehistoric use of hunting magic might explain why people seldom appear in cave art, the idea being that drawing the human figure could bring death or injury to other members of the group. It may be significant that cave art reached a peak toward the close of the Magdalenian period when herds were becoming smaller. Most of the great polychrome paintings seem to have been done during this period, which also saw an apparent increase in depictions of slain animals, suggesting one last ritual effort to restore the abundance of times past.

Another possible use of art was in initiation ceremonies. In many primitive tribes coming of age is a time of ordeals and revelations. To prove himself as a man and a hunter the adolescent may suffer mutilation and inflicted pain, starve himself, go without sleep, take hallucinogenic drugs and emetics—and then go out alone to sites in the wilderness to have visions and communicate with some sort of guardian spirit and perform a feat like catching an eagle and killing it with his bare hands, an old Blackfoot Indian custom. A cave would be an ideal place for such experiences. The darkness and shadows and eerie settings, enhanced by figures of animals and mystical signs, might well encourage a person to see and hear things during long vigils even without the suffering and fatigue and drugs. The feat might be to find hidden art, and leave your own work or mark to prove you had found it.

A hint of prehistoric initiations was discovered more than sixty years ago when a man and his son rowed a boat into the Tuc d'Audoubert cave in the French Pyrenees. A stream, the remnant of a swift river that had originally formed the cave, took them to a gravel beach and a passage leading to a hall with a pond in it and white stalagmites and stalactites. At the end of the hall they climbed a steep slope or "chimney." Breaking through a sheet of stalagmite at the top, they followed a tunnel several hundred yards through chambers and a torpedo-tube section, and found not far from the end of the cave a large circular room with two clay statues of bison propped up against a rock at the center. Near the statues is a clay area with small heelprints in a circle, as if children had danced there, perhaps preparing for a vigil or ordeal. Speaking of the dance, Aurignacian pipes made of hollow bone and containing well-cut fingerholes have been found in at least one French cave.

Several theories involve what may have been meeting rooms. There are several such places, including one not far from the Tuc d'Audoubert bison and another in a Spanish cave, where one climbs to the top of a natural platform and looks down on a chamber and practically sees the audience looking up at one. Engraved on a wall of the French chamber is a large figure of a man dressed in an antler headgear and reindeer skin, which may represent a sorcerer or a teacher. (The difference between the two was probably not great in prehistoric times.) Some of the art found on cave walls, as well as on bone and antler, hints at a kind of scorekeeping or counting. Alexander Marshack of Harvard, in a continuing study involving intensive microscopic examinations of many signs and symbols, suggests that certain sets of dots and parallel lines are calendars based on phases of the moon—and that seasonal rituals and a mythology may be represented in associations of plants, animals, fish, fishing and wading birds, and other figures.

These theories all have a measure of plausibility and should make one thing clear: no single notion, however ingenious, can account for even a major proportion of the observed facts. People were doing many things with their art and with their caves. The caves represent protoinstitutional sites before the coming of separate specialized institutions; from time to time they probably served as prehistoric archives, shrines, playgrounds, offices, schools, vigil places, theaters. Indeed, for limited periods at least some of them may have been as bustling for those times as downtown business and cultural centers are today. Generally speaking, the more we learn about settled communities in open-air sites like those near Kostenki and Fontainebleau, the more carefully we must reexamine our notions about how people used caves.

It should also be clear that investigators are long on guesswork and short on evidence. All they have to go on is a mass of unanalyzed observation and imagination, and that is not enough. In the past the tendency has been to present a theory as the last word, with a this-is-how-it-was attitude that discourages inquiry, rather than as a preliminary statement to be proved or disproved by fresh studies. This tendency was largely a result of the personality of the great prehistorian Breuil, who died in 1961 after dominating cave-art research as completely and almost as long as Louis XIV dominated France.

The priest was a jealous leader. At meetings he would shout down younger investigators who disagreed with him, and after a while they learned to keep their thoughts to themselves. One of his former students and a close friend for thirty years once dared to suggest in the mildest terms that Breuil might not have been entirely correct about the authenticity of the art in a certain cave, and he never spoke to her again. Another close friend summed things up as follows, after Breuil's death, of course: "As he got older and perhaps less sure of touch in his intuitions . . . he did not become less pontifical and it became more personally difficult to disagree with him."

Ideas have started to flow more freely during the past few years. The book by Ucko and Rosenfeld is an outstanding example of the new spirit, and so is a detailed study of more than sixty-five art caves by Leroi-Gourhan. He has made the first systematic large-scale effort to classify cave paintings and engravings, to find out what animals and signs are found most often in certain parts of caves, in different localities and at different times. For example, bison and horses appear more frequently than other animals in large chambers and passages, while such dangerous animals as bears and lions are usually found in hidden recesses and isolated places containing few other figures; and barbed signs and dots are found more frequently inside chambers and galleries off the main passage. Also, Leroi-Gourhan believes that the artists of 25,000 to 30,000 years ago tended to work near cave entrances, and that their descendants went deeper and deeper underground during the next ten millennia or so.

The French prehistorian, in short, is beginning to do for prehistoric art what Bordes has done for prehistoric technology. He is seeking significant associations, and at this stage that is more important than interpretations. (His notion that most cave art consists of sex symbols and deals almost entirely with sexual themes may reflect twentieth-century rather than prehistoric preoccupations.) Eventually the time will come for more sophisticated statistical techniques like the factor analysis which was used to analyze the Neanderthal tool data from Combe Grenal, and it may be possible to obtain more precise answers to some old unanswered questions.

The problem is to devise subhypotheses which if proved might lend weight to major hypotheses. For example, if superimposed figures included a high proportion of wounded animals, one would have more confidence in the hunting-magic theory. The initiation theory implies, among other things, that unusual objects might be found in vigil places. In primitive tribes persons undergoing such experiences generally bring good-luck pieces with them—polished or painted pebbles, clear quartz crystals, parts of animals, such as rabbit feet, and so on. Such items have been found in art caves, but they have never been looked for systematically. In fact, no major art cave has ever been excavated using modern techniques.

Research can take us only so far. We will never know what was in the mind of the artist who some 15,000 years ago forced himself into a "rathole" in the side of a cliff near Les Eyzies, slid into a pit, squeezed his way around two sharp turns, and when he came to a dead end rolled over on his back and, working on a surface only a few inches from his face, painted a little red and black horse. And what was the private mission of the other lone artist who walked nearly three-quarters of a mile through mud in a huge cave near Altamira and drew two horses in black outline, the only animal figures found in miles of chambers and galleries? There will always be awe and mystery, if that is what we want.

But it is also exciting to consider what may yet be discovered. The shift from intuition alone to intuition plus analysis, from speculations not designed for checking to scientific hypotheses, will bring us a great deal closer to prehistoric artists and to the roles they played in their communities. Perhaps, as a bonus, the new knowledge may affect our understanding of current insights and experiments. It may even bring us closer to the artists of our own times, and to a genuine awareness that they too are engaged in serious business.

The first great period of prehistoric art came to an end with the end of the Magdalenian culture about 12,000 years ago. Cultures had come and gone before, but this one had risen higher than any previous culture, and therefore subsequent events somehow seem like more of a letdown. What happened is plain in the record. Occupation layers at major Magdalenian sites are thick, extend far out beyond the area immediately in front of caves and rock shelters, and contain many tools and many varieties of tools. They represent the remains of a stable, powerful and prosperous people.

By contrast, the layers on top of the most recent Magdalenian deposits are meager. They are thin, so thin at certain sites that early excavators frequently missed them, and contain far fewer tools and more limited tool kits, including characteristically flat harpoons and many "microliths"—points, scrapers and other implements usually from half an inch to an inch long. Furthermore, they mark a kind of retreat, in general being confined to areas under sheltering rock and toward the face of the cliff. These are the remains of a shrinking and unsure people, the so-called Azilians (named after the Mas d'Azil cave in the French Pyrenees), who lived literally with their backs to the wall.

The Azilians hunted in the same regions where the Magdalenians had hunted and occupied many of the same sites. Like most dwindling people, they probably lived to a large extent in the past and told nostalgic legends about their ancestors, the mighty hunters of another age. On occasion they may have visited Lascaux and Altamira and other art caves, and wondered at the pictures on the walls. They left no art of their own, or at least no art worthy of the name. All we find at their sites are geometric designs painted on pebbles.

A world had passed, and for a surprising reason. The climate improved. There is always a danger in becoming too well adjusted, in developing practices and institutions that are too firmly established. The Magdalenians had mastered and flourished in the midst of bitter glacial conditions, but they were not ready for better times. Animal bones in an occupation layer at La Madeleine tell a familiar story of successful hunting, predominantly of reindeer together with the snow partridge, chamois and other subarctic species. But in the layer immediately above this one, the uppermost Magdalenian layer, reindeer are less abundant—and, especially significant, certain forest species such as the red deer and wild boar appear for the first time.

This change, also observed at many other sites, foreshadows the beginning of the end for the Magdalenian culture. The continuing retreat of the glaciers brought milder climates to the region and produced a series of further retreats. Species of grass which had adapted to glacial conditions and provided food for reindeer followed the glaciers north, the reindeer followed the grasses, and most hunters followed the reindeer or moved to coastlines and lived on other herd animals and seafood. The Azilians were descendants of those who stayed behind to carry on in the new environment as best they could, and, all things considered, they did well.

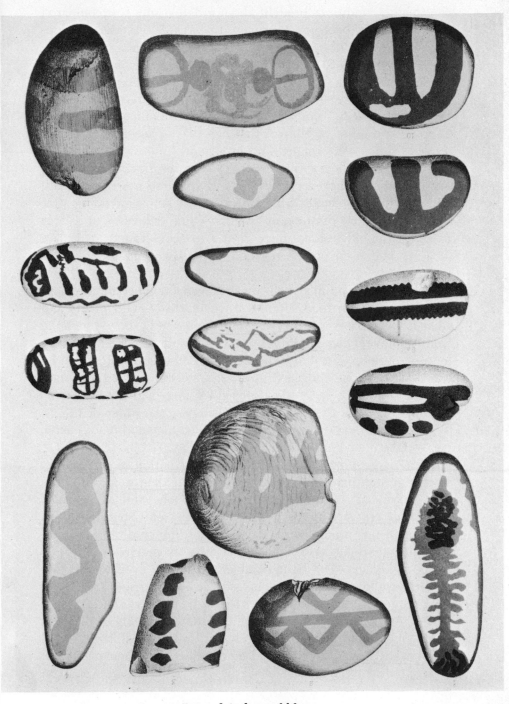

Painted Azilian pebbles

Although conditions brought about a defeat of a sort compared with what had been, one very positive result was the development of a new and ingenious way of life. Vast herds of game on the hoof were no longer around to be killed en masse by men lying in wait along traditional migration routes. The problem was to deal with more elusive forest animals which moved about in small groups and were agile, swift and camouflaged. Snaring, trapping and other techniques that had played secondary roles in reindeer times were refined and used more intensively; the bow and arrow may have evolved into a major weapon. The Azilians also leaned more heavily on fishing and acquired new food tastes, such as a taste for snails, which must have taken some doing after a diet of venison; presumably snails became delicacies at a later date. Incidentally, stone picks similar to those found at Azilian sites are still used on the northern coast of Spain to pry open mussels.

Up to this point man had always lived on what nature happened to offer, on food supplies in the form of wild plants and animals. The story of the Magdalenians shows how much he could achieve when conditions were right and remained that way for long periods. But it also shows, at the end, how vulnerable he was to changes beyond his control as long as he existed in a state of natural balance with other species. If man had not "cheated" by tinkering with the balance and changing the order of things, by producing food instead of merely collecting food ready-made, we would still be hunters and gatherers today.

The outcome of the tinkering was the invention of agriculture. That step took place in several areas independently, far from the river valleys of southwestern France, in such "underdeveloped" areas as Central America, the Near East and Southeast Asia which had not produced great art or hunting traditions. Significant changes may have been under way as much as 13,000 to 14,000 years ago. The basic change had begun even before that with the melting of the glaciers and the steady rise of sea levels which covered continental shelves throughout the world.

Different people adapted to the new environments in different ways depending on local resources and traditions. But in general populations soared, as they had among the Magdalenians, wherever settlements were established near shallow and abundant

waters and along the flyways of migratory birds, wherever supplies of fish and fowl existed to supplement diets based mainly on
meat and plant foods. One result was a widespread budding-off or
splitting process. Prehistoric pioneers left population centers and
moved on to less intensively settled lands. In Europe and elsewhere the migrants continued their hunting-gathering ways because they had no other choice, but in certain regions conditions
favored the development of crops and domesticated animals.

At present the evidence indicates that the world's first farmers
appeared in the Near East. Agriculture seems to have arisen in
the so-called Fertile Crescent along a 2,000-mile arc starting in
Israel and Jordan, extending up the eastern Mediterranean coast,
swinging around through southern Turkey and then southeast
following the Zagros Mountains of Iran to lands bordering the
Persian Gulf. A side branch of the arc runs 500 miles due west
along the coast of Turkey.

The region included plants and animals which did not exist in
Europe and which provided the basis for agriculture. There were
goats, pigs and sheep, and also massive stands of such common
weeds as wild wheat and barley. Many theories have been devised to explain how these species came to be domesticated. One
dubious but often-aired theory has it that people found the grain
good and stored it in their rock shelters for winter eating. Then
one spring day some leftover seeds started sprouting. Someone
noticed plants growing in a "magic spot" where nothing had
grown before, perhaps a dump pile where the earth had been
disturbed, and suddenly had the idea of planting seeds there on
purpose. Eventually the practice brought surpluses of food, some
of which could be used to nourish easily tamed animals.

This notion is in line with the Eureka theory of human progress, the idea that discovery comes in flashes to geniuses sitting in
bathtubs or under apple trees. But it is certainly not in line with
what we know about the evolution of *Homo sapiens*. It hardly
flatters our forebears to suppose that they spent their days in rock
shelters and used plant foods without recognizing why things
occasionally sprouted near living floors in the spring. It is likely
that the Neanderthals and their successors knew very well what
happens when seeds are planted in the ground, and that they
would have tried planting seeds if conditions had been right.

Furthermore, the Eureka theory implies the prompt, complete recognition and welcoming of discovery and all its results, and that rarely happens.

A theory involving the search for living space seems to jibe far better with the facts of life and with recent research findings. One of the most abundant occupation zones, for example, was located along the southeastern shores of the Mediterranean, where large communities existed in open oak parkland. People lived on a varied diet, a far better diet than any depending mainly on a single animal or plant, including deer, goats, wild cattle, fish, waterfowl, acorns, pistachios, and wild wheat. The very abundance created new problems as populations outran food supplies. Man had at last succeeded in multiplying beyond his means, at least on a local scale.

The time had come for a revolution whose leaders were anything but revolutionaries. The richest areas were becoming overcrowded, and some of the people had to move to less fruitful places. They were not crusaders or rebels. They were conservatives fighting to prevent change, to preserve the hunting-gathering way of life. But since there was not enough wild food in their marginal homelands, they took the all-important step of deliberately extending the range of a plant species, a point first emphasized by Kent Flannery of the University of Michigan. They transplanted wild wheat from its natural habitat on foothill and mountain slopes to places along seasonal streams where it would not normally flourish. This early venture in selective breeding worked because wild wheat, like many seeds, has a rich genetic potential and can adapt to a wide variety of conditions.

Agriculture was also taking shape at the other end of the fertile crescent in such sites as Ali Kosh, a village which flourished some ten millennia ago in the lowlands of southwestern Iran. The finding of more than 30,000 charred seeds indicates that wild plants were being gathered on a large scale. Furthermore, the collection includes one form of wheat which did not grow near the site and had to be brought in, perhaps for local cultivation, from zones some fifty miles away and about a thousand feet higher, in the foothills of the Zagros Mountains.

The general region also served as a natural habitat for wild sheep, wild goats, and other animals that have been domesticated. These animals were hunted here for at least 30,000 years before people settled at Ali Kosh, and the hunters may well have kept young animals as pets, a practice observed among such primitive tribes as the African Bushmen. (On occasion women will actually nurse the pets to keep them alive.) But there is no evidence of attempts at domestication. That step, like the domestication of wild grains, presumably came when the pressure was on—and the pressure was on at Ali Kosh, among other places. Studies of animal remains found in occupation layers show that about three-quarters of all the goats killed were yearlings, strongly implying systematic breeding and slaughtering, and domestication. There are also remains of domesticated sheep.

Early success favored further experiments. Pigs and cattle were domesticated after sheep and goats, peas and lentils after wheat and barley. Seeds became important items for trading, together with copper and obsidian, a black volcanic glass which makes very sharp tools, and bitumen, a brown tar used for cementing flint and obsidian pieces into hafts. (Bitumen was abundant in lands now exploited for petroleum.) Near Eastern foods and planting methods first appeared in Southeastern Europe about 8,000 years ago, and spread north and west during the next fifteen to twenty centuries. The polished stone ax, probably first developed to fell trees for dugout boats, became a major tool as people began clearing forests for farms.

Such activities were to finish off hunting as an essential way of life in Europe and the Near East. The hunters fought back for a time, particularly during hard times. What happened after that is another story. A new source of sustenance could be exploited, the stored food of people who had domesticated themselves in a new way by settling down to tend farms. In many respects, agriculture marked a sharp break with the past. It brought food surpluses and property, raids and conquests, thicker walls and fortifications, cities and population explosions. (Some 20,000 acres were required to support a single person in hunting-gathering days, and only about 25 acres in early village-farming communities.) It also brought writing and the end of prehistory.

But there was continuity, too. The shift from small- to big-game hunting, the use of fire, the invention of religion and art— these developments, like the invention of agriculture and all that has happened since, are part of a pattern. Everything man does to preserve the *status quo* is doomed to failure, because in the persevering effort to solve problems he always seems to create new and more complex ones. The human way of life is and has been from the beginning a permanent restlessness, and it is to understand the origin and nature of this restlessness that we continue to study the remote past.

■ The study of primates in zoos instead of in the wild as the cause of misconceptions about aggression; minimizing violence, a prerequisite for survival; varieties of animal societies; baboons, contemporary savanna dwellers; the collective wisdom of the troop; the importance of hierarchies; infant protection, grooming, affection

CHAPTER XII

Primate Studies and Revised Beliefs About Animal Behavior

■ Most knowledge about human prehistory comes from the archeologists, from dead evidence dug out of the earth. The preceding chapters deal in the main with deductions based on analyses of the remains and artifacts of creatures that have long since perished, fossil bones and soils and pollens, worked flints, living-floor patterns, burial sites and paintings and engravings. Research involving living material, baboons and chimpanzees and other species, has been cited chiefly for secondary reasons in connection with interpretations of archeological findings, to support arguments bearing on the origin of the erect posture, tool use and meat eating and hunting.

A shift of emphasis is called for at this stage. Living prehistory, information obtained from living rather than extinct species, is of major importance in its own right, but a great deal can also be learned from studies of other animals in their natural habitats. The problem is to see them as they are, and that seems to be about as difficult as reporting a political convention objectively. Depending on whom you read, animals are cute, charming and a bit bumbling and foolish (the Br'er Rabbit or Disney approach); noble, wise and pure; brutes and innate killers; and so on.

Such attitudes are poorly disguised messages, preconceptions rather than principles deduced from the evidence. They precede rather than follow the act of learning, and survive it. They show

277

that the writer is not really observing animals or even interested in them, but using them to make a point, to tell you what he thinks he knows—not what he thinks he knows about animals, but what he thinks he knows about people. For example, the odds are that if he belongs to the pure-and-noble school of animal behavior, he is commenting, implicitly or explicitly, on the Fall of Adam and the corruption of the human species. The temptation is strongest to moralize when it comes to primates, man's closest relatives and the species which have most to teach us.

Most primate studies are new and many have yet to be reported fully; their very newness is a phenomenon of some significance. As far as research on primates is concerned, biologists reacted strangely to Darwin's discoveries. In effect, they turned away from Darwin and turned their backs on the wilderness, investigating monkeys and apes in laboratories and zoos instead of in savannas and forests. In other words, instead of venturing into the great outdoors where the facts were, where they could observe primates living freely, they went indoors to observe primates locked in cages.

Such behavior, of course, was in part a matter of playing safe, because in some areas the danger of yellow fever and other diseases was greater then than it is now, at least until about half a century ago. Looking back, however, it appears to have been more than that. It amounted to a flight from reality, an evasion of nature which produced some spectacular results. Captive primates engaged in numerous and bloody fights, often to the death, killed their infants and indulged in a variety of bizarre sexual activity, all of which might have been predicted, if only by analogy with the actions of people subjected to prison conditions. Biologists had mistaken social pathology for normal behavior. Arguing from caged to free-ranging primates, they assumed violence to be an innate primate characteristic, part of the basic heritage of monkeys and apes, and unfortunately of men.

These findings were definitely in line with the Puritan-Victorian view of man as a Jekyll-Hyde creature, part the disheveled, lustful and violent animal and part the well-groomed and restrained gentleman. The discovery of Neanderthal man scandalized the Victorians because they saw him as a kind of Mr. Hyde built into the human past. The moral, of course, was that if only the beast in man could be curbed, life would proceed in a lawful and orderly fashion. But putting animals in cages had practically guaranteed that they would exhibit a high level of aberrant behavior, the "bestial" behavior generally expected of nonhuman primates, and thus confirm the notion of the beast-in-man. It was almost as if observers were deliberately creating conditions under which the gap between man and other primates would appear as wide as possible.

The first systematic study of wild primates came in 1931, when Ray Carpenter of Pennsylvania State University began observing howler monkeys in Panama. But extensive research did not start until the decades following World War II, a conflict which gave rise to second thoughts about the quality of human primates and a new and harder look at human origins. Powerful observing techniques were developed by investigators studying fish and birds, notably by Niko Tinbergen of Oxford, who has made a special point of the value of animal research in the analysis of motives and purposes: "The fact that animals cannot tell us what urges them to behave as they do might well be a blessing in disguise; at least they cannot tell us conscious or unconscious lies. They just behave." Tinbergen focused attention on repertoires of behavior patterns, repeated actions and reactions, and their inter-pretation in evolutionary terms.

These and other developments encouraged a new interest in primates, and for the first time observations in the wild became a major research activity. Early work created a certain amount of confusion as primates failed to behave as expected. Anthropologists and zoologists entered wildernesses expecting mayhem, and found peace. As a matter of fact, fighting was so rare that in the beginning each observer made a special point of reexamining his own results. Perhaps the species he was studying represented an exception to the rule of violence, or the animals were members of unusually amicable troops.

Later the observers compared notes and realized that they had not been dealing with exceptions, but with a common state of affairs. Their findings have since been confirmed by continuing field studies involving some hundred investigators in a dozen countries, including Japan, India, Kenya, Uganda and Borneo. Wild primates and most wild animals tend to avoid fighting with

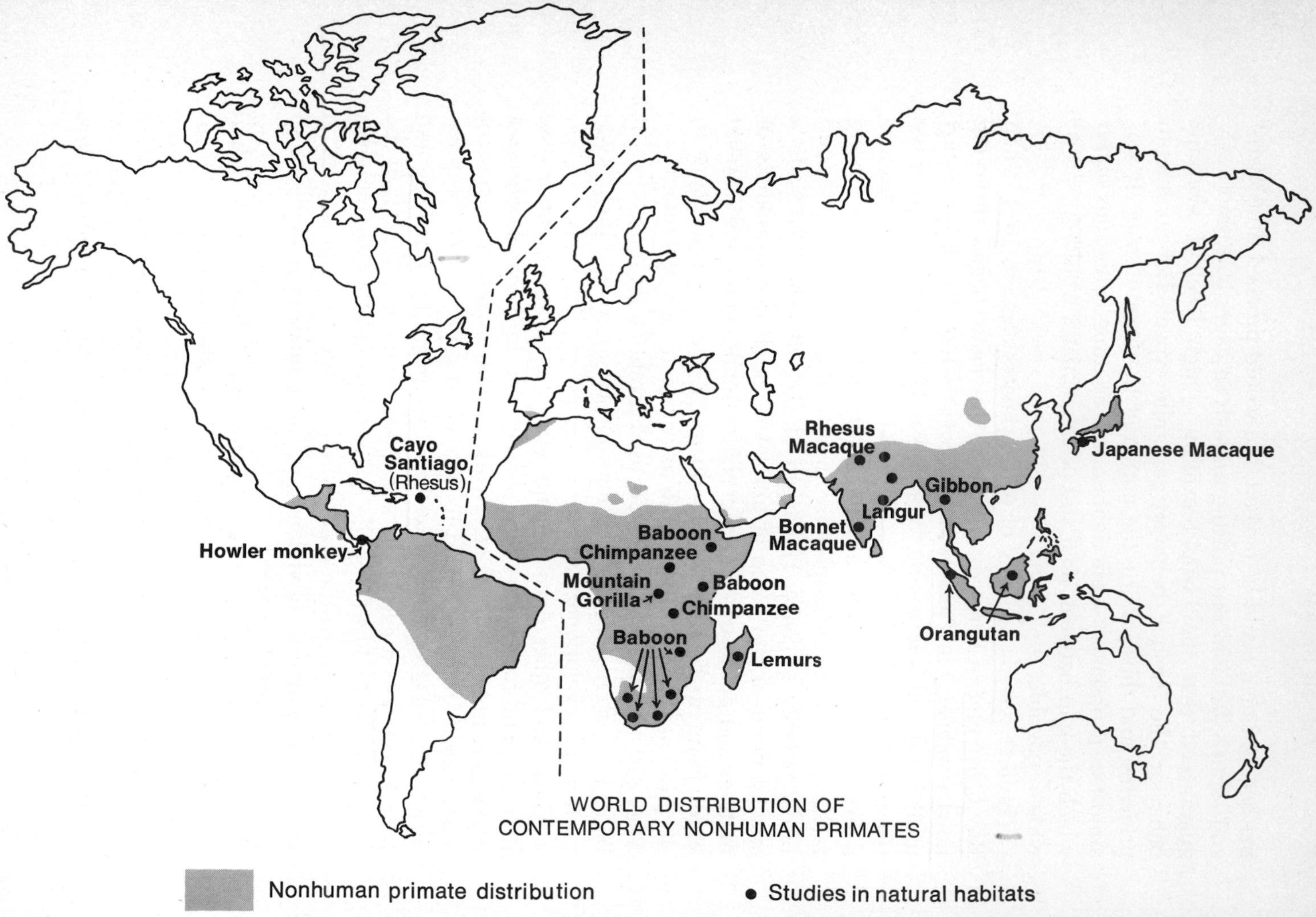

WORLD DISTRIBUTION OF
CONTEMPORARY NONHUMAN PRIMATES

Japanese Macaque

Gibbon

Langur

Rhesus
Macaque

Bonnet
Macaque

Orangutan

Lemurs

Baboon

Chimpanzee

Baboon

Chimpanzee

Mountain
Gorilla

Baboon

Cayo
Santiago
(Rhesus)

Howler monkey

Nonhuman primate distribution

• Studies in natural habitats

one another. Survival is too serious a business for the luxury of violent dissension within the ranks. If primates behaved as aggressively in the wild as they do in cages, they would have become extinct long ago.

The striking point about primates is not the existence of aggression but the uses and control of aggression. In them evolution has produced new orders of unity. The members of a troop of primates depend on one another as intimately and directly as if they were all physically connected by tough nerve fibers, which, in effect, is the way things are. The group is the adaptive unit, and the more that is learned about groups, the more notions about individuals and individualism will have to be revised. The evolutionary trend not only among primates but among mammals in general has been toward increasingly complex and close-knit groups.

The broad features of this trend have been analyzed by John Eisenberg of the Smithsonian Institution, in a survey of nearly five hundred studies. He describes four grades or levels of mammalian social organization:

1. Grade 1—the female-young unit. A mother caring for her offspring is the most elementary of all mammalian social units, a bare minimum in the sense that no species could endure with anything less. The wood rats of North America, for example, live alone in nests of twigs and come together only for mating. The female provides shelter and food and protection for her litter, and attacks and drives away males which come too close.

2. Grade 2—the mother-family group. Here again mothers and offspring make up the basic units but they may aggregate into large groups, a situation found among red deer. Fifteen or more hinds, each with two or three young, live together throughout the year under the leadership of an older female. A hind goes off alone to give birth, rejoining her group after a few days when the calf can walk and follow. The stags live separate lives, wandering more widely and foraging in loose all-male herds; during the breeding season a stag will associate himself with a female group and defend it against other stags. Stags and hinds may come together in good feeding grounds during the winter.

3. Grade 3—the male-female pair bond. This rare category includes a wide variety of specializations and living arrangements, the common element being that the male is part of the basic social

unit, the family, and that both male and female provide care and food for the young. Among wolves, for example, the male not only shares in protecting the litter but he is also the provider and may join with other males in hunting. At the kill site he will swallow chunks of meat without chewing them, and disgorge the food back at the den for family consumption.

4. Grade 4—the permanent male-female group, more than one male generally associating with a number of females. Certain primate societies represent this grade of organization, living in troops which may include more than a hundred individuals and are generally closed to outsiders. The males may act collectively in defending females and offspring. In such groups conflicts involving the individual and the organization may arise in acute form and demand new and complex control mechanisms.

Eisenberg points out that relatively unspecialized or low-grade social structures are typical for representatives of new orders of mammal, populations engaged in finding places for themselves in a world of established species. The newcomers are often small and inconspicuous, live in the shelter of forests rather than in open terrain, and do their foraging at night—all characteristics which favor Grade 1 female-young units. On the other hand, developments which appear later in evolution may have the opposite effect. Species frequently become larger in the process of adapting successfully, acquire greater freedom of movement, and forage actively during daylight hours; there is also a trend toward larger brains and more complex sense organs. Such changes favor the formation of more and more elaborate social organizations.

Similar patterns may be seen in the evolution of primates. The first prosimians, forerunners of monkeys and apes, were small forest dwellers, probably nocturnal. They depended largely on the sense of smell for communicating with one another and for detecting danger. Like some surviving prosimians, they probably lived solitary lives and were dispersed over wide areas. The trend has been in the opposite direction ever since, toward increasing brain and body size, increasing importance of sight and hearing in communications, and the formation of permanent troops. As far as human evolution is concerned, life in open country accentuated the need for tight group organization as a protection against big cats and other predators.

Detailed studies of nonhuman primates provide a more precise and dynamic picture of our own origins. It is particularly important to learn as much as possible about monkeys and apes in a variety of different environments. The more we know about the range of adaptations to open woodlands, for example, the better we will understand the behavior of the first hominids who depended increasingly on their ability to cope with such terrain. Going one step further, our ancestors gradually moved out of open woodlands into still more open grassy savanna lands, and the impact of that change can be appreciated more fully by considering how other primates have adapted to similar conditions.

This point has been emphasized by Woodrow Denham of the University of Washington in Seattle. After a systematic analysis of possible environments and possible adaptations, he indicates that the earliest hominids, like other primates living in open woodlands, tend to live in large groups because food, although ample, tends to be concentrated in a number of separate areas. Extreme territoriality among large groups, fighting to the death to defend feeding and living places from other troops, would hardly promote survival and is uncommon; within limits, troops may move in and out of one another's home ranges. Also, direct confrontation and fighting against predators is relatively rare, because it is usually possible to escape into trees, which means that the male is not often called on to defend the troop and hence is not likely to be much bigger than the female.

Early hominids lived in a comparable setting, until they moved into grassy savannas. At that point life became less relaxed, more highly organized. Denham suggests that in general food is more uniformly distributed in grasslands than in open woodlands, which encourages foraging by many small groups rather than a few large ones, the multiplication of home ranges, and a readiness to defend territories more vigorously. The male's role changes correspondingly, not only in keeping fellow primates out of his home territory, but also in confronting predators, escape being more difficult since trees are few and far between. The tendency under these conditions is for males to be appreciably larger and more formidable than females, and our remote ancestors may have gone through some such stage.

So something about the past may be deduced from the behavior of primates currently at large in grassy savannas, African baboons in particular. Baboons have received special attention from a number of investigators because they provide a dramatic example of adaptation to an exposed environment. The rest of this chapter is devoted chiefly to baboon troops I have observed myself, to those which DeVore studied in Nairobi Park and the

INCREASING SOCIAL COMPLEXITY

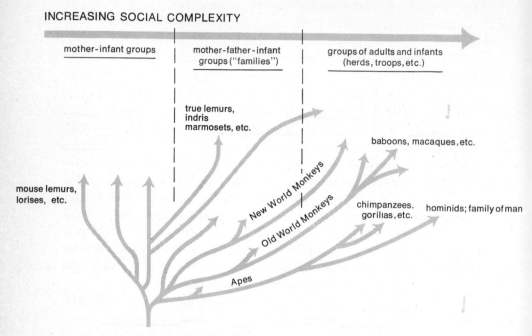

Social evolution among primates

Amboseli Game Reserve of Kenya. Their world demands a degree of alertness analogous to that demanded in baseball or cricket, in which nothing happens most of the time and most plays are routine. The challenge is always to be ready for swift and sudden action.

The difference between playing fields and savannas, of course, is that in savannas emergencies tend to be fatal. Under such conditions a lone baboon does not have much of a chance. Individuals living almost constantly within sight and sound of one another must experience shock when they find themselves isolated on a wide plain. It must be something like falling overboard and seeing the ship disappearing over the horizon. One young Nairobi Park baboon that was unusually bold as long as the rest of the troop remained reasonably close (it had earned the name "Brash" for leaping onto the hood of a fast-moving car and begging for food) lost its courage whenever the troop moved too far away, scampering back and emitting alarm barks all the way.

A sick or crippled individual does not survive long. It cannot keep up with the troop. Nor will the troop wait, although adult males sometimes drop back to accompany lagging females with infants. A sick baboon tries so hard to keep up that it does not take time to get enough food. It becomes weaker and falls farther and farther behind. Finally, it no longer moves. I once saw a sick female lying paralyzed in short grass, crouching as low as possible, fitting its body into every depression in the earth in a last effort to become invisible. Next morning she was missing, and presumably devoured.

Baboons in open country endure by moving together in patterns that depend on the lay of the land, food resources and the ways of predators. But the patterns are by no means self-evident. Following a large troop of baboons for the first time is likely to be frustrating if you expect to find clear-cut signs of organized behavior. The word "troop" implies some sort of coordinated structure, but what you generally see from a distance is baboons scattered over several acres of savanna, apparently paying little attention to one another, or to you. There are no neat rank-and-file formations and no mass movements in a particular direction, only baboons wandering about in small groups and baboons off by themselves, some sitting on branches and rocks as if surveying the terrain. (On closer inspection it turns out that a few of the sitters are asleep.)

Everything seems casual until observations can be made close up and for long periods, and that does not happen until troops grow accustomed to man. Some troops never learn to trust man and keep their distance. Others permit closer and closer approaches, and after several weeks they accept the investigator as a familiar part of the landscape, even to the point of falling asleep when he is only a few yards away.

A number of years ago DeVore devoted more than 1,200 hours to field observations, and practically became an honorary member of several troops. He came to know some eighty baboons by sight, and had names for all of them. He understood what they were "saying" to one another, a skill which helped considerably in interpreting their behavior—and, on at least one occasion, in interpreting his behavior to them. Baboons are reasonably tolerant of scientists, but one thing you must never do is frighten an infant. DeVore did just that by accident one day, the infant yelped, and immediately several large angry males dashed to the

Irven DeVore establishing contact with baboons

spot slapping the ground and lunging at him. Fortunately, he knew the appropriate signal. He smacked his lips loudly, which is a pacifying gesture among baboons and can be translated roughly as follows: "Sorry about that. It was a mistake. No harm intended."

DeVore followed troops all day for many days before he began to understand their way of life. Their comings and goings, which seem so haphazard at first, are actually quite predictable. Each troop confines its movements largely to a definite territory, a home range of about ten to fifteen square miles. The boundaries of the range are marked by an invisible "fence," by signs which we do not see but which are very real to troop members. Baboons become tense and watchful as they approach this line; they move away, and cannot be driven across it. They are not familiar with what lies on the other side. Novelty, always a reason for caution, repels powerfully when it becomes too vast.

The home range contains two or three core areas, areas where the troop spends more than 90 per cent of its time and does more than 90 per cent of its traveling and feeding. Each core area is further specialized in the sense that it includes at least one stretch of stream or river with trees growing along the banks, and trees are the only refuges on Kenya savannas. There is a calculus of escape involving such things as the probability of predators being abroad, conditions of visibility, and distance from the nearest trees. Where lions are numerous, baboons move within escape distance of trees, even if they are hungry and food in the area is scarce and abundant food exists outside the safety zone.

A collective wisdom exists in the baboon troop, as in every organized body of animals. As an organic repository of information, the troop knows more than any one of its members. The unique and unusual experiences of older individuals affect the behavior of the group. Once an investigator studying parasitic diseases shot two baboons from a car. More than eight months later, the troop was still giving cars a wide berth, although it had previously been quite approachable, and although the odds are that only a few of the troop's eighty-odd members saw what happened.

Such experiences may be remembered for years or generations and become part of troop culture. In fact, the larger the troop, the greater its store of accumulated information and its security from predators. If these were the only or the major factors operating, the forces of natural selection might well have produced larger and larger baboon troops and perhaps considerably more advanced social organizations. But other factors limit group size. When a troop has more than 100 members or so it tends to split. One of the reasons may be that there are too many large dominant males and they begin to form two rival groups.

Every activity is the result of a balance among opposing tendencies. You can see them at work in a baboon when it feeds, which is most of the time, in the way it moves its head and shifts attention periodically. It feeds with head down, scanning the

Lone baboon on savanna, fair game for lions and other predators

Baboon troop near trees, where they can find refuge from predators

Baboons at water hole

ground and missing nothing as it passes, pulling up grasses and shoots, digging for juicy roots in the dry season, snatching eggs out of nests, occasionally turning over rocks to find insects underneath. But it is built not to concentrate too steadily. Every five to ten seconds it stops and looks up and glances about for a second or two before resuming feeding. (This pattern is also observed among people eating alone and may be a throwback to man's primate days.) In an average-size troop, at any given instant about half a dozen individuals may be surveying the landscape.

Under certain conditions, particularly around densely overgrown places where predators may hide, baboons seem to live in a hair-trigger state. There are panic reactions when all of a sudden the entire troop, which has been sitting quietly, scatters and makes a break for the trees. Such behavior has obvious survival value, although many false alarms do occur. On one occasion a dozen baboons dashed away from a resting place, turned to look back, and promptly relaxed when they saw two young impalas stepping out of the grass. A rustling of leaves may be enough to produce frantic scattering, and, in general, troops are ready for flight at an instant's notice.

Perhaps the most fascinating and subtlest thing about a troop is the fit between its natural behavior and the demands of the environment. For example, any predator attempting to get at baboons during a resting session would probably confront one or more of the vigorous young males distributed around the central group of females and infants and older males. An effective defense system exists, an outer ring of aggressive troop members. But the young males are there not by choice or selection but in large part because their close presence is not generally tolerated by the dominant males of the inner circle. In other words, the natural structure of the group determines their function as guards or sentinels.

A similar phenomenon may be observed as a widely dispersed troop passes from open terrain into or near clumps of bushes and tall grasses. Again the baboons organize for defense. They move so as to form a more compact group, thus joining forces in a manner that tends to discourage predators crouching. But this cannot be considered a pure defense reaction. The mere fact that food is dispersed in the open and highly concentrated in the undergrowth would also tend to bring troop members together, so that a single natural maneuver serves a number of purposes at once.

|This sort of behavior illustrates the workings of evolution, the fine adjustment of group to environment. It is the result of natural selection operating over periods of hundreds of thousands of generations, and the process is no less impressive because it seems to be largely automatic. Baboons make self-conscious plans far more rarely than men do, one reason why they rank lower on the evolutionary scale. But the closer one studies them, the more human they appear. Incidentally, the reasons for man's own behavior are not always apparent. It also may often have an automatic quality.

|A central difference between men and baboons involves levels of organization. A baboon troop is a close association of individuals living together throughout their lives, and having little to do with other members of their species. Newcomers are not encouraged, although on rare occasions a baboon may leave its troop and join another if it is ready to fight for a place in the hierarchy. In densely populated areas troops may feed side by side without conflicts. When there is plenty of space, they tend to avoid one another entirely.|Superorganizations, alliances made up of two or more troops, have never been observed among baboons or any other nonhuman primate.

Seen from the outside in the broad context of social behavior, the troop operates as a closed and autonomous unit, a unified living system, moving about the savanna in search of food and avoiding danger. Seen from the inside, however, things become considerably more "personal." The problem as usual is to bring individual members of the troop, each with its own temperament and needs and aggressions, into a cohesive social structure.|Although living close together all the time may be essential for survival, it introduces stresses that must be given a measure of release and expression, and yet kept under control.

The solution involves periods of excitement and relaxation, a swell of rising and receding tensions. Every baboon receives a more or less continuous flow of information about the state of mind of other baboons and transmits information to them about its own feelings. The air is alive with signals: lip-smacking and soft grunts, which are most frequent and indicate peaceful intentions; hard direct stares (the most powerful gestures of all); and threatening

Yawn threat of adult male threatening competitors to hold place in hierarchy and maintain order

yawns revealing large canine teeth, individuals standing stiff with shoulders hunched and neck hair raised. Every now and then there is a chase accompanied by loud grunting and screeches of fear.

Glare threat of adult male baboon defending status

Little harm comes of the commotion. Most threats do not lead to a chase, for the threatened individual makes some sort of submissive gesture such as moving away slowly or screeching loudly with lips curled in an "appeasement grin." When chases do occur, they generally end with the fugitive pressing his body to the ground and the pursuer holding him there for a moment and then walking off. Bloodshed is rare, serious injury even rarer. As a rule, quarrels last less than half a minute. They can be interpreted as letting off steam or maintaining a certain level of excitement and alertness among individuals that really have little else to do. The net effect is to achieve stability through a sort of regulated turbulence.

All this activity goes on within the framework of a rigid social system, a hierarchy in which every adult member of the troop has a place. A few hours of observation are usually enough to figure out the status of various individuals in a general way. "The very bearing of a dominant baboon distinguishes it from the others," DeVore reports. "Besides having a confident gait, its fur is likely to be sleek and well-groomed. A subordinate animal will be less self-assured; it will have tousled fur and, frequently, many minor scars from old wounds."

More precise information can be obtained by noting which of two individuals gives way when both approach food or a shady resting place or a female in heat. Status also shows up during episodes of so-called redirected aggression. This is the baboon version of what happens when a man who has just been called down by his boss comes home and snaps at his wife—who then slaps her child, who, in turn, kicks the dog. The result is a flow of aggressive energy downhill through the troop's hierarchy. A dominant male usually starts things by chasing a subordinate male, who promptly expresses his feelings by chasing a still more subordinate individual. Low monkey on the totem pole during such activity is rarely an adult male, but often an adult female, the highest-ranking female still occupying a position below that of the lowest-ranking male. Sometimes baboons will even release their aggression on an inanimate object, bouncing against a tree or tugging at a large rock.

This sort of behavior may take place on a large scale when the troop has been frightened. The mere sight of a leopard, the most dangerous predator to baboons, was once followed by an extended burst of activity, dominant males chasing subordinate males and subordinate males chasing females to the accompaniment of much screeching and nipping. The episode lasted for more than five minutes before simmering down to a flurry of grunts, threatening yawns and lip-smacking. It was something like waves and ripples dying out in a pond after gusts of wind. On another occasion a lion charged at a troop and it took a full hour for the baboons to relax.

The hierarchy is not always a simple matter of A dominating B, B dominating C, and so on down the line. In one troop, for example, the strongest individual and the best fighter was Kula, an "aggressive, fearless, dominance-oriented" adult male in his prime. Kula could almost certainly have beaten any of the other adult males of the troop in single combat. But he never received privileges commensurate with his abilities because three older baboons, including a very old and formidable veteran, stayed close to one another most of the time and acted together as a coalition in putting down the challenges of others. In other words, Kula was the victim of the Establishment or central hierarchy.

Adult males, particularly the Establishment, bear the major responsibility for protecting the troop. The frequent quarrels and skirmishes among troop members serve constantly to reestablish and confirm status relationships and, like human fire or lifeboat drills, ensure that every individual will know his place and role in times of crisis. Most encounters with predators come to a quick conclusion, as when a pack of hungry wild dogs approached one troop. All individuals except the dominant male retreated, and left him sitting between themselves and the pack. He did not even bother to change his position; he merely turned his head and stared, and the dogs ran off.

As far as crisis within the troop is concerned, adult males maintain order and stop fights. The No. 1 male has a wide sphere of influence. If he walks toward trouble head up, leading with his chin, his presence may be felt at quite a distance. A long-range stare was once sufficient to break up a fight between two juveniles some sixty feet away and, on another occasion, to make a misbehaving infant scream as if it had been hit. On the other hand, the leader's power is not unlimited and even females may intervene successfully by ganging up on him if he treats one of their number too roughly.

Patterns of mating behavior favor the inheritance of physical strength, fast reflexes, and other qualities contributing to the attainment of top positions in the hierarchy. Although dominance alone does not guarantee success in mating, a high-ranking male will probably have access to a female at the height of her estrus period, when she is most receptive and most fertile. Furthermore, the higher his rank, the better his chances of monopolizing her as a partner. Consequently, a large proportion of the offspring born into a troop may be sired by the most dominant male.

As far as the hierarchy among females was concerned, there is not much to say except that it does exist and its workings are more difficult to figure out during a limited period of observation. On a short-term basis, relationships may change because of changes associated with the reproductive cycle. As a female in

The Establishment: (top) adult male threatens two members of central hierarchy (bottom), who turn and chase him

heat becomes increasingly aggressive, she arouses aggression within the troop, among females as well as males. She attacks other females more frequently and is more frequently attacked by them. Since she may be protected by adult males, her effective status in the hierarchy may rise a notch or two until the end of estrus (that is, for about ten days).

The behavior of the adolescent female is particularly ambiguous. She often joins forces with an adult female against another adult female, and may come to dominate some individuals ranking low in the female hierarchy. On the other hand, she generally makes it a practice to steer clear of dominant females, and is thus half in and half out of the hierarchy. In general, since status is always shifting with changes in physiological condition, females apparently do not have a chance to establish permanent coalitions. For the same reason they quarrel much more frequently among themselves than do males, although the consequences are not as serious. "There is more or less continuous minor bickering with very little real attacking and biting."

Females with young enjoy a very special status. In fact, in a sense the troop exists for them. DeVore points out that by far the most important force in binding the troop together, in creating a close-knit social unit, is the infant: "It is scarcely possible to overemphasize the significance of the newborn baboon. It becomes the center of interest, absorbing the attention of the entire troop. From the moment the birth is discovered, the mother is continuously surrounded by the other baboons, who walk beside her and sit as close as possible when she rests." An infant is likely to come in a time of relative abundance. About four out of every five offspring are born between October and December, at the onset of the rainy season in Kenya, when the food supply is about to reach a peak.

One of the important features about the primate way of life is that child rearing is essentially a group activity. Mothers aggregate at the center of the troop, and other baboons, drawn by the enormous attraction of the infants, join the cluster. Juveniles and adult females come near and smack their lips and try to touch one of the infants, although the mother prevents any outside contact for the first week or two. Adolescent females also approach, and learn how to care for the infants they will bear by carrying and fondling the infants of others. The central nucleus is ideally de-signed for the learning process, especially for infants, and infants born into complex primate societies have a great deal to learn.

Dominant males are also powerfully attracted. They may carry an infant the way its mother does, by letting it cling to the hair on their bellies. (Fortunately, it has a firm grasp.) In one troop a sickly female infant whose mother had died after nursing her was adopted not by an adult female but by an adult male, a member of the Establishment. As a matter of fact, adult males will con-tinue to protect a young baboon after its mother no longer does. After about two years she is busy with her next offspring, while they will come to its rescue for another six months or longer.

There is another interesting if somewhat perverse example of the significance of infants for adult males. One day in the Amboseli Reserve an adult male was running rampant through a troop, going after females and juveniles and practically every individual in sight. According to DeVore, he had just lost a fight to a higher-ranking member of the hierarchy. Another adult male, seeing the ag-gressor coming his way, snatched a nearby young infant and began to groom it frantically, knowing that with an infant in his arms he would probably be immune from attack. That is what happened. The aggressor passed him by for another victim, and he promptly released the infant. This sort of behavior, call it pretense or deceit, is peculiarly primate behavior; it is seen in no other species.

For the first month or so, mother and infant are practically a single organism. The infant is either in her arms nursing and being groomed or clinging to her belly upside down as she moves with the troop. From then on it becomes increasingly indepen-dent. At first it may wobble only a few steps away during rest periods, but as its coordination improves and it grows bolder, it spends more and more time feeding at a distance and playing with other infants and juveniles. In other words, at first the infant depends on its mother exclusively for both companionship and protection, and later turns increasingly to its peers for compan-ionship and to adult males for protection.

By the age of two to three, baboons are spending most of their time playing, chasing and tumbling over one another and dodging and wrestling. Special signals distinguish playing from fighting.

Mother-infant bond: infant in mother's arms

For example, in fights the pursuer comes on with a rush, grunting loudly and eyes fixed on the pursued, who may dash away screeching with fright. Play is generally silent, and the approach is made with a characteristic bouncing or hopping gait. It often seems to be a rehearsal, providing baboons with opportunities to maneuver body and face and teeth in appropriate positions for attack and defense.

Infant baboon looking for reassurance before exploring

The sexes differ in the way they play. Females chase one another for relatively brief periods, the chase ending gently with the pursuer simply touching the pursued. Furthermore, they devote increasing time to infants and drop out of play groups entirely by the age of three or four, that is, toward the end of their adolescence. Males are adolescent longer, until about the age of seven, and play longer and harder and rougher. Their chases generally end with romping and wrestling, and there is a greater tendency for excitement to build up until play approaches pain and serious encounters, which may have to be broken up by adult males.

At about the age of five the male is larger than adult females, and his time has come to rise in the troop. So he starts fighting the females, who fight back for a time, although one has the impression that they expect him to assert himself and offer only token resistance. Some of his greatest problems develop later with the ending of adolescence, when he is at the top of the female hierarchy but at the bottom of the male hierarchy and begins to fight older males. He may be physically ready for leadership, but socially the time is not ripe. Although completely mature, he may have to wait another two or three years before finding his place in the upper levels of the male hierarchy.

The males, defenders and defenders-to-be, represent the chief locus of tension in the troop. Except for members of the central hierarchy, they do not actively seek one another out, and within the structure of the group younger males seem to prefer being by themselves. They tolerate one another politely but without warmth, which is less unfriendly than it sounds, considering that males live at a high level of tension, particularly during periods when females are in estrus. Indeed, one test of any social group is whether it maintains its basic stability during such periods, and by that test the baboon troop is successful.

The locus of affection is definitely in the central group, among the aggregated females and infants, and of all expressions of affection grooming is by far the most frequent. Typically, one baboon sits or lies on its back as another baboon parts and searches through its fur, picking or licking off every speck of alien material. The picture is one of rapt concentration. The groomer scans the fur intently, section by section, while the individual being groomed closes his eyes or looks to the side, always avoiding a direct look at the groomer which is a sign of aggression, and wallows in contentment.

Grooming almost certainly serves a hygienic function. Africa is a paradise for all forms of life, including a rich assortment of insects and parasites. After walks through grass I have frequently had myself inspected and inspected others for the presence of omnipresent ticks. Among the Kalahari Bushmen, boys delouse one another beginning early in the morning. Among baboons, mothers groom newborn infants every few minutes, and morning grooming groups of two to eight individuals form as soon as troops come down from their sleeping trees. The licking and picking of wounds may also have a cleansing effect and help account for the fact that healing often proceeds very quickly.

Male baboons wrestling, playing more roughly than females

Above all, however, grooming brings individuals together. Sensual pleasure is involved, and the effect seems to be far more intensive when an individual is being groomed than when he grooms himself. The most common grooming cluster consists of two females, at least one with an infant. The next most common cluster is two females with infants and, in addition, an adult male. Although females participate in the activity more often than males and devote more time to it, it has a special significance for the male. The grooming of one individual by another tends to be more frequent among baboons and other primates with rigid hierarchies, as if the very rigidity demanded a compensating increase of affection.

Like all social relations, grooming can be exploited, used with malice aforethought. DeVore has seen a young female run over to a dominant male for protection against a young male who wanted to attack her. The young male came over and began grooming the female, but gave her a nip as soon as her protector looked away.

This can be cited as another case of deceit or, more broadly, of the evolving of complex tactics and strategies based on a knowledge of prevailing behavior forms. It is a characteristic developed to a fine point in man.

Grooming group, infant holding leg of dominant male

The baboon troop exists as a successful compromise, an equilibrium between individual aggression and cooperation. For all the tensions and chases, most of the day consists of peaceful feeding and resting and grooming. Affection represents the pervading force, and the power of affection is indicated by its durability and continuity. Fortunately, baboons do not have a great capacity for remorse. It is difficult to conceive of an organization better designed for the protection of infants than the troop with its inner cluster of mothers and dominant males. And yet probably less than half of all infants born survive beyond their second year, the rest becoming victims of injury, disease and predators.

An infant's death illustrates the persistence of affection, and also how abruptly it may cease. A mother may carry a dead infant for several days, clutching the corpse to her belly, letting it drop from time to time, and then going back and picking it up again. When the ultimate separation comes, it may be striking for its complete lack of apparent emotion. After clinging to her infant for four days, one mother simply let go of it without even breaking her stride or looking back, as if she were unaware of what had happened.

|Circumstances call for the shutting off of deep concern. The laws of necessity dictate that affection cannot be attached too strongly to any single individual. Death is too frequent. But affection itself must outlast all the endings and letdowns. In the case of the female, it must always be revived by the sight and touch of her next infant and the infants of others. The troop owes its existence to the fact that evolution and natural selection have made this enduring renewal possible.

CHAPTER XIII

Chimpanzees: Man's Closest Relatives

■ |A high order of <u>intelligence</u> is generally associated with <u>independence,</u> <u>individual initiative,</u> and a capacity for <u>novel</u> and <u>creative</u> behavior. This implies that the more <u>intelligent</u> a <u>primate</u> is, the greater the difficulty of limiting its <u>freedom</u> in the context of a rigid <u>hierarchy.</u> We see that tensions and frustrations have been observed even among baboons, and such behavior might well have caused more serious stresses among more intelligent prehuman apes.

|Severe <u>conflict</u> was probably a <u>basic</u> feature of the <u>hominid</u> line from the very beginning as a direct result of <u>savanna life</u> and the need for <u>rules</u> and <u>discipline,</u> of the clash between <u>individual</u> and <u>society.</u> Indeed, it appears that the clash was so severe that it could not be brought under the degree of control possible among less-advanced primates. It had a kind of life of its own as a seed of discontent, an ingrained nagging thing, a chronic restlessness which has become as characteristic of *Homo* as walking upright or making tools or talking.

The restlessness may have made survival somewhat more difficult, at least relatively early in the game. It has certainly worked with all the force of original sin against permanence, against all efforts to establish traditions and institutions so solidly that they would endure indefinitely. But in the course of time what once appeared to be a deficiency or flaw in the human makeup has acquired a more positive quality, as a stimulus to explore and do things that have never been done before. Human restlessness may represent for cultural evolution what genetic mutation represents for organic evolution, a built-in source of novelty and increasingly complex patterns of life—the source, indeed, of the human spark.

Baboon society provides a model of primate life in the grassy savannas of Africa, the sort of world man's ancestors encountered when they moved out of open woodlands. As indicated in Chapter IV, they, like baboons, may once have lived sunrise-to-sunset lives and slept in trees for safety and moved across open places in "covered wagon" defense formations with infants and mothers protected at the center. Their sons probably played rough-and-tumble games, while their daughters were attracted increasingly to infants and the care of infants. They also had hierarchies and Establishments, and the perennial problem of building individuals into a group.

But the comparison can be carried just so far, and no further. Other species have adapted in other ways to exposed conditions. Ronald Hall found that the patas monkeys of Uganda, perhaps the most terrestrial of all nonhuman primates, survive by scattering rather than aggregating as baboons do. Individual troop members are often separated by distances of more than a hundred yards, on the principle of offering predators isolated rather than concentrated targets. Built like greyhounds, they are outstanding for their fantastic running and dodging abilities; they show little aggression. Much remains to be learned about survival in wide-open spaces.

As for life in open woodlands, where the family of man is believed to have originated, attention focuses on the chimpanzee. Of all living primates, the chimpanzee is most like man, and the longer its ways are studied the more striking the resemblances become. It ranks high on the primate intelligence scale with a brain about twice the size of the baboon brain, spends much of its time on the ground, and reveals an impressive capacity for complex and enduring social relationships. Moreover, observations suggest the sort of forces that might have transformed its life style.

The wild chimpanzee prefers to keep its distance, at least in the beginning, and primate-watching for human investigators usually presents far more problems in forests than in open country. In

1960 when van Lawick-Goodall started her studies in the Gombe forests, she arose at dawn, about half-past five morning after morning, and spent most of the day on top of a rocky hill overlooking the forests and Lake Tanganyika, where she could observe and be observed as a harmless and unassuming fellow primate.

Social acceptance was slow in coming. Some days she spent twelve hours in the field, climbing up and down slopes and forcing her way through dense undergrowth without seeing a single chimpanzee. She often heard calls in the distance, but the animals had moved off by the time she managed to make her way to the area. "It wasn't just fear," she explains. "It was also resentment of your presence. Like people in an English village, they don't care to be stared at." During the first few months they would run away upon seeing her at distances of as much as five hundred yards.

The apes became tamer as they learned her ways, and as she learned theirs. Part of her strategy, for example, was pretending not to pay attention. Often a group that seemed nervous and about to take off when being watched intently would calm down and stay if she started doing something else, such as eating leaves or digging a hole. Gradually she was able to come closer and closer, to within fifty yards by eight months and within fifty feet by another half-year or so. In general males were bolder than females, displaying on occasion as they would to a fellow chimpanzee, with five or ten minutes of screaming and hitting trees and shaking branches. Then they would ignore her and go about their business.

The most striking single fact about chimpanzees is the flexibility of their social life, the lack of any rigid form of organization. It represents about as far a departure from the baboon type of organization as one can find among the higher primates, and serves to emphasize the great variety of primate adaptations. Chimpanzees are more human than baboons, or rather they jibe better with the way we like to picture ourselves, as free-wheeling individuals who tend to be unpredictable and do not take readily to any form of regimentation, and who are frequently charming. (Charm is relatively rare among baboons.)

Vernon Reynolds of the University of Bristol, England, describes what he and his wife Frances found during more than eight months spent among chimpanzees of the Budongo Forest of western Uganda: "We were quite surprised to observe that there is no single, distinct social unit in chimpanzee society. Not only is there no 'family' or 'harem' organization; neither is there a 'troop' organization—that is to say, no particular chimpanzees keep permanently together. On the contrary, individuals move about at will, alone or in small groups best described as bands, which sometimes form into large aggregations. They leave their associates if they want to, and join up with new ones without conflict."

The general practice is best described as easy come, easy go, although there are certain group-forming tendencies. As a rule chimpanzees move about in one of four types of band: adult males only; mothers and offspring and occasionally a few other females; adults and adolescents of both sexes, but no mothers with young; and representatives of all categories mixed together. The composition of bands may change a number of times during the course of a day as individuals wander off and groups split or combine with other groups. On the other hand, certain individuals prefer one another's company. Reynolds observed that four males often roamed together over a four-month period, and mothers often associate with their older offspring.

Such conditions do not make for the establishment of formal social structures. The largest and strongest males are often dominant, but they seldom have occasion to assert their dominance; strictly determined hierarchies do not exist. Aggression is rare. Van Lawick-Goodall once saw seven males, including an adolescent, waiting patiently for their turn to copulate with a female in estrus, and during her first two years in the field she noted only one case of fighting among adult males. Reynolds recorded only seventeen quarrels, none of which lasted more than a few seconds, in 300 hours of observing.

Chimpanzees are nomads. They generally sleep in different trees every night and travel, not in regular circuits confined to relatively small core areas, but widely and freely wherever food is abundant. Their tracks are everywhere in the forests, miles and miles of them, including tunnels through the densest stretches of undergrowth, "tubes" just about big enough for a chimpanzee to scramble through on all fours. (Many animals have such tunnels, perhaps the most spectacular being the great elephant tunnels of northern Bengal, long corridors ten feet high that wind through tangled places in jungles among the foothills of the Himalayas.)

There is nothing nonhuman for chimpanzees to fear in the

forest. The most formidable predators, leopards, tend to go after other game. Chimpanzees hunt more often than they are hunted, and the stalking and killing of a red colobus monkey has been discussed in Chapter VI. Sometimes, for no discernible cause, they will also hunt baboons, a strange state of affairs considering that the two species may intermingle freely and without friction. In the Gombe National Park young baboons and young chimpanzees frequently play together, and in at least one case an infant female chimpanzee formed a close friendship with a juvenile female baboon. Apparently an occasional killing does not affect such relationships, and baboons do not find being eaten now and then enough of a deterrent to discourage them from living within range of apes.

Hunting and sharing seem to go together, among chimpanzees as well as among men. In fact, the chimpanzee is the only non-human primate known to share meat in the wild, and van Lawick-Goodall has often seen a successful hunter tear a piece of meat off a carcass and give it to a fellow troop member begging with out-stretched hand. Sometimes the sharing is reluctant. One young female found that the only way she could get a banana from her mother (who usually had a boxful to herself) was to go into a full-fledged temper tantrum, hurling herself to the ground and flailing her arms and screaming, and even that did not work all the time. In general sharing is not practiced regularly, but the feeling is that it soon would be if hunting itself became a regular thing.

Chimpanzees may become highly aroused at the mere sight of a killing, screaming loudly as they watch the action and running about and throwing their arms around one another. In fact, a variety of conditions can throw them into a frenzy. They perform "rain dances" to the accompaniment of thunder and lightning during tropical storms, and one of their most outlandish perfor-mances is the "carnival," when as many as thirty individuals come together in a period of fantastic noisemaking which may last several hours. The sound is difficult to believe even when you have heard it.

Reynolds has described what it is like to be caught in the middle of a carnival: "The noise is terrific, like a tornado or an audience-applause machine turned way up. It can be very frightening, because there is also a great deal of running back and forth and the ground shakes, and you hear high shrieking and the thud of heavy feet coming toward you and violent drumming on trees." Carnivals may be elaborate greeting ceremonies which occur when two groups not familiar with one another happen to cross paths.

The mother-infant bond seems to be more enduring among chimpanzees than among baboons, one reason being the absence of any troop structure. A mother who lives more on her own has a greater individual responsibility for her offspring. If she is distracted or goes away, there is no permanent central cluster of individuals to protect her infant. Furthermore, chimpanzees mature far more slowly, requiring a prolonged period of infant dependency. The first separation between mother and infant, the first break in physical contact, does not occur for sixteen to twenty-four weeks, as compared to about four weeks among baboons.

Although juveniles no longer need to be nursed after four or five years or so, they may share their mother's nest for another three years and are dependent until about the age of eight. But that does not mean the severing of family ties. In fact, one of the most significant discoveries about chimpanzee behavior in the Gombe area, a discovery that would never have been made without long-term observations, is that family ties probably last throughout life. One mother estimated to be nearly fifty years old had two sons, both over twenty, who often kept her company and groomed her, while the two top-ranking males in a seven-male group support each other in times of trouble, look alike, and are probably brothers. Other examples of close ties, including brother-sister bonds, indicate the complexity of social relations within the community.

The period of extended youth provides ample opportunity for many kinds of play. As among baboons, this consists in the main of silent chasing and wrestling. The chimpanzee is unique among primates, however, in the amount of time it spends playing with objects. It seems to have a special predisposition for manipulating certain kinds of objects, notably sticks and twigs, and manipulating them in a certain way, by poking and probing. Such a built-in bias helps to ensure that learning will not proceed at random but along broad, genetically guided lines.

Chimpanzee family: sister nuzzling brother in mother's arms

One of the chimpanzee's outstanding accomplishments is the use of probes to extract termites from underground nests (see Chapter II). They do this sort of thing naturally. In captivity they have been seen poking sticks into pipes and holes in the ground,

Chimp mother playing with son

pulling the sticks out and licking off the ends. The same sequence performed casually in the wild at a termite hill might yield a mouthful of termites which provide protein and at least in the case of the red soldiers' heads, tasty morsels. Success encourages deliberate repetitions of the act.

Obtaining termites on a regular basis demands a variety of techniques. Sometimes twigs or vines or blades of grass must be broken to the proper length, and side shoots trimmed off to permit insertion into narrow holes. The object is in effect modified according to a purpose. An element of foresight and close observation over long periods is involved, since a chimpanzee will not wait for the termites themselves to open their holes and fly out. (Flying time occurs some weeks later, when many animals gather for the feast.) It takes the initiative by scratching away the covering dirt beforehand. It thus builds upon and expands the original act and creates the complex or constellation of interrelated acts required for tool use.

Another skill demonstrated by Gombe National Park chimpanzees represents the anthropoid equivalent of drawing water from a well. The "well" is the crotch of a tree where rain water has collected, and the problem is to get a drink. Thirsty juveniles and young infants bend over and squeeze their faces into the hollow, but they get nothing because their faces are too big. An experienced chimpanzee knows precisely what to do. It strips some leaves from a convenient plant, chews them just enough to form a crumpled ball, dips the ball into the hollow, and then withdraws the soggy mass and sucks the water out of it. In other words, it makes a kind of artificial sponge.

The full range of tool using among wild apes is yet to be understood. Junichiro Itani of the University of Kyoto, Japan, reports that chimpanzees in western Tanzania, occupying territories up to a hundred miles south of the Gombe Reserve, crack hard fruits with stone "hammers," scoop honey out of honeycombs with twigs and, as mentioned in Chapter II, sometimes use sticks to attack one another. This is definitely cultural behavior. Different practices are observed in different areas. Gombe chimpanzees employ the sponge method of getting at water in a tree crotch, presumably because the trick was discovered at some time in the past and has been transmitted from generation to generation ever since. But Budongo chimpanzees have another method which happens to be less efficient, simply dipping their hands into the natural bowls and licking the water off their fingers. Such knowledge is passed along by imitation. A juvenile may see its mother probing for termites and immediately try to prepare and use probes of its own, an activity that may go on for hours.

Termite catching points up the gap between wild chimpanzees and wild baboons. Baboons like to eat termites, and watch intently as their fellow primates eat the insects by the hundreds. They sometimes pick up sticks as well. But that is where it ends. The notion of a tool, of using an object to make up for their own limitations, apparently does not occur to them under these circumstances. They have never been observed trying to use probes, and seem to be completely incapable of making a connection between the sticks they hold in their hands and the activity of the chimpanzees they are watching. Instead, they wait until later in the season when termites are flying and grab the swarming insects on the ground or in midair, a far less efficient process.

Wild primates may tolerate the activities of novices, often to a surprising extent. Mothers allow inexperienced and awkward daughters to carry their infants, even when the carrying is done high in trees at the risk of the infant's life. But for all their permissiveness adults are passive in learning behavior; they have not yet been observed taking a more active part in such situations. The novice is entirely on his own. He imitates the behavior of his elders, but they do nothing to encourage him or make things easier for him. Nonhuman primates learn, but they do not teach.

Chimpanzees make extensive use of gestures and physical contact in expressing their feelings. Upon meeting in the forest, old friends kiss and embrace, or one individual may reach out and pat the other on the head or shoulder. Another common form of greeting is to rest the hand on the thigh or genitals. This gesture may also signify reassurance, and men as well as chimpanzees have used it for that purpose. (In the Bible, for example, laying a hand on a person's thigh is a way of sealing a bargain, of swearing to do what he asks.)

There are other actions one would have no difficulty in interpreting, for example, chimpanzees scratch their head when trying to make up their mind. Before picking a piece of fruit off a tree chimpanzees may squeeze it gently to test its ripeness, like a housewife selecting tomatoes at the local supermarket. Van Lawick-Goodall saw a male fidgeting and absent-mindedly eating a flower while waiting for a companion, presumably female, and looking for all the world like an "impatient man glancing at his wristwatch." Chimpanzees are perhaps most human when they are at play. Infants may play tug of war with a stick. Juveniles chase one another, and in the midst of a chase the pursued may burst out laughing, presumably in anticipation of being tickled by his pursuer.

All things considered, the chimpanzee's lot seems to be a relatively happy one. It lives the good life in a part of the world with plenty of food and water and no danger, the sort of safe uncomplicated place envisioned in all our Edens. Such a life prevailed far more widely fifteen to twenty million years ago, before the coming of man, in forests that formed a broad band stretching from Africa to the Far East. The most advanced primates of those times may have been animals rather like the chimpanzees observed today in the Budongo and Gombe forests.

These were the prehuman apes introduced in Chapter II. On the basis of recent studies, they can now be described as lively, easygoing and relatively independent creatures with a social system sufficiently flexible to allow considerable freedom of movement and individual action. As forest dwellers, most of them moved almost entirely in and out of shadows and along old ancestral trails. But some bands began to invade territory in which no ape had yet established a foothold, venturing away from the safe depths of forests and out into less dense woodlands toward the wide-open spaces of the savanna.

They came well equipped for life in the sun. They were large, agile, sharp-sighted, and had probably learned to use tools. Above all, they were intelligent and adaptable. Moving called for some radical changes. The invaders could not afford to travel through exposed places the way they had traveled among the trees, relaxed and with an almost careless lack of alertness. They had to contend with natives of the grassy plains, established species which were already admirably adapted for predation and had learned all the tricks of ambushing and harassing and killing. A reasonable guess is that the new primates did what all pioneers, human as well as nonhuman, must do when they enter hostile territory. They became "baboonized," as it were, joining ranks and traveling together in disciplined troops.

Evidence to support this theory has been gathered during the past few years. Observations in the wild indicate that primates are capable of adjusting to different environments. Budongo chimpanzees, for example, change their behavior drastically upon approaching open terrain. They may amble unconcernedly through their forest, but they are tense and vigilant when it comes to crossing a road, looking left and right at the road's edge, running back into the undergrowth, and finally making a dash for the other side. Gombe chimpanzees become nervous on the slopes of hills where the forest thins out.

The effect can be considerably more extensive, as indicated by evidence from Itani and his associates. They have observed chimpanzees crossing wide stretches of open woodland country along mountain ridges lying between dense riverine forests, and report that these apes move in structured groups more like baboon troops on grassy savannas. The effect may also work the other way around. According to Rowell, baboons living in the comparative safety of Uganda forests do not have hierarchies and generally live more relaxed, more chimpanzee-like lives with looser social structures. They are also freer to move from troop to troop, and adult males do not defend the troop during emergencies: "In fact, being larger they usually outdistanced the rest in a flight from danger, the last animals being females carrying the larger babies."

Similar changes may have occurred among the primates that were man's ancestors. At first perhaps it was a matter of occasional crossings and the finding of new foods on the savanna, occasional excursions into savanna regions bordering the forests and back to the shelter of the forests at night. Then there were moves farther and farther out into the open until the bond between apes and forest dissolved, and they left the forest for good and used tiny islands of forest, clumps of trees near water holes, for refuge and sleeping. This development, which required perhaps a million years or more, produced the first hominids. The new way of life was achieved at a price. Life in the open, exposed to predators in the relatively exposed environment of wide grassy savannas, demanded tighter troop organization and discipline. The process created new sources of tension, the rise of the human sort of restlessness and discontent, a built-in source of potential change.

Cultural evolution as well as organic evolution proceeds because nothing is perfect. Organic evolution continues because sooner or later in the reproduction of species there is always a mutation, an "error" in the replication of genes. (Perfection, errorless replication, would mean the end of evolution and life.) Similarly, there are always slip-ups, social mutations, in the workings of human laws and institutions. Man may strive to do just what his fathers and grandfathers did, to believe what they believed. He may even succeed for a time. But his self-feeding restlessness ensures the sort of failure that makes cultural evolution and survival possible.

Further insights are needed to help define more precisely what it means to be human. The German zoologist Karl von Frisch spent ten years studying some aspects of the behavior of the bee and, incidentally, raising as many questions as he answered; it is safe to assume that considerably more time will be required for a primate species. To be sure, a great deal of information can be gathered in short-term research. One ten-month study alone produced 2,000 pages of handwritten notes and 50,000 feet of motion-picture film, as well as numerous maps and photographs and tape recordings.

But for all the data, a year or a few years are not long enough. The period covers too narrow a slice of time, too short in comparison with the life spans of monkeys and apes, which may live up to forty years in the wild. It may furnish a good idea of the structure of a hierarchy, but tell us little about the dynamics of the hierarchy, how it changes and how individuals rise or fall in status. A troop must be observed over extended periods if insights are to be gained into such things as the development of personality, enduring bonds among individuals, and events which happen rarely but may be revealing.

The most systematic long-term study yet conducted involves a troop of macaque monkeys living on the northeast coast of Japan's Kyushu Island, the "see no evil, hear no evil, speak no evil" monkeys of the Buddhist religion. One troop, which lives in a forest on a mountainside sloping down to the sea, has been observed on a continuous day-to-day basis ever since 1953. Studies of this sort can establish the existence of relationships at best only inferred from short-term studies and often missed entirely, as well as the existence of some baffling problems.

For example, a remarkably effective incest "taboo" prevails in the troop. In thousands of recorded copulations not a single one involved a mother and her son, perhaps, as Robin Fox of Rutgers University suggests, because the rule for mating is that the female partner be subordinate to the male partner and a mother is dominant in relation to her son.

A different situation exists on another island, Cayo Santiago off the coast of Puerto Rico, among rhesus monkeys. According to Elizabeth Missakian of Rockefeller University, out of twenty-six mother-son pairs in which mating was possible, that is in which the son was at least three years old, mating actually occurred among eight pairs. Furthermore, she finds that more often than not the relationship is exclusive as far as the sons are concerned: "It appears that males with mothers in the group usually either mated with their mothers or did not mate at all. . . . The young males who do engage in mother-son mating seem to seek their mothers out as the first objects of sexual activity."

The reported difference between Kyushu and Cayo Santiago monkeys has not yet been explained. It may have something to do with species differences or traditions developed over the years or, more likely, with methods and conditions of observing. Perhaps the fact that the Japanese work was done at special feeding grounds is significant, although it is difficult to see how that particular setting would inhibit mother-son matings selectively. Clearly there is no simple answer to the problem of what forces determine the extent of incest among primates, nonhuman as well as human.

Another observation is that the sons of dominant mothers generally become dominant themselves, a state of affairs discovered more than ten years ago among Japanese macaques and subsequently reported among baboons. This raises a number of questions. Perhaps the mother is dominant by association since she keeps company more frequently with dominant than with subordinate males, and so her son tends to inherit dominant-male genes and has the opportunity to emulate the ways of leaders. But the explanation may be more direct, namely that the mother has "dominance" genes of her own and passes them on to her offspring.

But even with the best of backgrounds, males encounter many difficulties in trying to establish themselves among other males. In a special study Hiroki Mizuhara of Kyoto University has found that there is not enough room at the top among Kyushu monkeys. At one point the troop contained about 200 members and its male hierarchy was made up of sixteen adult males (that is, males about twenty to thirty years old), six leaders and ten subleaders. Several years later the troop had increased to 440 members, but without proportional representation. The hierarchy still consisted of sixteen adult males. Although most of the younger males stayed on as second-class citizens, more than a dozen left to lead solitary lives outside the troop.

Even after making it to the top levels, an individual must continue to assert his position, or else suffer the consequences. For more than three years an adult male, Pan, held No. 3 position in the hierarchy and, together with the other five leaders, occupied the favored central area of the feeding ground, located at the forest's edge on the site of a Buddhist temple. But then something very unusual happened. He began to lose status, without any decline in health or vigor and without any apparent pressure from other monkeys, as if he were relinquishing his position by choice.

The early part of the change took place gradually. Pan spent less and less time in the central area, and more time near its edges where the subleaders generally sit or play when the leaders are around. But if he represented a weak spot at the top, no other troop member took advantage of the situation until nearly ten months had passed. The first sign of a challenge came one afternoon from Siro, a male ranking No. 18 in the hierarchy. Siro lunged at Pan as if to chase him; Pan stood his ground.

The encounter ended there, except that Siro emitted a "gaa-gaa" cry, a threat frequently directed at solitary males which have left the troop. The cry proved to be prophetic. The next day Pan had a vicious and inconclusive fight with a subleader. A few days after that he permitted a young male to mount him three times, thus indicating quite clearly that he considered himself a subordinate and no longer part of the hierarchy. Within three weeks he had been chased from the feeding area. He was last seen alive sitting alone in a wheat field about three hundred yards from the rest of the troop.

Mizuhara cites this case and others in emphasizing that, as far as enduring security within the troop is concerned, striking differences exist between the sexes. The female's role is relatively clear-cut and stable; no Kyushu female has ever become a loner. On the other hand, the male must always be ready to fight if necessary to keep or advance his position. The social structure of the macaque troop is put to an especially severe test when it comes to assimilating younger males into the hierarchy, a problem that is found in many human as well as nonhuman primate groups.

In general, as new observations accumulate, the importance of female members of the group becomes increasingly evident. Indeed the increasing emphasis on the female's role is one of the chief developments of the past few years, and reflects continuing and extended studies of particular troops. Short-term studies generally yield information heavily weighted on the male side, because male behavior tends to be more vigorous and dramatic. Long-term studies, on the other hand, indicate that actual changes in the male hierarchy may be frequent and drastic, while the female hierarchy changes relatively little.

Certainly females have close relationships with more individuals, especially since fathers are not built into the family circle. In one Cayo Santiago troop, for example, 33 of its 89 members were related to a single female. Such ties become significant when major changes take place in social organization, a fact brought out in a study by Naoki Koyama of Osaka City University, who observed the splitting of a macaque troop of about 165 members into two roughly equal groups. He is convinced that a medium-ranking female named Mino was at the root of the trouble, which occurred as the result of a complex series of conflicts and status changes triggered off when she became dominant over her mother. This study and others, notably those of Donald Sade of Northwestern University, indicate that the social stability of a primate troop is related to the stable ranking of its older females.

Japanese investigators have also used feeding grounds in extended studies of the origin and spread of eating habits, for example, the habit of carrying sweet potatoes to the ocean's edge and washing the dirt off (see Chapter II). This trick was invented some sixteen years ago by Imo, a highly precocious female macaque only eighteen months old at the time, apparently young enough so that she had not yet learned to share the traditional primate fear of water. Her playmates were soon washing their potatoes, but the rest of the troop continued to use the old and less efficient method of brushing the dirt off with their hands.

Five years later, the new method had spread from Imo and her playmates to their mothers and later to their own offspring. Today only a few of the adult males have not switched. In another test the troop reacted in a similar fashion to a new food, caramels wrapped in paper. The candies were sampled first by young macaques, then by their more permissive mothers, and finally by adult males and mothers who had originally tried to discourage the practice. Acceptance required about three years.

The pattern differed considerably, however, in another macaque troop. This time the first to try a new food, wheat grains, was the dominant male and all troop members were eating the cereal within three days, a fine example of the power of the follow-the-leader principle. Troops differ in many other ways—in the intensity of aggression among leaders, the availability of females in heat to subordinate males, ways of seeking food, and so on. Long-term studies such as those going on in Japan, Cayo Santiago and the Gombe Stream Research Center are just beginning to indicate the possible range of cultural or protocultural behavior among non-human primates.

■ Macaque monkeys raised as human infants; the laboratory study of infant monkeys and mother surrogates and the development of abnormal behavior; Washoe and her security blanket; an orangutan that makes stone tools; studies of Ceylon elephants, wild dogs and lions; electrode implantation as a research instrument

CHAPTER XIV

Observation and Experimentation
with Living Primates and Carnivores

■ The colony of macaque monkeys of the Primate Laboratory of the University of Wisconsin was established nearly twenty years ago, at about the same time that Japanese investigators were beginning to study wild macaques on Kyushu Island. The original purpose of the colony has been described by Harry Harlow, the psychologist who founded the laboratory: "to provide a steady supply of healthy newborn monkeys for the intensive study of learning and intellectual development from the day of birth until the attainment of full capacities."

Infants were raised in surroundings designed to promote vigorous physical growth. Taken from their mothers six to twelve hours after birth, they lived in clean and well-lit individual cages where they could see and hear but not touch other infants. They were bottle-fed, transferred to solid foods at the proper time, and generally treated like human infants. As expected, the infants thrived on all the special attention. Their death rate was lower than that of infants reared by their mothers, and they gained about 25 per cent more weight. After a year they were moved to larger cages, to participate in a series of learning tests and eventually to provide offspring for continuing studies.

The monkeys never served as progenitors of a brave new laboratory breed, however. As they grew up, it became increasingly evident that they were physically fit but emotionally crippled.

321

They sat motionless in their cages, staring into space, or rocking sometimes for hours at a time. Some individuals would start biting themselves as soon as they saw a human being approaching. Also, they were sexually incompetent. One male was aroused when put in a cage with an experienced estrus female which had grown up in the wild. He tried several times to mount her, but did not know how and finally gave up trying and began to attack her viciously. Females raised alone behaved similarly with experienced males.

Studies carried out in the wild direct attention to special areas of behavior, such as relationships with predators, maternal care, communication, play, sleeping habits, and so on. They suggest interpretations and hypotheses which can be checked and modified by the results of experiments performed in laboratory environments. Experiments, in turn, may suggest things to look for when observing troops in their native surroundings. Sophisticated theories of primate behavior, theories capable of predicting new behavior patterns as well as explaining behavior already observed, are most likely to come from investigations which depend on an interchange of information between field and laboratory.

Expanding studies of our primate relatives in Africa and elsewhere are influencing work under way at scientific centers far from forests and savannas and predators. The effect may be traced in part to the long-overdue reaction against drawing broad conclusions about natural behavior from the behavior of animals in cages. That does not in any way imply a downgrading of laboratory research, the need for which has never been at issue. It has become more important than ever now that we are acquiring more and more information about life in the wild.

This represents a shift of emphasis. In the future, investigators may be expected to devote more time to the natural behavior of primates, and less time to the study of animals in cages or the traditional and still-prevalent kind of psychological experiment in which primates are tested for their ability to get at food lying beyond their reach, paint pictures, do arithmetic, or play tick-tack-toe. The effort increasingly is to discover how they solve their own problems rather than problems we impose upon them. The trend reflects a change in our attitude toward all animals, a new respect for them as individuals adapted to their native environments.

Field work involves observed events, the specific activities of free-ranging primates. But observing itself is an extremely complicated form of behavior, many times more complicated than anything being observed. There is something to the notion that we tend to see things not as they are but as we are. Since men come to studies of primates, as to all studies, with various preconceived ideas, the problem is to bring these ideas into the open as fully as possible so that they may be modified by experience. The French biologist Claude Bernard used to tell his students that "observation shows and experiment teaches," a statement which applies with special force to primate research. Early experimental findings such as those involving macaque behavior have given rise to a great many studies of normal and abnormal behavior.

Harlow and his associates investigated the response of infant monkeys to "mother surrogates" or "effigies," dummies built to serve some of the functions of real mothers. In one series of experiments infants were brought up in cages, each with two wooden-headed dummies, one made of bare wire and the other covered with terry cloth. There was no doubt which represented the preferred object to the infants. When bottles of milk were strapped to both dummies, infants invariably went to the terry-cloth dummy. Even when milk was available from the wire dummy only, they spent less than an hour a day there and seventeen to eighteen hours a day with the terry-cloth model. Softness and warmth were far more important than food in determining the strength of an infant's early attachment to its mother.

Further tests indicate that the mother is important for social rather than purely biological reasons. Infant monkeys raised with mother surrogates were put in a room where they had never been before, a traumatic experience in itself. More than that, the room contained a mechanical bear and a number of other playthings. For whatever it is worth, Harlow has found that the toys of human children are among the most frightening objects to infant monkeys. But if there was a terry-cloth dummy in the room, the infant would rush to it and cling. Then after a while it would start exploring, run back to the dummy, explore further, and so on, precisely as it would have behaved with a real mother. In the same room with a wire dummy instead of a terry-cloth dummy, however, infants found no solace or comfort or confidence. They were

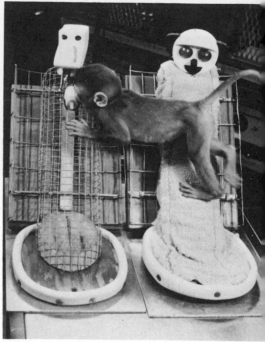

Love for mother surrogate: macaque infant clinging to warm terry-cloth surrogate (upper left); reaching for milk on bare-wire surrogate (upper right); using terry-cloth surrogate for protection against strange object (bottom)

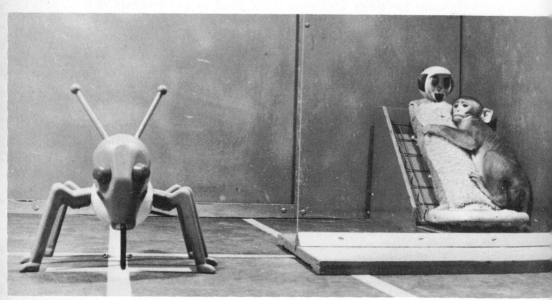

in effect utterly alone. They crouched and hid their faces and were generally too terror-stricken to do any exploring.

A recent case illustrates the "invention" of a sort of mother surrogate. Washoe, a young female chimpanzee currently being studied by University of Nevada psychologists, lives in a backyard trailer and does not usually venture out unless someone holds her

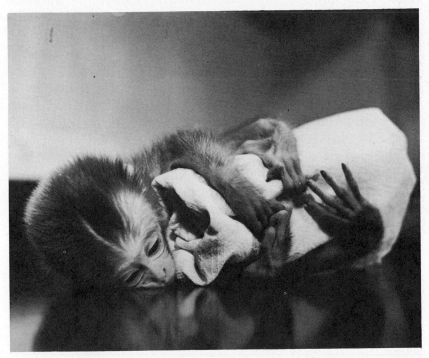

Macaque clinging reflex, prominent during first two or three weeks of life

hand and accompanies her. But one day she came out on her own dragging a blanket, putting it on her head, lying on it, and leaving it for brief exploratory excursions around the yard, only to rush back to it whenever her courage ran out. The spontaneous use of a mother or security symbol has also been seen in a young gibbon and hints that investigators may yet discover surprising examples of advanced behavior among wild as well as among captive apes.

But Harlow makes it clear that dummies providing warmth and comfort are not substitutes for mothers: "The surrogate cannot cradle the baby or communicate monkey sounds and gestures. It cannot punish for misbehavior." Individuals brought up with terry-cloth dummies are practically as pathological as individuals brought up in complete isolation, without surrogates or real mothers. As adolescents and adults they are incapable of getting along with other monkeys. The few motherless females which became pregnant, because of the persistence of males rather than through their own initiative, showed no traces of affection toward their infants. They were indifferent and rejecting at best; at worst they attacked and killed their infants. In the absence of normal social relations, there is no such thing as a maternal instinct.

On the other hand, it is rather startling to note that some of these females have given birth to a second infant and that they performed far more adequately as mothers the second time. This represents a most revealing example of learning ability in primates, an ability that has somehow managed to survive the trauma of being reared without a mother and alone. That a female can experience such extreme deprivation in early life and still arrive at an appreciable capacity for learning indicates how strongly she is predisposed to develop into an effective mother.

Judging by the experiments of Stephen Suomi, one of Harlow's colleagues, infants can also make remarkable recoveries. He put normal three-month-old females into the cages of six-month-old male isolates, monkeys reared without mothers or social stimulation of any sort. The first response of the typical isolate was to huddle in a corner rigid with fear, and the first response of the infant female was to come over and cling to her cage mate for warmth and affection. In the beginning the isolate remained rigid and unresponsive, but within a week he was clinging too, within two weeks the monkeys were playing with one another. Improvement was steady, and today, after more than two years, the ex-isolates seem completely normal.

This continuing study is of special medical interest, suggesting that the impact of even severe early deprivation can be appreciably reduced, a conclusion which runs counter to the views of some psychiatrists who feel that deprivation produces practically irreversible effects. From an evolutionary standpoint the experiments highlight the role of the mother. She has always stood between the infant and terror, and it is her function to help transform the infant into an individual ready for outgoing social relationships.

Techniques developed at the Wisconsin laboratory are being used in long-range research on learning by Seymour Levine of the Stanford University Medical School and William Mason, formerly associated with Harlow and now at Tulane University's Delta Regional Primate Research Center (one of seven such centers established by the United States Public Health Service). In general, they have found that infants with mother surrogates react to every variation of a standard test as if it were something entirely new, and react to novelty with screams of pain as if they were being tortured. One objective of current studies is to discover what biochemical changes accompany the emergence of pathological anxiety.

A great deal of fruitful work is also going on in an effort to bridge the gap between nature and the laboratory. The laboratory provides opportunities for precise observation under conditions that may be varied at will, but does so at the price of oversimplification, especially in the case of isolated mothers and infants. On the other hand, although the full range of primate activity is on display in the wild, it is difficult or impossible to vary conditions and obtain individual case histories. Therefore studies are being conducted to deal with social behavior which is somewhat more complex than that typical of most laboratory experiments, while at the same time permitting observations somewhat more precise than those usually obtained in the field.

Among investigators engaged in such work is Robert Hinde of the Sub-Department of Animal Behavior at Cambridge University, England. He has developed a most thorough procedure for recording the behavior of rhesus infants living in large outdoor cages connected with smaller indoor rooms. The procedure makes use of check lists on which observers indicate details of the behavior of an infant—whether it is on its mother's nipple, or off the nipple and on the mother, or off the mother and if so whether more or less than two feet away (two feet being about the distance within which the mother can pick up her infant quickly), whether mother is approaching infant or vice versa, various kinds of play activity, and so on.

The system yields an enormous amount of data. In one group of monkeys these and other items were checked off at 30-second intervals for 234 hours as part of a study that lasted a year, making a grand total of more than 28,000 observing intervals for each mother-infant pair—and the group included nine pairs. Such data can reveal, and pin down in quantitative terms, important aspects of social behavior. For example, Hinde found an unexpected set of relationships in a group consisting of an adult male, two adult females each with an infant, and an adolescent female.

Normal maternal behavior: mother protecting infant (left); pathological maternal behavior of females reared without mothers: abuse of infant (right)

The adolescent female showed a normal desire to hold, groom and play with the infants, and normally the mothers would have played a major and deciding role in granting or withholding the privilege. In this case, however, she was the male's favorite and he often intervened in her behalf when the mothers were trying to exercise their authority. They reacted by being extrarestrictive to their offspring. At the age of eighteen weeks the infants hardly ever stayed more than two feet away from their mothers for an interval as long as half a minute, while infants living in groups where their mothers could dominate other females stayed away in more than a third of the intervals.

This observation led to a year-long study planned especially to investigate, under more usual circumstances, the role of females other than the mothers in raising rhesus infants. The study involved four "isolates" or mother-infant pairs each living alone and, as controls, nine mother-infant pairs each living with a group of a male and three or four females and their young. Analysis of the results shows that, as compared with "isolate" mothers, group-living mothers maintain physical contact with their infants a greater proportion of the time and, when contact is broken, establish contact sooner. In other words, the fact that mothers restrict their infants more in the presence of other females is confirmed for conditions comparable to those prevailing outside the laboratory.

Notice that this effect would be difficult to demonstrate under natural conditions, although now that it is recognized it may be looked for more carefully. The same thing goes for possible effects on the psychology of infants. To test their initiative or curiosity, Hinde added "baby filters" to the main cages, cages which had openings so small that only infants could enter and which contained mirrors and other unfamiliar objects. As might be expected, the two infants raised in a group which included the male-supported adolescent female were more upset by a strange environment than infants raised with their mothers only, and tended to cling to their mothers longer after being exposed to such an environment, a cautiousness that would clearly increase their chances of survival in the wild.

As a rule, reactions to strangeness or novelty provide a very sensitive index to the existence and extent of emotional disturbance. Infants whose mothers had been removed from their cages for a brief period typically react to her return with a sharp increase in temper tantrums, distress calls and other signs of anxiety—all of which tend to decrease rapidly as time passes. But responses to strangeness persist. More than two years after their mothers had been absent for only six days, and after being with their mothers continuously ever since, young monkeys still showed aftereffects. They were extra-wary of strange objects such as a big ball or Hinde himself dressed in mask and black robe.

Later the British investigator decided to separate infants from mothers instead of mothers from infants, removing infants for six days of isolation and then putting them back in their home cages. He expected that this sort of separation would prove more upsetting to the infants. Actually there was a great difference, but in the other direction. The isolated infants were far less disturbed, chiefly reflecting the fact that they had to deal with far less disturbed mothers.

Combined findings from field and laboratory indicate how relationships favoring mother-infant ties have become intricately intermeshed during the course of evolution. The tendency to exclude younger subdominant males from the center of the baboon troop creates an outer defense ring, the attractiveness of the infant brings clusters of individuals to the center, the resulting restrictiveness of the mothers produces properly cautious offspring, and if a mother should die, one of the females that have been hovering about is available to adopt the infant. (Such an adoption occurred in one of Hinde's experimental groups. Harlow has records of rhesus females which actually produced milk for their new charges.)

These investigations have clinical as well as evolutionary implications. Researchers cannot afford to overlook certain analogies between the behavior of monkeys and apes and the behavior of man. Psychiatrists have been struck with the fact that such symptoms as rocking and vacant staring and self-mutilation observed among monkeys deprived of their mothers during infancy are also seen in some mentally disturbed children and orphans. Some physicians believe that women without practice in caring for young brothers and sisters have a less strong urge than more experienced women to care for their own infants, a phenomenon which probably exists among lower primates.

The appearance in experimental primates of behavior resembling human behavior encourages the investigator to feel that he is dealing with relevant situations, with principles that apply broadly. But it would be a mistake to deduce or expect too much from the parallels, and to foster the notion that man is "nothing but" an ape (another instance of what has been called "nothing-buttery" thinking). Man studies lower primates, and the similarities between them and himself, mainly so that in the long run he can arrive at a clearer and more precise understanding of the all-important differences.

Taking the full measure of our uniqueness demands further research along many lines. For one thing, we would like to know more about the bringing up of infants, and not only about the female's role. As far as the results of laboratory experiments to date are concerned, the absence of subadult and adult males does not seem to make much of a difference in the development of young males. There have been no long-term studies of the problem, but Harlow has recently started such a study. In any case, the matter is of special interest, considering that in most human societies sons know, and usually have a chance to identify deeply with, their fathers.

A wide range of possibilities exists for new kinds of experiments with chimpanzees and other apes, in the laboratory as well as under controlled field conditions. One study is concerned with the development of self-recognition in chimpanzees. Gordon Gallup of Tulane University put full-length mirrors just outside the cages of four wild-born chimpanzees, two males and two females, and observed their reactions. At first the image in the mirror was an alien thing, an object inspiring curiosity and fear, something to be bobbed and lunged at—a mixed response reminiscent of that exhibited by wild Congo chimpanzees when confronted with a photograph of a chimpanzee, in color and slightly larger than life.

After two days, however, the apes clearly began to realize that they were looking at themselves. They were soon making use of the mirrors for such activities as picking their teeth, and, most interesting, they promptly noticed red marks that had been dyed on their eyebrows and ears under anesthesia. In other words, they noticed changes in their image and responded by touching the marks repeatedly. Such behavior contrasts dramatically with the behavior of monkeys who were similarly confronted with full-length mirrors for three weeks and at no time indicated that they connected the image with themselves.

Gallup's research demonstrates that awareness of self is a sign of superior intelligence, advanced brain structure, among higher primates. It has implications beyond that. Self-awareness must have developed further during the course of human evolution from *Ramapithecus* to early *Homo sapiens*, which raises the question of what new quality of self-awareness came with the appearance of modern man within the past 50,000 years and the first evidence of personal adornment and art. Perhaps it was a new kind of power, the realization that one can somehow change the order of things by changing one's image deliberately and creating images and symbols outside oneself.

Apes may well have imagemaking capacities which are hardly called on in their normal lives, but which might be more fully developed in appropriately designed experimental environments and social structures. The same thing goes for toolmaking. Chimpanzees could probably make tools far more sophisticated than termite probes if they had sufficient reason to do so, at least judging by the accomplishments of a five-year-old orangutan named Abang currently resident at the Bristol Zoo in England. About a year ago Abang learned to make and use stone tools, his incentive being to have company and to please his teacher, Richard Wright of the University of Sydney, who was visiting England at the time.

In the first stage of the experiment Wright brought two items into the orang's cage, a smash-proof box of fruit which could be opened only by cutting a tough nylon string and, lying on the floor next to the box, a sharp flint flake. Abang put his heart into the game, trying everything from biting and tugging at the string to breaking the box and forcing the lid. At one point he stopped and turned to Wright with an appealing what-do-I-do-now look on his face. Following several demonstrations of the flake being moved back and forth across the string, Abang got the idea—and had his first success after 69 minutes of training. From then on he had mastered the trick, performing it fifteen to twenty times in a row.

The next stage involved the same setup, except that instead of a flake Wright put a large chunk of flint and a three-pound hammerstone into the cage. It was up to Abang to make a cutting implement for himself by bashing the flint with the hammerstone and knocking off a suitable flake, a more difficult problem than learning to use a ready-made flake. This time, after more demonstrations and tossing the hammerstone away at one point (his only sign of impatience), he took 134 minutes to learn the task,

Abang the tool maker: before knocking off flake; examining flake; eating fruit from opened box

for a total training period of about three and a third hours. Later for the benefit of British television he did it all over again in about fifteen minutes.

Wright has plans for more ambitious experiments. For example, he would like to find out how a flakemaking ape would go about passing its skill on to a novice, and whether it could work flakes into various shapes. Meanwhile Abang finds himself in a rather pathetic situation. At times during his training sessions he seems to have deliberately delayed opening the box, because he knew that once he succeeded Wright would probably leave him for the day—and the company was as important to him as the food. Now he sits in his cage with a rubber tire to play with, more bored perhaps than even his fellow apes who never had a chance to play really challenging games.

Apes participating in long-term projects in experimental colonies rather than zoos generally have more space, lead more interesting lives and provide investigators with more information. Van Lawick-Goodall spends three months a year carrying out research in a chimpanzee colony at the Stanford University Medical Center in California, one example of the increasing interplay between laboratory and field work.

There are also possibilities for experimental work in the field, particularly among wild chimpanzees. So far the emphasis has been mainly on observing. Except for confronting the apes with an occasional stuffed leopard or an awkwardly placed can of water or luring them to observing sites with bananas, the general policy has been not to tinker with natural conditions. But as accumulating evidence points up gaps in knowledge, some intervention may be useful. For example, the question whether chimpanzees in a savanna environment would form organized troops complete with hierarchies might be investigated by actually moving a band to a sufficiently large tract of open country.

Another suggestion concerns the social impact of habitual meat eating. Suppose that some kind of small game, say, hares, were fed to members of a chimpanzee band until they became accustomed to the meat as a regular and necessary item in their diet. Then suppose that the band was moved to an island or some other restricted area, where the only available food consisted of hares. Would the chimpanzees rise to the occasion and develop new hunting techniques? If so, would the techniques demand the development of appropriate new gestures and vocal signals, a more advanced communication system? (The problem of language is discussed in Chapter XIX.)

The current emphasis has been overwhelmingly on monkeys and apes for sound reasons, the most obvious being that they are our kind, members of the same order. It is a problem to account for the fact that the research under way now was not started half a century ago. Full-scale studies of the behavior of primates in the wild have been so long in coming that every consideration dictates a major effort along these lines.

Furthermore, the emphasis on primates comes as a healthy reaction against some emphases of the not too distant past. As recently as three decades ago the social insects were almost certain to be cited in serious consideration of the nature of man. The Aesop's-fable approach was on the way out—the tendency to present ants and bees as thrifty busy creatures, models of behavior—and the mood had become more somber. There were discussions about strict division of labor among ants and workers and slaves and armies, and warnings that in post-depression days of big government men might evolve regimented anthill societies of their own.

Such discussions are taken less earnestly today. But to veer to the other extreme and study the primate order only would also be a mistake. Man has much in common with mammals that live in herds and prides and packs as well as troops, with all species from hooved browsers and grazers to lions and other social carnivores. His ancestors, like many of their ancestors, had to cope with ice ages and wandered across wildernesses and land bridges in search of living and feeding space.

Eisenberg is studying the Ceylon elephant as an example of a large animal with a life span comparable to ours and a record of having been able to coexist rather successfully with us, at least until recently.

This elephant's basic social unit or "nuclear family" consists of a pregnant female with her offspring (aged about eight, five and three) closely associated with another female, often her mother or sister, with about the same number of offspring. Older bulls in the age range of twenty to thirty go about in less cohesive groups, occasionally accompanied by one to three male "satellites" eleven to fourteen years old. The oldest bulls, which may be forty or more years old, are usually loners or else travel with a crony of about the same age.

But during dry periods some three hundred individuals may form huge loosely organized herds, which provides Eisenberg with a chance to check the idea that "when an animal like man or the elephant attains a certain body size and brain size, it is capable of unique memory feats." Migration in Ceylon may mean moving over any one of a number of complicated routes from lowlands into lusher highland country, for distances up to forty miles, over high passes and into the mountains, and avoiding villages on the way to isolated feeding grounds with sufficient water.

In addition to the annual dry season there is a ten-year drought cycle. So details of certain special emergency routes must be remembered for periods of perhaps a decade or more by individuals which cannot have participated in many migrations during their lifetimes, and may have migrated only once. In other words, the elephant's bulk not only helps protect it against predators but also pays off in terms of proportionate brain size and memory capacity, permitting the shaping of long-term survival strategies. Since the same point applies to man, research on elephants may be expected to increase understanding of the role of memory in human evolution.

But as far as research on nonprimates is concerned, most of it can perhaps be expected from studies of predators and their prey. Early man became a carnivore, a carnivore that hunted in groups. Man can advance understanding of his nature by studying the ways of other hunting packs. Furthermore, when he started becoming a big-time carnivore himself, he probably profited from the efforts of his fellow meat eaters by imitating their stalking and hunting methods as well as by scavenging. Intent observations of wild carnivores is nothing new. Man's forerunners did so two or more million years ago. Today only the spirits are different and the motive for observing, now it is man who is feared.

Of all predators none comes closer to our ideals of cooperation than the wild dog. Work in Africa during the past few years certainly supports Campbell's comment: "It is not a coincidence that dogs and men understand each other so well today; until recently they both led the same kind of life, that of the social carnivore." The work has been done by Wolfdietrich Kühme of the Max Planck Institute for the Physiology of Behavior near Munich, Germany, Richard Estes of Harvard and John Goddard of the Ngorongoro Conservation Area in Tanzania, and George Schaller of Rockefeller University.

Kühme spent more than three months studying a pack of wild dogs on the Serengeti Plain, the general area which includes the Olduvai Gorge. The pack consisted of twenty-three individuals, six adult males and two females with litters of four and eleven newborn pups, all living together in a borrowed den, one of the numerous vacant burrows dug by aardvarks, wart hogs and hyenas. The females nursed and cared for all fifteen offspring on a first-come, first-served basis. They often competed for the privilege, even to the point of trying to steal one another's pups, a tactic which produced the only friction in the pack, mild bickering in the form of growls and snapping. Males were never seen fighting, and there are no hierarchies among wild dogs.

Both sexes performed guard duty, usually the same individuals taking on the job of remaining with the young while the rest of the pack hunted. In other words, unlike nonhuman primates, the wild dogs had a home base where the very young and their guardians stayed while the rest of the pack hunted. When the hunters returned with pieces of unchewed meat in their stomachs, pups and guardians met them with a characteristic begging gesture, the beggar pushing its nose against the hunter's mouth or biting at the lips or jowls. The meat was then disgorged, and every pack member received its allotted portion. The stomachs of the mothers serve as secondary storage depots and processing plants. On a number of occasions a female made a special point of chewing and swallowing disgorged meat intended for pups too young to handle the meat, providing them with small titbits which she redisgorged periodically during the next three to four hours.

Regular food sharing, a basic element in the pack's way of life, is unknown among nonhuman primates, as is regular communal hunting and division of labor in gathering food. As indicated in Chapter XIII, however, there are definite signs of a potential for sharing among chimpanzees at least, something which could be built upon and extended given the proper set of circumstances. But _man_ remains the only _primate_ to go in for _meat_ eating _habitually_ and, whenever possible, on a relatively _large scale._

Group hunting is another highly developed form of cooperation found among _wild dogs_ and other _carnivores._ Estes and Goddard used Land-Rovers to follow a pack in the crater of Ngorongoro, the volcano on the way to Olduvai which collapsed sometime during the past three million years. Some 25,000 herd animals and their predators live on the 104-square-mile crater floor, an open plain providing ideal observing conditions. The investigators obtained most of their information during the predators' two regular hunting periods, sessions which begin at the end of the day, early in the morning shortly before sunrise and in the late afternoon, and last about an hour or two.

During the _stalking_ phase of the hunt, wild dogs move with _shoulders_ hunched, _ears_ flattened and _hind legs_ in ready-to-sprint position like a runner at the starting block. The objective is to get within three hundred yards or so of a grazing herd, usually a herd of gazelles, before breaking into a run and stampeding the prey. The leader of the pack selects a victim from the fleeing herd, perhaps one of the slower individuals, one or two adult dogs follow at intervals of about a hundred yards, and the other members of the pack run behind at distances of as much as a mile.

Hunting _strategies_ are simple and effective. Dogs running immediately _behind_ the _leader_ are ready to _cut off_ the prey as it attempts to _dodge_, but as a rule by the time it starts dodging it is too tired to get away. At the end of the chase the victim is usually so exhausted and in such a deep state of shock that it does not fight back. Estes and Goddard describe a large female antelope which "did little more than stand with head high while the dogs cut it to ribbons, looking less the victim than the witness of its own execution."

About 85 per cent of all chases end successfully, that is, from the pack's point of view—not surprising in view of the fact that a wild dog can attain top speeds of more than forty miles an hour, and run at an average speed of thirty miles an hour for several miles. Most chases last only about three to five minutes and cover a mile or two. Schaller has found that when game is plentiful, hunting packs on the Serengeti Plain kill enough animals to provide about twenty pounds of meat per dog daily, at least four times more than is needed.

Wild dogs have developed some amazing rituals. A typical prelude to the hunt might find them lolling about in the grass. One restless dog will begin romping with a few of its pack mates.

Wild dog devouring young antelope

Soon others join in, and gradually the play and the chasing build up into a wilder and wilder climax, with the entire pack milling around in a circle and emitting, in unison, peculiar birdlike twittering calls signifying a high degree of excitement. The procedure has been compared to a "pep rally," and brings the pack to a fever pitch for the hunt.

Sometimes a chain reaction occurs in the midst of the milling about. It starts with two or three pack members engaging in particularly hectic play. The play in turn apparently triggers a response among other members, up to half a dozen dogs taking part in a strange melodrama. One dog seems to assume the role of victim and the others gang up on it, pushing it over and rolling it about but never biting. This so-called mobbing behavior is precisely what happens, more intensely, when the pack corners and starts ripping apart a large prey. Before the hunt, it may serve as a kind of dress rehearsal for the killing to come, a procedure as potent as drugs or fire dances in arousing excitement.

Kühme notes the existence of another ritual which has the opposite effect, in that it serves to prevent violence within the pack. Adults forestall aggression by habitually assuming postures of humility toward one another when greeting or soliciting food. Again, it is a kind of acting. An adult male may "pretend" to be young and use the same begging gesture infants and juveniles use, pushing its nose against the mouth of another adult. At other times adults behave like nursing pups, males licking the udders of females and females creeping under males as if seeking an udder. Such rituals achieve a "tolerance of competitors, which human beings find so difficult."

Research on wolves and hyenas and jackals as well as wild dogs is providing a richer background of knowledge against which to view human behavior. The abandonment of stereotyped notions about other social carnivores may prepare men to see themselves more clearly. For example, although hyenas have been too readily dismissed as uncourageous scavengers, the fact of the matter is that they function as effective hunters upon occasion. In early prehistoric times hyenas probably preyed on savanna apes and pre-men at least as much as lions and other big cats. As far as character is concerned, they display a rather subtle combination of shyness, persistence and incredible gall.

A solitary hyena during the day is relatively harmless, and perhaps the animal's reputation as a skulking coward is based on the behavior of such loners. But there is nothing more lethal than a pack of twenty or so hyenas at night. A lion will move away from its kill at the attack of a hyena pack, snarling but making no serious attempt to fight for its meat. Schaller once saw a pack that had worked itself into a state of excited aggression and was mobbing a large male lion. Under these circumstances the lion was anything but a king of beasts. It was plainly terrified.

The hyena is a superb waiter. According to Estes, "it will lie all day near an ostrich nest, anticipating the time when the eggs may be left momentarily unguarded . . . and cripples may be followed for days until too weak to resist." He also observed hyenas waiting hours for a pack of wild dogs to begin hunting, often crawling to within a few yards of the pack and staring almost purposefully at the dogs "as though urging them to get started." Furthermore, like jackals and lions and the Gonds of India and other tribes (and perhaps like early man; see Chapter VI), hyenas scan the skies for circling vultures and dash to the spot to share in the carcass.

Parallels exist between the evolution of canids, members of the dog family, and primates. As related species evolve increasingly complex social systems, they require increasingly complex signals to establish and maintain individual relationships within the group. In other words, there is selective pressure for more sophisticated communication, and one result may be an increase in the mobility of the face, in the number of possible expressions, a phenomenon being studied by Michael Fox of Washington University in St. Louis.

He points out that wolves, highly social animals with a system of cooperative hunting and sharing at least as elaborate as that of the wild dog, exhibit a far greater variety of facial expressions than canids like the red fox, which does not live in packs and tends to be a loner when it comes to hunting. Similar tendencies have been observed among primates, and as a matter of fact, social canids and social primates share a number of basic expressions signifying a playful mood (the so-called play face), threats, submissiveness, and so on.

Fox reports another difference between the wolf and red fox. Wolf cubs in a given litter seem to be born with widely varying temperaments, as judged by a series of tests designed to measure degrees of aggressiveness and fear of novelty, which is just what would be needed for pack formation and the establishment of stable hierarchies. The red fox, on the other hand, tends to have litters made up of cubs roughly on a par with one another as far as aggressiveness is concerned and all of them definitely "individualists," a feature which may help ensure that they will ultimately disperse and lead more or less solitary lives. Primates do not have litters, of course, but it might be interesting to study differences among primate infants from an evolutionary standpoint.

The behavior of the big cats is also of interest, and Schaller has spent a good deal of time among them, most recently during a three-year study of lions and other predators on the Serengeti Plain. His records show the advantage of hunting in groups. A lion alone, stalking its prey and lifting and placing each paw separately as it advances and selecting a moment to rush from its hiding place, has a batting average of about 0.150 or a success rate of one kill in every six or seven attempts—considerably better than a one-in-twelve estimate for tigers which always hunt alone.

On the average, group hunting involving two to four or five lions is about twice as successful. As indicated in Chapter VI, lions use elaborate encircling tactics, but they may simply move forward in an irregular line along a broad front and dash in for the kill when a herd panics. Sometimes in the confusion animals rush directly into the jaws of their predators. From the prey's point of view as well as the predator's there is an advantage in being a member of a group, provided the group is not too large. A lone zebra is far more vulnerable than a zebra in a herd of up to 75 individuals, but as herd size increases much beyond that level so does inertia. It may take longer to get moving, flight is inhibited, and the success of a killer rises correspondingly.

Lions, like most carnivores, conserve their energies and do not bother to kill if they can get meat in some other way. On the open savanna they do more scavenging than hyenas; about half their food comes from moving in and taking the kills of cheetahs and other predators. When lions are not hunting or scavenging, they do nothing in particular, spending about twenty hours a day lying down, generally asleep. Incidentally, wild dogs spend even more of their time doing nothing, probably because their killing success rate is so high; they lie down about twenty-two hours a day.

A pride of lions, like a troop of chimpanzees, tends to be very loosely organized, has no rigid hierarchy and may be scattered over a wide area. It is essentially a female-centered group, averaging about fifteen members. All males are ejected from the pride as soon as they reach sexual maturity, and become nomads wandering over the plains and joining prides for a time and then moving on again. Females, on the other hand, hardly ever change prides; they remain within a hunting territory of about a hundred square miles. In fact, Schaller suspects that generations of female lions have lived in their native ranges for centuries.

The ferocity of the big cats is often exaggerated, usually as an excuse for slaughtering them in the name of sport. Schaller never carries a weapon, and one of his closest calls came a number of years ago when he was studying tigers in the Kanha National Park of central India. He approached and failed to notice a large female tiger cub sleeping just over the rise of a large boulder. When she awoke and raised her head and looked over the rise, man and tiger suddenly found themselves eye to eye at a distance of three to four feet. Schaller leaped away and backed hurriedly toward a tree, with the cub bounding after "apparently out of curiosity." He reached the tree and the cub lay down to watch, later being joined by her two sisters. After about half an hour in the tree, he shouted just once and the cubs ran off.

Schaller has had a number of similar unexpected encounters with tigers, and they invariably make it a point to get away from him. In every case he was alone, on foot, and without weapons. On the basis of such experiences, he and other professional observers have little respect for teams of hunters who, supposedly at great risk to themselves, use high-powered rifles to bring down lions and tigers at distances of as much as several hundred yards. More often than not, tall tales about going out and braving wild beasts tell us much more about the characters of the hunters than the hunted.

As a general rule, different species of predators tend not to get along with one another. Lions have been known to chase and kill leopards and cheetahs and hyenas, leopards to kill cheetahs, hyenas to attack cheetahs and jackals, jackals to eat foxes. Furthermore, there may be within-the-species killing and cannibalism. Tigers may prey on tigers, lions on lions, and so on. Peace does not seem to prevail among carnivores. Such behavior contrasts with the behavior of antelopes, zebras and other plant-eating herd animals which normally live side by side without trouble, and the same thing is true within troops of nonhuman primates.

A rapidly growing body of firsthand knowledge about primates and other species, a wealth of new observations and experiences, now exists. At the same time, some investigators recognize that detailed accounts of how animals interact, and authentic anecdotes to replace the less reliable anecdotes of times past, represent an essential but only a first step. The facts cannot be expected to speak for themselves in the study of animal behavior any more than in the study of flint artifacts and other archeological remains. "Hard" science must follow "soft" science; a mathematical approach to relationships too complex to handle by intuition alone must follow the descriptive natural-history approach.

The beginning of systematic efforts along these lines may be seen in work such as that being carried out by Stuart Altmann and his associates at the University of Chicago. His basic information is descriptive, but in a rather special way. Some of it comes from a two-year study on Cayo Santiago, a forty-acre island off the east coast of Puerto Rico which serves as a home for some 400 rhesus monkeys. The pioneer primate investigator Ray Carpenter brought the monkeys from India more than thirty years ago, and they have been studied constantly ever since 1956.

During his field observations Altmann was not concerned solely with hierarchies, infant care, playing, and so on. He concentrated as much on the things a monkey does as on the setting or context of its doings, identifying and recording its concrete gestures and sounds and movements. In other words, he compiled a catalog of the "elementary behavioral patterns" of Cayo Santiago monkeys, listing "grooms," "gnashes teeth," "grimaces," "holds tail erect," and some 120-odd other items. This is a very restricted list in the sense that it includes only a fraction of all the things a monkey is physically capable of doing. But it does include all patterns which are known to serve in social communications and which thus make the survival of the species possible, a repertoire of behavioral units selected over millions of years of evolution.

The repertoire may be analyzed by using a mathematical theory originally designed to deal with the behavior of another type of primate, man, in his telephone and radio communications. Claude Shannon of the Massachusetts Institute of Technology developed the theory more than twenty years ago when he was at the Bell Telephone Laboratories, investigating how to plan systems for handling large numbers of messages as efficiently as possible. Part of the problem involves ways of predicting messages. Of course, the full information content of a message generally cannot be predicted; if it could, there would be little reason to send it in the first place.

On the other hand, a message is not entirely unpredictable. Certain rules for putting words together must be obeyed. The instant one is chosen, subsequent words are limited to an appreciable extent. For example, if a sentence starts with "I," the odds are that the next word will be a verb like "believe" rather than a noun like "apple," and the odds are that the next word after "I believe" will be "in" or "that" rather than "eat" or "elephant." According to Shannon, the English language is about 50 per cent redundant, which means that on the average, when writing in English, about half the words are chosen freely and half are determined by the structure or rules of the language.

This concept and others in communication theory are also relevant to the analysis of animal societies, which are living communication networks. Taking an analogy from the rhesus monkey's repertoire of 120-odd behavior patterns as a vocabulary, certain "words" or patterns occur far more frequently than others. In fact, the six most frequent patterns—"walks toward," "walks away from," "grooms," "presents for grooming," "grasps waist" and "grips legs"—account for more than half of all its observed activities. Furthermore, there is considerable "redundancy" in a monkey's life, a high probability that a certain pattern will be followed by a particular one of all the other patterns and those two by a third highly probable pattern, and so on, thus producing predictable sequences of stereotype behavior.

Such analyses represent one step toward the design of increasingly refined models of primate interaction, models that will prove more and more powerful in helping us to understand and predict social behavior. Furthermore, a new technology is now being developed which permits a spectacular degree of control over animal behavior. Altmann and others are interested in a procedure involving the capture of a wild primate, say, a baboon, and surgically inserting a dozen wire electrodes into as many different nerve centers of its brain. Attached to the electrodes is a miniature antenna unit capable of picking up and amplifying radio signals.

The complete unit of electrodes and associated circuitry and solar battery is smaller than a pack of cigarettes, weighs only about five ounces or less, and can be mounted firmly on the head. The baboon is then released to rejoin its troop. But it is not completely free. It has been wired for remote control; in fact, the so-called telestimulating equipment in its head was developed by space scientists for use in controlling and guiding satellites and interplanetary vehicles. An investigator sitting at a radio transmitter as much as half a mile away can change the monkey's behavior by pushing the right button or combination of buttons, sending radio signals to specific electrodes in its brain and stimulating specific nerve centers.

This technique provides an unusual opportunity to study the workings of social systems. For example, suppose the baboon happens to be the dominant male of the troop. How will lower-ranking males react if he suddenly becomes submissive? Or if he decides to go off and become a loner? Or supposing the wired baboon is the lowest member of the hierarchy, what would happen if he suddenly began behaving like a leader? These and other questions will be investigated in the wild as soon as experiments already under way make it possible to control aggression, sexual activity, maternal care and so on, to turn such responses on and off at will in a troop of wild primates or in a laboratory colony.

Telestimulating techniques offer especially interesting possibilities when combined with sophisticated mathematical analysis, when investigators can predict what would happen in response to an unusual type of behavior, and then create that behavior to order by remote radio control. Perhaps the problem of how many behavioral patterns make up the human repertoire can be investigated. According to one opinion, the repertoire is effectively infinite. Certainly the way will then be clear for measuring behavior and comparing in a precise way man's behavior with that of his fellow primates. New intuitions will follow analysis and controlled experiments, and the intuitions will radically change man's ideas about the social organization of human beings and other animals.

CHAPTER XV

Contemporary Hunter-Gatherers: Last Representatives of the Stone Age

■ Many "human" interludes, flashes or episodes of behavior reminiscent of human behavior, occur in the daily lives of monkeys and apes. We see ourselves in the baboon, top-ranking member of the hierarchy, scanning the horizon for danger and hesitating and finally leading his troop across a stretch of savanna —in the mother-infant pair surrounded by solicitous females, the rough-and-tumble play of male juveniles, the chimpanzee with a mischievous twinkle in his eyes or scratching his head in perplexity or laughing out loud at a bewildered playmate. Such similarities reflect the fact of continuity in human evolution, the existence of patterns which man and his ancestors share with lower primates.

A great deal more could be learned from in-the-wild observations of species even more closely related to man. If ancestral hominids still roamed river valleys and savannas and coastal plains, say, bands like those whose traces are found in Bed I at the Olduvai Gorge or at Torralba-Ambrona, investigators could obtain firsthand records of early hunting methods and social organizations. In the absence of such bands, however, we ourselves can serve as subjects for research in living prehistory. We are all relics to some extent and, as such, provide a legitimate source of clues to the nature of prehistoric man.

Much of what men do and think today is _conditioned_ by what

347

their ancestors did and thought long ago when they were half-wild and all the world was a wilderness. Investigators expect to learn more about how human beings behaved in the past from studies of contemporary human behavior.

|Much can be learned from contemporary hunter-gatherers, people who live on wild plants and wild animals. In March, 1966, at a native reserve on the southwest fringe of the Gibson Desert in western Australia, Richard Gould, an archeologist at the University of Hawaii, met an unusual two-family group of thirteen aborigines (three women, two men and eight children ranging in age from about four to fifteen). They were among the very few people in the world still making and using stone tools on a regular basis. A "lost colony," one of the last remaining pockets of Stone Age existence in the twentieth century, had stepped into the modern world from an isolation so complete that they had met their first white man only a few months before.

The aborigines soon had enough of the present and decided to step back into the past again, heading on foot for their homeland 155 miles away in the heart of the desert. Gould and his wife Elizabeth followed not long afterward in a Land Rover. They lived with this group and others for extended periods during the next fifteen months, learning their language and sleeping at their campsites and walking out with them in search of food among flat sand plains, long parallel sand ridges like ripples on a giant beach, and occasional cliffs and rocky outcrops jutting out of the sands.

This investigation is the first of its kind ever undertaken. The writings about the world's primitive tribes which have accumulated during the past century or two include page after page, volume after volume, describing myths and kinship and inheritance and systems and birth and puberty and marriage and death rituals, complete with details about rattles and masks and other associated paraphernalia—and, embedded in it all, a strikingly sparse amount of information useful in the framing of hypotheses. The focus has often been on the bizarre, on practically everything that makes people appear alien and exotic, a tendency which reveals as much about the authors as about their subjects. Going through such material is an ordeal, part of the initiation ceremony which students must endure on their way to degrees.

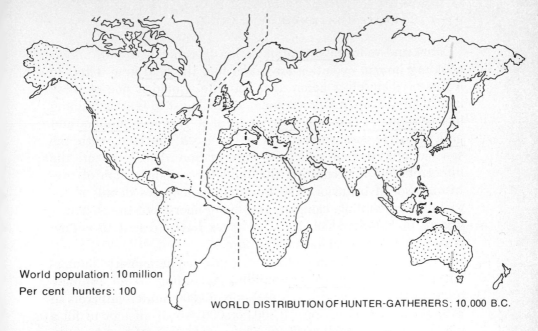

World population: 10 million
Per cent hunters: 100

WORLD DISTRIBUTION OF HUNTER-GATHERERS; 10,000 B.C.

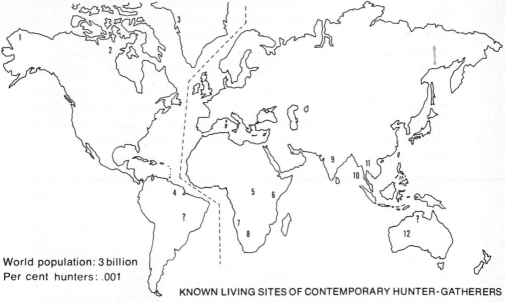

World population; 3 billion
Per cent hunters: .001

KNOWN LIVING SITES OF CONTEMPORARY HUNTER-GATHERERS

1	eskimos; Alaska	8	Kalahari Bushmen; South Africa, Botswana
2	eskimos; Northwest Territory	9	Birhar; Central India
3	eskimos; Greenland	10	Andaman Islanders; Andaman Island
4	Akuri; Surinam	11	Mrabri; Thailand
5	Pygmies; Congo	12	Australian Aborigines; Australia
6	Ariangulo; Tanzania	13	Tasadays; Philippines
	Boni; Tanzania		
	Sanye; Tanzania	14	Sevnany; Malaya
7	Koroka; Angola	15	Kubu; Sumatra
	Bantu; Angola	16	Panan; Borneo

|More and more investigators seriously concerned with understanding human evolution are going into the field in an effort to learn for themselves before it is too late. Gould is one of these investigators, the first professional archeologist to use his training in a systematic and intensive study of a group of hunters and gatherers. He has watched them living off the land, with the specific objective of collecting information that bears on the interpretation of prehistoric sites and the reconstruction of prehistoric social behavior. The information includes details about toolmaking, hunting, camping and living floors, and the elaborate system of beliefs which the aborigines have created to endow their world with meaning and purpose.

|Such studies are important, because contemporary hunter-gatherers are disappearing rapidly. According to an estimate made in 1966, the world included only 30,000 hunter-gatherers in a total population of some 3,300,000,000, about enough to fill a medium-sized football stadium. Their ranks have thinned appreciably since then, as they continue to die out or give up their ways and join farming and industrial communities.

|The past treatment of hunter-gatherers and others living in primitive societies whose behavior patterns resemble those that prevailed for more than 99 per cent of man's time on earth marks a low point in colonial history. A common notion was that they belonged to subhuman breeds, occupying "at best a middling position among the species," somewhere between apes and men but rather closer to apes as far as mentality and morals are concerned. In the name of this belief, they were widely dispossessed, enslaved, hunted, raped, slaughtered, fed poisoned food and otherwise exploited.

The classic case of this viewpoint in action involved the wiping out during the last century of 3,000 to 5,000 aborigines living on the Australian island of Tasmania. Rhys Jones of the Australian National University in Canberra comments on the process: "The fate of the Tasmanians constitutes one of the few examples in written history where an entire people has become totally extinct. . . . It is the example *par excellence* of genocide. . . . Savage and barbarian met face to face, and the savage died."

A later and somewhat more enlightened attitude, but one based on the same belief, was that they should be preserved together with other forms of wildlife as "living fossils" or lower species that never attained the evolutionary status of modern man. The report of a scientific expedition to central Australia in 1894 indicated the prevailing bias of the times toward members of all primitive societies, a bias found not only among laymen but also among specialists.

In appearance [the Australian aborigine] is a naked, hirsute savage, with a type of features occasionally pronounced Jewish. He is by nature light-hearted, merry and prone to laughter, a splendid mimic, supple-jointed, with an unerring hand that works in perfect unison with his eye, which is as keen as that of an eagle. He has never been known to wash. He has no private ownership of land, except as regards that which is not overcarefully concealed about his person. . . .

Religious belief he has none, but is excessively superstitious. . . . He has no gratitude except that of the anticipatory order, and is as treacherous as Judas. He has no traditions, and yet continues to practice with scrupulous exactness a number of hideous customs and ceremonies which have been handed down from his fathers, and of the origin or reason of which he knows nothing. . . .

After an experience of many years I say without hesitation that he is absolutely untamable. . . . Verily his moods are as eccentric as the flight of his own boomerang. Thanks to the untiring efforts of the missionary and the stockman, he is being rapidly "civilized" off the face of the earth, and in another hundred years the sole remaining evidence of his existence will be the fragments of flint which he has fashioned so rudely.

Today's attitudes are generally more in keeping with times that have seen the undermining of white supremacy and the passing of an empire upon which the sun never set. Anthropologists make a special point of recognizing all extant hunter-gatherers as members of the club, full-fledged representatives of *Homo sapiens.* They are people living exactly as we would be living if we had regarded nature in the same way and had adapted to the same conditions. Their societies are much simpler than ours, more primitive, but nonetheless sufficiently complicated to warrant continuing investigation.

A typical December or January day in the lives of the aborigine families who were the Goulds' hosts at the height of the Australian summer begins in darkness about half an hour before dawn.

The people are awakened by a natural "alarm clock," the sound of parrots and cockatoos and half a dozen other birds bursting into song. They join the chorus with yawns, throat-clearings, and exchanges of morning greetings and banter. There is no formal, communal breakfast. During the next hour or so each member of the group eats from a supply of food prepared the night before, usually cakes and loaves of ground-up seeds or fruit.

Work starts at about six or seven, when it is still cool by local standards, that is, when the temperature is below 95 degrees. The group divides into two parties. The women are responsible for the gathering of plant foods and may walk four or five miles—with long wooden bowls of water balanced on their heads and nursing children carried on their hips or slung over their backs—perhaps to one of the areas containing bushes of ngaru, an abundant pale green fruit about the size of a small tomato. Dogs and children old enough to walk come along too; no one stays behind at the camp.

Meanwhile the two men go off together to attend to their job of hunting, a less dependable way of obtaining food under desert conditions. In general they go to a place where they can ambush game instead of tracking and chasing it, especially in the summer heat. Perhaps they make use of a water hole as a kind of trap. They may travel a mile or two to the nearest creek bed, where they scoop out a pit or soak hole, exposing a small pool, and then select a spot on the bank overlooking the pit and about fifteen feet away to build a circular blind or hiding place of bushes (preferably in the shade of a tree). They lie there and wait, ready to hurl their spears at a thirsty emu or, very rarely, a kangaroo or a wallaby.

Everyone is back at camp by ten-thirty or eleven. By that time the temperature may have risen to 120 degrees, and not even the aborigines go out in that noonday sun. The women return the wooden bowls empty of water and filled with ngaru fruit. The men are usually not as successful. Sometimes they manage to kill a large animal, but on most days they have little to show for their patience, perhaps only a single goanna lizard. By rough estimate, about 60 to 70 per cent of the aborigines' diet is made up of plant foods; the meat consists chiefly of lizards, rabbits, snakes, birds, and other small game.

Yuwi, the hunter

Nyapurula, elderly aborigine woman, and child

Yutungka, drinking at clay pan

Close-up of aborigine branch shelter

The midday resting period is devoted to sitting in the shade, taking naps, making tools, gossiping. At three-thirty or thereabouts the women go to another area for a fruit, related to ngaru, which at this time of year is parched and looks something like large raisins. (Those two fruits provide more than half the aborigines' food during dry summer months.) One man decides to try his luck at the blind again; the other considers that a waste of time and goes lizard hunting. The people reassemble at camp before dark, in two hours or so, and the women prepare food for the evening and next morning. Fires are built even in the hottest summer nights to keep "mamu," or night cannibal spirits, away. There is much talking, and everyone is asleep by eight-thirty or nine.

The desert dictates rules governing the course, the rhythm, of daily activities. Some of the rules are harsh. In the absence of cultivated cereals and milk-yielding domestic animals, suitable children's foods are limited, and breast feeding generally goes on for three years or more. Since women can neither carry nor nurse two infants at once, there is no choice but to establish some form of birth control, and the most common type has been infanticide. Joseph Birdsell of the University of California at Los Angeles, who has gathered quantitative data relevant to the custom, estimates that in the not too distant past the aborigines killed at least 15 per cent of their infants and probably up to 50 per cent.

Killing the infant was the mother's decision and the mother's job. She disciplined herself to do it quickly, usually within an hour after birth. Her only consolation, and the only consolation for the group, was the belief that the soul of the infant would enter the body of another infant some time in the future. As indicated in Chapter X, this practice probably played a major part in limiting prehistoric populations, and the population boom believed to have occurred in Magdalenian times may have resulted in part from more settled living conditions and the decline of infanticide.

Nothing is denied to the children that are reared. Whenever they want food, either from the breast or from stored supplies, they get it. Aborigine mothers rarely spank or otherwise punish their offspring, even under the most provoking circumstances. In all his fifteen months of observing, Gould noted only one exception, when a mother reached out and smacked her son who was behaving in a particularly annoying manner. As children grow up they learn to resent being told what to do, so that perhaps the most insulting remark one aborigine can make to another is to call him "*wati tjukumunu*" or "bossy man." Adults are generally peaceful. Although personal clashes between individuals and kin groups occur fairly often, there are neither social hierarchies nor warfare.

The remarkable adaptation of these people to desert conditions includes a technology that would have been familiar to a tool-maker living 30,000 or more years ago. A distinctive and common tool, the so-called adz flake with a thick and fairly steep edge, looks much like the sort of scrapers archeologists find at prehistoric sites the world over. The edge may be made by removing tiny chips with a hammerstone or a wooden stick or, most unusual of all, with the teeth—a technique first reported by the Spanish explorer Coronado in 1541 among the Great Plains Indians of North America. Evidence for the practice in more remote times exists in the form of tiny chips of quartz found in human coprolites, fossil feces, excavated at a prehistoric cave in Utah.

The dental method involves placing the flake in a "nutcracker" position and nibbling with the side or premolar teeth. It requires teeth worn flat at the crowns to form an even working platform and exceedingly strong jaw muscles, both of which the aborigines have developed during years of using their teeth to chew tough meat, soften sinews, and rip the bark off branches. (They have no trouble in removing the top of a tin can by making successive bites along the rim.) There are reasons to believe that Magdalenian and Azilian toolmakers may have used this same method among others in the delicate job of fashioning microliths, very small scrapers and blades.

The need to travel light in the desert puts a premium on multipurpose or combination tools rather than elaborate tool kits. Of these the most impressive is the spear thrower, a flat wooden tool which may be used as a firemaker upon occasion. When an aborigine wants to start a fire, he splits a piece of wood, puts bits of dried kangaroo dung in the slot, and then rubs the edge of his spear thrower back and forth in the slot like a saw blade, hard and fast, until friction ignites the dung, a procedure that generally takes less than twenty seconds. This versatile tool serves other functions, such as shaper and cutter with the aid of an adz flake hafted to one end, mixing board for preparing pigments as well as a special blend of premasticated wild tobacco and ashes, and noisemaker for beating out rhythms at dances and other ceremonies.

Spear throwers also provide a crude kind of archives, the closest thing to written records among people who do not write. Decorations carved in the wood have practical and religious as well as esthetic purposes. The aborigines believe in a remote "dreamtime" before the coming of mortal men, when their ancestors, supernatural beings in the guise of humans and animals, rose from eternal sleeping places underground and roamed the earth's surface and created the world. In their wanderings they changed themselves into boulders, water holes, cliffs, trees, lakes, sand ridges, and other natural features which now mark their tracks through the desert. The features are represented on spear throwers by wavy and zigzag lines and a variety of irregular and geometric forms.

These symbols do not make up a language. They are not universal in the sense that only a fixed number of standard patterns exist and that each of them means the same thing to many men. They operate as personal symbols, different for different hunters and interpreted strictly on an individual basis. On the other hand, they can be regarded as private pictographs or hieroglyphics which help the hunter to establish firmly in his mind a "map" of his land, the locations of sacred places and water holes upon which his life may depend, and to pass the knowledge on to youths entering manhood. It is noteworthy that the Magdalenians also had spear throwers and also decorated them, often with abstract designs, suggesting that they may have used symbols for similar purposes.

The living-prehistory approach offers the enormous advantage of having men who make spear throwers and other tools right on the spot and ready to explain everything. Watching aborigines building and using blinds made of bushes or rocks, helping them at the task, is another way of bringing the past a bit closer and making it more vivid. Some of the blinds are natural rather than man-made, large boulders or rock shelters close to water holes or

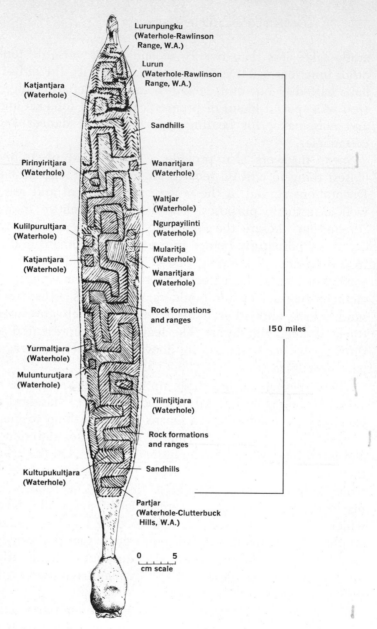

Lurunpungku
(Waterhole-Rawlinson
Range, W.A.)

Lurun
(Waterhole-Rawlinson
Range, W.A.)

Katjantjara
(Waterhole)

Sandhills

Pirinyiritjara
(Waterhole)

Wanaritjara
(Waterhole)

Waltjar
(Waterhole)

Ngurpayilinti
(Waterhole)

Kulilpurultjara
(Waterhole)

Mularitja
(Waterhole)

Katjantjara
(Waterhole)

Wanaritjara
(Waterhole)

Rock formations
and ranges

150 miles

Yurmaltjara
(Waterhole)

Mulunturutjara
(Waterhole)

Yilintjitjara
(Waterhole)

Rock formations
and ranges

Kultupukultjara
(Waterhole)

Sandhills

Partjar
(Waterhole-Clutterbuck
Hills, W.A.)

0   5
cm scale

Spearthrower as "map": Gibson Desert landmarks and water sources along a 150-mile track of a totemic snake in the dreamtime

Yutungka, in permanent water hole

in narrow gorges, and while a hunter waits he may take a piece of red ocher and draw animals on rock walls or designs representing animal tracks.

He may draw a line and side markings which look something like a feathered arrow or a branch with twigs. If there were not firsthand information to the contrary, the picture might well be interpreted as such or, even more likely, as another mysterious abstract sign. But actually it depicts the footmarks of a kangaroo as it hops slowly along dragging its tail behind through the sand. Such drawings are generally done as a loose form of magic, in the belief that they will attract animals to the blind, although now and then they seem to be mainly a matter of doodling to pass the time.

Stalking is done more rarely than waiting in blinds, but if an aborigine sees a possible kill he loses no time in going after it. "That happened late one evening about twenty minutes before sunset," Gould recalls. "There was not much wind, the landscape was very red from the setting sun, and a kangaroo was browsing about a thousand feet away. A hunter started walking directly at it, moving over the sand with the graceful and smooth motion which is second nature to the aborigines as sea legs are to sailors.

"He kept his eyes fastened to the animal's head and ears, and the instant it started to look up he froze in his tracks, sometimes for two or three minutes until it looked down again and continued feeding. Then he moved forward again. After about half an hour of stalking he came to within seventy-five feet of the kangaroo— but missed his prey! He used a rifle, and many Gibson Desert aborigines are still very bad with rifles. He would never have missed with a spear."

Gould has devoted much time to a study of contemporary living floors, occupation patterns representing the activities of aborigines he knew well, or the activities of their friends and recent ancestors. Such evidence can be used in interpreting prehistoric living floors not only in the Australian desert but elsewhere. For example he gathered considerable information during visits to Tika-Tika, a major open-air site covering several acres. The site includes ample supplies of fruit and berries in midwinter and late summer, small game and occasional kangaroos, and five water holes on a limestone flat, one of which can be counted on to furnish some water even during severe droughts.

Aborigine male making a spear thrower

Aborigine hunting blind

Aborigine food, a day's catch of lizards

One important feature of the layout here, and at other sites in the desert, is that the people never locate their occupation areas close to water holes. The general practice is to build camps at least two to three hundred feet from the nearest source of water, because if they were much closer camp noises would frighten game away. Another reason involves reducing social tensions, preserving peaceful coexistence among neighboring groups. A system of rules governs the behavior of relatives toward one another. For example, a man is strictly forbidden to talk with his mother-in-law, and if a family lived near a water hole it might be difficult to avoid awkward encounters.

In all, Gould and his wife spent the better part of a summer month living at Tika-Tika with the family group they originally followed into the desert. Shade is the primary concern during the summer season, when daily temperatures may average more than 100 degrees for four or five months in a row, and a typical shelter includes a basic structure of eight branches set into postholes about a foot deep and arranged in a rough semicircle. Thick clumps of grass piled on top of the branches provide protection from the sun, while the interior of the semicircle is scooped out to a depth of two or three inches to permit sleeping snug to the ground. The aborigines camped in two such shelters, making small fires just outside the entrances.

A winter visit to the same area called for different kinds of scooped-out shelters, for nights when the temperature may fall to freezing or below. One campsite consisted of a cleared oval area about fourteen feet long with a windbreak of dense brush constructed along the windward side. A large hearth was located at one end of the clearing between the windbreak and bushes growing nearby; two small hearths burned at the other end. The aborigines make no clothing for cold-weather living, and their custom has been to curl up naked near hearths and behind windbreaks. Dogs may furnish additional warmth, "wrapped" around the chest or legs like furs or blankets, a procedure which the animals seem to appreciate as much as the people.

A deserted campsite, located not far away, also had a windbreak and three hearths. What distinguished it was that the hearths were arranged in a row such as the rows found at the Abri Pataud in France and at Kostenki in the Soviet Union. The aborigines explained the pattern. It was the sort of camp constructed by all-male groups, probably two men in this case, since one man usually lies in each of the spaces between hearths. This modern site included signs of a hunting ceremony such as those found at Terra Amata on the French Riviera and at other sites, some of them 250,000 and more years old. A stone slab weighing about twenty-five pounds was covered with red ocher, indicating that the men had ground the pigment on the slab and painted their bodies, probably with designs representing water holes and the tracks of their dreamtime ancestors.

Artifacts collected from deserted sites at Tika-Tika included digging sticks, pieces of wooden bowls and spear throwers, and an unusual pad made of emu feathers and designed to be worn on the foot during "revenge" expeditions (organized when a group of aborigines believes one of its members has been bewitched by another group's sorcerer). Such items, of course, are perishable and may disintegrate within a couple of years under desert conditions, usually devoured by white ants. Among the durable items

Aborigine summer camp in the Gibson Desert

Aborigine women winnowing wanguna seeds

were grinding stones and slabs, several dozen adz flakes and hundreds of waste chips, all of them made of various forms of quartz obtained from quarries forty or more miles away. Such material may accumulate for many years, because campsites tend to be used over and over again.

Gould visited nearly a hundred sites, sites occupied by only a few persons and complexes including clusters of as many as twenty camps and more than eighty persons, ceremonial sites and butchering sites and ambushing sites. In all, his maps represent several hundred living floors and some new features of special archeological interest. At the dead end of a steep gully he came across a ring of rocks which, on the side facing a nearby water hole, were piled neatly to form a wall. A similar ring in another gully a quarter of a mile away, and near another water hole, had an even more carefully built wall almost three feet high.

Such structures had never been reported before, so Gould turned to the experts for an explanation. The aborigines identified them as blinds used by hunters at night. The gullies are natural traps for kangaroos and emus, and other hunters may hide in crevices along the gullies and at the entrances, ready to intercept animals trying to escape. Large animals killed far from camp are roasted whole on the spot in earth-oven trenches (another archeological feature that may endure for many years), butchered, and divided among the hunters, who may subsequently subdivide their shares among as many as fifty or sixty individuals back at camp.

There are also features of religious significance. Certain sites are transformation places, places on dreamtime tracks where special events occurred which caused supernatural ancestors to change themselves into various landmarks, often into rocks and rock formations. At one such site, the bed of a dried-out creek winds down from the Clutterbuck Hills about forty miles northwest of Tika-Tika through a low canyon, and on a terrace at the upper part of the canyon is a structure built centuries or perhaps millennia ago, a line of 436 rocks, 39 of them being upright slabs a foot or two high.

There is a tale behind these rocks, in Gould's words "a storyline that proceeds up-canyon from north to south." The story, as recounted by the two elderly aborigines who were his guides, concerns the legendary circumcision of a novice Kawan-kawan in the dreamtime. And signs of the ceremony are found all along the way to the terrace—depressions in the bedrock of the creek where the novice sat and knelt while waiting to proceed to the circumcision site, two slabs of rock marking the spot where he was picked up to be carried to the site, and, at the end of a billabong or long pool of water, a tall eucalyptus tree believed to be Kawan-kawan himself.

Of the 436 rocks on the terrace, one with red stripes on it is his freshly circumcised and bleeding penis; the other 435 rocks are dreamtime beings who assumed the shapes of marsupial cats and attended the ceremony. The canyon is a sacred place to these aborigines, who belong to the marsupial-cat totem or cult lodge. They identify themselves with the marsupial-cat people and believe themselves to be descended from these people in a direct male line going back to father and grandfather and so on to the beginning of the dreamtime.

It should be emphasized that circumcision, occurring at the age of fourteen to sixteen, is only the first of a series of initiations in which the male aborigine participates. Other initiations take place during the next ten or fifteen years, all designed primarily to impart knowledge of one of the most elaborate religions known. Songs and legends are memorized note for note and word for word, together with a vast store of details about numerous rituals, and everything is passed along from generation to generation.

Increase ceremonies ensuring the reproduction of plants and animals are involved as well as initiations. One increase site lies on a track where dreamtime water-snake ancestors became sick after eating the yellow flowers of a local shrub, vomiting up the flowers, which promptly turned to stones and are now represented by a cluster of eight piles of yellow rock. As one of the rare sources of sugar in the desert, the flowers represent a much-sought food, and members of the water-snake totem come to the site regularly to sprinkle their blood on the rock piles. The aborigines describe the act as "just like rain," indicating that they consider their blood as important as rain in bringing about growth of the shrubs. There could be no more vivid expression of the fact that they are laying their lives on the line in the business of survival.

Their art is intimately connected with religious themes, with preserving a unity with the world and the desert. They still paint on rock surfaces, and Gould has watched them applying pigments of charcoal and red and white ocher mixed in emu fat. He has also listened to explanations of various works from the artists themselves. Their rock paintings consist mainly of abstract designs, representing events that occurred along dreamtime tracks. In one rock shelter an artist of the water-snake totem drew a long wavy line in red ocher for the snake's track, elongated red dots for its eggs, and black dots for the hearths at its campsites.

The designs are basically different from those used on spear throwers. In fashioning the tools individuals use a variety of symbols which may be meaningless even to members of their own totem group. But rock-art patterns come from a set of recognized symbols, also used in painting the body for ceremonial dances. These symbols resemble the abstract designs found painted in the art caves of France and Spain—and suggest that prehistoric man may also have had a "vocabulary" of symbols to express his myths and beliefs. If so, investigators face a major job of deciphering.

The aborigines consider their paintings sacred but, being man-made, of a second order of sacredness. Thus it is no crime to paint over them, and superimpositions occur commonly, as in the pre-historic caves of Western Europe. Rock engravings and rock alignments and rock piles, on the other hand, belong to an entirely different category. They are not representations, but the real thing. To the aborigines the eucalyptus tree in the Clutter-buck Hills *is* the novice Kawan-kawan, and the aligned rocks *are* the dreamtime marsupial-cat people who attended his circumcision. Furthermore, Kawan-kawan and the people are alive, merely sleeping, and capable of moving and acting at any time.

Gould reports that the old guides who brought him to the canyon in the hills "spent about twenty minutes clearing away weeds and rubble which had accumulated around the rocks of the alignment since their last visit." And every time one of them set upright an aligned rock that had fallen over, he addressed it as "my father." The world of the aborigine has been described by Theodor Strehlow of the University of Adelaide, who has spent his life studying their religion:

Mountains and creeks and springs and waterholes are, to him, not merely interesting or beautiful scenic features in which his eyes may take a passing delight; they are the handiwork of ancestors from whom he himself was descended. He sees recorded in the surrounding landscape the ancient story of the lives and deeds of the immortal beings whom he reveres; beings who for a brief space may take on human shape once more; beings many of whom he has known in his own experience as his fathers and grandfathers and brothers, and as his mothers and sisters.

The whole countryside is his living, age-old family tree. The story of his own totemic ancestor is to the native the account of his own doings at the beginning of time, at the dim dawn of life, when the world as he knows it now was being shaped and moulded by all-powerful hands. He himself has played a part in the first glorious adventure, a part smaller or greater according to the original rank of the ancestor of whom he is the present reincarnated form. . . . Today, tears will come into his eyes when he mentions an ancestral home site which has been, sometimes unwittingly, desecrated by the white usurpers of his group territory.

In the last analysis the similarities among the aborigines and modern men and prehistoric representatives of *Homo sapiens* are much greater than the differences. On the other hand, this emphasis can be carried too far. Differences must be recognized, otherwise even logical and convincing hypotheses will never match the facts.

Perhaps the most obvious difference between the aborigines and prehistoric people living in Western Europe 35,000 to 10,000 years ago is their different environments. The technologies and philosophies that evolved in glacial climates with abundant big game naturally differed from those evolved under desert or semi-desert conditions. There were also differences among the aborigines themselves in prehistoric times, among those who lived in the desert and those who lived along coasts and rivers where food was considerably more plentiful.

Changes occurred even among the desert people. The original settlers of Australia probably did not have dogs, spear throwers, stones for grinding food, and spears as well designed as those of modern times. Over the course of millennia they borrowed techniques from others and developed techniques of their own. In fact, Gould has discovered a procedure that seems to have come

Aborigine art on rocks of a hunting blind: kangaroo tracks (left) and unidentified object

Water-snake pattern in aborigine rock shelter, illustrating a dreamtime legend

in quite recent times, a way of using rock slabs as foundations for shade-providing structures in summer camps. There are more than enough differences to keep investigators occupied for decades.

Meanwhile, the search for similarities goes on. The aborigines and the Magdalenians may or may not have had radically different religions, but what they had in common is more significant, a capacity for seeing beneath the surface of things and conceiving a meaningful world and expressing their ideas in art and ritual. More specifically, the similarities known to exist between some of the stone tools and living floors of prehistoric and recent times hint that further similarities remain to be discovered. Recognizing such things as rock blinds, rock alignments, earth ovens and so on in the occupation areas of the aborigines helps to free the mind when it comes to interpreting possibly related features of other living floors in Australia and elsewhere. According to Gould, "it suggests new possibilities and analogies to us, and helps us get unstuck from a limited range of ideas."

By the time he conducted his most extensive excavation, he had learned a great deal about aboriginal life styles in the region. He and a group of students dug for eleven summer weeks in a rock shelter at the foot of a steep cliff, under hot and dry conditions very much like those that prevailed in prehistoric times. Less than half an inch of rain had fallen there in two years, and all of it fell in a single day during the third week of the dig.

The shelter was first used about 10,000 years ago, and is still being used for brief visits today. In fact, within two years or so before excavating started aborigines had left a number of stone tools at the site, tools like those made and used throughout the history of the site. The original settlers, perhaps two families, found an ample shelter forty feet long and fifteen feet deep. One day after they had been living there for a long but undetermined period, and fortunately when no one was in the shelter, part of the roof collapsed, covering most of the living space with tons of quartzite debris. The people returned, however, and cleared two oval-shaped areas, presumably one for each family.

Gould drew on his knowledge about the behavior of living aborigines to help understand the behavior of their remote ancestors. The two oval-shaped areas are exactly the same size and shape, and contain many of the same kinds of artifacts as 41 current-style camps which he had mapped during the past few years, suggesting that then as now such areas were probably occupied by three to four persons. Some of the <u>stone tools</u> recovered from the site are <u>identical</u> to tools from other Australian sites dating back about <u>30,000 years</u>—and to tools still being used today. Furthermore, microscopic studies reveal that the wear patterns of modern woodworking tools are identical to those of similar prehistoric tools.

Experience gained from living with aborigines also helped explain one of the most unusual features of the site. Next to the main rock shelter is a smaller one, too small to live in but containing a pit five and a half feet deep, with many thin tilted layers of differently colored soil, some containing ash or charcoal. Excavators were surprised to find moist soil within the pit, suggesting that it had served as a water source, a trap for moisture percolating down through cracks in the cliff.

Gould believes the pit is a "<u>fossil</u>" well, and he has seen similar structures actually being used by modern aborigines. They are dug down to the water table, sometimes fifteen or more feet deep, and provide virtually permanent supplies of water. But it may be months or years between visits to a native well, and during that period the openings may be clogged with dense growth of grass and thorny bushes, which are cleared away by burning. The same procedure was probably practiced in times past, which would account for the thin layers of burned material found in the prehistoric rock shelter.

For all the information that has come from the aborigines during past investigations, considerably more can be expected in the years ahead as interest in living prehistory continues to grow. Findings in Australia already bear on problems encountered in the digging of European and Near Eastern sites. For example, Carmel Schrire of the State University of New York in Binghamton and Nicolas Peterson of the Australian National University have spent time in Arnhem Land along the north-central coast of Australia, the home territory of some 5,000 aborigines. They present reasons for believing that differences between the tool kits found at coastal and inland sites, differences once attributed to different cultures, actually reflect local adaptations to seasonal rains and flooding. In other words, the same people were doing different things at different times of the year, and comparable situations may have existed among prehistoric hunter-gatherers living at sites like Combe Grenal in southern France (see Chapter IX).

At the broadest level research on the ways of aborigines, past and present, furnishes an example of man's genius for adapting. Wherever he lives, he does what must be done in order to survive—and that includes finding a reason to survive in the first place, a harmony between necessity and belief. Necessity dictates that the land be used as effectively as possible, especially in inhospitable desert regions, and, as Peterson emphasizes in a recent study, belief ensures that this does indeed happen.

Where food is limited, people cannot live together in large groups. If they did, they would soon eat themselves into extinction, consuming food like a swarm of locusts and ruining the land in the process. Survival depends on living in small groups over a wide area, and on remaining dispersed. Men, not women, are brought up to be powerfully attached to their homeland. When a young man marries he may have to move a hundred or more miles to live with his wife's family. But as he grows older and accumulates daughters, perhaps another wife or so, and status, he generally returns to the region of his dreamtime ancestors.

This attraction, a kind of cultural homing "instinct," is created by rituals which include a whole series of painful procedures— knocking out a front tooth, circumcision, scarring of the chest, bloodletting, and so on. One function of the ordeals is to engrave as deeply as possible in memory an identification with place, to make knowledge about the features of the landscape and their meanings unforgettable, to ensure that the native son does indeed return.

Sometimes this may be difficult, for instance, when the homeland is not particularly attractive. Annette Hamilton of the University of Sydney points out that in the central Australian desert the tendency is to force young men to go through all the ordeals and mutilations, while in Arnhem Land, where rain and food are more abundant, the atmosphere is more permissive, and the more severe ordeal may not be compulsory.

Yet there is less tension in the desert; life is more equitable.

Young men are hostile toward the older men who initiate them, but they also feel admiration and respect, perhaps because women tend to be fairly distributed. As a rule, the practice is one man, one wife. But in Arnhem Land for some reason older men may have two or three wives, the young must wait until they are twenty-five or thirty to marry, and their hostility is mixed with less respect and more hatred. Also women have a higher status in the desert. They are excluded from initiations and other male rituals, but may have rituals of their own and generally seem more sure of themselves and less anxious than Arnhem Land women.

So there are differences among the aborigines, but the similarities are even more outstanding and enduring. In everything from artifacts to religious beliefs and practices they tend to be extremely conservative, and their past demonstrates the strengths and weaknesses of extreme conservatism as a way of life. For them everything had a completed quality; everything was accounted for, once and for all. The dreamtime was a kind of cultural high-water mark against which subsequent events could be measured, a lost golden age of heroes and heroic deeds and abundance and easy hunting. Every change since then had been a change for the worse, a step backward. The duty of the living was a rear-guard action to hold the line and prevent further changes that would result in a further falling away from dreamtime days.

The memorizing of songs and myths and dance sequences was a way of preserving the *status quo*. So were the mutilations which served to dramatize the desperate seriousness of remembering and doing things as they have always been done. Everything was spelled out detail by detail so that there would be no questioning. No one thought of modifying ideas about dreamtime tracks and sacred places, much less of inventing new ideas, because every feature of the desert had long since become part of a time-honored and firmly established legend. The landscape was effectively "used up."

This system stands as one more example of the fact, amply documented in civilized as well as primitive societies, that men can be "programmed" or indoctrinated with practically any set of beliefs—and that change itself can be put off if those beliefs are implanted deeply enough. The complexity of the aborigine's religion contrasts sharply with the simplicity of his technology, and suggests that he may have poured most of his creative energies into the dreamtime world. His struggle to preserve things succeeded for a long time and failed, not because of any change in himself or in his land, but because of the coming of people who had been programmed to regard change as both possible and desirable.

The old problem of observing, of registering what goes on as objectively as possible, is intensified as we study our nearest ancestors. The difficulty, serious enough in the case of simpler creatures such as baboons and chimpanzees, is multiplied many, many times in the case of man. Preconceptions are more massive and die harder the closer we come to our own species. There is a deeper commitment to belief and assumed knowledge, more to be justified and defended. But recent developments in every branch of the behavioral sciences indicate that a beginning has been made in breaking loose from notions no longer relevant to the times.

■ "Magic numbers" and social groups; recently vanished societies; living prehistory research among aboriginal hunting-gathering bands; study of living floors, fire sites, and bone deposits as indicators of hunting-gathering and cooking methods; food sharing; leisure; the rise of gambling; child dependency patterns; the religious dance and ritualistic trances

CHAPTER XVI

The Behavior of Primitive Peoples

■ The opportunity to see society "pure," to study groups living under relatively simple and uncluttered conditions, yields evidence that leads to the discovery of universal laws of human behavior. There is little doubt that laws exist which describe behavioral patterns, elementary responses and reactions common to all people whether they live in primitive or highly industrialized communities. But chances of discovering the laws may well be greater in primitive communities where basic relationships are often more readily detected. This is a major reason for doing research in living prehistory.

One basic relationship has to do with the so-called magic numbers problem. The magic numbers are 25 and 500, and refer to the sizes of hunter-gatherer bands and tribes, respectively. They have been the subject of discussion during the past few years, mainly because some investigators regard them as hints to the existence of social regularities which we do not yet understand. First, consider the number 25. More than fifteen years ago Birdsell, studying rates of population growth among the Australian aborigines, noted that their band sizes ranged from about 20 to 50, and selected 25 as a representative figure.

His choice has turned out to have a wider significance than he may have realized at the time. An unpublished census of ten bands of aborigines indicates an average size of precisely 25, and this number has also been reported in a survey of Kalahari Bushmen. The average for the Birhar, a hunting-gathering tribe of northern India, comes to 26. Other analyses involve similar figures. For example, evidence indicates that adult males tend to form working groups of six to eight individuals, which is the number generally included in a 25-member band. Incidentally, certain living-floor studies suggest about the same size for prehistoric bands.

There is nothing absolute about this number. Birdsell and others emphasize that it represents an "equilibrium" value, and that while actual counts may come to more or less than 25, they tend to cluster around that value. It is somewhat higher than the range for gorilla troops (about 12 to 17), fairly close to that for Indian langur monkeys (18 to 30), and lower than the averages for baboons (about 40) and forest-dwelling rhesus monkeys of north India (about 50). We do not know the reason for the human average, although, as indicated above, it may have something to do with the most efficient working groups of adult males. But it is not radically out of line with the general range for the order of primates as a whole.

The magic number 500, on the other hand, represents something really new. As a common average for a "dialectical" tribe of hunter-gatherers—that is, a group of bands all speaking the same dialect—it is a purely human number in the sense that comparable values do not exist among other primates. Birdsell also directed attention to the number during the course of his population studies of the aborigines: "The Australian data show an amazing constancy of numbers for the dialectical tribe, statistically approximating 500 persons. This tendency is independent of regional density. Since the data cover mean annual rainfall variations from 4 inches to more than 160 inches, the size of the dialectical tribal unit is insensitive to regional variations in climatic . . . factors."

This is an equilibrium value and not an absolute figure. Birdsell himself has noted that the sizes of individual tribes may range from extremes of about 200 to more than 800 persons. The phenomenon becomes clear and meaningful only after taking census figures for a large number of tribes. Such studies reveal a central tendency to cluster at the 500 level, and this tendency is widespread. It holds for the Shoshoni Indians of the Great Plains, the Andaman Islanders in the Bay of Bengal, and other peoples as well as the Australian aborigines.

This number apparently reflects certain fundamental features of human communication systems. The unity of a hunting-gathering tribe depends on face-to-face meetings, on a degree of intimacy among members of its component bands which creates the feeling of belonging to the same extended community, even though they may live many miles apart. The intimacy involves not only the same language and dialect but the same familiar intonations and expressions and gestures, a common store of idioms and jokes and myths and allusions. All this signaling or communicating activity is implied in the notion of sharing a common cultural background.

Apparently there are laws governing the extent of such sharing. There seems to be a basic limit to the number of persons who can know one another well enough to maintain a tribal identity at the hunter-gatherer level, who communicate by direct confrontation and who live under a diffuse and informal influence, perhaps a council of elders, rather than an active centralized political authority. It is difficult to define or measure "knowing one another well enough." George Murdock of the University of Pittsburgh, who has looked into the problem, provides some unpublished results.

To obtain a rough index of familiarity he asked students, colleagues and friends to estimate the number of people they associated with on a first-name basis. His main finding is that for most of us the number ranges from about 800 to 1,200, the unofficial champion being James Farley, an influential member of the Democratic party during the Roosevelt administration, who estimated that he knew between 6,000 and 7,000 persons by their first names. The range of 800–1,200 of course applies to citizens of a highly mobile and densely populated nation. Contacts are less frequent in the hunter-gatherer's world, however, where visits require long walks. The 500 figure for tribal sizes may be related to this limitation. As an interesting sidelight, there is an architect's rule of thumb to the effect that the capacity of an elementary school should not exceed 500 pupils if the principal expects to know all of them by name—and it has been stated that when a group exceeds 500 persons, it requires some form of policing.

The underlying phenomena which account for magic numbers have yet to be discovered, but some clues come from a recent study by Martin Wobst of the University of Massachusetts. It would be ideal to have detailed records indicating the success of hunter-gatherer bands over many generations, bands of different sizes and different social systems. Since this sort of information has never been collected, however, the second-best course is to play a kind of let's-suppose game and simulate what might have happened with the aid of a computer.

The first step involves feeding into computer memory some assumptions and probabilities and instructions—the original size of the group, the number and ages of all its members, certain social rules such as incest taboos and exogamy, and the odds that each individual will get married, have offspring, leave the group, die by accident or disease or old age, and other information. Then the computer can go to work and run through the probable history of the group over a specified period. Using a modern high-speed computer a single such "run" simulating the events of 500 years can be completed within six minutes.

Wobst has obtained a variety of theoretical prehistoric case histories. For example, he assumed for the sake of simplicity that the smallest possible "bands," lone adult male hunters on their own, have a half-life of about a year—which means that half of them will die within a year, half of the surviving half will die during the second year, and so on. Put five persons together, a family of father and mother and three children, and the half-life increases to a generation, while for a five-family band of 25 members the figure increases to 250 to 500 years. Cultural factors probably limited band sizes much greater than that, since the more members the greater the chances of conflict and splitting up.

Other computer runs suggest that what has been referred to as the magic number 500 concerns the size of the group from which mates may be obtained. The stricter the mating rules, the less chance a band member has to find a mate nearby and the greater the number of other bands needed to provide an adequate pool of possible mates. For example, for a band with incest taboos and a rule that a man can choose a woman of any marriageable age, the number of other 25-member bands would be seven for a tribal total of 175 persons.

This number increases to 19 bands or 475 persons if the age rule is stricter, if it specifies that a man must marry a woman younger than himself. Interestingly enough, removing the ban against incest has little effect on tribal size because, among other things, it increases the number of possible mates only slightly. The undesirable thing about incest in a prehistoric hunter-gatherer context is that it increases competition for mates within the band and requires more males to travel farther in search of mates, so taboos are of definite survival value.

There is certainly more to the 500 figure. The memory capacity of the human brain probably plays a fundamental role of some sort, since that influences the number of persons one can know by sight. Other problems are sure to arise as research uncovers other regularities and tendencies in the behavior of people adapting in complex ways to one another and to their environments. Evolution builds on these regularities and tendencies.

Funds may not be available soon enough for large-scale research into living prehistory, the behavior of living primitive peoples. It is already too late for further studies of the Hadza, for example, a group of some 400 Africans who occupied a remote area of bush country not far from the Olduvai Gorge and Ngorongoro Crater in Tanzania. About eight years ago they were living in beehive-shaped grass huts and, during the rainy season, in rock shelters. Although visitors from affluent lands described their land as "an inhospitable wilderness" and their life as a bitter struggle against starvation, they had a generous food supply and no enemies and a surfeit of leisure.

The people considered themselves to be hunters, and game was abundant. But more than 80 per cent of their diet consisted of wild honey and various plant foods collected by the women; about half the men did practically no hunting at all. From early morning until dark they spent a major part of their time gambling, betting arrows on whether wooden disks tossed against a tree would land barkside up or barkside down. (Gambling probably arose as an antimonotony device, a way of creating unpredictable events under all too predictable living conditions. Australian aborigines living on government reservations where there is little to do have taken to a weird form of poker with rules that seem to change from hand to hand.)

The Hadza had adapted successfully to their native territory. In 1960, visiting pediatricians from the Makerere University Medical School in Uganda reported that their children were among the healthiest in East Africa. Recently, however, most of the people were forced to change their way of existence. Government officials relocated them to a reservation fifty miles away, where they lived in much closer contact with one another. Within a year about a quarter of their children had succumbed to an epidemic, a turn of events that has occurred many times before during similar forced moves.

Another vanished society is that of the Ainu people, who are concentrated on Hokkaido, an island north of the mainland of Japan. Although some were still engaged in hunting and gathering no more than a generation ago, their world began changing rapidly in the early 1880's, when the Japanese government adopted the policy of encouraging them to become farmers. Fortunately, in a study based on extensive field work and interviews conducted by Hitoshi Watanabe and his associates at the University of Tokyo, their former way of life has been reconstructed.

The Ainu lived basically as our ancestors in Western Europe lived some 15,000 years ago. They also settled into river valleys and geared their existence to natural cycles, to the seasons and the predictable comings and goings of migratory animals. Their major source of food was the salmon, the "divine" fish which spirits living in the sea sent to the people and which returned year after year to the same spawning grounds. And every spring and fall deer came down from hills and mountains in the central part of the island along the same fixed trails through dense forests, and swam across rivers at the same points, the traditional places for ambushes.

Hunting and fishing served future as well as current needs. Provision had to be made for subsistence during a period of two or three months in the dead of winter when snows were deepest and deer retreated to the hills and salmon to the sea. Everything depended on the salmon. When they ran in large shoals, as they generally did, the people were assured of ample stores of sun-dried fish for cold-weather eating supplemented by sun-dried venison—and winter became a season of leisure, celebration, and visits from friends and relatives. Less abundant runs meant going after deer in their forest retreats and a greater dependence on nuts and other plant foods. One year in one valley salmon were extremely scarce, and during the winter some 200 persons died of starvation.

These studies put the past in perspective. In prehistoric Europe, longer and colder winters may have prevailed during glacial periods in the valleys of the Les Eyzies region, for example, confronting the Neanderthals and Magdalenians with the same essential problems that the Ainu recently faced. Survival for them as for the Ainu demanded ways of preserving and storing food and getting about in the snow when food was scarce.

Evidence has been obtained which bears on the storage problem. The Neanderthals almost certainly used natural permafrost and ice refrigeration, stockpiled meat in some of their caves, and possibly used saw-tooth flint tools to shred reindeer and horse meat into strips for drying in the sun or over slow-burning fires. The question is how they managed to cope with snow. Watanabe points out that they probably were able to follow game across open tundra country where winds freeze and harden the snow cover. But snowshoes are needed to move through forest areas where the snow is soft and deep, and that invention may not have come until Magdalenian times or later.

Current efforts to learn more about life in arctic and sub-arctic climates include the research of Binford and his associates in the Brooks Range of Alaska. Some of their archeological work has been mentioned in Chapter IX. They have also been observing hunting and other activities among some 135 Eskimos living near the main pass through the mountains, a pass used for millennia by man and caribou.

Last year Binford had a firsthand, unplanned adventure in the region. He came specifically to see the caribou, the people's major source of food, moving through the pass. But the herds did not appear. More than seven feet of snow fell during a six-day blizzard, the animals stayed in forests to the south, and the community faced its most severe food shortage in decades. Snows covered everything, changing the landscape of familiar contours and paths and willow stands into a vast blank, a white expanse with all the landmarks gone except for the tallest trees, the highest bluffs and the mountains themselves.

In this transformed world the people turned to strategies and tactics originally learned in prehistoric times. One group of hunters saw tracks in fresh snow, set 150 snares and caught 65 arctic squirrels, although as far as a square meal is concerned, a squirrel compares to a caribou as a hummingbird compares to a Thanksgiving turkey. The hunters also decided to try ice fishing in a nearby lake, but gave it up after hacking a hole more than four feet deep into the ice without any signs that water was near. They had better luck, but not much better, with meat put away in special places around the countryside for just such emergencies, locating two out of ten caches. Meanwhile the women were beginning to tap another source of food, marrow bones and the frozen carcasses of wolves and foxes kept on the roofs of houses where the dogs could not get at them.

At about this stage the situation started improving, and there was no need to use last-resort emergency foods such as fern roots and the inner bark of willow trees. A herd of moose headed south where there was food in the forests, hunters saw their tracks and came back with 3,700 pounds of meat. Not long afterward the caribou showed up, as temperatures soared from thirty or more degrees below zero Fahrenheit to a "warm" five or six degrees above.

But for nearly a month Binford had a glimpse of what things must have been like during prehistoric emergencies, when the weather often did not improve and the hunters were wiped out. Even today and even with the favorable change of weather, the community would have suffered far more severely if he had not brought an ample supply of antibiotics with him, because all but half a dozen of the people caught influenza.

Most of the information gathered in Alaska is still being analyzed. Binford and other investigators have hunted with Eskimos, observed their butchering methods, and obtained detailed records of the remains at some 280 kill sites at different seasons—all of which will help in reconstructing prehistoric activities. For example, skulls and necks and vertebrae are generally left behind at the kill site, while thigh bones and other long bones may be saved for their marrow and brought back to the main camp. The same sort of distribution exists among fossil reindeer bones excavated at a Neanderthal site in England, suggesting that it was a kill site and not, as had previously been concluded, a home base. Similar analyses are scheduled for material found at Olduvai, Torralba, Combe Grenal and many other sites.

Time is running out for hunters like the Eskimos, and for the scientists who would learn from them, even in the few remaining areas where civilization has not yet produced radical changes. Such territories still offer sufficient supplies of food, but human resources continue to dwindle. In Australia only an estimated forty to fifty aborigines are still living the old hunting-gathering life, and they can no longer stay away from missions and reserves and farming communities where most of their people have settled. They must find mates for their sons and daughters, which means visiting civilized centers and often never returning to the desert.

So the emphasis in living-prehistory research has been increasingly on immediate large-scale projects conducted in depth. One such project involves a region thousands of miles from the aborigines' home country, a region in Southern Africa where about a third of all existing hunter-gatherers (some 9,000 persons) are concentrated. Specifically, it has focused intensively on a very small area of unusual interest, a speck in the 350,000-square-mile Kalahari Desert of Botswana. The area has a radius of less than twenty miles, is surrounded by vast stretches of waterless terrain and includes eleven permanent water holes and wells, between 400 and 500 plant and animal species, and about 450 Bushmen living in hunting and gathering bands.

In 1967 a group of Harvard scientists, working under a grant from the National Institute of Mental Health, began a long-term survey of these people. DeVore, who has shifted his attention from primate to human societies, his co-worker Richard Lee, and ten others are engaged in one of the most comprehensive investigations yet undertaken of hunter-gatherers—an investigation including special studies of health, nutrition, family and group structure, child training, personal relationships, rituals, and so on. The project is continuing, and accounts of various phases of the work are to be published during the next few years. But some important findings are described in preliminary reports.

For one thing, there are intensive studies of contemporary

living floors, studies along the lines of those conducted by Gould at Tika-Tika and other sites in western Australia. DeVore has observed how the Bushmen use fires and has drawn attention to facts that may influence interpretations of many prehistoric sites in Africa and elsewhere. Excavators there and elsewhere uncover a number of living floors with dwellings and the remains of fires. By assigning one family group to each fire or "hearth," they estimate the size of the band that lived there. This is the approach used at Terra Amata, Kostenki, and other sites.

Kalahari mongongo forest

But if Kalahari practices are any indication, the actual situation is somewhat more complicated. A Bushman band may consist of thirty to forty persons, eight to ten family groups living in as many little beehive-shaped huts made of saplings and palm fronds and grass, and arranged in a circle or semicircle. (The remains of such huts have been found at a 4,500-year-old site in central Zambia, together with preserved wooden tools which a Bushman visitor recognized as practically identical to those being used by his people in the Kalahari today.) Each group maintains a number of different fires for different purposes. In front of the entrance to each hut is a fire that burns all night and helps keep sleepers warm, particularly during the winter when temperatures fall to freezing or near-freezing levels.

Fires for cooking, a morning fire and an evening fire, are located at various places outside the hut so that cooking may be done in the shade. When a man returns from a hunt with a small animal such as a buck or warthog or porcupine, he goes to a spot perhaps twenty to thirty yards from his hut, digs a pit, makes a large fire with big logs, and roasts the animal whole. If a band of eight family groups occupies a site for a month or so and then moves on, it will leave twenty-four cooking and warming fires and, depending on the success of the hunters, eight to twenty-four roasting pits—and perhaps several ceremonial fires and ash dumps. The remains of the fires will endure long after the huts and other features of the camp have disappeared.

Such observations will help archeologists to speculate more precisely about the meanings of living-floor patterns, especially patterns uncovered by excavations extending over wide areas. The word "hearth" may be far too general to describe the fires of prehistoric hunter-gatherers, as it certainly is to describe the fires of their living descendants. The Kalahari studies will lead to new ways of interpreting the evidence. For instance, hunter-gatherers probably tend and tended to eat more meat in the evening than in the morning, which suggests that the remains of evening fires might include more bones than the remains of morning fires. One would expect, further, to find few if any traces of food in warming fires.

This is only one example of research conducted by DeVore and John Yellen, the archeologist of the Harvard group. Yellen's richest site lies in the very same area as an important contemporary site. Located near a pan or natural basin which contains standing water four months of the year, it includes the remains of a pit very much like those used today, and the odds are that then as now hunters hid here on moonlit nights ready to attack when animals came to drink.

Findings at this site, among others, suggest that the Kalahari Bushmen may not have been forced to live in the desert during recent colonial times. If these people were driven out of more abundant lands and the desert is indeed a refuge area, it happened long before the coming of Europeans, perhaps more than

20,000 years ago which is the minimum age of the oldest excavated occupation layers.

Lee, who is now at the University of Toronto, has concentrated on economics, specifically on the amount of effort individuals put into the business of living. Local Bushmen are fortunate in one respect, namely, that they have an abundant and dependable food staple, a "staff of life" in the form of the high-energy, high-protein nut of the mongongo tree. Although some eighty-five desert plants are considered edible and may be used for variety or as second-best fare, this single species provides from half to two-thirds of the total vegetable diet. The selection of campsites is determined by the locations of mongongo forests found on the crests of long sand dunes or, more precisely, by the distances between the nearest water sources and the forests.

According to Lee, "the Bushmen typically occupy a camp for weeks or months and literally eat their way out of it." During January or February, when most of the rain falls, they may camp at a temporary pool within a mile or so of the nearest trees, and exhaust that supply of nuts in a week. Then on successive weeks they may have to walk two, three and four miles to progressively more distant forests, all the time camping at the same pool. They will never walk more than six miles, however, since women are not willing to undertake longer trips in a single day at temperatures averaging 100 degrees and carrying twenty to forty pounds of nuts on their backs, plus infants or tired children.

This is the departure point, and the group will then move to another water source near other forests, that is, in relatively wet weather. But in the driest season, in October and November, there is no choice because all temporary pools have vanished, and the people must stay near one of the permanent water holes. Most of them forgo mongongo nuts and other preferred foods, living on poorer fare which can be gathered within a few miles of their homes. Some hardier groups, however, travel up to twenty miles to mongongo trees in waterless places where they may camp for a week or two.

Life becomes exceedingly difficult under such conditions. Indeed, it would be impossible without a certain type of shrub that has bulbous root organs which are about the size of a football and store water in the form of milky juice. Even with these natural

Kalahari woman gathering food with child on back

reservoirs the campers barely make a go of it in dry seasons, since so much of the water they get from the roots is needed simply to replace the water lost in the process of digging for the roots, which lie a foot or two underground in the hard compacted soil of basins between sand dunes. Incidentally, on one occasion Lee asked a group of Bushmen to go through this ordeal, even though he could easily have driven them to a mongongo forest and back again in his Land Rover, which is something like asking city dwellers to walk to work in blizzard times without using available buses and subways. But the Bushmen promptly agreed after he explained that they were the only people in the world who could cope with the Kalahari at its worst, and that he and others wanted to know how they did it.

Food gathering requires only a bare minimum of equipment. The basic tools include a pair of unworked hammerstones to crack nuts with and a sturdy digging stick about three feet long and three-quarters of an inch in diameter and sharpened to a blade at the business end. The most important item of equipment is the "kaross," a combination garment and receptacle made of antelope hide, which women wear draped over the shoulder. It forms a pouch for carrying nuts, berries and edible roots and bulbs as well as ostrich-shell water containers, firewood, and babies. These three simple items are all that is needed to obtain vegetable foods.

Going after animals demands more ingenuity and a correspondingly more elaborate set of tools—including bows and arrows and arrow poisons made from crushed beetle pupae, rope snares and nets, firemaking kits, knives, and a dozen other items. Yellen has gone with Bushmen on hunting trips and studied their tracking techniques. Judging by a variety of scuff marks and indentations in the sand, they can tell the kind of animal as well as its size and sex and which way it is going. They can also tell how old the track is. Some tracks are so recent that sand is still falling into the hollow, while old tracks may be blurred and faded. Such abilities are relatively routine, roughly the equivalent of reading and writing.

The finer points of the art come into play in deciding what the animal is doing and whether or not to go after it, decisions based on an intimate knowledge of the land and animal behavior. Yellen emphasizes that an eland's tracks may be only half an hour old, but if the Bushmen feel it is "going somewhere far" and moving at a steady pace, they will not bother to pursue it. On the other hand, tracks several hours old may represent a call to action if they indicate that the animal is moving irregularly within a limited area, which may mean that it is stopping frequently to rest or keeping watch on a young offspring hidden in some bushes.

One of the most impressive things about these and many far subtler deductions is what they imply about the quality of the brain required for advanced forms of hunting. During the following of game trails Bushmen discuss the nature and meaning of tracks, assess the probable merits of different theories about what is happening, decide on a course of action, and frequently check and recheck their theories in the light of fresh evidence. They distinguish clearly between fact and hypothesis. The hunter's brain is also the scientist's. Whether he is predicting the movements of game in a wilderness or satellites in space, man uses the same basic thought processes.

Big game is not as plentiful in the Kalahari as it once was, so considerable effort is devoted to smaller animals. The most commonly caught game, the springhare, is taken in its burrow with the aid of a flexible pole thirteen feet long. The hunter pushes the pole into the burrow slowly as it bends to follow underground turns, proceeding by "feel" and ready to detect vibrations or sounds that indicate the location of the cornered prey. Then at the proper moment he moves the pole backward in a swift thrust, impaling the hare on a hook attached to the probing end, and uses a digging stick to get at the animal and kill it.

The Bushmen are also experts at trapping, a skill which involves far more than merely finding tracks where snares may be placed. The trick is to influence patterns of animal movement, deliberately creating places suitable for snares. For example, hunters may notice antelope tracks on a sandy area of bush country, and toss some branches across them. Coming back to the area a day or two later, they notice changes in the tracks and put down more branches. After a number of days there is a seemingly haphazard brush fence with gaps two or three feet wide. The next step is to add just enough branches to narrow the gaps still further, and then set nooses in them. By this time, and it requires considerable patience, the animals have been conditioned to walk right into the traps.

There is also a clever way of catching guinea fowl. If a hen sees that one of her eggs has rolled out of the nest, she tries to roll it back with her head and beak. This is an automatic reaction, triggered by the sight of the misplaced egg, and a hunter will take advantage of it by removing an egg from the nest, placing it about eight inches away and laying a buried noose around it. As soon as the hen returns to her nest and notices what has happened, she is doomed because she cannot help nudging the egg toward the nest and springing the trap.

The Bushman has an enormous repertoire of hunting techniques which he can call on and modify to fit special circumstances. After all, that is his job and he spends his life learning what his ancestors developed to a high level. So despite the hard times of hot dry seasons, he is remarkably successful at extracting a living from desert lands. Lee has measured the success in a detailed study of one group of about thirty persons camping near a water hole. (Numbers varied from day to day as families left to visit other groups and visitors arrived from other camps.) The study continued for twenty-eight consecutive days in July and August, an "average" time when food was neither exceptionally abundant nor exceptionally scarce.

It yielded a precise and revealing subsistence balance sheet. During this period, meat made up 37 per cent of the diet, mongongo nuts 33 per cent, and other vegetables 30 per cent. Sufficient supplies were obtained daily to provide each member of the group with 1.4 pounds of food or some 2,140 calories, about 165 calories more than the basic daily requirement. Furthermore, obtaining food is by no means a full-time job. Individuals engaged in hunting and gathering devoted only from one to three days a week to the job, and had the rest of the week free for resting and playing games and visiting friends at nearby camps.

As a matter of fact, earning a living is even more efficient than these figures indicate. During their few days of working time the providers manage to obtain sufficient food not only for themselves but for dependents, individuals under fifteen and over sixty years old, who make up about a third of the group and contribute nothing or very little to food supplies. It is worth noting that about 8 per cent of all 248 hunter-gatherers in the Kalahari area were persons sixty to more than eighty years old. A final point—the study was conducted during a year of drought, a year which had less than seven inches of rain, and foraging achievements would have been even more impressive in better times.

There are many reasons to carry out such analyses. For one thing they tend to pin down, and sometimes to show up, anecdotal information and general impressions. In this instance they have contributed to an entirely new picture of the hunting-gathering way of life, contemporary and prehistoric. The old picture was less a solid theory than a fine example of our aptitude for seeing all human beings in our own image, that is, based on the way things are in an affluent society. Many investigators assumed that people who have few and relatively primitive possessions are impoverished, long-suffering, and pitiable.

Certainly that assumption does not hold for the Kalahari Bushmen. Their way of adapting stands as a living reminder of earlier adaptations, details of which can only be inferred from patterns of fossils and artifacts found in excavated occupation layers. Their success illuminates earlier successes which set the stage for the coming of modern man. Evolution that was uniquely human arose with the rise of hunting, the expansion of the brain, the prolonged period of infant and child dependency, the need for a home base, and a kind of division of labor hitherto unknown in the order of primates.

Society changed when men specialized in outwitting animals and women specialized in collecting vegetables, and the change can be measured in terms of work schedules. The result was a degree of leisure unattainable in a troop of primates in which there are no home bases or stored foods and every individual except nursing infants must spend time seeking food every day of its life. A hunting-gathering society probably provides more free time for all its members than any other type of society yet evolved. For most people leisure vanished with agriculture and cities and the Industrial Revolution; it may yet return with computers and automation.

Research on the economics of the hunting-gathering way of life involves not only man's origins but also his future. Using Lee's subsistence balance sheet, Harold Thomas of Harvard's Division of Engineering and Applied Physics has made some preliminary studies of the productivity of the Kalahari Bushmen and their land. His work indicates that with their present tools and knowledge and at their present population level, the people could approach but never exceed a daily food supply providing about 3,200 calories per person, no matter how hard they worked. In other words, the 2,140 calories which they are currently producing represent about 60 per cent of the theoretical maximum.

Kalahari dietary staple: roasting mongongo nuts

The calculations may be taken several steps further by estimating the effect of an improvement in food-getting techniques. For example, the Bushmen use metal points on their arrows instead of the bone or stone points used by their ancestors—a step which, by increasing range and killing power, has increased food production by an estimated 1.5 per cent and made it possible to support four more working members of the group than could have been supported by hunters using the old-style arrows. Thomas believes that Bushman economics provides a simple model of basic forces and relationships encountered in the study of all communities, technologically advanced as well as primitive. He is interested in developing a broad and mathematically based theory which can be applied to the problems of a world far more complex than that of the Kalahari, a theory which would permit planners to predict more precisely the impact of new programs in industry, public health, and education on the course of social development.

The Harvard studies are concerned with values and customs in addition to economics. Along with a continuing analysis of the Bushman's economic system, special efforts are being made to probe factors which are closely related but much more difficult to measure, such as the way people get along with one another, the way they handle the vital and by no means simple problems of living together in a desert. Insight into such matters may be obtained from methods of bringing up children which, like hunting techniques, have evolved as a result of long experience and represent a program or repertoire of behavior selected to ensure the production of appropriately socialized adults.

For example, what is the significance of the tendency to prolong further the already prolonged period of dependency? Among Bushmen, as among Australian aborigines, breast feeding may continue until the child is three or four years old. Furthermore, until the age of five children are carried most of the way during hikes from camp to camp, and responsibility is delayed for a long period after that. Although seven-year-olds regularly take care of their younger brothers and sisters in many primitive societies, in Bushman societies young children have nothing to do but play, and they are still playing at the age of twelve or more when boys of the same age among neighboring Bantu peoples are herding cattle. As a matter of fact, Bushman girls do not begin regular food gathering until they are about fourteen, while boys generally do not begin hunting seriously until at least two years later.

These and other practices are part of a pattern that was once universal, the pattern of raising children for a life of hunting and gathering. The first stages of the process are of special interest to Melvin Konner, who is focusing on development and behavior during infancy and early childhood. Among other things, he has been studying the reflexes which Bushman infants are born with, the same repertoire of reflexes observed among infants born in urban societies—except that more of them seem to be important in a hunter-gatherer context.

Some reflexes such as sucking, blinking and crying are useful to infants in all societies. Others seem to be useful only in primitive societies. For example, an infant placed on its stomach a few days after birth is very likely to try raising its head, turning its head from side to side, and dragging itself along by a crawling action of its legs. Also, if held upright with its feet touching a flat surface, it will probably exhibit stepping and walking movements. These reactions serve little purpose for a baby who spends most of its time lying on its back in a crib.

But they may be important to a Bushman infant who is held upright in a sling on its mother's side or hip, particularly when it is sleeping with its face pressed against her. Under such circumstances automatic moving of the head and body can be expected to reduce discomfort as well as the risk of smothering. Konner points out that other reflexes considered "vestigial" may also play an important role in primitive societies where infants spend practically all their time in a vertical position rather than in the horizontal position typical of urban-society infants. Further research will be required to learn what effect, if any, the difference in positions has on subsequent development and behavior.

Perhaps the most striking difference between Bushman and urban infants, although in most respects they are very much alike, is how they react to strangers. Infants of all societies generally begin to fear strangers at about seven to nine months, but the response tends to be relatively mild among American and European babies, who may frown and turn away and cry in protest if a stranger does not leave. But the response of the Bushman infant is spectacularly more intense.

One day Konner and a British colleague stopped their Land Rover to pick up a family of Bushmen, including a mother with a sleeping infant. During the ride the infant woke up, lifted its head, saw the Britisher in the back seat, and unleashed an ear-splitting scream—the same sort of scream which babies emit when they are in severe physical pain. This was a typical response. Furthermore, tests show that practically identical responses occur whether the stranger is a white visitor or a Bushman native to the Kalahari. The reaction probably has a sound basis in experiences of the prehistoric past. At least until recent times, the appearance of a stranger was presumably a rare event, and an event that often meant trouble.

Studies are also being conducted of the behavior of Bushman children after the first two years of life. Patricia Draper has concentrated on this problem, although she also has information about infancy. Her approach depends on the keeping of detailed records, which include data on the activities of about 35 children up to fourteen years old, each of whom was observed for a total of three to four hours over a period of 12 months.

Analyses based on this evidence provide a quantitative and vivid picture of the intimacy of life in the wilderness. Taking the entire age range from birth through fourteen, children were in physical contact, actually touching another individual, about a third of the time. For the age range from birth through five the proportion of contact time was more than 50 per cent, and in only four observed cases was the child unaccompanied, that is, without another person less than three feet or so away. (In two of the four cases, the child was asleep.)

From the young child's viewpoint the camp is a self-contained world, an island in the bush which extends pathless in all directions without obvious landmarks. The child grows up in a group of forty to fifty individuals among whom relationships are intense, very close and personal. Families sitting at night in front of their huts, around their fires, do not have to raise their voices to speak with one another across the camping area. A disturbance of any sort moves swiftly like a ripple through the group; the people, in Draper's words, live together "almost like a flock of birds."

In such an atmosphere there is little aggression and no sustained fighting among children. Potentially disruptive encounters are halted at the very start by an adult, usually but not necessarily one of the children's mothers, who is within arm's reach and more often than not separates the would-be antagonists casually, without interrupting work or conversation. "Aggression is never allowed to build up," Draper comments, "and children do not get a chance to learn the satisfaction of making someone cry or humiliating a person."

All this is part of the preparation for a life designed to minimize aggression, and maximize sharing. Food and water are shared among bands and among individuals within bands, as well as with scientists and other visiting white men. Goods are shared in continuous trading and the exchange of gifts. Everything, pots and spoons and arrows and buttons, tends to circulate. Most Bushmen feel uncomfortable if they have a particularly beautiful ornament, a skin decorated with colored beads, a fine knife, or any other distinctive possession. They fear that they will be envied and resented, and the item is passed on to others who will eventually feel the same way.

There is much to be learned about the early development of sharing, but some aspects of the process have been observed in modern communities. One study indicates that some children begin sharing candy and other valued items with companions at about the age of two or three, on a fifty-fifty basis. Generosity, defined as giving more than half the items away, appears later and is observed in more than 40 per cent of six-year-olds; it increases after the sixth year, only to drop sharply at twelve or so. The same study finds no difference in sharing between boys and girls. It would be interesting to compare these patterns with those of Bushman children, relate the differences to differences in upbringing and environment, and perhaps speculate about similar changes that might have occurred during the evolutionary shift from hunting-gathering to agriculture.

Further patterns exist which might reveal more if we knew how to interpret them, for example, living-floor patterns found at sites long deserted. People have many reasons for selecting a place to camp and for choosing spots within the camp for their shelters and hearths. The land itself has a great deal to do with the choice, the presence of water and shade trees and edible plants and so on. The site may be abandoned as soon as natural resources begin to dwindle.

But subtler forces are also at work. We seem to depend on instinctive rules for placing ourselves, for keeping our distances, with respect to other individuals. The rules can be observed in action when a person enters a living room or subway train and selects a seat near other people, but not too near. Gould has found signs of analogous behavior in the course of observing families of Australian aborigines who locate their camps not near a water hole but some distance off, partly to reduce chances of crossing the paths of other families in the area.

All such responses and adjustments are part of the delicate business of being sociable, of relieving tensions and avoiding conflicts. There is nothing at all natural about living together, if by natural we mean easy or effortless. Every individual must devote a considerable amount of time and energy to maintaining a reasonably peaceful place in the scheme of things, to keep from rubbing people the wrong way or being rubbed the wrong way. The continual building up and spilling over of tensions is as characteristic of human as it is of baboon groups. Sometimes a set smile and a "thank you, do come again" is the equivalent of a chase that ends with a bite and a submissive grimace.

Another major phase of the Kalahari project concerns the relationships between behavior and beliefs. At the core of the Bushman's religion is the healing dance, and at the core of the dance is the trance of the healer. The Bushmen believe that medicine lies cold in the pit of the healer's stomach, and that it can be released and transferred to sick persons by a laying on of hands. But first the medicine must be brought to a boil, which is the purpose of the dance.

Proceedings usually start in the evening as women, and often children, make a fire and sit about it clapping and singing. Soon some of the men move into the area to dance for brief periods in circles around the fire, shoulders hunched and feet stamping and arms pressed against their sides, in a casual sort of warm-up period that may last for two hours or so. Then the frenzy comes. A vacant stare appears in the eyes of the dancer and he trembles, sweats heavily and stamps so hard that, in Lee's words, "shock waves can be seen rippling through the body."

The trance state is marked by moaning, shrieking and intense physical exertion. Sometimes a dancer, a novice as a rule, loses control and runs wild into the bush or burns himself by dancing through the central fire. One man described the experience as follows: "I see all the people like very small birds; the whole place will be spinning around and that is why we run around. The trees will be circling also. You feel your blood become very hot just like blood boiling on a fire and then you start healing. . . . When I lay my hands on a sick person, the medicine in me will go into him and cure him."

As a rule, healing hits a peak between midnight and two in the morning, simmers down for a while, hits a second peak at sunrise, and comes to a close around ten or eleven. During this period a large proportion of the group participates in the sessions. Healers are not members of an elite, exalted beings regarded by the rest of the people with fear and trembling. The ambition of all boys is to become "doctors" and, after many trials and several years of apprenticeship for promising candidates, about half of them make it. A few women, especially very old women, may also go into trances, while some of the younger men simply use the occasion to demonstrate their dancing skills.

These rituals serve a number of purposes besides healing. The people may also organize dances out of sheer exuberance, to celebrate the killing of a large antelope or to greet old friends

Beginning of Kalahari trance dance: preparing for laying on of hands and healing

coming for a visit. Looking at things in a wider context, Lee draws attention to a point involving the resolution of conflict. He emphasizes that in the course of their dancing activities the Bushmen experience hallucinations, distorted body images and related effects which members of other societies, primitive and otherwise, experience with the use of drugs—and that certain features of the dance, such as violent exertion and shrieking, help provide harmless relief for resentments and fears and insecurities.

A number of techniques, such as psychological testing and extensive interviews, have been used in an effort to gain a deeper understanding of what the trance ceremony expresses. Ritual has always been difficult to get at. Like poetry, it has meanings at many levels and demands complex types of analysis. But if fruitful studies of poetry are any indication, such work may yet yield important insights. Meanwhile it is evident that the ceremony can no longer be viewed as a sort of circus display put on by quaint savages, that they are by no means as exotic or remote from us as was once believed. Their rituals and ours express common needs and frustrations, and have common roots in human prehistory.

All phases of survival in the Kalahari are interrelated in the sense that they represent an adaptation, one of many possible adaptations, to a particular type of environment. The Bushmen live in a diverse and scattered world. Food is available in different areas at different times of the year, and since rainfall is not always predictable, they must be able to take advantage of every local opportunity as it arises. Henry Harpending of Yale stresses that this flexibility shows up in a number of genetic and breeding patterns.

For example, he has studied nine areas containing a total of about 2,300 Bushmen, and finds that only about 60 per cent of the parents in a particular area were born in that area, as compared to a figure of 95 per cent or more for some settled agricultural villages of similar population size. This situation reflects the basic nature of the band. The band does not exist as a fixed group of individuals living and moving together as one big family. It is a dynamic unit where people, singly and in groups, arrive and depart according to such things as the availability of food as and how well they happen to be getting along with one another.

Their adaptation has been an effective one. Reports by Nancy

Howell-Lee of Princeton University's Office of Population Research, who has gathered and is analyzing records of about 850 Bushmen, indicate that their population has been increasing slowly over the years—and that their death rates have been moderately low in the recent past and probably for a long time before Europeans came. Their maximum life span seems to be the same as it is for human beings everywhere, with perhaps one person in a million living to the age of 110. (The oldest known Bushman is almost 90.)

There is an increasing interest in living among today's hunter-gatherers, studying them, and at the same time conducting local excavations which they can help to interpret. A number of people have never been observed by modern methods, although their existence has been known for some time, among other places, in the forests of Borneo, Thailand, Malaya and South America. More such groups are still being found.

For decades explorers, anthropologists and other strangers have moved through forests without coming across people camped unobtrusively off ancient trails. Now new kinds of strangers include such commercial pioneers as road builders and mining engineers and land prospectors who go increasingly into places without paths. The first contact with natives may be a glimpse of forms retreating into the shadows. Face-to-face encounters come later, and there are headlines about the discovery of "lost tribes" such as those recently reported in Colombia and the Philippines.

The problem of introducing these newfound people constructively into the modern world is taken more seriously than was once the case. So is the closely related problem of how to learn most effectively from them. In the days when all primitive people were regarded as bizarre inferiors, it was customary to come in with beads and other gewgaws and come out with the traditional sort of information which features ancedotes and general descriptions and impressions, generally romantic. The tendency is still with us, as indicated by Anthony Pfeiffer of Rutgers University in a recent analysis of research on Congo pygmies, an analysis which draws attention to some "neglect in collecting quantitative data on pygmy economics" and presents a tentative economic interpretation of one of their major ceremonies.

The current swing toward quantitative data and toward statements precise enough for checking has been stimulated to an appreciable extent by the presence on university campuses of high-speed computers, which can be extremely powerful tools but are no good at all without numerical information and a set of unambiguous instructions. Although the machines have yet to play their full role in the study of prehistory, indications of a change are already evident.

One sign of the change is the interest in magic numbers. Another sign is renewed thinking about what June Helm of the University of Iowa calls "a life style transcending grossly different environments." As examples she cites three features which seem to be widely found in hunter-gatherer societies: the basic right of a man to live and work with any group that contains a relative of his or of his wife to serve as "sponsor"; bride service, involving a man's duty to live with and help support his wife's parents for a period of months or years, a custom which reinforces alliances between local groups and expands hunters' knowledge of terrain and resources; and an ethics of sharing, the readiness to give generously of one's time and goods. These and other practices are "continually reweaving a set of localized camps into a greater society," an effort which concerns man still.

■ Participant observers' reenactment of prehistoric man's way of life; relearning of extinct skills in use of tools and survival techniques; necessary revision of old theories of hunting and farming; construction of artificial "prehistoric" sites for experimental and teaching purposes

CHAPTER XVII

Experimental Archeology

■ There are ways of entering more actively into the life of prehistoric man, ways that take us out of the laboratory and into the open wilderness and a small step closer to his world. And sometimes opportunities for experiments arise unexpectedly. One July evening in 1966 a group of excavators was camping in an isolated part of the Fort Apache Indian Reservation of eastern Arizona. Among them were William Longacre, an archeologist at the University of Arizona, and a group of students engaged in a continuing long-term project, digging an 800-room pueblo community dating back to the fourteenth century.

The camp routine was upset an hour before midnight when a student stringing up a hammock heard a rustling in the leaves and turned his flashlight on a big black bear, attracted by the smell of baking banana bread. The animal was fair game since the bear population in the area had increased rapidly to a point where the Apaches were losing cattle regularly, and several nights earlier bears had killed a couple of calves at a nearby dam. The cattle manager for the Indians was called to the scene, and killed the animal with a single 30-30 carbine shot.

The problem of what to do with the carcass became a valuable lesson. It happened that Don Crabtree of Kimberly, Idaho, a specialist in stoneworking, was visiting the camp to demonstrate toolmaking techniques to the students. The bear represented an unprecedented chance to see his tools actually in use by an expert hunter and skinner, the man who had killed the bear. The expert, Gene Seely, gracious if not highly enthusiastic, obviously preferred rather more conventional methods, but agreed to give it a try.

Everything was ready early next moning. Crabtree had prepared a "little kit" of eight tools, all made of the hard volcanic glass obsidian. The students had gathered around to watch and there in the center of the circle were the bear and Seely, chewing tobacco and shaking his head skeptically. He took a backed blade, and had started the first cut from below the jaws down the chest when he was shocked to find himself "off balance" in a peculiar way. On the basis of his experience with steel knives, his muscles were set to overcome a certain amount of resistance in cutting through the tough skin. The obsidian blade had gone through the skin as if it were butter.

From there on it was smooth sailing and a clear-cut victory for the stone tools. Seely, muttering to himself in surprise, completed in less than two hours a task that would have taken up to three and a half hours using his favorite Swedish steel knife. Of course, the one advantage of steel is its superior durability, although the volcanic glass can be resharpened in a few seconds by removing tiny chips along working edges. After the demonstration, Seely requested and received a kit of obsidian tools to commemorate the occasion.

As indicated in Chapter V, Louis Leakey conducted a number of similar experiments. He skinned and butchered wild game with stone tools of his own making, for example, the antelope dismembered one Christmas Eve at Olduvai before wondering Masai tribesmen. Moreover, his experiments also involved activities which come earlier in the chain of food-getting events. They included efforts to duplicate methods which prehistoric man may have used to capture animals in the first place, such as the technique of running down hares by anticipating which way they will dodge.

One of his most successful performances occurred a number of years ago in open country near a lake outside Nairobi. Leakey saw a herd of nine fleet-footed Thomson's gazelles or "Tommies" about 250 yards away, and decided to stalk one of the group that was grazing apart from the others. First he fastened leafy branches to his belt as part of a crude camouflage, not to hide himself, but to break up the telltale silhouette of the human body. Then he started closing in: "The essence of stalking is not to appear to move."

The trick is to move directly forward and to move very slowly, because that way the shape of your silhouette does not change and the size increases imperceptibly. But any sideways movement, particularly of the hands, which are a sure sign of man, changes body shape and may cause animals to flee in panic. So Leakey kept his hands against his sides, moved his legs straight forward, and kept his eyes on the gazelle he was stalking as well as on the rest of the herd.

As long as the animals were feeding, as long as their heads were down, he advanced steadily. But the instant they looked up in his general direction, he had to freeze to the spot, and he knew how to anticipate that instant: "There's a subtle movement just before a Tommy lifts its head. One shoulder seems to rise just a bit higher than the other." Leakey advanced in a series of stops and starts and changes of direction as his prey moved about. Several times he had to wait motionless for birds, which emit sharp alarm calls when startled, to fly away. Finally, after two solid hours of stalking, he reduced the distance between him and the gazelle from 250 yards to about six feet, and brought it down with a perfectly timed flying tackle.

During the entire period Leakey played two roles alternately. Part of the time he identified himself with the gazelle he was stalking, drawing air through his nostrils for the scent of predators, listening for a snapping twig or the rustle of branches, and anticipating, not only by overt signs but with a sixth sense for its rhythm of alertness, the moment to stop grazing and look up. When the animal pricked up its ears and turned suddenly, Leakey felt an uncertainty, a tension, that was not relieved until it resumed feeding. And a split second before the final tackle he felt the burst of fear and confusion of his prey.

At other times he was a prehistoric hunter, applying what he had learned as a child from Kikuyu hunters who lived near his home in Kenya. He observed a thousand details while frozen in position, noting things nearby as well as at a distance, particulary things that meant food—a large snail, an anthill, tracks and trails where snares might be set, weaverbirds' nests lined with grass on the inside so that there are few openings and little light gets through, a sign that rats or mice have moved into the abandoned nests. "You try not to take risks, not to strike until you're quite certain," Leakey explained. "But I've failed many times and Stone Age man did, too, so he always noticed second-best foods as he stalked, in case his quarry escaped."

Such attempts to learn as much as possible about life in prehistoric times go one step beyond observation. No matter how hard most observers work at recording and reconstructing the past, their approach is necessarily passive. They are always on the outside looking in. Investigators like Crabtree and Leakey chafed at being perpetual spectators. They found a way to enter, however briefly and superficially, the world of prehistoric man.

An analogous process takes place in acting. When an actor learns to move as he believes a character would have moved, when he assumes the gestures and intonations and garments and bodily rhythm of the character, he is beginning to feel another's feelings and to live another's life. We say he lives his role. No investigator has gone to the extreme of immersing himself so deeply into the role of a prehistoric man. On a more restricted scale, experimental, do-it-yourself archeology has made efforts to re-create a small part of the past so as to obtain by direct action a measure of insight into what it might have been like to work in, say, Magdalenian times or earlier.

It is primarily an active approach, a matter of trying out a technique to see how it works, modifying it if necessary, seeking fresh archeological and behavioral evidence, and trying again. Anything that helps translate hypothesis into action helps to make prehistory come alive, and thus serves teaching as well as research purposes.

Many experiments concern the making of stone tools, by far the most numerous traces of prehistoric man. Tools can be found in isolated places everywhere, on all continents, often in fantastic abundance. I have seen stretches of semidesert peppered with artifacts lying exposed on the sand, sites where you can still collect several dozen hand axes and cleavers and other tools within half an hour or so, even though amateur archeologists, professional archeologists, and tourists in search of sourvenirs have been collecting from the area for twenty years or more. One part of South Africa alone, the Springbok Flats just outside Johannesburg, contains an estimated 17 billion artifacts.

No material is familiar to us in the way stone was familiar to our ancestors. Toolmaking was second nature to them, part of their daily lives, something like driving a car is today, only learned much younger. They acquired a feel for the qualities of stone, for the way it had to be held and struck and the way it broke, and every step of the shaping proceeded according to traditions thousands of years old. They accumulated a kind of "muscular knowledge," only a fraction of which could be conveyed by words.

Prehistoric children probably learned mainly by watching and imitating rather than by verbal instruction, at least as far as most early tools are concerned. A number of experiments suggest that such instruction is not necessary to make reasonably good hand axes or, according to Gould's observations, to make the sort of tools produced by the Australian aborigines. On the other hand, when it comes to the most refined techniques and the shaping of such items as Solutrean blades and some of the projectile points to be discussed in the following paragraphs, experts almost certainly had to tell novices what to do.

Much of what we infer about prehistoric stoneworking techniques comes from the experiments of modern stoneworkers. Among them, one of the acknowledged masters is Don Crabtree, whose tools skinned the Arizona bear. For more than forty years Crabtree has devoted a major part of his time to this highly specialized work, first as an expert on American Indian artifacts at the Ohio State Museum in Columbus and more recently at the Idaho State University Museum. He has made more than 50,000 blades, scrapers, projectile points and other stone tools, and probably broken three or four times that many in the course of his research.

In flintworking, technique is everything, and during recent years Crabtree has become far more interested in techniques and the behavior of materials than in making artifacts. As part of an effort to understand more fully the muscular habits of prehistoric hunters, he may spend hours trying out a single style of removing flakes. When he finds a good source of flint, he may make several hundred pounds of blanks and preformed pieces for future practice sessions. Sometimes he will take pieces worked on both sides and make them thinner and thinner until they break or practically "melt" away, just to develop a mastery of the thinning process.

One of his major projects is a continuing effort to duplicate the work, to learn the "extinct skills," of certain virtuosos among the American Indians. Outstanding examples of stone toolmaking include the laurel-leaf points of the Solutreans described in Chapter X, Danish daggers and Egyptian bracelets—and, when stone was already on the way out, beautiful flint knives made in Europe and the Near East in a lost-cause attempt to imitate and compete with the new metal blades, even to the point of reproducing in the stone seam lines made during the casting process. Incidentally, to the expert toolmaker many rough and ungainly-looking items represent the work of craftsmen who were fully as skilled as the makers of museum pieces, but who had to cope with inferior material.

The project, which has occupied Crabtree's attention on and off ever since the start of his career, involves a New World tool as remarkable as any produced in the Old World, a projectile point discovered in 1926 at a buffalo-kill site near the town of Folsom in New Mexico. Folsom points come in a variety of forms. But Crabtree has concentrated on a type which in his opinion "reflects the very ultimate in working skill and control . . . being as thin and perfectly shaped as the technique would allow"—an artifact generally about two inches long, shaped something like a rowboat, and featuring a full-length groove or fluting along each side.

Crabtree has taken the measure of the vanished craftsmen whose work he is trying to reproduce. He has examined many of these points, as well as the waste chips produced during their manufacture, with all the care of an art student examining the brush strokes of a da Vinci or an El Greco. For example, he notes the delicate retouching along the edge, of 152 tiny flakes all of which are practically identical in shape, their widths varying by no more than a few hundredths of an inch. Crabtree emphasizes that such uniformity indicates a high order of skill: "For each flake removal requires the same platform preparation, the same spacing, the same downward and outward pressure, and the force must be applied each time at exactly the same angle."

He has tried eleven different methods of making this type of Folsom point, each calling for the control of up to thirty-five variables from the selection of suitable flint to final retouching. One of his current methods is based on a procedure observed half a century ago in Mexico. It includes use of a "chest crutch," a wooden tool which may have an antler tip at one end and a crosspiece at the other. The crosspiece rests against the chest of the stoneworker, and by leaning forward he can apply forces of as much as 300 pounds to the working end of the tool and remove flakes from a flint piece held firmly in a special clamp.

The technique is extremely difficult. Although Crabtree can turn out almost-perfect notched arrowheads at a rate of one every five or ten minutes, it takes him three hours or more to make a single Folsom point. The final product may look very much like the real thing to less-accomplished stoneworkers, which includes the great majority of archeologists. But the Idaho stoneworker knows that he still cannot duplicate the craftsman-ship of people for whom properly made tools meant survival. He feels that his most important contribution to date has been to demonstrate that certain previously suggested methods will not work. For example, he has ruled out a number of notions about the making of Folsom points and believes they could have been produced either by the chest-crutch or other pressure-flaking methods or by indirect percussion, that is, by using a punch to strike off flakes. Indirect percussion appears to be more conve-nient and less demanding.

Crabtree has conducted many other experiments. He has used rounded stone hammers as large as basketballs to obtain pieces of raw material from quarries, tried flaking tools made of ivory and horn and wood and a dozen other materials, compared the qual-ities of hundreds of varieties of flint by feel and appearance and sound (a piece that rings sharply, for example, will probably be of good working quality), and used the tools he made to produce other tools. In every case the objective of such studies is to learn by doing, to come closer and closer to a working knowledge of stone and of the stoneworkers' original purposes.

There are no final answers, but we know a great deal more than we did about the significance of our finds, including the Folsom

Don Crabtree demonstrating chest-crutch to make Folsom point

Contemporary flintworkers: Don Crabtree and François Bordes in Crabtree's Idaho workshop

point. For one thing, it appears that the striking beauty and symmetry of the tool is purely a coincidence from an esthetic point of view, a by-product of practical considerations. Crabtree does not believe in the art-for-art's-sake theory which suggests that Indian craftsmen took extra pains to embellish their work, going beyond strictly functional requirements. He is convinced that every feature of the Folsom design is necessary to produce a point that can be hafted securely to a spear shaft, plunged into an animal, and easily withdrawn for subsequent thrusts in a repeated stabbing action.

His work on Folsom points and other tools has resulted in a discovery that provides further evidence of the ingenuity of prehistoric stoneworkers. Some time ago he observed a difference between flint as it came from the mine and flint used in artifacts.

Four Crabtree-made Folsom points

For example, finished arrowheads usually have a characteristic greasy or glasslike luster, while the same material is relatively dull in its "green" freshly quarried state. He also found that the shinier material is less brittle and easier to work, and, after many trial-and-error experiments, learned how to convert the native material to a glassy form by heating it for at least twenty-four hours at more than 400 and less than 900 degrees Fahrenheit under carefully controlled conditions.

The procedure is a form of annealing or tempering like that used to toughen steel. In flint as in steel, tempering reduces crystal size, transforming a coarse-grained into a fine-grained material which is more elastic and more readily shaped. All the evidence indicates that the American Indians preheated most of their flints and other coarse minerals, and what may have been a flint-heating pit has been reported from one western site. Furthermore, similar pits may be identified in the Old World, because there is reason to believe that various forms of heat treatment were used widely during prehistoric times by the Solutreans and perhaps earlier peoples.

So museum and home workshop experiments have had widespread repercussions, suggesting new features to look for in artifacts and at prehistoric sites. The National Science Foundation has provided funds for the publication of Crabtree's research as well as for high-speed motion pictures of his toolmaking techniques. (The filming of certain phenomena, such as detachment of a blade from a flint core, requires speeds of more than 10,000 frames per second). It also supported a special conference on "lithic technology" or stoneworking, which, fittingly enough, was held at Les Eyzies, the unofficial capital of French prehistory.

Such activities represent a new trend in archeology. Not that working with flints and other materials is anything new; it is as old as archeology itself. But it has not always attracted funds or the active attention of most professional investigators, and only a decade ago it was generally tolerated as an absorbing if rather unfruitful hobby. The increasing interest in experimental toolmaking is significant as one further example of the current focus on behavior in all areas of evolutionary research. It expresses the idea that exploring possible ways of doing things may help in arriving at theories of what people did in times past.

Often the result is to eliminate or at least to cast considerable doubt on theories which have little evidence to support them, and yet are commonly cited in research papers and textbooks. Another experienced present-day stoneworker, John Witthoft of the University of Pennsylvania, has commented on the hammerstone as "the basic implement used by Stone Age man in tool manufacture." He emphasizes that in many cases it is mistaken for something else, mainly because if it has a roughly spherical shape to begin with, it tends to become increasingly spherical with use since irregularities and projections wear away faster than other surfaces.

Investigators insufficiently acquainted with stoneworking procedures have offered a variety of interpretations of objects which experienced toolmakers immediately recognize as hammers. Spherical stones found at Neanderthal and earlier sites have been interpreted as evidence for the use of the bola, a weapon consisting of two or more stone balls which are attached to leather thongs, whirled around, and flung at the legs of escaping animals to trip and entangle them. Witthoft mentions another case of mistaken identity: "The stones of the Pyramids were shaped by pecking with spherical hammers, but most of the Egyptologists have identified these hammers as ball bearings used to roll the masonry blocks into place."

Perhaps the most important contribution of experimental stoneworking to our understanding of prehistoric behavior was made by François Bordes (see Chapter IX). His theory that there were four different Neanderthal cultures or tribes, a theory which has opened the way for a new approach to the study of tool assemblages, arose directly out of his firsthand experience with the use and making of stone tools. It depends on the careful identification of more than sixty types of scrapers and other implements which make up the four basic Neanderthal tool kits— and the odds are that this analysis could have been carried out only by someone with a worker's knowledge and feel for the shaping of flint tools.

Other experiments have been conducted in line with studies of the evolution of the human hand. The use of tools involves two types of grip. In the so-called precision grip, the grip you use in such delicate work as starting to insert and turn a small screw in its socket, the tool handle is held between thumb and fingertips. But as soon as the screw is in place and you want to tighten it, you shift automatically to a power grip for the last turns, with fingers flexed around the handle of the screwdriver and thumb acting as a kind of clamp. This is the standard grip for applying full force.

According to John Napier of London's Royal Free Hospital, whose studies of the hand are mentioned in Chapter IV, the precision grip has evolved to its highest form in man, and the trend can be deduced from studies of tools and toolmaking. Napier believes that certain primitive tools could have been made without a fully developed precision grip, which requires a long and mobile thumb capable of being placed readily opposite the tips of the other fingers, or without any precision grip at all. To prove the point he has performed some stoneworking feats with his thumbs glued firmly to the sides of his hands, thus in effect permitting him to use a power grip only.

Under such conditions the English anatomist found he could use a hammerstone to strike flakes off a large pebble and produce the sort of chopper found in ancient occupation layers at the Olduvai Gorge and elsewhere. He even managed to turn out a crude hand ax. He believes that the manufacture of more advanced tools, however, required not only a larger brain and new purposes and plans but also a more advanced hand with a fully opposable thumb. The human hand may have evolved to its present form a million years ago, or a million years or so after the earliest known tools.

The fact remains that we still can only guess at the functions of many tools, and here again experiments can help us obtain a better picture of prehistoric workers in action. Making a good replica of a specialized tool and then successfully cutting or scraping with it demonstrate only how it could have been used. But further research may be needed to indicate how it was actually used, and one effective approach takes advantage of a kind of built-in evidence, evidence which can be obtained from the original implements themselves, as they are found in excavated sites.

For more than thirty years Sergei Semenov and his associates at the USSR Institute of Archeology in Leningrad have been studying "microwear," tool marks which cannot be detected by the naked eye. Certain gross features, such as gloss or polish and nicks and scratches, provide general clues to the way a particular implement was used. But a far more detailed record can be obtained by treating tool surfaces with metal powders and other chemicals, and then examining them magnified as much as several hundred times under the microscope. This procedure reveals an entirely new "landscape" of wear, a <u>topography</u> of lines and pits, scars, facets, cracks, dull patches and so on. It is something like the difference between viewing the moon from an earth-bound telescope and from a telescope mounted on an artificial satellite flying only a few hundred miles above the lunar surface.

For example, on the basis of naked-eye inspection, archeologists had tentatively identified one flint tool from Neanderthal times as a knife, since the working edge was polished on both sides as if it had been used repeatedly to cut down through some material. Microscopic examination, however, revealed a system of many fine grooves and indicated a different function. The grooves are not parallel to the edge as they would be if it had been used in a regular back-and-forth cutting action. They run at various angles, often crisscrossing one another, which is precisely the sort of pattern produced with experimental tools serving as scrapers.

The fact that the edge appears rounded under the microscope, as well as the presence of grooves on both sides of the tool, shows that it had been used with a two-way motion, left to right and right to left. Furthermore, the material involved could only have been animal skins, because previous skin-scraping tests had created identical microwear patterns, and different patterns result from the scraping of wood, bone, stone and other materials. A final deduction: the skins were probably fresh and damp, because skins dried in the open generally contain tiny wind-blown sand grains which produce grooves considerably deeper than those actually observed.

Another study concerned a more recent flint tool, perhaps about 15,000 to 20,000 years old, found at Kostenki on the Don River. It is about five inches long and almond-shaped, with a point at one end and a rounded butt at the other; the working edge on the butt contains nicks and scars produced by heavy blows. For a number of years investigators had debated about the nature of this tool, a debate settled by microwear analysis. The microscope shows very slightly curved grooves on both sides of the working edge, most of them parallel to one another at an angle of about 25 degrees to the line running longitudinally from butt to tip. This pattern is a fingerprint of a sort, a positive identification for ax blades whether made of flint, bronze or high-grade steel.

Engravers, saws, perforators and other stone tools also have characteristic patterns, although not all mysteries are solved as completely as those cited above. So do many tools made of bone and antler, which are often only slightly worked or not worked at

Working edge of scraper used by Australian aborigines, magnified 25 times, showing typical fractures. Same kinds of fractures found on the Quina-type scraper of the Neanderthals

all, so that shape may not be a clue to use and identification may depend entirely on microwear studies. Similar research at laboratories outside as well as inside the Soviet Union confirms Semenov's basic finding that tools may bear permanent records of their motion through and across various materials, records of the movements and rhythms of workers who vanished tens of thousands of years ago.

Getting the most out of the microwear approach calls for a three-stage process, as illustrated by one of Gould's laboratory experiments. First he took two dozen scrapers obtained from

Australian aborigines who had been using them to make spear throwers and other wooden objects, and examined them under the microscope. In every case he detected "terminated" fractures on the working edges, characteristic markings produced by the breaking off of tiny irregular chips.

Then he made an aboriginal-type scraper out of native stone, hafted it to a handle of native mulga wood with a resin made from a special kind of native grass, and used the tool to trim a mulga-wood shaft the way the aborigines do in preparing a spear. After exactly 1,000 strokes, he examined the tool under the microscope and found fracture markings identical to those on the aborigines' own scrapers.

Finally, Gould located a number of Neanderthal scrapers, Quina-type scrapers which were used by prehistoric people living at the La Quina rock shelter in southern France—and, again, the same markings appeared under the microscope. In other words, he has made a strong case for the notion that the prehistoric tools were used for working wood or some other hard material like bone, and indications are that future microwear research will involve this sort of comparative study on a larger scale.

Prehistoric farming has also been investigated experimentally. For example, several years ago Jack Harlan of the University of Illinois, a specialist in early plant domestication, joined an archeological expedition to southeastern Turkey, one of the Near Eastern regions where farming was first practiced. The region is still rich in plant foods. Harlan saw "vast seas of primitive wild wheats" still growing on mountain slopes, the same varieties of wheat used by early farmers some ten to twelve thousand years ago, and one day he went out into the fields to see how much grain he could harvest.

During his first tests he used the simplest of tools, his bare "urbanized" hands, which soon became red and raw. But even so he had no trouble gathering an average of about 4.5 pounds of grain per hour. Then he made himself a crude sickle by gouging a slot in a sturdy branch and inserting a flint sickle blade obtained from a 9,000-year-old early-agriculture site in Iraq. The blade cut wheat about as well as a steel sickle blade, yielded nearly an extra pound of grain per hour, and spared his hands. His conclusion: "A family group . . . working slowly upslope as the season progressed, could easily harvest wild cereals over a three-week span or more and, without even working very hard, could gather more grain than the family could possibly consume in a year."

He also tried various ways of preparing wild wheat. He removed hulls by using an Osage Indian mortar and pestle, a process made somewhat easier by pretoasting in an oven for fifteen to thirty minutes at 350 degrees. The pounded material could be cleaned by passing it through a sieve of woven grass, or simply by winnowing it in the wind, and then made into a soup or boiled like rice. Harlan reports that wild wheat is nutritious as well as tasty, chemical analysis showing that it contains nearly 60 per cent more protein than modern cultivated varieties.

Of course, those who have actually lived with primitive people on a day-to-day basis gain a kind of firsthand knowledge that can be obtained in no other way. In his studies of the Bushmen, for example, Lee had to learn their difficult language, which includes four different clicks and five tones. He has gathered mongongo nuts with them, and lived for three weeks on a diet consisting mainly of this staple. On one occasion he managed to keep up with hunters walking through the Kalahari at a speed of five to six miles per hour, although doing that as a regular practice was something else again. His most arduous experience was an effort to live as Bushmen live at the height of a drought, accompanying a group on an overnight hike to a mongongo forest where the only local source of water were the juices in deep underground roots.

This was too much for Lee. After spending hours looking for game and digging for roots and walking some nine miles under the sun in temperatures of well over a hundred degrees, he realized that he would be a burden to the others. He felt feverish and dry, could not swallow, and decided to go back to the base camp near a permanent water hole. Upon his return early the next morning, Lee made a dramatic beeline for the nearest water bag and emptied it with evident relief, a sight that set the Bushmen laughing for an hour.

There is an advantage in trying to share a way of life and a language, an advantage beyond coming closer to people and earning their confidence and good will. Although one can never learn to think as prehistoric man thought or learn exactly how he did things, every increase of knowledge adds a bit to reconstructions of times past. And the problem of improving the reconstructions, of understanding human origins better, is sufficiently important to merit the exploration of every possible lead. Perhaps the ultimate step, the ultimate experiment in living archeology, is to become a prehistoric individual for a time and live entirely on what you can get from the wilderness.

As far as I know, no one has yet undertaken an organized effort to "go prehistoric" in this sense, although there have been occasional efforts in that direction. One archeologist in his undergraduate days spent several months hunting and trapping alone in the wilderness, and provided very well for himself. But his motive was personal rather than scientific; he simply wanted to get away from people. And more than a decade ago ten French investigators spent three weeks in a cave living off the land in what they considered to be the style of Neanderthal man.

Leakey evolved a more ambitious plan. It covers several million years of human evolution in six weeks, each week representing a different stage of development. During the first week he would live the way hominids presumably lived before the regular making of tools, say, some three million years ago. Equipped with clubs, rocks for bashing, digging sticks, and cord for snares and traps (made from the inner bark of trees), he would subsist chiefly on plant foods and small game which can be ripped apart with bare hands.

During the second week, the second evolutionary stage of perhaps two million years ago, he would make simple choppers and flake tools. That permits systematic scavenging for the first time, because such tools make it possible to cut through tough antelope skin and separate joints and do general butchering, all of which cannot be accomplished with hands and fingernails and teeth. (Leakey has tried.) The third week involves man's increasing independence of other killers, the decline of scavenging and the rise of big-game hunting, the development of hand axes and cleavers and other heavy-duty butchering tools, and the invention of wooden spears with whittled and perhaps fire-hardened tips, or antelope-horn tips.

The plan calls for reliance on more and more advanced techniques during the last three weeks, which cover the period from about 100,000 to 10,000 or 15,000 years ago. Leakey would begin by making stone points and hafting them to spears with natural resins and gums and sinews, and later turn to backed blades and spear throwers and harpoons. Up to this point all his weapons would be designed primarily to cripple animals and slow them down, but the final week would see the first "shooting to kill" with finely balanced spears and, above all, an efficient bow and arrow. Throughout the six-week period he would live in increasingly advanced quarters: rock shelters, caves, crude tents and half-sunken pit houses or "artificial caves," and huts with solid walls and roofs.

Leakey had an explanation for not undertaking such vigorous living off African savanna lands: "I'd have done it long ago, but Mary wouldn't let me. She thought it was too dangerous." But a review of what has already been done and of what has not yet been done indicates that the time may be ripe for some such plan. Making tools, using them to make other tools and butcher animals and gather plant foods, trying out primitive hunting techniques—these and many other studies have all contributed blocks of information to our understanding of hunter-gatherers.

On the other hand, each study has been a piecemeal effort in the sense that it is isolated from the others, representing the skills and enthusiasm and interests of the individual investigator acting pretty much on his own. The next step might well be a coordinated series of field expeditions designed to do the whole thing at once, as it were. The objective would be to duplicate the complete range of actual Stone Age living as closely as possible by organizing volunteers into prehistoric-type bands and having them camp out in the wilderness for extended periods.

There is another type of experimental archeology which has many unexploited possibilities, the construction of artificial "prehistoric" sites, full-scale living floors prepared mainly for research purposes. A number of such sites exist on the Santa Barbara campus of the University of California, for example. In one series of studies John Chilcott and James Deetz used a machine to dig square pits seven feet on a side and some five feet deep, put artifacts and other materials in predetermined positions, filled the pits up again, and planted grass on the surface. Six months later, after the elements had "aged" the area, they returned to excavate.

One of the pits was designed to test the effectiveness of various digging techniques in recovering small objects, in this case glass beads about the size of BB shot. Among other things, the study indicated just how important the type of soil may be in this connection. Ninety-six per cent of the beads placed beforehand in the natural silty soil of the region were recovered by simply scooping up the soil in a trowel and sifting through it. But the recovery rate dropped to less than 60 per cent in damp earth formed by decayed organic matter, which is oily and tends to cling to the beads, a fact underlining the need for special measures when working in such soils.

A second site served as a proving ground for students. It had three made-to-order occupation layers, the deepest containing a hearth, scrapers, projectile points and other carefully placed items that might be found in Indian deposits 6,000 or more years old. Above this layer the California archeologists arranged a more recent type of living floor, including coyote and human bones and pottery, and above that a modern or "historic" layer, including a beer bottle, pieces of glass, a metal bank and more human remains. Five crews of students representing different age groups and different degrees of experience worked at five parts of the site. As expected, the more experienced students did a more careful job of excavating than novices (breaking fewer items and leaving more items in their original positions). In other words, this sort of setup provides a good way of training and testing students.

Even with the best of excavating techniques, however, there is always the problem of how to interpret the evidence. For example, it is often taken for granted that if bones are relatively scarce at a living site, the people probably did not eat much meat—and that a predominance of small-animal bones means a diet heavy on small game. Actual tests show that these assumptions are not necessarily valid.

Glynn Isaac once dumped 55 large bones and bone fragments and more than 60 bone splinters on a one-square-yard plot in the Rift Valley. He came back four months later to see what was left, and found that more than 70 per cent of the material was gone, destroyed and scattered mainly by hyenas and other scavengers. In the Kalahari, Yellen observed that large bones are often splintered for their marrow and the splinters tend to disintegrate swiftly, while small bones tend to become buried and remain intact. Such factors must be taken into account before drawing conclusions about early hunting practices.

A more elaborate experiment designed to last a hundred years is being conducted by investigators working in southern England under the direction of Peter Jewell of University College London. In 1960 they built an earthwork such as prehistoric villagers built to defend themselves and "seeded" it with cremated human bone, human bone with marrow of different blood types, pieces of pottery each numbered, cooked and uncooked animal bones, burned and unburned wood, leather, and half a dozen types of textile. The position of each item was recorded exactly. Different parts of the site will be excavated at set intervals to determine not only how and how fast materials decompose but also how their positions change as the result of the "heaving" of freezing and thawing soils, the activities of rodents and earthworms, and so on. Excavations are scheduled for the years 1974, 1990, 2022, and 2060.

Incidentally, Jewell and his associates have already learned a great deal from their project. Part of the earthwork was built with primitive tools such as antler picks and shovels made from shoulder blades, and this phase of the experiment has provided the most interesting results to date. The tools turned out to be "amazingly efficient." For example, the antler picks stood up under rough treatment which included not only the breaking up of hard layers of soil but also the splitting of solid rock.

Unfortunately, professional archeologists have not used the experimental approach as widely as they might have in their own research work. But their greatest failure lies in education, where the gap between what has been accomplished and what could be accomplished is enormous. Indeed, there is no better example of missed opportunities to bring significant and exciting activities into the classroom. Although much effort has gone into the preparation of more stimulating and challenging courses, the shortage of really imaginative ideas continues.

A promising exception is a course in experimental archeology offered at Virginia Commonwealth University in Richmond. Errett Callahan and his students have been shaping a variety of materials from tough Virginia quartzite to a ton of imported

Texas flint into Oldowan choppers, Acheulian hand axes, Neanderthal points and other stone tools. They have used the tools to make spears, dig holes, chop down trees and prepare hides—and as part of a broadening program, they have spent weekends living off the land with primitive brush shelters for sleeping quarters.

Some of the most interesting work is being done in the lower grades. For example, several years ago teachers at the Solebury School in New Hope, Pennsylvania, used artificial sites for the first time in a new way that goes considerably beyond the University of California project as far as creative pedagogy is concerned. Part of one experiment involved a carefully planned game between eighth and ninth grades. Eighth-grade pupils dug a large square hole about a yard deep and made a triple-decker "sandwich" consisting of three layers.

The deepest layer included a hearth with ashes, a stone anvil, flint chips, a broken scraper and some fossilized bone, arranged to represent the sort of occupation that might be found in an actual Indian site 10,000 or more years old. The uppermost layer represented a camping place about 1,000 years old. For each layer the pupils made a map indicating the position of each object, and then they covered the site with leaves and branches. In the spring, ninth-grade pupils excavated the artificial site, the aim being to plot the position of the uncovered objects precisely enough to duplicate the maps drawn by the eighth-grade pupils —and although the soil was clayey and difficult to work in, they managed to reconstruct appreciable proportions of the original patterns. This experiment gave pupils a chance to think up their own living-floor patterns, and in the process to gain a firsthand feeling for the basic notion of living floors and the importance of slow and careful excavating.

Such experiments and many variations on the same theme are beginning to interest a few educators. Experimental archeology can do as much for students not planning to enter the field as for professional archeologists and archeologists-to-be. There is much to be gained by making the past come alive in a truly meaningful way, by introducing into a "humanities" course the notion of evidence and experiment—for one thing, a better understanding not only of human origins but also of the culutral process itself.

Solebury School students at
experimental site

■ The beginning of the "smile" before birth; the use of the eyes, then the social smile as a tracking, reaching, communicating method; its origins and prehistoric behavior; the evolutionary modification of the "grin" as cringing submissiveness; crying, maternal responsiveness and feeding schedules

CHAPTER XVIII

The Human Infant: A Study in Living Prehistory

■ The study of the human smile, as it develops in infants, has given scientists a more vivid and detailed picture of what might have happened in the remote past, a picture consistent with archeological and fossil evidence as well as with evidence provided by research on primate behavior. The fact that the pattern of smiling is universal, appearing in all human societies, suggests that it must have deep roots and hints at the intensity of prehistoric needs and demands.

The development of the smile is a process of unusual interest to investigators as well as parents. The act itself, the mechanics of drawing back the corners of the mouth and associated facial movements, appears very early in life. In fact, the first smile of the infant appears so early that it is usually never seen. Judging by observations of premature babies, it may occur in rudimentary form two or more months before birth. The role of subsequent learning is to attach that reflex to appropriate things in the environment, and that involves other biases.

The first "public" smile comes several months later. It appears as early as the third week after birth, as late as the twelfth week, and in most cases between the fourth and sixth weeks. In the beginning the infant smiles not at its mother but at a visual symbol of its mother, an abstraction related to her the way pictographs are related to actual objects. The symbol may involve

424

sounds and physical content and other sensations. But the central factor is the sight of the face—and at first the sight of only a part of the face, that part which the infant, with its primitive capacity for seeing, finds most compelling, namely, the eyes, especially when the face is moved about a bit.

Studies indicate that the minimum image required to arouse early smiling consists of the eyes. Investigators have used masks to eliminate every other feature, lips and nostrils and hair, and the infant still smiles at what remains. Both eyes are necessary. Smiling stops when one eye is masked or when the investigator shifts from a full-face to a profile position with respect to the infant so that it can see only a single eye. Incidentally, it need not actually be a pair of eyes. Two glass balls or any other pair of shiny objects will also produce smiling, as long as they have roughly the same size and shape and spacing. Human eyes are most compelling, however, because they stand out against the more uniform background of the forehead and cheeks. They have color and movement, and reflect a high proportion of the light falling on them.

This reaction involves the decided preference for variety and contrast which babies seem to be born with. The reason an infant looks away from a black background is partly because of the monotony of a scene without features, and it naturally glances toward places where the "action" is, where there are edges and areas of dark and light. So all shiny objects are of unusual interest, and the infant's world is full of them: keys and dishes and chrome-plated handles and all highly reflecting surfaces of polished wood and glass and metal.

But the infant goes beyond the mere taking of a general inventory. Out of the entire collection of attractive items it begins to learn to know the one that is and will continue to be most meaningful, the pair of bright objects which at first represents all it can notice of its mother. It picks out one image from all the rest, the one usually associated with soothing sounds and other pleasant sensations, and answers that particular brightness with a brightness of its own, the brightening of its eyes when it smiles. The infant learns to smile at a selected image in its new world because of a built-in ability that will serve it throughout its life, an ability to sort things out and distinguish those of special importance.

A great deal is going on along with the subsequent development of the smile. After two months or so, an image consisting of two bright "eye spots" no longer causes the infant to smile. It requires something more before it will respond, the outline of a nose in addition to two eyes and later still more, a mouth and lips and hair and so on. In other words, the infant's impression or picture of the face is filled out in finer and finer detail until it becomes complete and is identified with a specific person, generally the mother.

This process has been studied intensively by Anthony Ambrose, director of the Behavior Development Research Unit of St. Mary's Hospital in London. His technique was to stand before a baby and simply look at it for thirty seconds without moving and without expression. Then he stepped away, recorded observations of the infant's smiling responses and other behavior for thirty seconds, returned to watch for another thirty seconds and so on until he had completed a run of twelve consecutive observing periods. In one of many experiments he conducted thirty runs, one a week, on four infants starting when they were six weeks old.

Among other things, he found that the total smiling time per run, a measure of response strength, changes in a characteristic way. For example, one infant did not smile at all during the first three runs, smiled only a few seconds during the fourth run, and not at all again during the fifth run. Practically nothing happened between the ages of six and eleven weeks, a situation which contrasted with the infant's response to the face of its mother, to which it smiled increasingly over this period—because the sight of her face was usually accompanied by movement and by her voice, touch and warmth. So the first part of the experiment showed that during the early weeks the image of a face alone, without movement or other accompanying sensations, produced hardly any response.

Then a striking change appeared in the record. The infant rapidly became more and more responsive until at the age of fourteen weeks it was smiling more than 40 per cent of the observing time, about two and a half out of six minutes, indicating that it had learned to react with feelings of pleasure to the image of a face by itself, isolated from voice and touch and other sensations. At this stage the infant was responding to a general, broad-gauge symbol rather than to a particular human being. Any appropriate image would have produced a smile, a properly designed mask as well as its mother or Ambrose.

The next change came even more rapidly one week later, a sharp decline of smiling. The infant smiled only fleetingly at the British psychologist, and for no more than twenty seconds in all. The rest of the time it stared without expression, turned away, sucked its thumb, or whimpered. But during that same week its smiles had become even more frequent and brighter for its mother. The infant had passed a peak, the peak of indiscriminate and impersonal responding. Mother had suddenly become a unique individual. The image of her face had "filled out" in sufficient detail so that it could be compared with and distinguished from other faces. Later the infant's response to Ambrose reached a second peak which was considerably lower than the first peak and represented a level of habitual smiling reserved for all people not members of the family.

This is a representative record. Other infants differed widely as far as the timing and intensity of their changes were concerned, but they showed the same general changes in the same order. The sequence of little or no response, sharp increase in smiling, sudden decline, and so on turns out to be a basic pattern which involves not only certain built-in biases but also a bias to learn in a certain way.

A fuller understanding of human development can help in the task of reconstructing prehistory. The stages of growth unfold at their own pace according to genetically determined schedules, when the time and the individual are ripe and not until then. Changes come throughout the course of life. But the swiftest and most spectacular changes, like the smile, come during infancy, nature having arranged things so that we do most of our growing up when we are most helpless. As a matter of fact, certain major changes take place so rapidly during infancy that they are extremely difficult to observe and analyze.

The human condition contrasts sharply with that of other animals. In general, the lower a species ranks in the hierarchy of

Smile of human infant: straight face, low, medium, and high intensity

evolution, the more likely its young are to be born "ready-made" and prepared to participate in life with a minimum of learning. The leopard frog, for example, comes fully equipped for keeping itself alive. Its brain and sense organs are built to perceive only those elements in the environment strictly necessary for survival, and to exclude everything else. It sees only what it is designed to see. Its world is a mere fragment of the real world.

Experiments conducted by Jerome Lettvin and his associates at the Massachusetts Institute of Technology show that a frog is blind to stationary insects. It actually sees nothing in its field of vision until they move and move in a certain way, namely, toward it. Insects moving away are invisible, and do not exist in the frog's world. Furthermore, the things it sees are not insects as we know them, creatures with six legs and wings and iridescent colors. As far as the frog is concerned, all that information is utterly useless. It sees abstracted insects stripped of everything but a few essential details, standardized symbols like the black dots used on maps to represent cities, small objects with curved front edges.

The frog operates largely as an automaton, and automata are notoriously vulnerable to experimental tricks. If a frog is put in a cage with freshly killed flies, it will starve to death unless it is rescued and provided with a supply of live flies. It cannot see motionless food. But in the context of evolution and adaptation, such behavior is a strength rather than a weakness. Frogs are admirably designed for a real-life world where small objects that have curved leading edges and move are almost always insects. The probability of being confined in a place where the only insects are dead insects is exceedingly low, so low that the frog has endured for some 200 million years.

Whether or not man manages to survive that long, and there are powerful arguments on both sides, he is committed to survival by different means. Man's forte is flexibility of behavior, which depends as heavily on inheritance as rigid behavior does. In fact, his behavior is being studied with the aid of techniques developed by Tinbergen and other investigators during research on less flexible species, techniques being applied increasingly to human as well as to nonhuman primates (see Chapter XII). This is the field known as "ethology," roughly speaking, the biology of behavior.

The marks of the past are deeply embedded in us. The past has given us a selective advantage that enables us to survive and multiply. Although the range of observed human patterns is vast, it is still only a fraction of the even vaster range of possible patterns. We do not move along narrow and strictly determined paths like robots on monorails, but we are not completely at liberty either. Like all species, we represent a compromise between freedom and constraint.

The infant is born with enormous potentialities. Its brain will develop a system for storing and rapidly retrieving a vast number of memory traces, enough information, according to a recent estimate, to fill a thousand twenty-four-volume sets of the *Encyclopaedia Britannica*. There are nerve centers where the traces can be put together into new combinations representing possible actions, and a kind of switching circuitry which permits choices among many alternatives.

The special structures develop automatically. They take shape according to the same genetic schedules which shape the rest of the body. They dictate the human way of life. In the last analysis man has no choice but to be true to his genes. It is as impossible for man to stand pat as a species, to resist the forces for change embodied in his brain, as it is for animals of lower species like the frog to unlearn their built-in habits. Man is born free in comparison with other animals. His world is wider and richer in events because of inherited behavior patterns, products of an evolutionary process involving prehistoric man and pre-man in a hominid line that goes back some 15 million years.

Some of the patterns that appear earliest in life seem to have no use although, as indicated in Chapter XVI, other patterns may be more important in a hunter-gatherer than in an urban context. Infants have an amazingly tenacious grip as early as the first or second week after birth, in some cases hanging from a stick and supporting their weight up to fifteen seconds or so, an ability that might have saved lives when our ancestors lived in trees. A more complex pattern which also involves grasping and has been called the "embrace" reflex may be a vestige of the infant monkey's efforts to obtain a firmer hold on the belly hair of its mother as she rises to walk. These reflexes disappear within a few months.

Other early patterns come to stay. The baby enters the world with a bias to explore actively and almost immediately. In fact it starts exploring not long after it leaves the womb, just about as soon as there is anything worth exploring. It proceeds promptly to divide the world into parts, to make out the differences and boundaries that distinguish objects from one another. Experiments show that on the very day of their birth some infants "track" triangles displayed in their field of vision, following the outlines with their eyes. Also, when a newborn baby is confronted with a plain black background, it keeps looking away, looking from side to side and up and down as if in search of something more interesting.

In other words, the human infant is designed to seek out features, edges and discontinuities and shiny objects including those which turn out to be its mother's eyes. Such tendencies are innate in the same sense as the frog's tendency to go after small moving objects with curved leading edges. We enter the world with a whole battery of built-in biases, and a number of them involve getting along with people. In a study of 25 mother-infant pairs Mary Ainsworth of Johns Hopkins University has observed a definite "disposition to obey," which she suggests may have evolved in prehistoric hunter-gatherer times when obeying was a matter of life and death.

There also seems to be a general tendency toward rather than away from people, at least in the beginning. The baby loses no time in learning to communicate with the world. All newcomers face the need to establish relationships with others; of all human undertakings there is none more important than the infant's first efforts to find its place in society. The infant starts out as well equipped for entering into and maintaining relationships as it is for breaking them off if they turn out to be irritating or damaging. Whatever happens later on, it has a tendency to reach out and approach and bring things closer, as in the use of the smile. Varieties of avoidance and withdrawal come afterward.

Ambrose has used his observations and the observations of others to develop a theory of the origin of smiling. As a matter of fact, his theory goes further than that and, in effect, includes a partial analysis of the evolution of facial expression in primates and elaborates on some of Michael Fox's ideas presented in Chapter XIV.

The process started more than 65 million years ago among practically dead-pan prosimians or premonkeys, the first primates to take up life in the trees. The most primitive surviving prosimians, such as the lemurs of Madagascar, simply do not have the proper equipment for a fine play of emotions. Their facial muscles consist mainly of broad bands of fibers which tend to contract all together and produce gross movements. It happens that lemurs are capable of only a single clear-cut facial gesture, the original primate expression. It consists of a drawing back of the lips to bare the teeth for biting, a sign of fear or anger.

Refinements of this fighting "posture" came with the reshaping of the face. The earliest prosimians had long terrier-like snouts, and lived mainly by the sense of smell as their ground-dwelling ancestors had lived. But chases and escapes and games played high in the trees favored the rapid development of vision at the expense of the sense of smell. The snout retreated, the face shortened and flattened somewhat, and the eyes shifted from the sides of the head to an up-front position. Evolution in effect created a kind of natural "screen" or surface for visual displays.

The muscles of the face became more specialized among higher primates and primates living in more complex social groups, forming small bundles of fibers which branched off from the broad bands like secondary roads and side lanes from superhighways. A particularly elaborate system of muscles developed around the eyes and lips, and nerves running to and from the brain permitted finer control and greater variety of expression. For example, laughter seems to have emerged in apes as a composite form of behavior. When a chimpanzee laughs it draws back its lips and bares its teeth as if confronted with a dangerous situation, but at the same time its muscles are relaxed and its eyes brighten as if it is playing.

These and other mechanical characteristics of laughter may be regarded as signs of an ancient emotional conflict between two opposing tendencies. The dominant tendency was enjoyment and an attraction toward the object or situation being enjoyed; the subordinate tendency was fear or anger, and running away. This interpretation fits in with what we know about the arousal of human laughter, which generally occurs in response to a surprise of some sort, sudden or startling stimulation such as takes place in tickling or in mock attacks and chases during games. Of course, a delicate balance is involved. The lightness and good humor can vanish swiftly as a result of overstimulation, too much tickling or play-fighting that becomes too rough.

Ambrose believes that smiling evolved from laughter, and that the social smile, which is unique to man, evolved as a special adaptation designed to strengthen bonds among people. The first such bond is with the mother. In prehistoric times, however, there were forces tending to weaken that bond. Imagine that you are observing a troop of hominids on an African savanna perhaps 15 million years ago, not long after the start of the hominid line.

A troop of small slender near-apes or pre-men, the earliest representatives of the family of man, is taking its midday rest; at its center is a cluster of mothers with offspring and young females and dominant males.

The cluster exists as an island of stability and safety in the wilderness. The main social task of every adult member is to look after and protect the infants. One mother sits near a tree and is being groomed by another female, while its infant, which is only a week old, clings to her hair as it will continue to cling for another three or four months. Another mother moves off to a spot where fruits are growing and ignores her infant, which is old enough to follow her. When the entire troop moves, it moves as a single unit. No one stays behind. There is a certain amount of evidence to support this picture. It is based to a large extent on observations of wild baboons which have been living reasonably well-adjusted savanna lives for more than 25 million years. Their early prehuman ancestors probably lived according to the same fundamental patterns.

This situation began changing in *Australopithecus* times. The earliest human infants had to contend with conditions different from those confronting the earliest hominid infants. Their parents were practicing a new kind of division of labor, with hunting and gathering chiefly performed by men and women, respectively. As a result, in one sense at least the human band was, and is, less of an organic unit than the prehuman troop. Its members no longer went everywhere together. There was a home base where the women and the young and the old remained and waited while most of the men went away to hunt, often staying away for long periods.

The infant was still a major center of attraction. It was still carried practically 100 per cent of the time during the first year of life, or somehow in contact with its mother, judging by Draper's observations of the Kalahari Bushmen. But it no longer enjoyed quite as much undivided attention as infants had enjoyed in earlier times. Society had become a great deal more complicated and its parents had more things to do, making tools and preparing meals and talking as well as collecting wood and plant foods and taking care of fires. Furthermore, it found itself in a frustrating position largely because of the rise of hunting, which favored an increased learning ability, larger brains, and a longer period of development and dependency after birth.

The infant was not only born helpless and remained helpless longer than the offspring of monkeys and apes, but it was physically ill-equipped to do anything about it. Presumably upon occasion its mother had to put it down and walk off to perform a chore if only for a few minutes. When that happened, it could neither cling to her nor follow effectively. It could only watch as she moved out of sight, a predicament guaranteed to produce emotional disturbances in the young of any primate. At least as frustrating was the effect on the tendency to explore. The prehistoric infant depended completely on its mother for transport. Unless she carried it, it could not go where it wanted to go and establish contacts with new people and new objects.

The smile may have evolved as a signal or communication specifically to help make up for the handicap of infant immobility. Of course, crying could always be used to bring the mother to the spot. But crying alone was not enough. The infants of other primate species have vocal signals of some sort which indicate at a distance the nature and intensity of their distress, and something extra was called for to deal with the human predicament, something to hold the mother's attention longer and after the nursing and the burping were done. The infant represented only one of several alternative social contacts available to her. It had a high priority, to be sure. But it still had to compete for her time against other individuals and groups of individuals with demands of their own. Smiling became an essential way of meeting this competition.

The forces of natural selection come into play under such circumstances. Ambrose's research indicates that the smile is simply mild or low-intensity laughter minus chuckling and other sounds, and more relaxed. When it first appeared after nursing, mothers no doubt responded with cooing sounds or the prehistoric equivalent thereof, and other forms of affection. Infants capable of making a ready connection between such pleasant responses and their mothers, at this stage seen merely as pairs of shining dots, learned to smile more and more and received more care and attention than other infants and prospered accordingly.

In other words, it was extremely important for the infant to form a deep attachment to its mother and to form it swiftly. Conditions existing in prehistoric times favored rapid learning at an early age. Judging by the records of contemporary infants, the process may have started during the third month of life with a sudden decrease in smiling at any human face and an increase in smiling at the mother's face. The odds are that if an infant had not formed a firm attachment by the age of six or seven months, it never would. So the evidence suggests the evolution of a sensitive or critical period, when the infant is particularly ripe for learning the smiling response and associated behavior.

Certainly critical periods exist in other species, notably birds. For example, a newly hatched gosling separated from its mother and all other adult geese will accept a substitute mother. It will attach itself to any one of a wide variety of moving objects, a blue balloon or a cardboard box or an investigator interested in mother-infant bonds. The gosling responds to the object as to a real mother, follows it closely, and cries when it disappears. Studies indicate that in many cases this phenomenon, known as "imprinting," must take place within twenty-four hours of hatching or else it may not take place at all.

For obvious reasons no comparable research has been conducted on human infants, and if it were, the situation would certainly turn out to be far more complicated. But evidence exists for a critical period in monkeys, and many aspects of the behavior of the human infant indicate that similar reactions are involved. For example, consider one of the ways a four-month-old baby may behave when its mother comes into the room. It has just learned to distinguish her face from other faces, and as soon as she enters it turns its eyes on her and smiles and tracks her while she moves about, looking and smiling intently all the time.

This is an impressively powerful response, a silent response. The infant seems to be compensating with all its might for its immobility. It is doing with its eyes and its smile what other primates can do more directly by clinging or following, keeping in close touch with its mother. The tracking could hardly be more efficient if its eyes were actually connected with the target. Such observations indicate strongly that tracking can be regarded as a substitute for following; that imprinting or something like it played a major part in the evolution of the human smile and continues to play a major part in the development of the smile during infancy.

The infant had much to gain by its positive reactions. The longer its mother remained close, the greater the chances that its immediate physical and emotional needs would be satisfied. So it would presumably be healthier, and even a small raising of the odds in that direction could have had an appreciable selective impact among populations in which more than half of all infants died before they were twelve months old. But helping to meet the demands of the moment was probably not the only, or even the most important, function of the smile.

Everything points toward its predominant role in a long-range social context, in promoting the capacity to get along with other individuals. The increase in complexity of social systems during hominid evolution, everything from toolmaking and meat eating to the shift from small-game to big-game hunting, put increasing pressure on the infant. Indeed, evolution seemed to be painting itself into a corner. It was shaping an infant which had to learn more sooner, and which at the same time remained helpless longer. In such circumstances its first close associations with an adult inevitably assumed an overriding importance.

Judging by activities in primate societies simpler than ours, the trend seems to have begun much earlier. For example, in troops of macaque monkeys the infant may obtain many things from its mother over and above the satisfaction of immediate needs. Perhaps the most telling point in this connection is the finding, originally reported by Japanese investigators (see Chapter XIII), that the offspring of dominant mothers tend to grow into dominant adults, another indication of the fact that it pays to start at the top. In general the infant's relationship with its mother also serves as a model for future relationships in gorilla and chimpanzee troops.

The uses of the smile reveal a great deal about the position of the mother in human societies and her special meaning to the infant. One interesting response may occur after it tracks her movements around a room. Notice that such behavior implies that it is not hungry or cold or uncomfortable in any way. For such things crying serves and has long served as a highly effective protest and summons. In this case the infant wants something else, and what it wants is indicated the instant its mother comes over and picks it up and holds it in her arms.

At that point smiling usually ceases abruptly, almost as if shut off by a switch, in a gesture that says, more plainly than words, "mission accomplished." Then, secure in physical contact with its mother, it proceeds to look around the room. This is the exploring tendency in action. It is the beginning of an adventure, a brief adventure to be sure, but a prototype for all subsequent adventures. Later, when the infant crawls, it continues to use its mother as a base of operations from which to explore the mysterious world. It leaves her to play with things it cannot touch by reaching, and then comes back to her and leaves again. Still later there will be other departures and returnings.

The mother also has problems, although they are more complicated and more difficult to investigate than the infant's. Evolution has confronted her with dilemmas and conflicts. The same forces that increased the dependency of the infant increased her dependency as well. The longer it remained helpless, the longer she had to stay nearby and be ready to come at its call. At the same time, her own security was threatened by the departures of hunters. She often had to watch people whom she needed passing out of sight, and often felt a fear of being abandoned analogous to that experienced by her infant when she left it to carry out other duties.

Mother love, like infant love, had to be learned and learned quickly. The mother's natural bias, like the infant's, was toward the positive, toward all the feelings and actions that would foster a close and deep coming together. Her smiling and associated behavior became part of a self-enhancing communication that worked both ways. But there were negative as well as positive aspects of infant care. Upon occasion, especially after prolonged crying, the mother came to her infant with resentment and anger, and one of the main functions of its smile was probably to help soften her feelings.

Incidentally, a related function can be traced back long before the coming of man. Some time quite early in primate evolution a modified form of the baring of the teeth developed as a sign of submission displayed by a low-ranking member of the hierarchy to a dominant member, a so-called appeasement grin, and the

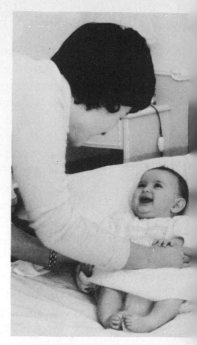

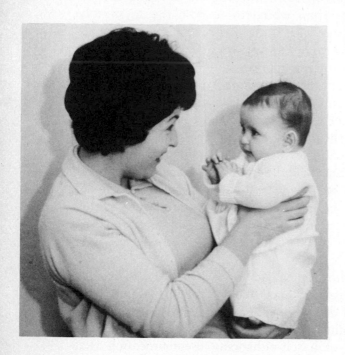

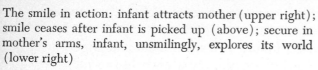

The smile in action: infant attracts mother (upper right); smile ceases after infant is picked up (above); secure in mother's arms, infant, unsmilingly, explores its world (lower right)

human smile may serve a similar purpose in adult life as well as in infancy. Under such conditions smiling loses its warmth, and it and the gesture that evokes it may be an extremely ugly thing.

I remember how one man responded to a hard look from his superior. It was toward the end of a conference in the vice-president's office of a large corporation, and he flushed and his smile was a cringing and a humiliation. All of us in the room, all human relations, seemed to shrink as he turned and left the room. It was a perversion of the smile, and we were all back in earlier times, behaving like members of a troop of prehuman primates.

The smile is only one aspect of infant behavior which has been studied for what it may suggest about possible courses of early social change. Crying also has evolutionary implications, although it seems to be more complicated than smiling, at least during infancy. For one thing, it is more difficult to classify. There are degrees of intensity and tone which make all the difference between hunger cries, pain cries and so on. Also crying may come in regularly or irregularly spaced bouts, and distinctive patterns may exist within individual bouts. Preliminary studies suggest that it may be necessary to consider eight or more types of infant crying.

In most cases, however, the general message is clear and basic. Crying is designed to elicit a fast maternal reaction, and the faster the better. But the infant requires time to learn how effective its crying is, and to adjust its behavior accordingly. Ainsworth and her associate Silvia Bell report that although the amount of crying varies widely during the first three months of life, from more than twenty minutes per hour to practically no crying at all, it has little to do with maternal responsiveness. At this stage babies tend to cry at their own individual levels no matter what their mothers do.

Differences begin showing up during succeeding months. By the end of the first year there is appreciably less crying among babies whose mothers are quick to respond than among babies whose mothers delay responding or do not respond at all. If myths were not so enduring, such findings would be enough to discredit once and for all the notion that a crying infant is trying to get away with something and, for the good of its character, must not be spoiled by paying too much attention.

The primal urgency of most crying, its deep-rooted nature, is revealed by the observation that what counts most is the promptness of the response. Some mothers know better than others why their babies cry and precisely what to do—whether to feed the baby, change its diapers, pick it up, or simply to utter soothing words. But as long as she appears promptly, its crying will tend to decrease.

The real point of appearing promptly is what it does for the baby's expanding world view. Equipped with its appetites and desires and biases, it must identify objects and events, learn their regularities, and to some extent control their movements. When crying brings a dependable response, its world makes that much more sense—and making sense of things can be extremely difficult, perhaps even more difficult during infancy than later on. What happens outside and around the infant must often seem erratic and unpredictable.

The work of Ainsworth and other investigators indicates that a rather high proportion of mothers, perhaps one out of every three, frequently misinterpret infant signals or even overlook the signals entirely. Part of the problem is a tendency to underrate infants, to treat them as if they were too small and too undeveloped to have anything to communicate. A baby may feel hungry and cry, but its mother, who may or may not be going by some sort of schedule, figures that the last feeding was too recent for another one just now. So she comes over with a toy. A while later the baby, having been distracted for a while, is busy playing with the toy and suddenly finds it must stop, its mother having decided that the time has come for a feeding.

It is on the basis of many many such strange incidents that the infant must learn to modify its wants in appropriate ways and build its model of reality. Feeding seems to be a perennial problem. The notion of a feeding-every-four-hours schedule, originally recommended without benefit of evidence by a discipline-minded German physician about a century ago, is no longer as popular as it once was. On the other hand, modern living conditions do not permit the baby to obey its natural inclinations.

Evidence relating to feeding during prehistoric times has recently been considered by Nicholas Blurton Jones of the Institute of Child Health in London, who, in addition to studying English

children, observed Kalahari children during a visit to the Kalahari. (As a matter of fact, he is the British stranger mentioned in
Chapter XVI, the sight of whom caused a Kalahari baby to
scream.) Comparative studies of a hundred mammal species
show that the chemical composition of mother's milk provides
clues to the frequency of infant feeding. Milk containing high
proportions of protein and a fat is characteristic of rabbit and tree-
shrew mothers, for example, which feed their offspring about
once every twenty-four and forty-eight hours respectively. At the
other extreme, among some rats, some marsupials and most
monkeys, the young are fed every half-hour or so, and the rat
mothers have low-protein, low-fat milk.

Human mothers, and chimpanzee and gorilla mothers, have
milk very low in these essential compounds, indicating that frequent, almost continuous feeding was the rule in the remote past.
The same conclusions follow from the observation that frequent
feeders tend to suck slowly, and human infants are very slow
suckers. Judging by Konner's estimate for the Kalahari Bushmen,
infants who are carried most of the time and have ready access to
the breast probably feed at least twice an hour, each time for
thirty seconds to ten minutes.

Such behavior represents the result of intensive selection, and
suggests some of the fundamental characteristics which man
shares with other mammals. It may serve the special purpose of
developing a close bond between mother and infant. Blurton
Jones asks the question: Why carry babies? His provisional answer, based on admittedly incomplete evidence: "The association
in the mammals between frequent feeding and a following or
carrying system of child care is not nutritionally necessary, but
rapid onset of hunger and satiation in the baby would be a simple
mechanism for ensuring that it stays with the mother."

The fact that the infant can adapt to a rich variety of feeding
practices and schedules, most of which are hardly geared to its
basic biases, is as significant an example of man's unique flexibility as the capacity for surviving and multiplying in widely different environments. Studies of smiling, crying and other forms of
infant behavior reinforce the notion of the infant as an active
participant in its own development. It is not waiting, unformed
and undirected, for us to make impressions upon it. It takes the

initiative in responding and approaching and establishing relationships, and makes up for its physical helplessness by a surprisingly advanced ability to communicate.

Ainsworth emphasizes an interesting point in this connection, namely that you can often tell a great deal about the quality of an infant's communications with its mother by watching its face. A highly mobile face, a face that shows a varied and vivid interplay of emotion, is usually a sign that the infant has established satisfactory and sensitive communications. On the other hand, less fortunate infants tend to be "pudding-faced," a bit on the deadpan side. It may be that a close evolutionary relationship exists between prolonged infant dependency and the importance of a close mother-infant bond, and the increasing capacity for facial expression.

Facial expression, and the expression of emotion, may also have a racial basis according to a report by Daniel Freedman and his Chinese wife Nina Chinn Freedman of the University of Chicago, who studied 24 Chinese-American and 24 European-American infants. The infants were only 7 to 75 hours old, yet even at that early age sharp differences in temperament occurred between the two groups. In one test a cloth was placed over a baby's face for a few seconds, a procedure which proved highly upsetting to most European-American newborns, who struggled to remove the cloth by trying to brush it off with their hands and turning their heads. Chinese-American babies did far less thrashing around, most of them simply lying still until the cloth was lifted off.

This test and several others yielded similar results. Chinese-American babies are not only born more imperturbable than their European-American counterparts, but they also tend to calm down sooner when they do become upset. Such findings raise many questions. If they are confirmed by other investigators, it should be possible to learn more about the origin of modern races during the past 10,000 to 30,000 years, and how long it takes to establish genetically based behavior changes in man. (A number of investigators believe that in some cases it may take less than 500 years.)

Research in living prehistory includes living infants and all representatives of *Homo sapiens,* not just members of the last remaining bands of aborigines in desert places. It was only a few hundred generations ago that we, the citizens of technologically advanced nations, were also hunter-gatherers, that all the people in the world were hunter-gatherers. Contemporary man is close enough to those days to behave "prehistorically" upon occasion. His behavior provides clues to the behavior of prehistoric people.

The differences between the most civilized and the least civilized among us are striking, but hardly basic. They are cultural differences chiefly, learned programs of behavior expressed and conveyed to us in traditional codes, and such programs are completely interchangeable. Any child from an American or Japanese family, for example, could be brought up to believe as firmly as the Australian aborigines in dreamtime beings and a world that can only change for the worse. What we want to understand better are things relatively independent of upbringing, the sort of biases all humans share, the built-in tendencies for all individuals to feel and think and react alike under comparable conditions.

The tendencies must first be identified and then accounted for in evolutionary terms. In the process of reconstructing the past through studies of contemporary behavior, we can also work things the other way around, using what we learn about prehistory to see ourselves more clearly here and now. It is a matter of obtaining new perspectives on life in our times. The present and the future are also part of human evolution, the part that must concern us most directly in times of accelerating transition. So it may help to turn in a serious and systematic manner to prehistory as part of our current efforts at self-understanding.

For example, evolutionary studies indicate that the mother-infant bond may not be as adaptive as it once was. In fact, any other conclusion would be amazing considering how much the world has changed. Society was much simpler in prehistoric times. There were fewer people and fewer kinds of people. Not only that, but customs and traditions endured to an extent that we can hardly conceive. Individuals lived their entire lives in societies that had not changed appreciably for thousands of years, and would not change for thousands of years to come. They faced exactly the same dangers that their ancestors had faced, chiefly swift and sudden attacks by predators.

Survival in this kind of world favored rapid learning and, even more to the point, once-and-for-all learning, the formation of relatively fixed actions and attitudes. It was a steady-state, predictable world, the sort we yearn for in our weaker and more nostalgic moments. Time and life had a monolithic quality. Expectations were high that everything would endure in its present form forever, that the future would continue to be very like the past. In other words, what the infant learned fast and early would in all probability serve it admirably for the rest of its life.

Ours is a different world, with the wilderness gone. Even danger is not what it used to be, and instead of predators we face diseases that tend to develop slowly and strike late in life, a kind of violence which is as uniquely human as mercy or tolerance, and the enduring insecurity of change itself. The emphasis must be increasingly on flexibility. The mark of the new evolution which sweeps us along is that unlearning and learning anew have already become as important to survival as learning used to be. What man knows is far less important than his capacity for modifying or discarding what he thinks he knows.

So self-examination includes a harder look at the mother-infant bond, and the speed and depth and intensity of early learning. Much of what the infant learns during its first years may block its ability to learn later in life and create rigidities, an outcome somewhat more appropriate for prehistoric than for modern societies. The question for the future is whether built-in flexibility, one of the most distinctive marks of being human, is great enough to permit the erasing if necessary of information learned early— whether in a sense we can be taught to forget as effectively as we remember.

■ The infant's discovery of language; his inherent sense of grammar; the nonverbal conversation of trained captive animals; tool using and children's play as steps toward prehistoric language, call systems and development of abstractions; invention of a "vocal" alphabet; the anatomy of learning

CHAPTER XIX

The Evolution of Language

■ More than half the people in the world can neither read nor write, but practically every individual everywhere speaks his native tongue. And, at the deepest levels, all languages are built according to the same fundamental blueprint. They all involve a very small number of basic voice or speech characteristics, about fifteen or so, ways of producing vowel and consonant sounds. These sounds are building blocks which in various combinations make up a very large number of words (several million words in the English language, which is increasing at an estimated rate of 200,000 to 300,000 words a year). The number of sentences, the hierarchies and patterns of words used, is infinite.

The origin of language is one of the great problems of science. To know how human speech emerged as something distinct from a system of calls—the assorted grunts, barks, screams and hoots typical of nonhuman primates—demands nothing less than a step-by-step reconstruction of the evolutionary process, and for that the evidence is still lacking. There are no fossil clues to the nature of man's earliest languages and no living representatives of possible in-between stages on the way to present-day languages.

A fuller understanding of the prehistory of language will depend on the observation and analysis of behavior, human behavior mainly but also that of other surviving primates. The trend is away from reliance on anecdotes and casual reports, and toward the far more difficult task of investigating what actually goes on in intensive detail and over long periods.

445

Of particular interest is what happens during infancy and early childhood, the only chance we have to see language taking shape. The development is part of a larger process. As a newcomer, a recent arrival from the womb, the infant faces a problem it will never solve completely. It is born into a turbulence of noises and odors, smooth places that suddenly become rough, cold places that suddenly become warm, lights and shadows that rise and fall and appear and disappear. Plunged into this commotion, the infant must start to find a way and a place for itself. Its job is to create out of all the random strangeness a system of familiar objects and landmarks, and rhythms and laws.

So the infant investigates because it must, because that is what it is designed to do. It seeks and sorts out the elements of its world, including the sounds. It distinguishes meaningful from meaningless sounds, which sounds to heed and which to ignore, and among the heeded sounds which have the precisely patterned qualities of words. And it eventually makes what is probably the greatest discovery it will ever make, a discovery which is no less great because it is made over and over again by every infant. It proceeds to discover language.

This is a true discovery in the sense that the child learns but is not taught. Most of us have little or no knowledge about the intricacies of syntax and semantics, and even if we did, we would not be able to impart such abstruse information to our offspring in the nursery. We play a vital but more passive role, supplying language to them as we supply food and shelter. We provide them with a flow of sounds, words and intonations which they may imitate, and that is the full extent of their imitating. Given this raw material, this sample of adult speech, they go to work and create language anew on their own.

In little more than two years the child progresses from baby talk to an excellent command of its native tongue. It begins forming simple sentences at about the age of eighteen months, six months or so after uttering its first words. By the age of three and a half to four it has a speaking vocabulary of up to 1,500 words and, since the ability to comprehend language outruns the ability to use it, probably understands another 3,000 to 4,500 words which do not appear in its sentences. This situation continues throughout life, and the reading vocabulary of the average adult may be some 100,000 words, or ten times larger than his speaking vocabulary.

By the time the child is four or five years old it has learned the great majority of more than a thousand basic rules of grammar. But many fine points remain to be mastered. For example, consider the difference between "John told Mary to go to Boston" and "John promised Mary to go to Boston." The first sentence obeys the rules, in that it is Mary who is to go to Boston. The agent, namely Mary, and the verb "to go" are next to one another, in accordance with the so-called minimum distance principle.

In the second sentence, however, the principle does not hold. "John" is the agent of the verb "to go," but the two words are not next to one another, and a child may be confused and unable to use the verb "promise" properly until it is nine or ten years old. Another difference which may confuse children even more is that between "Tell Mary what to put in the box" and "Ask Mary what to put in the box." There are several thousand more rules and exceptions to rules, most of which are learned unconsciously by the age of ten or so, although some people never learn some rules.

The full-scale investigation of language development among young human primates is a demanding task, which may be one reason that until recent times it has been generally avoided. Roger Brown and his associates at Harvard University have summarized their problems in tape-recording the utterances of children between the ages of two and three: "There were those who warned that the child would be shy and speechless in our presence; this was not the case. Mothers told their children that visitors were coming and, in general, we were eagerly welcomed, shown a parade of toys and games, and talked to rather steadily.

"It became clear that the child expected a guest to put in some time as a playmate, and so the recording was a two-man job with one of us taking data and the other prepared to play cowboy, horsie, coloring, trains, and the mule in 'kick the mule.' . . . We found that by about noon we needed a rest and so we went away for lunch, returning about two; the child took his nap in the interval."

The patience and endurance required to cope with such conditions have proved rewarding in a number of ways. For one thing, the evidence shows quite clearly that the child takes the initiative in learning language. Its first sentences, mostly strings of two or three words, are not formed at random. They indicate an inherent feeling for subject-predicate and verb-object relationships. Furthermore, they are often completely original. The child continues to surprise us with a rather high proportion of phrases like "that doed," "more up," "allgone shoe" and "hi, milk" which cannot be the result of any parroting process, since it does not hear any such remarks from its elders.

Other observations reinforce this point. David McNeill of the University of Michigan has analyzed thousands of sentences, in records he has obtained himself as well as in the records of Brown and other investigators (and in Russian and Japanese as well as English), and reports the existence of learning patterns that have all the marks of built-in biases. For example, by the age of two or so the child has already divided its speaking vocabulary into two broad classes. There is a small group of so-called pivot or heavy-duty words like "my" and "green" and "the" and "that" which are used repeatedly in combinations with all other words, the other words being lumped together to form the second large class.

The classifying process continues during the course of development. Within two or three months the child indicates by the way it uses words that it has learned some of the differences within the pivot-word class which starts as a mixture of several types of words. It forms three subclasses: the articles "the" and "a," the demonstative pronouns "this" and "that," and a miscellaneous subclass made up of all the other pivot words. In another two or three months the child's utterances indicate that it has divided the miscellaneous subclass still further into adjectives, possessive pronouns, and another "all others" group. So the original class has been broken down into a total of five subclasses, and more distinctions come later.

Details vary from child to child. Different individuals include different words and different types of words in their original pivot groups. But the main point of interest is the nature of the underlying phenomenon, and in all cases that happens to be the same, the formation of finer and finer distinctions for nouns and verbs and all other parts of speech. Learning language, like learning to pick up and manipulate objects and learning to walk, obeys its own laws and develops according to a definite timetable.

On the one hand, it develops almost no matter what anyone does about it. According to Charles Hockett of Cornell University, language acquisition "is practically impossible to prevent, save through environmental insults so drastic that the child has little chance to survive at all. . . . The earliest steps, moreover, are remarkably alike for children in all different speech communities, suggesting that all the languages of the world are, and for a long time have been, erected on a single groundplan." On the other hand, the coming of language cannot be rushed. Children make progress when they are ready to make progress, and not before.

For example, at about the age of three, when they are still learning the rules of negation, they tend to produce double negatives and, as the following exchange indicates, until they grow out of this stage nothing can be done about it:

> CHILD: Nobody don't like me.
> MOTHER: No, say "nobody likes me."
> CHILD: Nobody don't like me.

The mother put up a game but losing fight. After the above dialogue was repeated word for word eight times in a row, she tried one last time:

> MOTHER: No, now listen carefully; say "nobody likes me."
> CHILD: Oh! Nobody don't likes me.

The double negative was ingrained in the child's mind. It could not change, because no matter how often its mother repeated the correct sentence starting with "nobody," it heard something else. It listened with its inner ear and heard not one but two words, "nobody don't." Of course, within a month or two it had learned to hear differently and was producing perfect negatives. So let the teacher, parent or otherwise, beware. Individuals younger than we are may not always be ready to profit by our greater experience and wisdom.

Language develops with the pace, the sweep, of a biological force. When it comes to the crucial matter of origins, we can no longer beg the question and assume with the theologians of three or four hundred years ago that man was created fully articulate, that Adam and Eve spoke Hebrew in the Garden of Eden. Incidentally, one Scandinavian authority dissented from prevailing opinions and suggested that God addressed Adam in Swedish, Adam answered in Danish, and the snake tempted Eve in French.

These are some of the less plausible theories about the origin of language. A complete listing of all theories and variations of individual theories and related studies has yet to be made, although Gordon Hewes of the University of Colorado has taken on the formidable task. His published bibliography contains about 2,600 references, and a more inclusive and more up-to-date version has nearly 4,000 additional titles.

All investigators agree that producing a solid theory is still a job for the future. The problem is to devise some sort of evolutionary scheme, a sequence of step-by-step developments—and, among other things, that means further research on communication in societies of lower primates. Everything we know would lead us to expect something special from chimpanzees as the most human of nonhuman primates, something as impressive as their use of tools, for example, the use of combinations of calls to form crude sentences. But for all their intelligence, and their intelligence is considerable, observations have been disappointing, at least in studies conducted in the wild. Although further observations may reveal subtleties that have eluded us to date, the record has not yet yielded clues to the origin of language. According to van Lawick-Goodall, chimpanzees have about two dozen calls which, like the calls of many other primates, express such things as threats and rage and greetings and satisfaction, but exhibit no "prelanguage" features.

On the other hand, interesting and surprising results are coming from studies of captive animals. As far as linguistic accomplishments are concerned, one of the world's most advanced nonhuman primates is an African-born female chimpanzee named Washoe after Washoe County, Nevada, the site of Reno and her home until recently. For five years, starting in June, 1966, when she was one year old, she has lived in a trailer with free access to a yard containing trees and a jungle gym. All her waking hours were spent in the company of one or more human beings, usually psychologists Allen and Beatrice Gardner, a husband-wife team at the University of Nevada. Washoe never heard human speech. Observers never uttered words in her presence, only hoots and other chimpanzee calls, and gestures based on those of the standard American sign language for the deaf.

There is a logic behind this unusual experimental arrangement. Chimpanzees cannot learn to talk, a point proved once and for all nearly twenty years ago when another husband-wife team brought up another female chimpanzee named Viki. Viki learned to brush her teeth, dust furniture, open cans and bottles, and eat at the table with manners at least as respectable as those of the human children who were her only playmates. But she could utter only three words, "mama" and "papa" and "cup," and only with extreme difficulty. In fact, she often rocked back and forth and exhibited other symptoms of severe emotional distress when called on to say her words.

The Gardners designed their experiment partly as a consequence of seeing motion pictures of Viki's behavior. They did not conclude that the chimpanzee is inherently incapable of language, but simply that it is incapable of imitating human speech sounds and acquiring spoken language. On the other hand, gestures come quite readily to it, and it often imitates human gestures when playing. So it seemed reasonable to take advantage of this natural ability and explore the chimpanzee's linguistic potentialities by using sign language.

Washoe responded enthusiastically. She learned her first word at about the age of fifteen months, an insistent "come-gimme" represented by a beckoning gesture with fingers or wrist. Her second word, "more," which involves bringing the fingertips of both hands together, came within another week or two—and by the time she was about three and a half to four years old she used more than fifty signs, including those representing "hear-listen" (index finger touches ear), "toothbrush" (index finger rubs front teeth), "flower" (index finger touches one or both nostrils), "dog" (slap thigh), "cover-blanket" (one hand moved over the back of the other and toward the signaler's body), and "please" (draw open hand across chest).

When Washoe was about two she spontaneously made the "come-gimme" sign and then wagged her tongue and touched it with her index finger, the sign for "sweet." It was her first sentence. But even more significant, it was a creative sentence. Although she had learned the individual signs by imitating, the combination was not imitated and could not have been because Washoe had never seen that particular combination of gestures. The Gardners had never used sign language to ask her or one another for candy. Many of her subsequent sentences were also original combinations like "come-gimme tickle" or "please up" or "hurry open." She has used five gestures in a single sentence ("more more more sweet drink") and as many as four different gestures ("drink sweet please hurry" and "out open please hurry").

Washoe recognizes herself in the mirror, an ability she shares with other chimpanzees such as those studied at Tulane University and discussed in Chapter XIV. The big difference is that in their case the ability had to be inferred indirectly, because they did not know how to communicate with people. In Washoe's case the evidence is direct. While looking into a mirror one day, she was asked, "Who is that?"—and promptly responded: "Me, Washoe."

Like human children at a comparable age, Washoe at about the age of four had a number of pivot words or, rather, pivot gestures which she used in more than 80 per cent of all her combinations of signs. They were mainly demand gestures such as "please," "come-gimme," "hurry," and "more." Her understanding of gesture words can be very human on occasion. When she went riding in a car with the Gardners and they used the sign for "dog" in communicating with one another, she "overheard" and looked out the window in search of a dog, indicating that she had acquired a kind of built-in cerebral dictionary which matches gestures and images.

The Gardners are engaged in a continuing analysis of Washoe's "utterances." Often sign-order seems to be unimportant to her, and "please hurry sweet drink" could probably just as well have been "hurry sweet drink please." But in many cases she shows a sense of sign-order. For example, the odds are better than ten to one that she will signal "you me go" rather than "me you go."

Washoe's accomplishments have attracted widespread interest, and many other investigators are speculating about her ways of putting sentences together, and how her rules of grammar compare with human rules. McNeill notes that her earliest signs were predominantly action signs, verbs or prepositions used as verbs, and included only a few nouns, just the opposite of what happens among normal human children. They tend to utter nouns first, the names of things, and use verbs very rarely in the beginning. But deaf children are more chimpanzee-like; they include more verbs in their early vocabularies, perhaps because they depend on the sense of sight, on seeing activities around them.

Other things seem to be more important to Washoe, as McNeill has pointed out: "This may be an example, the first example ever encountered, of a language just beginning to evolve in another species, an alien language based on principles quite different from our own." Human language evolved to express propositions, statements that can be either true or false, and demands a sort of precision which may not come naturally to chimpanzees. Emphasis and intensity may be the principles that guide their language. Washoe seems to think mainly in terms of degrees of urgency, stressing repetitions of words like "hurry," "more," "please" and so on.

But chimpanzees are quite capable of learning many of the rules of our language. Also assured of a prominent place in the annals of man-animal communication is another African-born female chimpanzee, named Sarah and ten years old and retired because of "orneriness." She is the protégé of David Premack at the University of California in Santa Barbara, who started her off with a simple procedure some four years ago. In the first step, designed mainly to achieve a good working relationship between ape and teacher, he put a ripe banana on a table and watched benevolently as she ate it.

Having established that routine, he put a banana just out of her reach and, within reach, a small pink plastic square with a steel backing. Sarah quickly learned that to get the banana she had to pick up the piece and place it on a magnetic language board. In similar fashion she learned that a purple triangle meant "apple" and so on for a total of half a dozen different fruits and their corresponding plastic pieces. Confronted with two pieces and one fruit, two fruits and one piece, and various combinations, she showed that she knew which pieces and fruits went together, and had chances upon occasion to indicate her preferences.

The next stage was teaching Sarah a new class of words, the names of her different teachers. She found that to get a banana from Mary Morgan, a research assistant working with Premack, she had to place a plastic M on the language board and under it, since Sarah writes vertically Chinese style, the square banana symbol. After learning the names of several teachers, she learned that fruit would not be forthcoming unless she constructed a three-word sentence—for example, M for Mary, the purple triangle for apple and, between the two, a third piece shaped something like a vertical bow tie and representing "give."

Give

Chocolate

Sarah

Sarah and trainer: learning to "talk"

So, slowly and step by step, Premack built up Sarah's linguistic skills. By the time of her retirement about a year ago, she knew some 125 words, 125 plastic shapes which she could manipulate to produce sentences on the language board. She had learned to use proper word order—for example, that "Mary give apple" works, while "apple give Mary" brings no results—indicate whether two objects are the same or different, and answer yes-no questions.

Premack feels that up to this point Sarah was actually learning very little which was new to her: "Mostly our procedure had been merely teaching her the names for concepts she already knew." Subsequent training sessions showed definitely that she could advance to new and more sophisticated concepts. She dealt with the equivalent of the question "What is the relationship between an apple and the plastic triangle word for apple?" by indicating that the triangle was the name of the fruit. She also learned to answer questions involving abstract ideas of color, shape and size.

The problem currently is how far we can go linguistically with chimpanzees or, for that matter, with other species, nonprimates as well as primates. Recent research demonstrates quite clearly that in the past the limitations were not primarily on the side of the apes, but rather on the side of human investigators who failed to create experimental conditions that would bring out the talents of their animal subjects. Now that the possibilities are evident, a number of more elaborate studies are planned or already under way.

The University of Oklahoma has a chimpanzee colony consisting of about half a dozen members. The oldest and most learned member of the colony is Washoe, who at the age of seven and with a vocabulary of about 175 words has been moved from her former home base in Nevada. Her colony mates are being trained to communicate with their teachers using sign language, and it is hoped that they will eventually begin communicating regularly with one another. If that happens, the result might be direct and new insights into the structure of chimpanzee society.

Premack's plans include a shift from pieces of plastic to television displays. Instead of learning and manipulating the tokens, his current chimpanzee trainees are sitting at electric typewriters with about a hundred keys, each of which has a small image of a word symbol. By pressing the appropriate keys in the appropriate order they can produce sentences of up to eight or nine words which appear on a color television screen. The Santa Barbara psychologist also intends to find out whether, by creating suitable environments, he can convert a troop of chimpanzees into hunter-gatherers with a developing language of their own.

Another proposed project involves the Yerkes Regional Primate Research Center in Atlanta, one or two chimpanzees or orangutans, and a computer-controlled teaching machine. The apes will learn to operate a special typewriter keyboard which, as in the Premack experiment, flashes word symbols on a television-type screen. Their training will consist of a series of automatically programmed tests designed to simulate basic steps in the growing up of a child, and they will be able to communicate their needs and desires 24 hours a day. According to the investigator who conceived the project, Duane Rumbaugh of Georgia State University, this study should yield a better idea of the linguistic limitations of nonhuman primates, provide new information about how children learn to talk—and "perhaps even lead to training devices that will facilitate language formation in the young and mentally retarded."

The gap between human and nonhuman is still enormous as far as language is concerned, and the odds are that no ape will ever learn more than a fraction of what the average two-year-old learns automatically. Nevertheless, the gap is not quite as large as once thought. Laboratory investigations may be expected to lead to new studies of wild primates, and to a new appreciation of their powers and limitations. Perhaps the main point is that chimpanzees may be capable of far more sophisticated communicating than they are actually called on to demonstrate in their native forests. They certainly seem to outdo themselves linguistically under the pressure of associating with psychologists.

The great evolutionary question is what pressures were at work on man's remote ancestors, and part of the answer seems to be the steady increase in the complexity of things. Even before the appearance of hominids, the world was richer and more diverse for primates than for most other species. Equipped with an outstanding visual apparatus, they saw more objects more vividly and in finer detail. Items viewed in three dimensions and in color stood out with a new prominence and demanded a new degree of attention. As a matter of fact, from one standpoint objects did not exist in the fullest sense of the word before the coming of advanced stereoscopic color vision.

The quality of objects was further enriched by the evolution of hands with mobile fingers. In contrast to most of the earliest prosimians, monkeys and apes could reach out and pick up things for inspection, for feeling and sniffing and mouthing. Things were moved more readily from their "natural" positions, and regarded more closely and from more angles. The brain, particularly the most recently evolved cortex or outer bark, took over the task of synthesizing new information from a number of

Nonhuman primate learns to "talk": Washoe says "drink" to Beatrice Gardner

Signs That Washoe Uses

(Listed in approximate order of appearance from June, 1966, to December, 1967)

Sign	Description	Context
Come-gimme	Beckoning, with wrist or knuckles as pivot.	To persons, dogs, etc., also for objects out of reach such as food or toys. Often combined: "Come tickle," "Gimme-sweet," etc.
More	The fingertips are brought together, usually overhead. (Correct American Sign Language [ASL] form: the tips of the tapered hand touch repeatedly.)	Asking for continuation or repetition of some activity such as spinning, tickling, second helpings of food, etc. Also used to ask for second demonstration of some performance such as a somersault.
Up	Point up with index finger or thumb.	Wants a lift to reach object such as grapes on vine, leaves, etc.; or wants to be placed on someone's shoulders.
Sweet	Index or index and second fingers touch tip of wagging tongue. (Correct ASL form: use index and second fingers extended side by side.)	For dessert; occurs spontaneously at end of meal. Also, when sweets are offered. (A common interchange: —*W:* "Gimme, gimme." P: "What do you want?" *W:* "Sweet.")

Sign	Description	Context
Go	Opposite of "Come-gimme."	While walking hand-in-hand or riding on shoulders of companion. Usually indicates direction desired.
Hear-listen	Index finger touches ear.	For loud or strange sounds: bells, car horns, sonic booms, footsteps, etc. Also, solicits someone to hold a watch to her ear.
Tickle	Draw the index finger of one hand across the back of the other hand. (Related to ASL "touch.")	For tickling or for chasing games.
Open	Place the flat hands side by side, palms down. Draw them apart while rotating to palms up.	At house, room, car doors. Also, refrigerator, cupboards, and containers such as jars.
Toothbrush	Using index finger as brush, rub front teeth.	At end of meals. Once when W noticed toothbrush in strange bathroom.
Hurry	Shaking the open hand at the wrist. (Correct ASL form: use index and second fingers extended side by side.)	Frequently follows signs such as "Come-gimme," "Out," "Open," "Go," particularly when there is a delay before she is obeyed. Also, when watching her meal being prepared.
Funny	Tip of index finger presses nose, and W snorts. (Correct ASL form: use index and second fingers, no snort.)	Soliciting interaction play, and during games. Occasionally, when being pursued.
Hurt	The extended index fingers are jabbed toward each other. Can be used to indicate location of pain.	To indicate cuts and bruises on herself or on others. Can be elicited by red stains on a person.
Drink	Fist with thumb extended, thumb placed in mouth.	For water, formula, soda pop, etc.
Sorry	Rub bent hand on chest. (Correct ASL form: rub fisted hand, circular motion.)	After biting someone, or when someone has been hurt in some other way (not necessarily by W). When told to apologize for mischief.
Please	Draw open hand across chest. (Correct ASL form: use fingertips and circular motion.)	Asking for objects and activities. Frequently combined: "Please go," "Out please," "Please drink," etc.
Food-eat	Several fingers of one hand are placed in mouth. (Correct ASL form: fingertips of tapered hand touch mouth repeatedly.)	During meals and meal preparation.
Flower	The tip of the index finger touches one or both nostrils. (Correct ASL form: the tips of the tapered hand touch first one nostril, then the other.)	When sees or wants flower. Elicited both by actual flowers and by pictures of flowers.

sensory channels and creating more detailed models of objects. The result was a partial taking apart or fragmenting of the environment. It became less of a continuum, less an uninterrupted expanse of blurred and merging forms, and more a system of distinct items.

It should be pointed out that this development was characteristic of primates in general. Something more must have been involved in the origin of language among those primates that were members of the family of man, something that further increased the complexity of life. The change was essentially a matter of behavior. They must have been doing things which increased the number of meaningful objects in their world and the number of possible relationships among the objects, for example, using tools. Tool use drew attention to certain objects not merely out of curiosity or as possible food, but as items representing food indirectly, once removed as it were, items like digging sticks and stones.

Early steps toward language may have taken place among upright tool users who made a practice of hunting small game, shared food, had home bases of some sort, and established rules of sharing and cooperation. The chief innovators were children, at least if vocal communication depended on built-in hereditary factors in remote times as it does today, and if it was not taught but acquired automatically. Prehistoric parents were no more aware than modern parents of the rules governing their communications, and hence no more capable of conveying important changes to their offspring.

So the evolutionary spotlight focused on children and, more specifically, on children at play. The very nature of play makes for invention in language as in other forms of behavior; novelty flourishes wherever there is freedom and a certain lack of responsibility for taking care of the world's immediate business. At one time man's remote ancestors presumably had a call system not too different from that of contemporary chimpanzees, which means that as far as vocal communications were concerned they lived almost exclusively in the present. Their calls were generally immediate responses triggered by the emotional impact of immediate events. The bonds between calls and intense emotion were loosened somewhat during play only, with its elements of make-believe and incomplete involvement.

Radical changes came later, in all likelihood among the children of tool-using hominids who were preparing to participate in a more elaborate world and were playing more elaborate games. Of course, their repertoire must have included such perennial primate favorites as chases, mock fights, and various versions of hide-and-seek. But probably some games were being played that had never been played before. Pursuers may have carried rocks in their hands and may have thrown the rocks, the chases sometimes ending with something more serious than a playful nip or an appeasement gesture.

Mock danger may often have turned into real danger, mock pain and terror into real pain and terror. Perhaps such pursuits were gradually modified or abstracted, stripped of the fear and much of the excitement and the risk of pain and injury, stripped of everything except the elements needed to improve throwing accuracy and coordination. The result may have been something like the game of catch, which can be regarded as a watered-down or domesticated pursuit, a disguised target practice in which the participants take turns at throwing and being thrown at, at being predator and prey.

New symbolic activities which developed during play were probably accompanied by new symbolic vocalizations. Action and utterance were part of the same behavioral process, with natural selection always favoring "detachment," the ability to free objects from their positions in the environment and to free utterances from their connections with intense emotion and the present. A ball game required some delay, some anticipation, as compared with the old standard primate games. It called for organization, perhaps a choosing up of sides, and an object— often a prepared object at that, something worked into a roughly spherical shape to remove sharp edges and projections.

A rich system of calls could have evolved in such a setting. Before the start of a play-chase many primates approach with a kind of hopping gait, a signal which indicates that what is about to happen is all in fun, and perhaps an analogous point was expressed vocally as a prelude to games with objects. Perhaps a hominid who wanted to play catch went through the pantomime of throwing, and at the same time uttered a standard excitement call modified by a sound signifying a game. If the game became popular, the combined gesture and modified call could have spread rapidly to other children in the group, and later the call by itself could have meant "Where is the ball?" or "Let's play catch."

And at some later stage a child acting on the spur of the moment, or as the outcome of an accidental turn of events during play, may have invented a more complicated game, say, a game involving throwing and then running, and uttered the "throw" and "run" calls together, specifically in that order. Perhaps the two-part call came first and inspired the idea of the two-part action, or it might have happened the other way around. But in either case the result would have been a dual creation, a new game and a sentence or protosentence.

What would adults have been doing all this time? For one thing, they may have wondered then as they sometimes do now at the offbeat utterances of their children. Part of their influence would have been negative in the sense that mothers warning players to be more careful probably helped to transform violent chases and the hurling of missiles into something as innocuous as the game of catch. Also, on occasion adults may have adopted some of the new calls and the new games that went with the calls, although it can be assumed that as far as acceptance in general was concerned, they always lagged a bit behind their offspring then as they do now.

The most receptive adults, however, were those who had participated most actively in innovation during their youth. The longer the period of infant and childhood dependency, the longer the delay in assuming responsibility, the greater the opportunity for playing together and forming close associations. Games and utterances learned during childhood provided the sort of experience in cooperating found among team members who have competed so long together that they can anticipate one another's intentions and actions. Linguistic habits carried over into adult life served well in hunting and fighting, thus setting a prehistoric precedent for the notion that Britain's wars were won on the playing fields of Eton.

This is only one of many possible processes. But it seems reasonable to suppose that some sort of transition stage existed between call systems and language and that it took place not within the confines of a single band but in many bands over very long periods. There was certainly time and energy enough, millions of years and billions of individuals interacting with one another. Evolution put a premium on detachment, the survival of bands including members who could reconstruct the past in their minds and express their images and conceive new sequences of actions to serve as the basis for future plans.

Certain elements of this faculty can be seen among nonhuman primates. Only primates seem to be capable of the sort of behavior described in Chapter XII, in which a male baboon threatened by an angry and higher-ranking male snatched up an infant and began grooming it, because he knew that he was safer from attack with an infant in his arms. This form of pretense has a deliberate, plotting, symbol-using quality. It requires not only a second-nature familiarity with complex hierarchal relationships but also a certain ability to disengage oneself, to stand apart and observe the relationships and exploit them for new ends. It amounts to a kind of tool use in which a behavioral pattern is displaced from its natural setting and put to work in the service of a special purpose. Using the grooming of an infant as a device for turning away wrath demands a certain detachment not unlike that involved in the early evolution of language.

Detachment implies certain things about the structure and workings of the brain. It implies the development of the negative sort of ability discussed in connection with the increasing need for self-control, for biding one's time in an increasingly complicated world (see Chapters I and VII)—namely, the ability to inhibit flight, the display of anger and other actions. If language evolved from call systems, it demanded not reacting to sounds as emotion-laden, here-and-now signals, but as abstractions referring to something that had happened or was yet to happen. Incidentally, the same basic ability to postpone impulses, perhaps indefinitely, is heavily involved in two other uniquely human characteristics, in incest taboos and the use of tools to make tools, say, a stone to sharpen a digging stick. George Miller of Rockefeller University emphasizes that the stone acquires a value not only as something immediate but as something to help in fulfilling a delayed purpose.

The first crude language or prelanguage may have appeared a long time before the making of stone tools, even before life on savannas became a full-time proposition. It may have appeared when hominids still maintained bases deep in the forests, ventured for brief excursions into open country stretching away from forest edges, and hurried back to the forests before sunset. After all, chimpanzees living in present-day forests use tools and sometimes hunt. It is possible that the first steps toward language were under way as much as 15 million years ago and that some form of language existed among *Australopithecus* populations about 3 million years ago.

Subsequent developments came with the fuller exploitation of savanna lands. If tool use had made life more complicated and led to a multiplication of objects and relationships among objects, the trend must have accelerated with a vengeance when hominids broke their ties with the forest. Forests generally have a continuous, uninterrupted quality. Food tends to be abundant; shelter offers no serious problems, practically any area having trees suitable for refuge or sleeping. The topography of the savanna is considerably more varied. There are open areas, dry and dusty stretches of semidesert, clumps of tall grasses and thorny bushes, swamps and water holes, groves of trees along river banks. Resources are not evenly distributed, and primates must range widely in search of food.

So from the very beginning savanna-dwelling hominids had a great deal more to cope with than their arboreal ancestors. They led a more public, a more exposed, life among vast populations of other species. They became aware of new events and sensations and new regularities involving the habits of herd animals and predators such as lions, cheetahs, hyenas and wild dogs. Theirs was a "spotty" world of many discontinuities and many little environments. It contained more significant places than the forest, more places to seek out and to avoid, places where food was abundant and, when the food was consumed, second-best and third-best places.

During the course of evolution, hominids found reasons to visit other places, traveling miles from their campsites in search of materials particularly suited for the manufacture of tools. They brought back the best stones in the region, as far as size and shape and working qualities were concerned. They learned the steps and the sequences of steps necessary to produce a variety of tools, including tools to make tools, for example, to sharpen digging sticks and spears. Such work created new objects, and not only the tools themselves. It also created objects in the sense that things once ignored, such as unworked rocks and other selected raw materials, things once "invisible" as part of the general background, acquired special importance and reality.

Also, there was the hunt and its repercussions—small-game hunting at first and the increasing emphasis on big game, the use of human flexibility in exploiting the rigid behavior of herds and preparing pitfalls and ambushes in advancing along age-old migration routes, the development of implements and techniques for killing and butchering, and a basic division of labor with women responsible for gathering plant foods.

All this contributed to the multiplication of new experiences, and the mounting need for more elaborate communication. Big-game hunting had a special impact. Hunters had to make plans and share those plans with the people who stayed behind. They had to convey such information as: "We are going into the valley over there," "We will be back tomorrow before sunset," and perhaps even "If we are not back by sunset, come and look for us."

At the same time the family was becoming a more complex institution with the change from closed inbred groups to open groups in which matings outside the band became a policy supported by ritual. This development marked the creation, the invention, of the uniquely human sort of group made up of a number of bands held together by kinship systems. Such systems, of course, could not have come until our ancestors had brains and languages sophisticated enough to conceive and identify a variety of elaborate family categories.

All this and more involved new pressures. It added up to a flood of objects and relationships and activities to be named, a pile-up of calls, perhaps several hundred of them. Perhaps a major reason for the near-doubling of the size of the brain which marked the transition from *Australopithecus* to *Homo erectus* was the need for a larger memory to house expanding vocabularies, and at some stage the strain on memory may have approached the breaking point. At some stage our ancestors were hard pressed to invent new and distinguishable calls.

The problem can be illustrated by a hypothetical case of picture writing in which each symbol is a simplified sketch or caricature of a house, a man running, a wounded animal, and so on. If an evolving tribe kept adding new pictures for every new object and relationship generation after generation, it would sooner or later run out of symbols which were simple and compact and at the same time sufficiently different so that the eye could tell them apart readily. This situation, or something very close to it, arose about four centuries ago in Chinese writing, which had accumulated an overwhelming total of more than 45,000 pictographic characters.

Comparable difficulties may have arisen in the development of spoken language. If some of the differences between calls became so subtle that they could no longer be recognized readily or uttered as distinct patterns, one result would have been a high level of ambiguity. Bands with such overloaded communication systems may have tended to cross their signals rather frequently. Presumably there were misunderstandings and ineffective or confused responses, a situation which might have been particularly unfortunate in matters involving complex plans and social relationships. In other words, pressures of living favored the ability to reduce ambiguity, to make further refinements in the classification and interpretation of sounds.

Specifically, they were able to dissect calls into their components and discover categories, common elements. Hockett suggests that the change required a heightening of awareness or sensitivity, a shift of attention from whole calls to parts of calls. It was something like the difference between writing with pictorial symbols, representations of familiar objects and activities, and writing with the individual letters of an alphabet, which are not intended to be images of anything in particular, but which make possible the invention of an indefinite number of readily distinguished words. What happened, in fact, was the invention of a kind of vocal alphabet, a small set of acoustic units, the vowel and consonant sounds which we use to form words.

We have no direct evidence concerning this important development. But it may have been under way some 200,000 or more years ago among early representatives of *Homo sapiens,* during a time when human evolution was beginning to accelerate faster than ever. Indeed, it may have had something to do with the making of very special kinds of tools, tools which seem to have been shaped primarily for their beauty and symmetrical proportions. As pointed out in Chapter X, although such tools have been uncovered at sites several hundred thousand years old, they first appear in relative abundance at Solutrean sites dating back 18,000 years or so.

Strictly speaking, laurel-leaf blades and a number of other flint artifacts are not tools. Too thin and too brittle ever to have been used for serious cutting and piercing, they definitely represent something beyond technology. In them the esthetic far outweighs the practical. They are above all symbols, and their existence may be a sign of new trends in the evolution of language, trends which in some way gave wings to expression by opening up the possibility of fashioning an unlimited number of words and sentences. A common element may link the fashioning of beautifully shaped tools with the freeing of language, as well as with the origin of art.

Many things are beginning to come together here, and there is a feeling among archeologists that important new findings will come during the next few years. François Bordes sees a significant connection between the evolution of toolmaking and art, and the evolution of a capacity for abstract thinking. An early stage involved the concept of a cutting edge, as something which is absent but imminent and possible to create in a suitable unworked pebble. We can credit this insight to *Australopithecus* about three to four million years ago.

The trend since then has been toward more and more abstract concepts. The concept of shape in addition to cutting edge developed perhaps 350,000 years ago with the making of hand axes like those found at Torralba, while in the Levallois technique as established perhaps 150,000 years ago (see Chapter IX) man not only pictured the desired shape in his mind but actually predetermined it, by trimming the stone beforehand in such a way that the shape would come into being all at once with the final striking off of the flake.

A higher degree of abstraction was expressed some 30,000 years ago in the rise of art. Bordes speaks of "an ability to separate the shape from the object shaped . . . reproduction of a real shape, taken from the outside world and transferred in two dimensions to a flat surface." As far as we know, the concept of depicted shape was used in the main to represent animals rather than inanimate things like tools.

The existence of such stages in the evolution of thinking and technology strongly implies corresponding stages in the evolution of language. Perhaps the concept of cutting edge marks a time when language consisted chiefly of simple nouns, names for specific objects such as a "thing-for-cutting"; the concept of shape involves broader notions, say, classes of things and words like "tool"; and the concept of predetermined shape, requiring a carefully planned sequence or chain of flintworking operations, came with the increasing use of word chains or sentences. The artist's depicted shape might signify a new ability to make images, to picture or imagine things, fictitious as well as real, a language richer in symbols and theories and similes.

For the record, it should be stated that some investigators regard spoken language as a product of relatively recent times, something which certainly did not exist in the days of *Australopithecus* and probably not until the appearance of modern man. Hewes has a new theory which was inspired partly by the achievements of Washoe and Sarah, and is a refined version of ideas first presented two hundred or more years ago—namely, that man's original language was a silent gesture language.

He suggests that *Australopithecus* probably got along with a small number of gestures, perhaps fifty or so, for landmarks, common plant and animal foods, water sources and directions such as up-down and near-far and here-there. Later advances, primarily learning how to make hand axes and other more sophisticated tools, required more and more gestures until, say, 50,000 to 75,000 years ago at about the 1,000-gesture level the number approached the limit of readily distinguishable signs, at which point selective forces brought about a greater and greater emphasis on spoken language.

Notice that the theory of gesture origins, like the theory of call origins, assumes a pile-up stage when overloading of the communication system became so severe that something radically different had to evolve. Also, both theories indicate that modern-type languages appeared during the final stages of prehistory, that major changes took place during the past 50,000 years or so. A report by Philip Lieberman and Edmund Crelin, of the University of Connecticut and the Yale University School of Medicine respectively, tends to support this view.

The first part of their analysis is mainly the work of Crelin, a specialist in the anatomy of the newborn. He studied the skulls of modern newborn infants and adults and Neanderthal man, concluding that the Neanderthal skull resembles the skull of an infant more closely than it resembles that of an adult. Going by this comparison, he produced a reconstruction of Neanderthal man's vocal apparatus, which differs fundamentally from ours in permitting less variation of the size and shape of air passages controlling sound production.

Lieberman, a linguist, then used the model to figure out how Neanderthal man might have talked, by simulating its operation on a computer. The results indicate that our ancestor could not utter *a, i, u,* the vowel sound in *brought, k* or *g*—and that he probably spoke in a nasal, baby-talk fashion. Furthermore, these limitations affected his rate of speech so that he could produce only fifteen or so words a minute, or about a tenth of our rate, which was apparently enough to conceive and convey burial rituals and notions about life after death.

In any case there seems to be a good argument for the general point that our sort of language represents a refinement of the Neanderthal sort. It arose during the period which saw population increases and larger settlements and confederations, mass cooperation for mass killing in the hunt, burials and cave paintings and advanced ceremonies and kinship systems. The continuing rise in social complexity, the continuing pile-up of words, almost certainly put extra pressure to bear on the further development of grammatical rules.

According to a theory proposed by McNeill, there may simply have been too much to remember. For example, every form of every verb may once have been a distinct word; at one time men may have had completely different words for "he is running," "he was running," "he will be running" and so on. Learning such a language might take at least twice as long as learning a modern language with its rules for the use of auxiliary verbs and special endings. McNeill believes that the child learns so rapidly today because prehistoric children invented rules which their own children acquired by the usual process of inference. So perhaps, like the new artificial languages man is devising to communicate with electronic computers, natural languages began as rather complicated and unwieldy systems and became increasingly easy to learn and use.

Present knowledge, taking account of some recent findings about the behavior of chimpanzees and human children, can carry the story no further. New findings will certainly alter current ideas. What seems central to all arguments is the notion of increasing complexity, of a world becoming steadily richer and wider with the successive phases of hominid evolution, and the rise of increasingly complicated mechanisms to deal with it. To put it in the most direct terms, if objects of significance to ancestral primates in the trees could be numbered in the dozens, hundreds of thousands of natural and man-made objects had special importance for prehistoric *Homo sapiens*. Taking command of the world means classifying the objects and imposing regularities upon them, and language is our most effective way of doing precisely that.

In the last analysis, understanding these and other basic processes depends on understanding the relationships between brain and behavior, the biological basis for language acquisition. Something in the brain, some structure or set of structures, is designed to scan the environment from infancy on and to seek and discover out of all the hubbub certain very special kinds of order. Just enough is known about phenomena at the cerebral level and the organization of cell-to-cell nerve connections to hint at some of the problems that lie ahead.

One of the elementary aspects of learning language is the ability to associate things seen and things heard, to learn that certain sound patterns or words are the names of objects and persons. Laboratory experience shows that it is very difficult to produce such associations in most lower primates. According to one investigator, "you have to hit them in the guts to accomplish anything," which means that if you want a macaque monkey to associate the word "circle" with the image of a circle, you must subject it to considerable emotional stress. You must punish it for making mistakes by applying an electric shock or some other painful stimulus, or keep it hungry and then reward it with food. And even under such conditions the experiment may not succeed.

Anatomy suggests one of the most important reasons for the difficulty. A certain visual area on the surface of the monkey's brain, on the sheet of nerve cells forming the cortex, is concerned with the shaping of images; another auditory area is concerned with patterns of sounds. Learning to associate an image and a sound is primarily a matter of establishing communications between the two areas. But it happens that there are very few direct connections from one to the other.

The main pathways in the macaque brain take an indirect course. They include nerve fibers running from the auditory area down beneath the cortical surface to nerve structures which appeared relatively early in evolution and are involved in emotional and biological needs. The fibers then make connections with other fibers ascending from these structures to the visual area at the surface. Many problems encountered in the laboratory arise because such roundabout routes are involved in efforts to train monkeys to associate complex sounds and images.

The situation in man is entirely different. The human brain includes a rich system of direct routes, fibers within the cortex itself which by-pass the depths and connect not only visual and auditory areas to one another but also both these areas to a similar area concerned with the feel and texture of things. In fact, the fibers are so numerous that a special switching station or "superassociation" structure has appeared during the course of hominid evolution. It is somewhat bigger than a half-dollar piece and occupies a strategic position on the side of the cortex just behind the temple, at the junction of the three areas.

Medical research indicates that this structure may be involved in the development of language. According to Norman Geschwind of the Harvard Medical School, it plays a major role in the formation of connections which enable children to associate the image and the feel of a teddy bear with the sound pattern "teddy bear." Injury to the center later in life may produce strange disorders of language, disorders which result from difficulties in establishing connections between things heard and things seen. For example, a patient may have only minor difficulties in speaking, but he may lose the ability to read or write.

Notice that the anatomy of the superassociation structure helps account for something we know from observations of behavior. The calls of lower primates are bound to emotion, occurring almost invariably in response to immediate satisfactions and dissatisfactions, a fact which makes sense considering the strong links that connect their visual and auditory areas to underlying nerve centers concerned with emotion. On the other hand, since such links are much weaker in the human brain, we are capable of a certain detachment and can even upon occasion communicate dispassionately. By the way, although the superassociation structure is absent or exists in only very rudimentary form in monkeys, it may be somewhat better developed in the chimpanzee, which helps explain the talents of Washoe and Sarah.

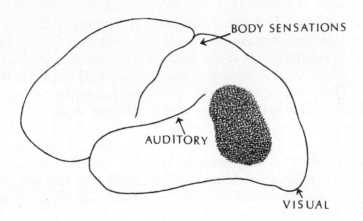

The "superassociation" center, a brain area believed to be involved in language acquisition

Here is an example, however hypothetical it may be at the current stage of human ignorance, of what it means to know. The point is not that we have an answer or a partial answer to our problems. Geschwind's ideas will surely have to be revised and they may well be discarded within a few years. But the approach, the fundamental nature of the search, is meaningful and appropriate. Sooner or later things must be confronted at the biological level, seeking explanations in the behavior and organization of nerve cells.

We do not really know unless we know anatomically and

physiologically, and in most cases even conceiving plausible models is enough of a problem. How would one design a brain so that it automatically classifies things? The information received through sense organs passes into some kind of sorting structure, some system of precisely interconnected nerve cells or molecules within cells. It must be categorized, arranged in hierarchies of classes, subclasses, subdivisions of subclasses, and so on. The information is stored in retrievable form so that answers can be given, usually in short order, to questions like "Have you ever eaten at the Golden Horn?" and "Do you know an elderly carpenter named Jim?" The anatomy of grammar will be better understood when we learn how the brain cross-indexes its remembrances of things past.

In general it seems that the mechanisms involved are not primarily a matter of brain size. Size is important if only to provide sufficient storage space, and the elephant's famous long memory is related to the massiveness of its cerebral hemispheres. But language may be acquired with surprisingly little nervous tissue. There are dwarfs with perfectly proportioned bodies scaled down to a height of two and a half feet or so, and their brains weigh only some fourteen ounces, the weight of the chimpanzee brain (and about a third of the weight of the average human brain). They are mentally retarded, but they speak fluently. Their undersized brains still retain intact the uniquely human mechanisms which embody the capacity for language and probably arose early in hominid evolution.

These mechanisms have certain built-in biases, as indicated by the observation that all children acquire certain habits of using words. For example, Joseph Greenberg of Stanford University points out that in all languages studied to date the word for "good" appears more often than the word for "bad." (In English, "good" appears five times more often than its opposite.) The phenomenon may reflect at the linguistic level our tendencies to expect the best and to start by approaching things rather than turning away. But what are we to make of the fact that "long" occurs far more frequently than "short," "many" than "few," "deep" than "shallow," "wide" than "narrow"?

Also, it may be significant that some rules of grammar are learned later than others. The fact that proper use of the verb "promise" does not generally come until the age of nine or so may imply a later appearance in the language itself of the complete notion of promising—and that, in turn, may imply something about the nature and sequence of evolutionary events. The order in which individuals learn rules of grammar may reflect the order in which the species encountered and dealt with various social problems.

Perhaps language is full of such relics, clues to prehistoric experiences and ways of thinking. Perhaps language, like the brain itself, is a thing of many coexisting structures which are inherited from times past and can provide insights into our remote heritage. The past has not vanished or been discarded in the continuing process of becoming human.

■ New studies of mothers and children, the significance of giving and the need for relaxing current tensions; play and art as sources of novelty; man's unique restlessness; crowding and intertroop conflicts among rhesus monkeys; war as the most human form of hunting; social interactions in cities; evolution and mental disease; Freud's concern with primate behavior and the irrational past

CHAPTER XX

Study of Man: The Power of the Past, the Potential for Change

■ Everything that is being learned about human evolution points unequivocally to the power of the past. In a sense prehistory is happening to man today. He is quite capable of responding prehistorically to present-day situations, thinking and acting in flashbacks as it were, living upon occasion in a world that ceased to exist a long, long time ago. He may at times revert to a dreamtime of a sort, responding to contemporary events as if he were still a wild species at large in a wilderness.

We may see the past most clearly in our children, whose behavior has not yet become too complicated and civilized to interpret with some degree of sophistication. Sometimes, indeed, the past is obvious. Like lesser primates, nursery-school children may form hierarchies, and aggressiveness is part of the basis for their ranking. According to observations made by William McGrew at the University of Edinburgh, those individuals who are most successful at wresting toys from their playmates tend to occupy dominant positions in the social order.

There are further suggestive findings. In studying children, McGrew and other investigators are using the same sort of approach that Altmann used in studying rhesus monkeys (see Chapter XIV), compiling lists of behavior elements to describe as objectively as possible what the child is doing. McGrew reports striking similarities between patterns in play groups of human

474

and nonhuman primates, practically identical "flashing" or eye-brow raising and other common elements such as "play face," "play crouch," "gaze fixate," "kiss," "stamp," "beat," "hug" and so on: "I would estimate that at least 80 per cent of the behavior patterns we have defined for preschool children have counter-parts in nonhuman primates."

Differences can be as significant as similarities. On a dozen separate occasions he observed the introduction of new children, six boys and six girls most of whom had just turned three, into a group of about fifteen children—and to his surprise noted no aggressive responses, a sharp contrast to the violence with which the members of most nonhuman primate troops greet newcomers. In the human group girls were generally warm in their responses, to girls and boys alike, often displaying "a remarkable degree of maternalistic attentiveness"; boys could also be friendly, but were generally indifferent.

Many factors are involved in these observations. But one evolu-tionary interpretation is that hominids may have differed from other primates in having more open societies, in being more hospitable or less hostile to outsiders. One advantage in accepting strangers is indicated in a study by Valerius Geist of the University of Calgary in Canada, who cites work indicating that the offspring of wandering reindeer bulls tend to be healthier than those produced by bull members of the same herd. Introducing new genes may have had comparable advantages among our early ancestors.

Incidentally, in an important trend investigators who have been studying children exclusively are becoming more and more interested in the ways of nonhuman primates. McGrew is spend-ing the next two years studying chimpanzees with van Lawick-Goodall at the Gombe Stream Research Center, and Denham, whose work on nonhuman primates is referred to in Chapter XII, has made a switch in the other direction by studying the ways of Australian aborigines.

Blurton Jones is also studying nursery-school children with strictly observational techniques. In fact, he pioneered in the use of such techniques several years ago. From his viewpoint young human beings, like the young of other primates, have a repertoire or "vocabulary" of standard gestures and movements, and an analysis of these elements can yield objective information about the causes and development of human behavior. Trained as a zoologist by Tinbergen, he is using the same basic techniques on children that he used in studying fleeing reactions, threat and attack displays, and meeting ceremonies among chickadees and geese in England and seagulls off the Bering Sea coast in western Alaska.

His early work included more than a hundred hours spent among children three to five years old at a London nursery school. He simply sat on a chair in a corner, notebook in hand, and began watching: "On your first visit the children make an enormous fuss about you. They either stand and stare or run up and give you things, and then go away if your response is polite but uninvolved. They make a fuss again at the beginning of the second visit, but it does not last as long. It takes about three visits to be completely ignored practically from the start."

In many ways, the rough-and-tumble play of children is identical to that of other primates. There are chases and flights and wrestling, all typically preceded by a kind of I-dare-you pattern or posture and expression. A child about to be chased often stands side-on to the prospective chaser, slightly crouched and with a mischievous play face resembling the play face of the macaque monkey or chimpanzee under comparable circumstances, an open-mouthed smile with the teeth hidden. Another characteristic play pattern, jumping up and down on both feet, is reminiscent of the baboon's hopping gait in mock fights. There is also an open-hand beating movement without actually hitting, an overhand movement very much like that used in throwing a ball or spear. As might be expected from studies of wild primates, boys indulge in such activities more often than girls.

The patterns for fighting, such as frowning and a cold stare and real blows, are entirely different. In fact, the differences are greater and more clear-cut for children than for the offspring of any other primate. Play fighting has been underlined as it were, isolated or set apart from real hostility, identified by a special system of signs so that the chances of misunderstanding are reduced to a minimum, which has a double implication for what apparently happened in the remote past. Hostility became extra-dangerous, extra-lethal, in a species that wielded rocks and clubs

Play-fighting face, open mouth and sparkling eyes

Real hostility: human primate

and hurled missiles. At the same time play acquired an extra importance not only in preparing for fights and escapes but also in developing social competence and imagination and a mastery of language.

During these studies Blurton Jones became especially interested in interactions between mothers and children when they separated at the beginning of the nursery-school day and when they came together again at the end of the day. Subtle things were going on, related to how much a child needed and liked its mother. In some cases it would run to its mother and hug her, while in other cases it would walk toward her and, instead of hugging or making contact of any sort, would give her a toy or some other object, as if trying to distract her and keep her at a distance emotionally.

Such observations led to a full-scale research project which called for patience, plenty of space for storing data, and greeting-separation records for ten different days for each of 35 children. Blurton Jones and his associate Gill Leach recorded 33 different behavior elements such as child running or walking toward mother, child reaching out to touch mother, child showing or giving something to mother, mother touching child, and mother talking to child. Then he found which elements tended to cluster or occur together, using a factor-analysis procedure similar to that used by archeologists to study tool kits (see Chapter IX).

The analysis has yielded nothing simple, except perhaps the observation that nothing is simple. It has done much to reveal the full complexity of child-mother interactions, the need for a re-examination of such concepts as attachment, and the existence of some intriguing problems. For example Blurton Jones points out that when a child presents an object to its mother, the act may have "some social significance over and above the object given, and possibly even independent of the response to the object." Older children commonly do the same thing upon meeting a stranger, and the feeling is that in some way giving of this kind is a deeply symbolic act involving fear and appeasement.

This type of work inevitably draws attention to our current ways of bringing up children. Studies in prehistory suggest that there is room for improvement. Throughout the main course of human evolution, during the 15-million-year period from the earliest hominids and *Australopithecus* to the rise of agriculture, children lived continuously from birth until the age of five or older in a world of people close at hand, as individuals in intimate contact with many other individuals.

Middle-class customs have tended to work against the child's capacity for wide intimacies, to tie the mother-child bond too tightly. The child is ready to associate with other individuals, particularly its peers, earlier than most people realize, early in its second year or some two years before nursery school usually starts. The child is also ready to form the closest sort of ties not only with its mother but with other individuals, notably an older brother or older sister.

Prehistory suggests that a great deal of the strain and pressure of child-mother relationships would be relieved if society were only organized to provide more opportunity for the child, and the mother, to circulate a bit more widely. Increased freedom of this sort would increase rather than decrease the closeness between mother and child, the stability of the family as a whole.

Real hostility: nonhuman primate

We may also have a lot to learn and unlearn from new studies of play, another highly complex form of behavior. It has long been a loaded notion, implying something frivolous, an admonition to grow up and put your toys away. This is the voice of puritanism, and Darwin heard and was influenced. It still speaks out strongly today. It speaks in the tendency to concentrate in evolutionary studies of man and other animals almost exclusively on feeding, reproduction, and fighting—and to underrate the significance of casual leisure-time activities, all varieties of behavior without immediate relevance to the "important" things of life.

The notion of play can be overextended. Corinne Hutt of the Park Hospital for Children in Oxford, England, has observed nursery-school behavior in a test situation, a familiar playroom including familiar toys such as a truck and a panda doll—and a brand-new object, a red metal box with four brass legs and a kind of four-position gearshift lever on the top. Under the conditions of one series of experiments, moving the lever operated a bell, a buzzer and four clicking counters.

Children were set free in the room for six ten-minute sessions, usually two days apart, and their actions at first were decidedly not playful. At first they were afraid. When an adult was in the room with them, the fear did not last long and they approached the red box within thirty seconds or so, generally after asking what it was. But when they were alone they delayed longer and approached more hesitantly, and never approached without bringing a familiar toy along. Boys brought the truck, girls the panda doll.

And even then the children did not play. As might have been predicted, they paid special attention to the new object, spending up to half their time with it, holding the lever in one position, listening to the noise and watching the counters, shifting positions rapidly, and trying to twist it and pull the lever off. Such activity might have passed for play in this study, as has been the case in many other studies, except for the key observation that the children did not seem to be having fun. There was a certain amount of tenseness in the air as they concentrated on the object with intent, earnest attention. The entire pattern of behavior, from the first hesitation on, was clearly serious business.

Novelty is a threat to children as well as to their elders. The fear comes from the remote past, when the sight of a stranger or an unfamiliar object had the impact of a criminal loose on the street or a house on fire. Children and adults then react appropriately for that early world if not for their own. Working against the fear of novelty, however, is the tendency to approach and inspect and above all to remove the mystery and the insecurity. Novelty is also a necessity. It cannot be wished away. It can be assimilated and transformed into the familiar and made part of the environment. It can be built into the scheme of things as a landmark, as something dependable and therefore something that can usually be ignored. All this represents a special need for the human child who is dependent for so long.

So the Oxford nursery-school children first hesitated and then investigated, an activity that tapered off rapidly after the third or fourth experimental session, after the red box had lost its mysteries. Now at last they were ready to enjoy themselves. Starting at the second session and reaching a peak at the fifth, their posture and facial expression relaxed and they spent more and more time treating the box as a familiar thing. In effect, it became a toy for the first time. One boy ran around the room pulling the truck, and every time he passed the lever he shifted it to produce bell-buzzer sounds. He had finished exploring and had turned to play.

Hutt stresses the significance of the shift: "The emphasis changes from the question of 'what does this object do?' to 'what can I do with this object?' " Play is thus active in a creative rather than a purely exploratory way. It is a fragile thing, as fragile as joy itself, which vanishes with the first hint of fear or uncertainty. It flourishes among familiar objects in a familiar setting, at savanna feeding grounds with dominant males nearby and at home bases. Among hominids it has become increasingly associated with pretending and acting, the invention of games, and in all likelihood the evolution of language. Incidentally, when it comes to pretending, boys do more of it and do it more elaborately than girls, at least they did in Hutt's studies. She observed twenty out-of-the-ordinary cases of playing with the red box, such as using the gearshift knob as a microphone and crooning into it, and in sixteen cases the player was a boy.

These and many other observations are being summarized and extended by Owen Aldis of the Behavioral Science Research Fund in Menlo Park, California, as part of a work in progress, a

Make believe crooning

major survey of all aspects of play. Among other things, he is interested in the evolutionary role of play fear which attracts and excites children, and may in an instant turn into real fear. He also points out that aggressive play during childhood had obvious survival value in prehistoric times when the risk was high of meeting a predator or human enemy, but questions its value today, particularly if a suspected relationship between it and adult aggressiveness can be established.

Finally, play is related to the arts, to music and song, sculpture and painting and dancing. The element of pretending, of something standing for or symbolizing something else, is prominent in both play and art. So are the elements of surprise, adventure, pleasure, experimentation in the sense of trying out new patterns and contrasts, and "uselessness" in the sense of not fulfilling any immediate biological function. And so is the element of fragility because, for all the banalities and nonsense about the benefits of starving in attics, creative activity generally thrives in more congenial and happier circumstances.

A consideration of these similarities is found in a recent analysis of the origin of art by Ellen Eisenberg, who comes to the problem as "someone right in the middle, not quite in tune with either the mystics or the measurers." She is possessor of a degree in art history and a student of animal behavior and the wife of John Eisenberg, cited in Chapter XII, who has written on the social organization of mammals. Her basic notion is that art arose from play and went its separate way, acquiring its formal and ritualistic qualities in the course of serving social functions.

The precursors of art may have been a variety of representations used originally in games—pieces of wood resembling animals and infants, circles and other shapes drawn in the dirt with sticks and fingers, colored clay smeared on faces and pebbles and cave walls. Art may have been associated with religion from the very beginning. The archeological evidence indicates that religion became an established institution at least 75,000 years ago, or some 30,000 years before the first signs of painting, suggesting that the earliest art, like the art of medieval times, may have been "sponsored" by individuals in charge of memorial ceremonies, burials and other rituals. Art was probably also involved in teaching, in designing ornaments and marks of social status, and in arousing men to a pitch of excitement for fighting and the hunt.

Eisenberg's work draws attention to the value of careful speculation and also to the need for combining the humanistic and behavioral approaches in intensive studies of children of all ages in the process of creating art. Such studies, like studies of smiling and language acquisition, would widen understanding of recent as well as remote times. Art has never lost its original social function and continues to be a medium of assertion and rebellion and commemoration. But somewhere along the line it achieved a life of its own and became, in addition, a type of abstract and highly disciplined innovation like mathematics.

In other words, art became one of a larger class of behavior patterns, the class which includes all forms of exploration. Men share the need for novelty with many other animals. The classical model of how monotony may affect a living thing built for action is the lone tiger pacing back and forth in its cage, following the same narrow route hour after hour, eyes wide open but seeing nothing. It is dying on its feet, dying from lack of surprise. This is obviously a disease of captivity; tigers in the wild do not suffer from it. They are at peace in the sense of being adjusted to their natural environment, which offers sufficient variety to keep them healthy, and which has offered sufficient variety for millions of years.

Artists are specialists in creating, in replenishing, surprise. And so are scientists, who certainly concern themselves with solving problems, but whose passion is discovering problems. Change arises in a thousand forms out of man's attempts to keep things from changing, to preserve life and his ways of living. In recent times, as if to make the best of a bad thing, human evolution has taken a new tack and arrived at a new kind of permanent and deliberate instability. It is no longer a matter of adjusting to change, to the variety which the world offers. Apparently an important part of being human is to discover and invent more and more variety.

Some day perhaps, when investigators study adults as intensively as they are beginning to study children, we may know considerably more about these things. Until then we will have to go mainly by impressions and a minimum of solid data in approaching such basic problems as the sources and control of man's chronic restlessness. There seems to be no peace for him. Even as he strives to create stability he upsets things anew, because his way of striving is increasingly to change his environment, his social and physical milieu—and then he must adapt all over again by changing his environment again, and so on. Life is further complicated by the fact that he has never yet been able to foresee most of the important consequences of the changes he brings about.

Man is continually trying to adapt and, in the process, making new adaptations necessary. Changes occur continually because of his own activities, because of the growth of knowledge and everything else that contributes to the accelerating complexity of things. The irony is that he began so innocently, as anything but a revolutionary. Man was, and may still be for all we know, basically conservative. But his relationship to the world is "antinatural" in the sense that events seem to thwart his conservatism at every turn. It is as if he and life were chronically at odds, even as he moves creatively to adapt himself.

There is no better example of this tension, this strange quality of the human condition, than the story of fire (see Chapter VII). It all began in a rather straightforward fashion. The first fire users were probably hunters who curled up near red-hot embers on cold nights to keep warm. They wanted no new worlds. They simply wanted to make the world as they knew it more comfortable, and they had no idea of what they were getting themselves and their descendants into. They could not begin to know the consequences of their invention.

They could not know that fire would bring light as well as heat, creating a new and longer day and bright glowing places around which people gathered after sunset and talked to one another and looked back at yesterday and forward to tomorrow; that fire would bring pain and fear, and would be used more and more over the millennia to drive other animals out of their lairs and caves, and into a variety of deathtraps; or that fires would bring wonder at the flickering of shadows and visions among the shadows and intimations of spirits and demons and other worlds. In short, the first fire users could not know that the simple act of bringing warmth into their camps would play a leading role in transforming their lives radically and irrevocably.

The same forces came into play as a result of the eating of meat. An apparently simple extension of the diet to include meat on a regular basis as well as the usual plant foods led to a new kind of cooperation and the expansion of the brain, and to all the other aftermaths and repercussions of the hunt and hunting psychology. And the same forces continue to operate in our times, only far more swiftly. For example, we move to forestall death and save the lives of a greater and greater proportion of our young, and confront in all its stark ramifications the prospect of exploding populations and a hungry and overcrowded world. The effort to decrease suffering increases the threat of suffering on a wider scale than ever before.

The rise of meat eating and the hunt tended to help counteract or inhibit the divisiveness of those who confronted the dangers of the open savanna. It put a premium on cooperation, provided increasing opportunity to take out aggressions on big game rather than on one's fellow men, and accentuated the male behavior pattern of running down or trapping prey and closing in and finding consummation in the kill. On the other hand, hunting brought a new order of organized aggression and group excitement. A new ambiguity had come into being, a new potential for instability. That same pattern of behavior could now be turned inward against other hunters and groups of hunters.

The later development of larger and larger communities doubtless created new tensions. Living close to other people may have created dangerous conflict, as it does today, and as it does among recent hunter-gatherers and among nonhuman primates subjected to similar conditions. Charles Southwick at Johns Hopkins University reports that encounters among rhesus monkeys of northern India are particularly vicious in and near temples, a phenomenon observed also among human beings.

The chief problem is the crowding. Monkeys occupy the same sort of position around Hindu temples as pigeons do around churches and other buildings in American cities. They are fed by local people and treated as semipets; they multiply freely to produce large troops, larger and much more aggressive troops than those found in the forests. Fighting breaks out more often not only within the ranks but among entire troops. There are dominant and subordinate troops, hierarchies of hierarchies, whose positions are usually determined by the number of members. Subordinate troops always retreat when they see a higher-ranking troop approaching.

But not infrequently, perhaps once every three or four days, sudden encounters take place. A subordinate troop may be so absorbed in its feeding that it fails to notice the approach of a dominant troop, and then violence flares up. Adult males generally begin the fighting, but females and juveniles also join in. According to the Johns Hopkins investigator, temple monkeys are particularly vicious aggressors: "These fights were ferocious and dangerous . . . often resulting in severe wounds, and most adult males bore wound scars around the face, shoulders or rump. Wounded individuals were fewer among the rhesus monkeys in rural habitats and forest areas."

Most fights end after only a few minutes with the retreat of the subordinate and smaller troop. Now and then, however, the sides happen to be evenly matched and a pitched battle results, lasting as long as fifteen to twenty minutes. On one occasion, part of the top-ranking troop suddenly came upon the full No. 2 troop. For a while the subordinates seemed to be enjoying a distinct advantage until the rest of the dominant troop, like reinforcements of Federal cavalry in a Western movie, arrived to save the day.

Even though war like language is uniquely human, it has roots at the subhuman level. Indeed, the case of the temple monkeys suggests how war may have arisen as an established institution among men. As long as men lived in the wilderness, the excitement and glamour of the hunt had meaning in the context of survival, in promoting aggression against prey and predators. But agriculture and the domestication of animals gradually reduced hunting from a truly important activity, a vital part of the world's work, to a sport for people with time on their hands. Agriculture also accelerated the growth of populations and cities, bringing more people and more different kinds of people closer together than ever before.

Men deprived of hunting as a major source of prestige, deprived of wild species as a major focus of aggression, began playing the most dangerous game of all. Men began to go after other men, as if their peers were the only creatures clever enough to make hunting really interesting. So war, the cruelest and most elaborate and most human form of hunting, became one of the most appealing ways of expressing aggression—war has always been more exciting than peace, robbers than cops, hell than heaven, Lucifer than God.

Counteracting tendencies are nevertheless at work in men's efforts to reduce the tensions they create for themselves. When asked why they live in small groups, the Bushmen of the Kalahari reply that they fear fights. The solution of living in small groups is closed to most people, who are no longer hunter-gatherers. But something related to it may be observed in urban and suburban communities. An instinctive cutting down of social contacts occurs which in its pathological form may become a total shutting off and withdrawal from the world, but which normally amounts to behaving continuously as if one is living in a small group. It also re-creates the possibility of privacy.

The traditional readiness of men to form and join organizations has become if anything more intense in urban settings. Men tend to associate themselves with certain fellow workers at the office and, outside the office, with a widening variety of community and business associations, political clubs and hobby clubs, historical societies and so on. An individual has roles in many organizations, and on his way from one to another he may pay little attention to his other fellow men—one reason for the impersonal atmosphere newcomers feel in cities and for the reluctance of many passers-by to come to the aid of strangers in trouble.

The tendency to form social islands in population oceans can be regarded as a kind of provincialism, a throwback to the small-band living and small-band psychology of prehistoric times or as another example of mass pathology. But it is more than that. A countertendency exists to form larger and more inclusive organizations at national and international levels. There is no reason to believe that the two tendencies are incompatible.

Local joining, furthermore, serves to relieve tensions as well as to get things done. Local organizations include some of the trappings of rank and status, presidents and vice-presidents and treasurers and executive committees. They are hierarchies, but hierarchies without the tensions and intensities of the past. Swearing blood brotherhood in secret by the light of the full moon is an inappropriate way of joining a stamp club or a group dedicated to keeping the countryside beautiful. The more archaic qualities of rituals, such things as vigils and ordeals, and fighting for positions in hierarchies, somehow seem more obvious when people meet to enjoy themselves or to cooperate rather than compete.

Much human behavior has a strong hereditary bias, and tends to be automatic and stereotyped. The power of the past is indicated by what comes easy to man and what comes hard. It is hard to think things through before acting, to develop long-range master plans and abide by them. It is easy to act quickly for quick results on a day-to-day basis.

In many ways modern men still behave like members of a small-band species with a small-band mentality, still creatures wandering in close-knit groups through wilderness. It is easy to love family and a few friends, hard to love more widely and care about anyone outside one's immediate circle and to trust people who look different—easy to be aroused to quick anger and a fight, even when the arousal works against one's interests, hard to become aroused about a project involving a community or several communities. Men respond too readily to the call of the wild.

People interacting with one another show many of the characteristics found in troops of nonhuman primates. Direct stares, frowns, forward movements of the lips and other expressions indicate aggression; hunching the shoulders, drawing the chin in toward the chest, closing the eyes, and moving away are among our natural flight reactions. People living together in groups, in hospitals and homes and offices and military units, use such signs to establish hierarchies much like those observed among wild baboons, including coalitions of two or three individuals to form dominant cores or "Establishments" (see Chapter XII).

The fact that man is partly geared to the past is reflected in physiological processes over which we normally have no control. Body temperature falls about three degrees Fahrenheit during the course of a night's sleep, reaching a low point at about four in the morning, and begins to climb sharply from then on. Blood pressure follows the same general pattern and so does the concentration in the blood stream of certain adrenal-gland hormones which mobilize natural body fuels. Dreaming tends to increase during the last hour or two before awakening, and heart and breathing rates become more irregular.

This entire complex of changes which exists in certain lower primates has been interpreted as an alerting mechanism. Men no longer live in open country, sleeping on the ground or in trees or on rocky ledges. But the brain does not "know" this, at least those parts of the brain responsible for such reactions. Morning after morning we are prepared for events that no longer occur, for responding to emergencies that confronted our ancestors. The hours before sunrise on the savanna represent a period of special danger as far as stalking predators are concerned.

The past is with us also when we wake up and go about the day's business. Unpleasant encounters and frictions, a bitter argument at home or an accident barely avoided while driving or a belittling remark from a superior at the office, produce changes which prepare the body for violent and sudden exertion on the spot—for bursts of anger or fear, and attacks and flight. Many of the predawn reactions are accentuated. To cite one example, a sharp rise in the output of adrenal hormones produces a corresponding rise in blood levels of fatty substances which can be burned or metabolized rapidly to provide energy for the muscles.

Usually men do not act impulsively, because they have learned not to act; certain parts of the brain play an inhibiting role on other parts. But self-control may take a toll in the long run. The excess fatty substances in the blood are ready for burning and they do not burn, and, in the opinion of David Hamburg of the Stanford University Medical Center, man may suffer accordingly as a consequence. Most of the substances are excreted unused, but very tiny amounts may accumulate and form deposits on the inner walls of arteries, including the arteries that bring blood to the heart itself. As the deposits thicken, the arteries become narrower and narrower until blood supplies are seriously reduced or cut off entirely and a heart attack results.

Such attacks are far more common among men than among women. Women burn fatty fuels more completely, one possible reason being that they are brought up to be less ashamed of emoting and hence tend to release tensions more openly and directly. In a sense they live more in harmony with their metabolism, with their inherited physiology. Men probably emote less readily and are called on more often to disguise their feelings. They often encounter situations demanding inhibition, so they seethe inside and smile and delay the settling of accounts. Vital statistics suggest that the woman's way may be healthier than the man's; she lives seven to eight years longer than he does.

Evolutionary factors may also be partly responsible for a number of other diseases that come increasingly after middle age. The body's immune system reflects the notion that in the remote past people too old for hunting and fighting and reproducing played minor roles at best in society. Active participation after the age of forty or fifty is a relatively new phenomenon, and the body has not caught up with the times. It is precisely during this period that the immune system, which not only combats bacteria and viruses but may also destroy abnormal cells, begins to go into a decline.

This amounts to a lowering of the guard. One result may be increasing vulnerability to a variety of infections which were held in check during earlier years, and to cancer and other conditions involving uncontrolled cell growth. Robert Good of the University of Minnesota Medical School comments: "After all, nature is not basically interested in individuals who have passed the age of maximum reproductive efficiency. The coming of language and brains capable of intricate learning and long memories, factors that helped make old people important as bearers of tradition, is a very recent development in evolution."

Mental illness may also involve evolutionary throwbacks, behavior patterns more appropriate to prehistoric times than to the contemporary scene. Primate studies indicate that the shift from forests to savannas, the same move that presumably brought about an increase in meat eating and hunting, was accompanied by a shift from the relaxed and loosely organized hierarchies characteristic of chimpanzees to a more rigid baboon-like hierarchy. The change was a matter of survival. Individuals can go about alone or in twos or threes in the forests, but not in open country, the hunting grounds of lions and wild dogs and other predators.

Evolution favored bands made up of individuals who knew their places and behaved accordingly. John Price of the Maudsley Hospital Institute of Psychiatry in London believes that mental disease originally appeared in the hierarchies of early man, and that many present-day patients behave as if they were still living in such a context. For instance, certain disorders may have been associated with low-ranking members of the hierarchy who fitted into the scheme of things, because they were predisposed to be sensitive to and expect trouble, and adjusted by responding with apprehension, appeasement gestures and withdrawal.

Price suggests that the first cases of anxiety neurosis and schizophrenia were diseases of humility, arising among subordinate individuals subjected to unusually severe stress, perhaps during periods of food shortage or overcrowding. Dominant individuals, on the other hand, would have been vulnerable to other conditions. Endowed not only with physical strength and fighting ability but also with a suitable temperament, in readiness to fight and a capacity for impatience and anger, they suffered from diseases of arrogance—megalomania, delusions of grandeur, and abnormally aggressive behavior. Depressive states could have arisen among individuals losing caste and on the way down in hierarchies, manic states among individuals on the way up. Our current disorders may be reversions to such behavior under stress, reenactments of conflicts in prehistoric hierarchies.

There are two important things about this theory. In the first place, it is a theory thoroughly in line with and in spirit with recent research findings. It has an evolutionary perspective, takes account of what has been learned about primates, and is based as far as possible on direct observation in the wild and in the clinic. In the second place, it can be tested. If the theory is sound, patients should benefit from any measure which works against the formation of hierarchies, thus reducing rivalries among them.

According to Price, one measure might be a no-nonsense approach involving clearly specified and strictly enforced rules and regulations in mental wards: "The allocation of beds, places at meals, and ward chores . . . should be seen to be rigid, immutable and insusceptible to influence by any behavior on the part of the patients or their relatives. All social activities would be controlled by the staff, and no opportunity allowed for jockeying for position." He and his associates are planning to investigate the beneficial effects, if any, of this approach and others calculated to discourage competition and dominant or submissive behavior.

Another interesting development in research on mental illness comes from Christopher Brannigan of the Department of Psychiatry at the University of Birmingham in England and David Humphries of the University of Aston in Birmingham. They report an episode that occurred during a group therapy session. The group was discussing one patient's homosexuality when, at the uttering of the word "homosexual," another patient, Mr. X, responded with an involuntary gesture, a characteristic movement in which he placed his hand on the back of his neck.

The gesture was a message, and the British investigators were prepared to read it because they had conducted studies of child behavior. Their studies, like those described earlier in this chapter, were based on detailed observations of gestures and expressions—136 separate elements including forty-two hand-arm gestures, seventeen eyebrow patterns, seven types of smile, and so on. Mr. X's hand-to-neck gesture made sense in the context of this silent language and its special vocabulary.

Preschool children preparing for fights raise their hands to a ready-to-strike position, assuming a so-called beating posture. As they grow older, usually starting at about the age of five, they begin to modify this reaction, because they are learning other ways of settling disputes, mainly exchanging well-chosen words instead of blows. But often they are unable to prevent early patterns entirely. At the start of trouble the hand goes up by instinct, and then as controls take over, instead of moving forward for a blow, the hand retreats and hides as it were, ending up concealed at the back of the neck.

The gesture in childhood is a sign, a sign in disguise, something like a message written in code. It expresses hostility and feelings of being threatened and a readiness to fight if necessary, and is carried over into adult life. For Mr. X the word "homosexual" uttered in an open group discussion represented the threat of being discovered, and it came out later that he had strong homosexual tendencies.

So the child appears in the man—and the species appears in the child. The case of Mr. X is more than part of the history of an individual. It is also part of man's history, since the hand-to-neck gesture is a pattern developed in remote times when words were just becoming a serious alternative to violence. There are many other basic gestures of this kind, most of them yet to be interpreted with any degree of precision, and all of them making up the elements of an evolutionary sign language. The ability to read this language will advance our understanding not only of emotionally disturbed persons, but also the forces that shaped prehistoric man and made him vulnerable to new varieties of mental disease.

Prehistoric ways of life may be reflected in other behavior patterns, which as a rule are considered solely as abnormal states with no particular evolutionary significance. One recent study suggests that epilepsy or something very much like it may once have served a useful purpose in human survival, at least if one can judge by the results of certain animal research. Michael Chance, head of the University of Birmingham's Sub-Department of Ethology, who has conducted a special investigation of this condition in man and other species, points out that in many cases it can be better understood in terms of the prehistoric past.

For example, laboratory tests show that certain strains of deer mouse inherit a tendency to have violent epileptic seizures upon hearing sudden loud noises. The reaction is clear-cut, swift and dramatic. Typically an individual runs and crouches alternately;

lapses into a running "fit" during which it runs blind and collides with anything lying in its path; then attacks cage mates and inanimate objects, sinking its teeth in and holding on; and finally collapses, stopping dead in its tracks and going rigid all over. The entire reaction generally lasts only a minute or so.

This behavior appears to have nothing to do with survival mechanisms when observed among caged animals; investigators have usually dismissed it as the result of an undesirable mutation. But it makes more sense when one considers the behavior of deer mice in the wild. They do not make burrows. They live on the surface in sparsely wooded country where at any moment they may encounter a predator out in the open. Under such circumstances, chances for survival would be increased by a pattern of automatic flight, vicious fighting if flight fails, and if fighting fails freezing or playing dead. So epilepsy among hypersensitive deer mice, as well as among other animals, seems to be a hereditary and pathological form of normal defensive behavior.

The same principle may apply to human epilepsy. Early man also lived in open country with few places to hide, and had to develop a variety of flight tactics. There seems to be a connection between this behavior and an observation of sexual behavior. According to the Kinsey report, about one out of every six preadolescent boys and a small proportion of men occasionally have violent convulsions during or after orgasms, which may reflect the well-known and very ancient association of flight and aggression with sexual activities.

Also, certain forms of seizure may have acquired special importance by helping to control the flow of fuel to various parts of the body. Brain cells demand liberal supplies of oxygen, and suffer irreparable damage when supplies fall too low. The threat of such emergencies must have arisen frequently 2 million to 1 million years ago when the brain was expanding rapidly with the coming of *Homo erectus*. If so, epileptic attacks may have served a protective function by prostrating the body and increasing the flow of oxygen-rich blood to the brain.

In general, the more that is learned about human behavior, the more patterns seem to be rooted in prehistory. A growing concern with such problems is one of the reasons for the relatively generous if somewhat belated support of long-term primate research. In fact, some of the most prevalent notions about the underlying causes of human behavior, about human drives and impulses, might have been considerably different if such research had been carried out half a century or so ago. Robin Fox of Rutgers University points out that Freud recognized what most biologists and few psychoanalysts recognize today, namely, the importance of basing any theory about the origins of human behavior on the behavior of other primates.

Unfortunately, the best sources available to Freud were highly colored and unreliable. The only evidence he had during the early 1900's consisted of second- or third-hand tales about gorillas. Their basic social unit was supposed to include a single dominant male, a number of females whom he monopolized, and younger males continually trying to gain access to the females and continually being outfought. Using such material, Freud conceived of a "primal horde," the original human family made up of an all-powerful, jealous, and aggressive Jehovah-like father who maintained a harem and drove his sons out of the household when they became sexual rivals, thus providing the basis for Oedipus and Electra complexes.

Freud, like Darwin, was influenced by the puritanism of his times. His picture of the folks at home, as well as the stories upon which it was based, reflected the attitude that sexual passions, the root of all evil, were "animal" things inherited from devilish sub-human savages. The observations of Schaller and others do not support these notions. Gorilla bands usually contain more than one adult male; the head of the hierarchy may be completely unconcerned when other males copulate with receptive females, even males who have only recently joined the troop; and younger males are not driven off. Aggression of any sort is rare.

Human violence and conflicts cannot be foisted on less-advanced primates. On the other hand, tendencies that exist within primate troops bear on the nature of human problems, and Freud was apparently on the right track in directing attention to the adult male animal. The beginnings of a more intensive study along these lines are evident in the recent work of Lionel Tiger. As indicated in Chapter VII, his is an evolutionary and biological approach, and a very tough-minded approach, to the nature of all-male associations.

Many familiar observations acquire new significance when one begins to regard groups of men in a strictly behavioral context, in the same spirit which guides recent studies of children and wild primates. The basic fact which emerges is that men seek each other out and find pleasure in being together. They engage in a wide variety of activities from which women have long been excluded —war, the top councils of organized religion, finance and politics (all essentially male monopolies) to the tendency of men at parties to converse in groups away from the womenfolk.

According to Tiger, men are attracted to one another and the attraction is powerful and deep-rooted, as powerful and deep-rooted as that between men and women or between mothers and infants. He suggests that the very pleasure involved in all-male associations, particularly in sports and fighting, is an index to the intensity of the attraction: "An emotional current or perhaps an esthetic excitement adheres to manly militant strength which seems biologically equivalent to the sexual excitement between men and women." In this connection many ceremonies such as the circumcision rites of the Australian aborigines, initiations into fraternities and secret societies and, at a somewhat less ritualized and communal level, businessmen's luncheons may play a role in male-male relationships analogous to the role of courtship in male-female relationships.

Men are predisposed to associate with men, another way of saying that the tendency has a genetic basis and a long prehistory. It may have arisen very early in hominid evolution, at least judging by certain observations of wild chimpanzees. One of the most remarkable features of their remarkably relaxed and informal life in the trees is the spirit of camaraderie which prevails among top-ranking adult males. Even investigators trained to avoid easy comparisons between apes and human beings describe what they observe as "friendship."

The biggest and most powerful chimpanzees in a given territory seem to enjoy one another's company, and often travel about together in groups of half a dozen or more individuals. Such behavior probably arose out of necessity, and group action had an important selective value when it came to defending the troop in times of emergency. But eventually it may have come to serve some other function as well, perhaps helping to promote and maintain amicable social relations. In any case, the attraction of males for males continues in contemporary forests, even though dangers are few and chimpanzees have little to fear from predators.

As forest dwellers, the earliest hominids in the male line may have been very much like chimpanzees in their readiness to form close associations. Furthermore, developments during the subsequent course of evolution almost certainly worked in a positive way to reinforce the tendency. The existence of a home base where individuals met at the end of the day, a specific site to be protected and defended against all comers, certainly fostered feelings of solidarity among the defenders. Long hunting trips must have had a similar effect, particularly hunting trips that called for camping out overnight away from the home base in unfamiliar and uncertain territories.

Male-male bonds had to be strong, because opposing forces came into play. If the tensions of the human condition emerged in the shift from forests to savannas, as suggested in Chapter XIII, the shift affected males in particular. DeVore and others have observed that things may be anything but relaxed among highly organized primates of the savanna. Dominant male baboons, like male chimpanzees, associate with one another upon occasion. When trouble appears they come together to form a formidable wall between would-be predators and the rest of the troop; in peaceful times they are close at hand as part of the core group that includes females with infants.

Adult male baboons may act together, but they do not become friends. Most encounters involve mild but firm assertions, tensions and latent threats in which the dominant male expects and receives standard gestures of appeasement, almost as if he were deliberately reminding lower-ranking males of the way things are. There is little real warmth or affection, even among members of the central hierarchy or Establishment who may join forces to keep stronger individuals in subordinate roles. At best adult males tolerate one another with a cool and restrained politeness. They do not seek one another out.

Life in the open may have produced a similar tendency among forest-dwelling hominid males. When they moved into savannas on a full-time basis, their natural warmth must have been somewhat tempered by a guarded tension which, like that found among male baboons, involved elements of fear and aggression.

The savanna subjected them to a special strain, bringing threats from new predators and demanding a higher degree of alertness. One result may have been a divisive tendency: if trouble is sought and prepared for long enough, it may be found—if not from the outside, then within the ranks.

In all areas a realistic picture of human behavior is only beginning to emerge, and, as indicated in Chapter XII, nothing discovered to date is more remarkable than our long resistance to such studies. The resistance has been so intense and so effective that it must have been of special value to the species, serving some vital adaptive need. Perhaps it was a matter of survival for early man to feel supremely confident and all-powerful, most of all at times when the wilderness seemed most alien and daily routines most futile. Feelings of superiority are not easy to maintain in the face of too much self-knowledge.

In any case, if insight once threatened man's security, today ignorance is an even greater threat. More than 90 per cent of current knowledge about primate behavior has come during the past decade. New studies indicate how much remains to be discovered. Considering our biases, our deep-rooted tensions and instabilities, one can no longer be quite so confident about the future of man as was the fashion before our most recent world war. The new study of man starts off with a new realism. It avoids the unwholesome spirit that causes us to speak of black Americans as one-third middle class instead of two-thirds impoverished, that impels us to put rouge on the faces of corpses, and to suggest that the effects of atomic radiation be measured in "sunshine units."

On the other hand, man has an unprecedented capacity for adapting culturally, for passing on things that are not inherited. His brain is designed precisely to permit flexibility, learning, imagining and a certain amount of unlearning. It is at least conceivable that he may yet eliminate war and mass violence. His efforts to domesticate himself are only a few thousand years old, after some 15 million years of hominid life in the wild, and from that perspective man is often surprisingly civilized. For all its current popularity, naïve pessimism is as useless as naïve optimism.

■ The probability that species outside the solar system confront problems like man's; the symbiosis between man and computer; computers as devices that speed the pace of evolution; the interaction of man and environment, an experiment in violence; an urban environment to meet the need for close human contact; the limited value of hierarchies in the modern world; conditions promoting aggression in young people; the future of home and family

EPILOGUE

The Future of Man, an Ex-Hunter, in a World That Has No Place for Hunters

■ The problem of the future is whether there will be a future fit for human beings to live in. The question arises now after some fifteen million years of evolution in the hominid line, after the transformation of a clever ape into a creature with unprecedented and increasing powers to create and to destroy. The crisis man faces is the first of its kind on earth, the first involving the entire species. As the only remaining members of the family of man, we may or may not survive. The issue will almost certainly be decided within the next hundred years.

There will be a future if man can avoid nuclear warfare for that long. If he is sufficiently impressed by the sheer horror and impracticality of the "ultimate solution," he will probably survive to create and surmount other crises, and human evolution will probably continue for millions of years on earth and other planets. If he does not avoid nuclear warfare, he can expect extinction and not the swift and sudden "big bang" sort. Such an ending would amount to mercy killing, and we dare not count on that. It would probably be a slow process, the fading of a species that had lost will and purpose and the capacity for caring.

One's notions about what will actually take place must in the last analysis rest on a personal, essentially an esthetic, basis. No precedent exists for the human situation, that is, no known precedent. Looking at the problem from a wider point of view,

499

however, there is good reason to suspect that man is not the first species to find itself facing a similar crisis. The Milky Way is one of many islands or galaxies in the universe, a concentration of some hundred billion stars, and practically every one of them is a solar system complete with central sun and set of planets.

It would be a miracle if life had arisen only on the planet earth, if evolution were not taking place in billions of solar systems. There is good reason to believe that the universe contains planets in various stages of development—planets forever barren because conditions there are not right for life of any sort, planets so young (say, half a billion to a billion years old) that life has not yet appeared, planets with species just starting to make nuclear weapons and nuclear power plants. On slightly more advanced planets, species have recently formed stable world governments and are well on the way toward creating life in the laboratory, tapping unlimited sources of thermonuclear energy, establishing permanent settlements on other planets, communicating with crea- tures in other solar systems, and accomplishing other feats that man may yet accomplish. Planets also exist which have had their all-out nuclear wars and have passed out of the community of civilized worlds.

There are a great many possible universes, and this universe of evolution everywhere, survival of the fittest on a cosmic scale, may not be the real one. But it is a probable universe, sufficiently probable so that those convinced of the complete uniqueness of what is going on here must bear the burden of the argument. The notion that the human species will be among the survivors may turn out to be unduly optimistic, since there may be a tendency for new civilizations to destroy themselves. In that case, our consolation will have to be that others probably survived before us and will survive after us.

Assuming that man does not succeed in bringing about his own destruction, he will certainly be involved in changes more radical than any which have occurred in times past. And of all inventions the one that hints most strongly at the spirit of things to come is the large-scale electronic computer. This machine has the feel of the future about it, marking an area where evolutionary forces are active and change seems to be particularly intense. It repre- sents a taking-off point, a new direction in the human journey, and its effects promise to be as far-reaching and unpredictable as those of fire.

As a matter of fact, it is the fire story all over again, the sort of story that opens uneventfully, almost in a humdrum manner—and then, slowly at first and later at an accelerating pace, takes on the aspect of a major evolutionary adventure. The first electronic computer was not intended to blaze any trails, and was not regarded as a bold experiment. A development of World War II, it was designed primarily to do something that had been done ever since the invention of guns, to prepare ballistics tables indicating the trajectories of shells for different elevations, wind directions, and so on. Under peacetime conditions such tables had generally been produced by groups of mathematicians working at hand-operated desk calculators, but the war brought a serious shortage of mathematicians and the only alternative was to turn to automatic methods.

Today the computer has become far more than a device for the solution of routine problems. It permits investigators in all fields to deal with problems which would not even have been considered or conceived of in precomputer times, because they would have taken centuries to solve. It permits the doing of things that could never have been done, and thus helps promote basic changes in the nature of research and planning. A new man-machine relationship is in the process of being formed, a relationship amounting to a kind of organic union. Computers are strong where we are weak, and weak where we are strong.

The hunting-gathering life did not foster an ability to do arithmetic efficiently. Man is sloppy and inaccurate when it comes to working with large numbers and cannot even carry out a moderately difficult series of calculations without making a dozen or more errors. A large electronic computer, on the other hand, may operate for a month and perform billions of calculations before a defective part results in an error. Furthermore, man works slowly. It would take a mathematician two years to do what a computer does in a minute or so, or a millennium to do what a computer does in an eight-hour day. On the other hand, no machine can yet think creatively in the sense of dealing with novelty, recognizing and discovering and exploring new problems.

The symbiosis between man and computer takes on a special

significance from an evolutionary perspective. The computer serves as an accessory to the brain, a thinking aid built specifically to carry out operations which the brain cannot carry out by itself, logical as well as arithmetical operations. Man is inclined to view the world in terms of chains of events, to see things as cause-and-effect sequences, a phenomenon reflected in written sentences. Sentences, as formal items each starting with a capital letter and ending with a period, are symbols or models of "linear" approach.

This tendency is another example of living partly in the past. The world of modern man is by no means linear, but the world of his prehistoric ancestors was. Most tasks were one-man, one-material tasks like making scrapers, which involved four broad activities in a fixed order: finding a flattish flint nodule, trimming the edges, striking off flakes, and retouching the flakes. Setting a blade in a handle or a spear point in a shaft was somewhat more elaborate, involving more materials and more activities. But any hunter could readily carry out the entire task on his own.

Today's tasks reflect enormously more complicated lives. They require hundreds of materials, thousands of men and activities, hundreds of thousands of parts to be assembled. Furthermore, the essential relationships are not straightforward sequences where one activity leads to another in a simple way; there are lattices and networks and nests of intricately related activities. Activities A and B and C and D may be carried out simultaneously, activity E cannot be started until A and C are completed, F depends on the completion of B and D, G depends on F and A, and so on. Producing a new-model automobile or airplane, a space vehicle or a housing development may require tens of thousands of inter-dependent activities all of which must be coordinated in flow charts and master plans.

Such problems, problems featuring the interaction of a great many variables, are a sign of the times. They may be found every-where, not only in factories and on production lines but also in projects involving urban renewal, medical care, crime control and the administration of justice, economic opportunity, and education. The brain alone cannot handle them, but the combination of brain and computer can. The computer, programmed or instructed to apply special mathematical techniques to the analysis of complex systems, enables things to be seen whole. It happens that so far these techniques have been used widely to deal with business and military projects, and not so widely to deal with matter of public welfare. More attention seems to have been devoted to the mathematics of competition and warfare than to the mathematics of cooperative endeavors.

Computers have been developed to serve man, and their duties have been amply publicized. The most impressive are general-purpose machines which do anything they are "told" to do. At any time any one of them may be calculating payrolls or insurance premiums or the orbit of an artificial satellite, checking income-tax returns, simulating a flood or the evolution of a star, predicting election returns, or playing a tournament-level game of chess—depending on the set of instructions, the program, which investigators have prepared for it.

But the computer has already exceeded its role as servant. Upon occasion it may function as an electronic goad, a helpful and necessary and at the same time an upsetting thing which often seems to acquire an impetus of its own. It is not capable of creative thinking. But it forces people to think creatively, perhaps more creatively and precisely than they would if computers did not exist.

The history of the Japan Broadcasting Corporation provides one of the best examples of this effect. The corporation "let a computer into the house" a number of years ago, and the net effect has been a widespread reorganization. The first computer served as an aid to program planners, helping them to schedule shows and allocate studio space well ahead of time. Later, communications were speeded up when it was hooked to half a dozen terminals, including television-type screens on which schedules were displayed for immediate information or revisions. Success along these lines created a demand for still more ambitious plans to coordinate the activities of some 5,000 directors, engineers, and technicians concerned with producing shows—and these plans, in turn, demanded a special control center and other basic changes.

The company now has an entire system of computers, including some 200 terminals, and handles more than 1,800 programs on two television and three radio networks. The system is involved in everything from scheduling programs months in advance to putting programs on the air automatically a fraction of a second before broadcasting time. Among other things, this is the way to cut down on paper work and endless conferences and red tape of all sorts. The use of visual displays has eliminated more than 90 per cent of the 1,800 daily telephone calls and meetings and the 5,000 daily memoranda and reports formerly required to run the business.

This, the first company-wide computer system of its kind, provides a model for research and development in many areas. Organizations in the United States, the Soviet Union and other countries are at work on similar systems to handle their own routines, and it is only a matter of time until larger organizations, including entire industries and government agencies, will proceed along the same course. Computers will bring about radical structural and management changes at these levels as they have already done at the company level in Japan.

They will also bring about a widespread amplification of intelligence. A man at a computer terminal is in effect many times more intelligent than a man without a computer at his service. In colleges freshmen sitting at terminals located in classrooms, laboratories and dormitories are already solving easily problems far too difficult for seniors to solve in the days before computers, and the same increase in brain power will continue throughout life. The computer, one of the latest and most remarkable products of human evolution, permits individuals and groups to cope with new complexities of their own making. It is thus actively speeding the process of evolution.

Finally, and this could turn out to be the most significant effect of all, the computer may be used to increase the effectiveness of human adaptation. The brain evolved in times of great physical danger and little social change, but must now cope with times of little physical danger and great social change. Once it was appropriate that ideas and ways of doing things should endure for millennia. But the pace of contemporary developments suggests that the ability to unlearn swiftly is becoming at least as important as the ability to learn swiftly.

In such a context computers may serve as powerful weapons against the persistence of habit, the tendency of people to stay the same as the world changes. Electronic memories are erasable. They can be wiped clean at the flick of a switch and prepared for a fresh start. Computers do not become more and more biased as they age, a distinct advantage in solving new problems.

So all things, even man's most ingenious "thinking" machines, seem to be pushing him along, emphasizing the pace and the prevalence of change, the need to reorganize himself in transit as it were, on the run. He has yet to develop artificial environments as appropriate for contemporary populations as natural wilderness environments were for prehistoric hunters and gatherers. But that is his job, and a renewed search for such environments is under way. It is characterized by increasing efforts to understand people in groups, grownups as well as children, and to base the design of living and working places on observations of what they do and prefer.

A number of studies indicate the existence of biases that seem to hold for people in many cultures. For example, Dutch investigators find that visitors to parks and other public recreation areas tend to concentrate in transition zones where two different kinds of terrain merge, along seacoasts and the banks of rivers and the edges of forests. At the same time they naturally seek out locations providing some cover at their backs, a cliffside or a sand dune or a dense growth of trees, and in front of them expanses of open space.

This tendency is made up of many things. There is a feeling for freedom and privacy, a preference for shady spots, and a strong attraction to panoramas and unobstructed views of distant horizons. One thinks immediately of forest-dwelling hominids or prehominids venturing into the plains and ready to dash back into the trees—and later of bands of early hunters living in shelters and caves high on rocky ledges, relatively safe from predators and with a wide view of valleys and grazing animals. Such places offered beauty and security in a world where men were few and bands rarely came across one another.

Today beauty and security must be sought in man-made settings, practically all developed with other things than beauty and security in mind. Man moves about in environments which often promote tension and anxiety and conflict as effectively as if they had been designed for that very purpose. Not long ago a special conference was held in Washington, D.C., to consider "the office building as a current-day artifact in our society . . . not only

what an office building is but what it could be—what it should
be."

One discussion concerned the headquarters of the Central
Intelligence Agency, about as unattractively and unimaginatively
designed as most government buildings, only a bit more so, being
dominated by gray, narrow tunnel-like corridors 400 feet long
and a generally dismal décor to match. In such a "wasteland
environment" people tended to dress drably and be suspicious of
one another, and on at least one occasion fighting broke out in a
corridor. The simple expedient of painting walls and doors with
brighter colors produced a notable effect. Employees, female
employees in particular, soon began wearing more cheerful and
colorful clothing, and there was a marked improvement in
morale.

Another case cited at the conference concerned an unplanned
experiment in violence, a situation involving two school buildings
built at the same site for the same group of high-school students.
One building was designed according to the notion that young
people naturally tend to rip things apart. It incorporated so-called
maintenance-free construction consisting of "hard" spaces enclosed in massive bare walls which are easy to keep clean and
difficult to destroy. Vandalism was common in this building;
extensive repairs were required. The setting, like most institutional
settings, was alien to the student and represented an invitation to
trouble.

The other building was based on an entirely different notion of
human behavior, the notion that people respond positively to
places which they feel belong to them and which incorporate
some of the elements of a home setting. The building was designed
from the beginning with the needs of the students in mind. There
were carpets on the floor, as much for warmth as for appearance,
large windows and plenty of light and informal comfortable
spaces. Students have done very little damage here.

These examples come as no surprise to architects, who have long
been sensitive to the impact of environment on behavior and of
behavior on environment. They know how often people have
painted walls brighter colors, put in large picture windows, and
added extra wings in an effort to undo what has already been
done, to humanize the inhumanity built into structures. They also

know how much a creatively designed setting, a house or a housing development or a city, can help reduce tensions and contribute to a fulfilling life.

In fact, one of the most original preliminary designs for an urban environment grows directly out of a consideration of human needs and the causes of human anxiety. Christopher Alexander of the University of California at Berkeley starts from scratch with the notion of cities as meeting places and with the most elementary human need of all, the need for intimate contacts with other individuals. He defines an intimate contact as one in which people see one another very often, almost every day, not in offices or public places but under informal and private conditions.

Contacts of this sort were commoner in prehistoric times and in times not long past. Small farms and villages were commoner, and homesteads with large families made up of representatives of three or more generations. Contacts were closer then, although we should guard against becoming overnostalgic because in many cases the contacts were too close and people tended to be ingrown and conservative and to regard all outsiders and outside ideas as alien. But the modern city, for all the opportunities and variety it may offer, produces another form of alienation. Although people may accept or tolerate one another more readily, it is often distant and impersonal.

Alexander approaches the problem directly with a plan for a new kind of made-to-order city, including, within densely populated areas, zones designed to encourage certain living features once provided by village-farm settings. He cites psychiatric studies suggesting that mental illness is extra-likely to develop among persons with few intimate contacts or none at all, and that an individual needs at least three or four such contacts. The environment must be organized so that close friends can drop in on one another on the spur of the moment, which means that they should live no more than ten minutes apart. (In today's cities friends or, rather, potential friends usually live half an hour to an hour apart, enough to prevent casual dropping in.)

This general requirement leads to certain design requirements. Each house must be located on a through street for automobile traffic, the street being a thousand feet long at the most and connected with a major traffic artery at both ends. Each house must lie within a hundred yards of twenty-seven other houses, and have private bed-living rooms as well as a transparent communal room which opens on a private garden and can be looked into from the street. Also, the entire residential area must consist of uncluttered countryside and rolling hills.

In all, there are twelve requirements or "geometric considerations," and a residential area that meets them all consists of an artificial landscape, including hills constructed so that the highest and steepest may be nearest the theater-shopping-commercial center of the city, and the lowest and flattest hills furthest from the center. All roads and houses in the area are underground, providing unbroken expanses of countryside. Each house is located so that while its street-side entrance is buried, its garden-side entrance lies on a hill slope and is wide enough to let in daylight for communal and other rooms.

According to Alexander, planners starting with his objective, namely, to create an urban environment fulfilling our need for one another, will arrive at a design that may differ from this one in details but not in any fundamental way. He is also stressing something even more important, a principle that holds independent of this or that particular plan. Design is no cure-all; it cannot by itself solve problems of mental illness and violence. But it is not arbitrary either. It depends on and is determined to a large extent by human needs.

The fundamental concepts of urban design are bound up with what is known about those needs and will change as more is learned. For example, there are no carefully controlled studies to support the notion that every individual needs three or four intimate contacts or, as a matter of fact, to support most notions about the negative and positive aspects of living in large groups. Most knowledge about the effects of living and working spaces consists of impressions and anecdotes like those discussed at the Washington conference on office buildings.

Solid evidence can be obtained from research on behavior. Cities and communities designed today must take account of tendencies and biases shaped during the course of prehistory, a period representing more than 99 per cent of man's time on earth. Until recently this approach has received little more than lip service, partly because architects were preoccupied with other matters and partly because computers and other tools for the analysis of complexity were not widely available. The work of Alexander and others, however, indicates that the approach will play a larger role in planning and building of the future.

The problem is whether thinking and feeling can evolve accordingly, whether man can design institutions and philosophies as imaginatively as he designs machines and structures. There is certainly a need for new designs. Living in a hierarchy is often about as appropriate for modern times as living in a cave. In small savanna-dwelling bands including only a few adult males, the hierarchy was a most effective way of controlling aggression and maintaining order. Dominant individuals were always close at hand to curb fighting and, when necessary, to inflict punishment with a minimum of mayhem. Furthermore, during most of prehistory each band lived alone and isolated from other bands most of the time, so that conflicts among competing hierarchies were rare events.

Under certain circumstances the hierarchy is still an effective way of doing business. In fact, studies indicate that it is still by far the best way of organizing individuals to deal with situations involving firmly established rules and regulations, where procedures have already been spelled out to the letter and must simply be applied. It flourishes along with rituals and rote learning in settings dedicated to preserving traditions. But it is completely ineffective when, as frequently happens in a modern context, there are no precedents and the task is to discover new rules and patterns.

Current demands for dominant and submissive behavior often clash sharply with our purposes. In a troop of baboons, keeping the peace is a matter of establishing subhierarchies within a hierarchy. Males are ranked in order from the most to the least dominant, but as a rule the lowest-ranking male dominates the highest-ranking female, and naturally the subhierarchy of infants and juveniles is the lowest of all. Man is biased to organize things along similar lines, only with a few variations. For example, he tends to keep older and older individuals in the lowest-ranking subhierarchy, prolonging too long the already prolonged period of juvenile dependency. (Legally an infant is generally any individual less than twenty-one years old.)

It is difficult to conceive of a situation better calculated to promote aggression. In certain respects a traditional role of the school has been to serve as a social isolating or excluding mechanism, separating students as completely as possible from essential community activities. For many children the word "school" has acquired the same negative and thoroughly belittling connotations that the word "home" has acquired for many women, as a place where one is put to be kept busy and out of trouble. The practice of taking students outside the classroom to visit museums, laboratories, factories, courtrooms and so on may be a step forward, but not by itself. If that is all they do, if they only watch, visiting becomes a spectator sport and may heighten feelings of being excluded.

Meanwhile, at home as well as at school, they learn to want to rise in hierarchies. As far as reaching the upper levels within any large organization is concerned, however, most of them will never reach the top simply because there is not much room there. Only a limited number of high positions exists, and pressure from below increases steadily with increasing population. At the same time submissive behavior, the type of behavior traditionally expected from the vast majority of people, is not as widely accepted as it used to be. So to the extent that we instill in children the notion of dominance as a goal in life, we are educating them for frustration and defeat.

Other trends help aggravate the situation. As organizations become larger and more complicated, more education is needed to qualify for important positions. Young people must stay longer in school and away from places where the action is. As if that were not enough, there is a final aggravation. All along, as young people have had to wait longer and longer to participate in the world's work, sexual maturity has been coming at an earlier and earlier age. Records from many countries show that they are reaching puberty three to five years sooner today than they did a century ago, largely as a result of improved nutrition. Biological as well as social factors are heavily involved in student unrest.

A massive movement is under way in an effort to meet needs that have been ignored for decades. It is not yet coordinated, and its most spectacular developments to date have been student demonstrations and riots. But there are other developments designed to permit earlier and more constructive involvements, for example, so-called community service programs. Starting as early as the first or second year of high school, students are beginning to participate actively in local affairs by helping to take care of retarded and disturbed children, tutoring slow learners among grade-school students, joining conservation and civil-rights groups.

This is only an indication of what is coming. Only a few schools, less than one in a hundred, have organized such programs—and even there the tendency is to regard the programs as if they were somehow not really a major part of education, like gym or manual training or driving lessons. We are not quite ready to accept the notion that working in the community should be built into academic courses, that it can play the same sort of role in the humanities and social sciences that laboratory periods play in physics and biology. But everything points to an accelerating breakdown of the traditional discrimination against the young.

Similar changes are taking place in the home, and have been for some time. The infant is designed to learn many things fast, to reach out and cling and explore, to smile at the right faces at the right time, and later to talk and ask questions. It seeks love and security in the home, and the early relationships it establishes with its parents, particularly with its mother and particularly during its first few years, determine to a large extent its future capacity for affection and sharing.

This is as it has always been. What is changing is the relationship between home and community. As the human family evolves, it becomes less and less like anything observed in any other primate. Its ties are based more on the evolving needs of independent individuals than on strict rules of dominance and submission. The child is obtaining more of what it needs from the outside world, and obtaining it earlier. In line with preschool training programs, for example, educationally underprivileged children four and five years old are attending classes, and with such promising results that the practice is sure to be extended to all children.

The parent's role will also involve the outside world to a greater extent. The bond between mother and offspring may be as intense as it ever was but, at least after the period of infancy, it demands less and less of her time. This is the latest phase of a development that started perhaps a million or more years ago when the woman assumed major responsibility for gathering plant food, cooking, and keeping the home fires burning while the able-bodied men were out hunting. Her most important concern was still the infant, but it was not her only major concern as it is for the mother in a chimpanzee or baboon troop.

Today for the first time prolonged juvenile dependency need not mean prolonged maternal dependency. The increasing availability of outside services such as preschool training and day nurseries means that mothers can share on a larger scale responsibility for the care and education of their children. Furthermore, the attitude toward having children is changing and will have to continue to change. Overcrowding was once somewhere else, in slums and across oceans. Now it is here among us, to be seen in the dwindling of the wildernesses and villages, in traffic jams on Main Street, streams clogged with garbage, paper cups and beer cans left on river banks.

Under such conditions, and they can be expected to become much worse, birth control ranks with the control of aggression and nuclear weapons and pollution as a prerequisite for survival. Unlimited motherhood and unlimited fatherhood cannot be supported quite so wholeheartedly and without serious qualifications. We will be as proud of our children as ever, but considerably less proud of large families. So for many reasons women will have more time available earlier in their lives for activities outside the home, associating more with other adults and other people's children.

How will men, the ex-hunters among us, behave in such a setting? Even today, even during times of violence, there are still signs that all is not well with a number of the more violent manifestations of male-male bonding tendencies. In this connection man seems to be obtaining assistance from an unexpected quarter, from television and from engineers and technicians as well as directors and writers and performers. We can forgive television most of its offerings, and that is a lot to forgive, if it continues to show and show up some of the most archaic all-male activities.

Seeing is believing, and the eye of the television camera has a way of putting behavior in perspective. Prizefighting was an early victim of the cold, hard camera look, which showed people at large the things that a few people had been viewing all along—men being battered long past the point where they could offer any defense, rabbit punching and butting, and the passions of the fans themselves. Fights were "cleaned up" somewhat in response to public protests: referees stepped in sooner to stop the action when a fighter was obviously helpless. But prizefighting lost its appeal as regular television entertainment.

More recently, political conventions have received the camera treatment. Goings-on at the 1968 presidential conventions in Chicago and Miami exposed the nation and the world to some incredible demonstrations of violence and raw power. Some of the candidates felt the vulgarity at best and called for shorter speeches and more subdued demonstrations, rather like actors calling for less applause. There was a sense of national embarrassment at the events in Miami and Chicago, events hardly appropriate for the citizens of a world power in a time of crisis, and one has the feeling that conventions, like prizefighting, will never be the same again. And, finally, we cannot yet evaluate the long-range effects of television coverage on war. But we can hope.

It is not only research in the social sciences, in prehistory and primate behavior, which puts up a mirror to man. Many developments heighten self-consciousness and self-understanding, indicating more clearly the forces that tend to divide men and bring men together. Most of prehistory has been a record of small bands on the loose, the efforts of a minority species to survive in an alien and mysterious world. Most of history has been a record of a painful but steadily increasing inclusiveness, of letting more and more people into the club of first-class citizens, commoners as well as kings, nonwhites as well as whites, women and children, all minorities and pseudominorities. Human lib, if you will.

Human evolution proceeds, as it has during times past, in an atmosphere of uncertainty and adventure—just beginning to explore outer space, the final wilderness. Nothing in the record proves that man will become extinct, or that he will endure. Whatever our viewpoint, it is and will continue to be a matter of belief, an act of faith. We shall continue to behave as we are designed to behave, proceeding positively on the assumption that man represents not an ending but a beginning.

Bibliography

(The following is a personal bibliography in the sense that it includes primary sources only, publications of most direct use to me in developing the main ideas of this book. The publications themselves, of course, include bibliographies which the reader may consult for a fuller listing. The references for the Prologue are made up chiefly of general works about human evolution and prehistory, while those for subsequent chapters deal with specific studies.)

Prologue: Techniques and Prospects in the Search for Man

BATES, MARSTON, and HUMPHREY, PHILIP S., *The Darwin Reader,* New York: Scribner, 1956.

BEER, GAVIN DE, *Charles Darwin,* New York: Doubleday, 1965.

BORDES, FRANÇOIS, *The Old Stone Age,* New York: McGraw-Hill, 1968.

BRAIDWOOD, ROBERT J., *Prehistoric Men,* Glenview, Ill.: Scott, Foresman, 7th ed., 1967.

BUTZER, KARL W., *Environment and Archeology,* Chicago: Aldine Atherton, 2nd ed., 1971.

CAMPBELL, BERNARD G., *Human Evolution,* Chicago: Aldine, 1966.

CLARK, GRAHAME, *Archeology and Society,* New York: Barnes and Noble, 3rd ed., 1957.

CLARK, J. DESMOND, "Early Man In Africa," *Scientific American,* July, 1958.
———, *The Prehistory of Africa,* London: Thames and Hudson, 1970.

COUTTS, PETER, and HIGHAM, CHARLES, "The Seasonal Factor in Prehistoric New Zealand," *World Archaeology,* February, 1971.

DOBZHANSKY, THEODOSIUS, *Mankind Evolving,* New Haven: Yale, 1962.

GOLDING, WILLIAM, *The Inheritors,* New York: Harcourt, Brace and World, 1962.

GUMERMAN, GEORGE J., and LYONS, THOMAS R., "Archeological Methodology and Remote Sensing," *Science,* April 9, 1971.

HOWELL, F. CLARK, *Early Man,* New York: Time-Life Books, 2nd ed., 1971.

HOWELLS, WILLIAM, *Mankind in the Making,* New York: Doubleday, 1959.

KELSO, A. J., *Physical Anthropology,* Philadelphia: Lippincott, 1970.

LACK, D., *Darwin's Finches,* New York: Harper Torchbooks, 1961.

LEAKEY, L. S. B., *Adam's Ancestors,* New York: Harper & Row, 1960.

OAKLEY, KENNETH P., *Man the Tool-Maker,* Chicago: University of Chicago, 5th ed., 1961.

————, *Frameworks for Dating Fossil Man,* Chicago: Aldine, 1964.

OSBORN, HENRY FAIRFIELD, *Men of the Old Stone Age,* New York: Scribner, 3rd ed., 1925.

PFEIFFER, JOHN, "DNA," *Natural History,* December, 1960.

————, *The Search for Early Man,* New York: American Heritage, 1963.

————, "Man Through Time's Mists," *Saturday Evening Post,* December 3, 1966.

SIMPSON, GEORGE GAYLORD, *The Meaning of Evolution,* New Haven: Yale, 1949.

I. Primate Origins

EIMERL, SAREL, and DEVORE, IRVEN, *The Primates,* New York: Time-Life Books, 1965.

FOODEN, JACK, "Breakup of Pangaea and Isolation of Relict Mammals in Australia, South America, and Madagascar," *Science,* February 25, 1972.

KURTEN, BJÖRN, "Continental Drift and Evolution," *Scientific American,* March, 1969.

MARTIN, R. D., "Towards a New Definition of Primates," *Man,* September, 1968.

SIMONS, ELWYN L., "The Earliest Apes," *Scientific American,* December, 1967.

————, *Primate Evolution—an Introduction to Man's Place in Nature,* New York: Macmillan, 1972.

VAN VALEN, LEIGH, and SLOAN, ROBERT E., "The Earliest Primates," *Science,* November 5, 1965.

II. The First Members of the Family of Man

BARTHOLOMEW, GEORGE A., and BIRDSELL, JOSEPH B., "Ecology and the Protohominids," *American Anthropologist,* October, 1953.

CLARK, J. DESMOND, "Human Ecology During Pleistocene and Later Times in Africa South of the Sahara," *Current Anthropology,* July, 1960.

CURTIS, GARNISS, "A Clock for the Ages: Potassium-Argon," *National Geographic,* October, 1961.

ECKHARDT, ROBERT B., "Population Genetics and Human Origins," *Scientific American,* January, 1972.

GOODMAN, MORRIS, "Immunochemistry of the Primates and Primate Evolution," *Annals of the New York Academy of Sciences,* December 28, 1962.

HEWES, GORDON W., "Hominid Bipedalism: Independent Evidence for the Food-Carrying Theory," *Science*, October 16, 1964.

HOCKETT, CHARLES F., and ASCHER, ROBERT, "The Human Revolution," *Current Anthropology*, June, 1964.

HOWELL, F. CLARK, "Hominidae," *McGraw-Hill Yearbook of Science and Technology*, 1971.

JOLLY, CLIFFORD J., "The Seed-Eaters: A New Model of Hominid Differentiation Based on a Baboon Analogy," *Man*, March, 1970.

LAWICK-GOODALL, JANE VAN, *In the Shadow of Man*, Boston: Houghton Mifflin, 1971.

————, "My Life Among Wild Chimpanzees," *National Geographic*, August, 1963.

LEAKEY, L. S. B., "Adventures in the Search for Man," *National Geographic*, January, 1963.

————, "An Early Miocene Member of Hominidae," *Nature*, January 14, 1967.

PFEIFFER, JOHN E., "When Man First Stood Up," *New York Times Magazine*, April 11, 1965.

PILBEAM, DAVID, *The Ascent of Man*, New York: Macmillan, 1972.

————, *The Evolution of Man*, New York: Funk and Wagnalls, 1970.

————, "Man's Earliest Ancestors," *Science Journal*, February, 1967.

SARICH, V. M., "A Molecular Approach to the Question of Human Origins," in *Background for Man*, Boston: Little, Brown, 1971.

SIMONS, ELYWN L., "Some Fallacies in the Study of Hominid Phylogeny," *Science*, September 6, 1963.

————, "On the Mandible of *Ramapithecus*," *Proceedings of the National Academy of Sciences*, March, 1964.

————, "The Early Relatives of Man," *Scientific American*, July, 1964.

————, and ETTEL, PETER C., "Gigantopithecus," *Scientific American*, January, 1970.

SIMPSON, GEORGE GAYLORD, "The Biological Nature of Man," *Science*, April 22, 1966.

VERCORS, *You Shall Know Them*, Boston: Little, Brown, 1953.

WASHBURN, SHERWOOD L., *The Study of Human Evolution*, University of Oregon Press, 1968.

————, "Tools and Human Evolution," *Scientific American*, September, 1960.

————, and AVIS, VIRGINIA, "Evolution of Human Behavior," in *Behavior and Education*, New Haven: Yale, 1958.

III. "Southern Apes"—Links in the Evolution of Man

BRAIN, C. K., "New Finds at the Swartkrans Australopithecine Site," *Nature*, March 28, 1970.

CLARK, W. E. LE GROS, "The Importance of the Fossil Australopithecinae in the Study of Human Evolution," *Science Progress*, July, 1947.

DART, RAYMOND A., "*Australopithecus Africanus:* The Man-Ape of South Africa," *Nature*, February 7, 1925.

——, *Adventures with the Missing Link*, New York: Viking, 1961.

DEGENS, EGON T., and ROSS, DAVID A., "The Red Sea Hot Brines," *Scientific American*, April, 1970.

HEEZEN, BRUCE C., "The Rift in the Ocean Floor," *Scientific American*, October, 1960.

HOWELL, F. CLARK, "Omo Research Expedition," *Nature*, August 10, 1968.

HOWELLS, WILLIAM, *Mankind in the Making*, New York: Doubleday, 1959, Chap. 17, "Piltdown Man: His Rise and Fall."

ISAAC, GLYNN L., LEAKEY, RICHARD E. F., and BEHRENSMEYER, ANNA K., "Archaeological Traces of Early Hominid Activities, East of Lake Rudolf, Kenya," *Science*, September 17, 1971.

LAWICK-GOODALL, JANE VAN, "My Life Among Wild Chimpanzees," *National Geographic*, August, 1963.

——, *My Friends the Wild Chimpanzees*, Washington: National Geographic Society, 1967.

LEAKEY, R. E. F., *et al.*, "New Hominid Remains and Early Artefacts from Northern Kenya," *Nature*, April 18, 1970.

PATTERSON, BRYAN, BEHRENSMEYER, ANNA K., and SILL, WILLIAM D., "Geology and Fauna of a New Pliocene Locality in Northeastern Kenya," *Nature*, June 6, 1970.

——, and HOWELLS, W. W., "Hominid Humeral Fragment from Early Pleistocene of Northwestern Kenya," *Science*, April 7, 1967.

TAZIEFF, HAROUN, "The Afar Triangle," *Scientific American*, February, 1970.

IV. Fossils and Tools as Clues to Man's Beginnings*

COLE, SONIA, *The Prehistory of East Africa*, New York: Macmillan, 1963.

CONNOLLY, KEVIN, and ELLIOTT, JOHN, "The Evolution and Ontogeny of Hand Function," in *Ethological Studies of Child Behavior*, New York: Cambridge University Press, 1972.

HALL, K. R. L., "Variations in the Ecology of the Chacma Baboon, *Papio Ursinus*," *Symposia of the Zoological Society of London*, No. 10, 1963.

LEAKEY, L. S. B., "Olduvai Gorge," *Scientific American*, January, 1954.

——, "Finding the World's Earliest Man," *National Geographic*, September, 1960.

——, "Exploring 1,750,000 Years into Man's Past," *National Geographic*, October, 1961.

LEAKEY, MARY D., "A Review of the Oldowan Culture from Olduvai Gorge, Tanzania," *Nature*, April 30, 1966.

* A special 87-page section in the October, 1965, issue of *Current Anthropology* includes articles on the dating of finds at the Olduvai Gorge as well as on the finds themselves, together with comments from investigators throughout the world.

Napier, John, "Studies of the Hands of Living Primates," *Proceedings of the Zoological Society of London,* September, 1960.
———, "The Evolution of the Hand," *Scientific American,* December, 1962.
———, "The Antiquity of Human Walking," *Scientific American,* April, 1967.
Payne, Melvin M., "Family in Search of Prehistoric Man," *National Geographic,* February, 1965.
Pfeiffer, John E., "Dr. Leakey and His Olduvai Digs," *Think Magazine,* September, 1963.
Washburn, S. L., and DeVore, Irven, "The Social Life of Baboons," *Scientific American,* June, 1961.
Zihlman, Adrienne L., and Hunter, William S., "A Biomechanical Interpretation of the Pelvis of Australopithecus," *Folia Primatologica,* 1972.

V. Early Migrations of Man's Ancestors

Butzer, Karl W., *Environment and Archeology,* Chicago: Aldine Atherton, 2nd ed., 1971, Chap. 2.
Chard, Chester S., "Implications of Early Human Migrations from Africa to Europe," *Man,* August, 1963.
Howell, F. Clark, "Observations on the Earlier Phases of the European Lower Paleolithic," in *Recent Studies in Paleoanthropology,* American Anthropologist Special Publication, April, 1966.
Howells, William W., "Homo Erectus," *Scientific American,* November, 1966.
Ju-Kang, Woo, "The Skull of Lantian Man," *Current Anthropology,* February, 1966.
Shapiro, Harry, "The Strange Unfinished Saga of Peking Man," *Natural History,* November, 1971.
Washburn, S. L., and DeVore, Irven, "Social Behavior of Baboons and Early Man," in *Social Life of Early Man,* Chicago: Aldine, 1961.
Watanabe, Hitoshi, "Running, Creeping and Climbing: a New Ecological and Evolutionary Perspective on Human Locomotion," *Mankind,* June, 1971.

VI. The Rise of Big-Game Hunting and the Psychology of the Hunt

Bordes, François, *The Old Stone Age,* New York: McGraw-Hill, 1968; Chaps. 3 and 4.
Cole, Sonia, "A Spanish Camp of Stone Age Elephant Hunters," *New Scientist,* October 18, 1962.
DeVore, Irven, and Washburn, S. L., "Baboon Ecology and Human Behavior," in *African Ecology and Human Evolution,* Chicago: Aldine, 1963.

EDELMANN, CLAUDE, "Camping on the Riviera in 2,000,000 B.C.," *Réalités*, English ed., September, 1968.

HOWELL, F. CLARK, "Observations on the Earlier Phases of the European Lower Paleolithic" (Torralba-Ambrona), in *Recent Studies in Paleoanthropology*, American Anthropologist Special Publication, April, 1966, pp. 111–140.

ISAAC, GLYNN, "The Diet of Early Man: Aspects of Archaeological Evidence from Lower and Middle Pleistocene Sites in Africa," *World Archaeology*, February, 1971.

———, "Studies of Early Culture in East Africa," *World Archaeology*, June, 1969.

MOVIUS, H. L., "The Lower Paleolithic Cultures of Southern and Eastern Asia," *Transactions of the American Philosophical Society* (New Series), Vol. 38, Part 4, 1948.

OAKLEY, KENNETH P., *Man the Tool-Maker*, Chicago: University of Chicago, 5th ed., 1961, pp. 39–70.

———, *Frameworks for Dating Fossil Man*, Chicago: Aldine, 1964, pp. 217–240.

PFEIFFER, JOHN, "Man the Hunter," *Horizon*, Spring, 1971.

SCHALLER, GEORGE B., and LOWTHER, GORDON R., "The Relevance of Carnivore Behavior to the Study of Early Hominids," *Southwestern Journal of Anthropology*, Winter, 1969.

SOLHEIM, WILHELM G., "Southeast Asia and the West," *Science*, August 25, 1967.

VII. The Impact of Big-Game Hunting on Human Evolution

CAMPBELL, BERNARD G., *Human Evolution*, Chicago: Aldine, 1966, Chap. 9.

CRAIK, K. J. W., *The Nature of Explanation*, Cambridge: Cambridge University Press, 1952.

EISELEY, LOREN C., "Man the Fire-Maker," *Scientific American*, September, 1954.

FOX, ROBIN, "The Evolution of Human Sexual Behavior," *New York Times Magazine*, March 24, 1968.

———, "Sexual Selection and the Evolution of Human Kinship Systems," in *Sexual Selection and the Descent of Man*, Chicago: Aldine Atherton, 1972.

LASHLEY, K. S., "Persistent Problems in the Evolution of Mind," *Quarterly Review of Biology*, March, 1949.

LAWICK-GOODALL, JANE VAN, *In the Shadow of Man*, Boston: Houghton Mifflin, 1971.

———, *My Friends the Wild Chimpanzees*, Washington: National Geographic Society, 1967.

MACLEAN, PAUL D., "New Findings Relevant to the Evolution of Psychosexual Functions of the Brain," *Journal of Nervous and Mental Disease*, October, 1962.

MANN, ALAN, "*Australopithecus* and Its Behavior," paper presented at annual meeting of the American Association for the Advancement of Science, Philadelphia, December, 1971.

OAKLEY, KENNETH P., "Fire as Palaeolithic Tool and Weapon," *Proceedings of the Prehistoric Society,* Vol. XXI, 1955.

PFEIFFER, JOHN E., *The Human Brain,* New York: Harper, 1955, Chaps. 2 and 3.

——, "When Homo Erectus Tamed Fire He Tamed Himself," *New York Times Magazine,* December 11, 1966.

REYNOLDS, V., "Open Groups in Hominid Evolution," *Man,* December, 1966.

THOMAS, ELIZABETH MARSHALL, *The Harmless People,* New York: Knopf, 1959.

TIGER, LIONEL, and FOX, ROBIN, *The Imperial Animal,* New York: Holt, Rinehart and Winston, 1971.

TRIVERS, ROBERT L., "The Evolution of Reciprocal Altruism," *Quarterly Review of Biology,* March, 1971.

YOUNG, J. Z., "The Organization of a Memory System," *Proceedings of the Royal Society,* Vol. 163B, November 23, 1965.

VIII. The Search for Remains of the Earliest Modern-Type Men

CAMPBELL, BERNARD, "The Centenary of Neanderthal Man: Part I," *Man,* November, 1956.

——, "The Centenary of Neanderthal Man: Part II," *Man,* December, 1956.

——, "Quantitative Taxonomy," in *Classification and Human Evolution,* Chicago: Aldine, 1963.

HOWELL, F. CLARK, "The Evolutionary Significance of Variation and Varieties of 'Neanderthal' Man," *Quarterly Review of Biology,* December, 1957.

HOWELLS, WILLIAM, *Mankind in the Making,* New York: Doubleday, 1959, Chaps. 13 and 15.

SOLECKI, RALPH S., "Neanderthal Is Not an Epithet but a Worthy Ancestor," *Smithsonian,* May, 1971.

——, "Shanidar Cave," *Scientific American,* November, 1957.

——, *Shanidar—The First Flower People,* New York: Knopf, 1971.

STRAUS, WILLIAM L., and CAVE, A. J. E., "Pathology and the Posture of Neanderthal Man," *Quarterly Review of Biology,* December, 1957.

SULLIVAN, WALTER, "200,000-Year-Old Skull of Man Is Found," *New York Times,* October 13, 1971.

IX. Developments in the Scientific Study of Neanderthal Man

BANFIELD, A. W. F., "Migratory Caribou," *Natural History,* May, 1961.

BINFORD, LEWIS R., *An Archeological Perspective,* New York: Seminar Press, 1972.

——, and SALLY R., "A Preliminary Analysis of Functional Variability in the Mousterian of Levallois Facies," in *Recent Studies in Paleoanthropology*, American Anthropologist Special Publication, April, 1966.

BINFORD, SALLY R. and LEWIS R., "Stone Tools and Human Behavior," *Scientific American*, April, 1967.

BORDES, FRANÇOIS, "Mousterian Cultures in France," *Science*, September 22, 1961.

———, *A Tale of Two Caves*, New York: Harper & Row, 1972.

HOWELL, F. CLARK, "Isimila: A Paleolithic Site in Africa," *Scientific American*, October, 1961.

KELSALL, J. P., *The Caribou*, Ottawa: Canadian Wildlife Service, 1968.

KLEIN, RICHARD G., "The Mousterian of European Russia," *Proceedings of the Prehistoric Society*, Vol. XXV, 1969.

PFEIFFER, JOHN E., *The Search for Early Man*, New York: American Heritage, 1963, Chaps. I and IV.

X. The Disappearance of Neanderthal Man, the Appearance of Modern Man

BAKER, JOHN R., "Cro-Magnon Man, 1868–1968," *Endeavour*, May, 1968.

BINFORD, LEWIS R., "Post-Pleistocene Adaptations," in *New Perspectives in Archeology*, Chicago: Aldine, 1968.

BINFORD, SALLY R., "Early Upper Pleistocene Adaptations in the Levant," *American Anthropologist*, August, 1968.

———, "Late Middle Paleolithic Adaptations and Their Possible Consequences," *Bioscience*, March 1, 1970.

BRACE, C. LORING, "The Fate of the 'Classic' Neanderthals: A Consideration of Hominid Catastrophism," *Current Anthropology*, February, 1964.

BROTHWELL, DON, "Where and When Did Man Become Wise?" *Discovery*, June, 1963.

CORRUCCINI, ROBERT S., "A Numerical Taxonomy of Some Fossil Hominids," *Student Anthropologist*, Vol. 3, No. 2, 1971.

FREEMAN, L. G., and ECHEGARAY, J. GONZALEZ, "Aurignacian Structural Features and Burials at Cueva Morin (Santander, Spain)," *Nature*, May 23, 1970.

GARROD, DOROTHY A. E., "The Relations Between Southwest Asia and Europe in the Later Paleolithic Age," *Journal of World History*, July, 1953.

HOWELL, F. CLARK, "Upper Pleistocene Stratigraphy and Early Man in the Levant," *Proceedings of the American Philosophical Society*, Vol. 103, 1959.

MONGAIT, A. L., *Archaeology in the U.S.S.R.*, Baltimore: Penguin, 1961.

MULVANEY, D. J., "Prehistory from Antipodean Perspectives," *Proceedings of the Prehistoric Society*, Vol. XXXVII, Part II, December, 1971.

PERICOT-GARCIA, L., "A New Site with the Remarkable Parpallo-Type Solutrean Points," *Current Anthropology*, October, 1961.

PFEIFFER, JOHN, "Man the Hunter," *Horizon*, Spring, 1971.

————, *The Search for Early Man,* New York: American Heritage, 1963, Chap. VI.

SACKETT, JAMES R., "Method and Theory of Upper Paleolithic Archeology in Southwestern France," in *New Perspectives in Archeology,* Chicago: Aldine, 1968.

SMITH, PHILIP E. L., "The Solutrean Culture," *Scientific American,* August, 1964.

————, "Solutrean Origins and the Question of Eastern Diffusion," *Arctic Anthropology,* Vol. 1, No. 1, 1962.

SONNEVILLE-BORDES, DENISE DE, "Upper Paleolithic Cultures in Western Europe," *Sicence,* October 18, 1963.

WHITMORE, FRANK C., *et al.,* "Elephant Teeth from the Atlantic Continental Shelf," *Science,* June 16, 1967.

WORMINGTON, H. M., *Ancient Man in America,* Denver Museum of Natural History, 4th ed., 1957.

XI. The Golden Age of Prehistory

BAUMANN, HANS, *The Caves of the Great Hunters,* New York: Pantheon, 1954.

BORDES, FRANÇOIS, "Physical Evolution and Technological Evolution in Man: A Parallelism," *World Archaeology,* June, 1971.

BRODRICK, A. H., *Father of Prehistory,* New York: Morrow, 1963.

COLLINS, DESMOND, "Prehistoric Art," *Discovery,* May, 1965.

FLANNERY, KENT V., "The Ecology of Early Food Production in Mesopotamia," *Science,* March 12, 1965.

————, *et al.,* "Farming Systems and Political Growth in Ancient Oaxaca," *Science,* October 27, 1967.

GIEDION, S., *The Beginnings of Art,* New York: Pantheon, 1962.

GRAZIOSI, PAOLO, *Palaeolithic Art,* New York: McGraw-Hill, 1960.

HARLAN, JACK R., and ZOHARY, DANIEL, "Distribution of Wild Wheats and Barley," *Science,* September 2, 1966.

HARRIS, DAVID R., "New Light on Plant Domestication and the Origins of Agriculture," *Geographical Review,* January, 1967.

HOLE, FRANK, and FLANNERY, KENT V., "The Prehistory of Southwestern Iran: A Preliminary Report," *Proceedings of the Prehistoric Society,* Vol. XXXIII, 1967.

KUHN, HERBERT, *On the Track of Prehistoric Man,* New York: Random House, 1961.

LAMING, ANNETTE, *Lascaux,* Baltimore: Penguin, 1959.

LEROI-GOURHAN, ANDRÉ, "The Evolution of Paleolithic Art," *Scientific American,* February, 1968.

MARSHACK, ALEXANDER, "Lunar Notation on Upper Paleolithic Remains," *Science,* November 6, 1964.

————, *The Roots of Civilization,* New York: McGraw-Hill, 1972.

PFEIFFER, JOHN E., "Man's First Revolution," *Horizon,* September, 1962.

SIEVEKING, ANN and GALE, *The Caves of France and Northern Spain,* London: Longacre, 1962.

UCKO, PETER, and ROSENFELD, ANDRÉE, *Paleolithic Cave Art,* London: Weidenfeld and Nicolson, 1967.

XII. Primate Studies and Revised Beliefs About Animal Behavior

DEVORE, IRVEN, "Mother-Infant Relations in Free-Ranging Baboons," in *Maternal Behavior in Mammals,* New York: Wiley, 1963.

————, and HALL, K. R. L., "Baboon Ecology," in *Primate Behavior,* New York: Holt, Rinehart and Winston, 1965.

DENHAM, WOODROW W., "Energy Relations and Some Basic Properties of Primate Social Organization," *American Anthropologist,* February, 1971.

EISENBERG, JOHN F., "The Social Organization of Mammals," *Handbuch der Zoologie,* Vol. 10 (7), 1965.

HALL, K. R. L., and DEVORE, IRVEN, "Baboon Social Behavior," in *Primate Behavior,* New York: Holt, Rinehart and Winston, 1965.

RUSSELL, W. M. S., "The Wild Ones," *The Listener,* November 5, 1964.

WASHBURN, S. L., "Behavior and the Origin of Man," *Rockefeller University Review,* January-February, 1968.

————, *et al.,* "Field Studies of Old World Monkeys and Apes," *Science,* December 17, 1965.

XIII. Chimpanzees: Man's Closest Relatives

CHANCE, M. R. A., "Kohler's Apes—How Did They Perform?" *Man,* September, 1960.

HALLOWELL, A. IRVING, "Behavioral Evolution and the Emergence of the Self," in *Evolution After Darwin,* Chicago: University of Chicago Press, 1960.

ITANI, JUNICHIRO, and SUZUKI, AKIRA, "The Social Unit of Chimpanzees," *Primates,* Vol. 8, 1967, pp. 355–81.

KORTLANDT, ADRIAAN, "Chimpanzees in the Wild," *Scientific American,* May, 1962.

KOYAMA, NAOKI, "Changes in Dominance Rank and Division of a Wild Monkey Troop in Arashiyama," *Primates,* December, 1970.

LAWICK-GOODALL, JANE VAN, *In the Shadow of Man,* Boston: Houghton Mifflin, 1971.

————, "Mother-Offspring Relationships in Free-Ranging Chimpanzees," in *Primate Ethology,* Chicago: Aldine, 1967.

————, *My Friends the Wild Chimpanzees,* Washington: National Geographic Society, 1967.

————, "My Life Among Wild Chimpanzees," *National Geographic,* August, 1963.

———, "New Discoveries Among Africa's Chimpanzees," *National Geographic,* December, 1965.

Missakian, Elizabeth A., "Genealogical Mating Activity in Free-Ranging Groups of Rhesus Monkeys (*Macaca Mulatta*) on Cayo Santiago," in press.

Pfeiffer, John E., "The Apish Origins of Human Tension," *Harper's Magazine,* July, 1963.

Reynolds, Vernon, "Chimpanzees of the Budongo Forest," in *Primate Behavior,* New York: Holt, Rinehart and Winston, 1965.

———, "Kinship and the Family in Monkeys, Apes and Man," *Man,* June, 1968.

———, "The 'Man of the Woods,' " *Natural History,* January, 1964.

Rowell, T. E., "Forest-Living Baboons in Uganda," *Journal of Zoology* (London), Vol. 149, 1966, pp. 344–364.

———, "A Quantitative Comparison of the Behavior of a Wild and a Caged Baboon Group," *Animal Behavior,* October, 1967.

———, "Variability in the Social Organization of Primates," in *Primate Ethology,* Chicago: Aldine, 1967.

Sade, Donald Stone, "Determinants of Dominance in a Group of Free-Ranging Monkeys," in *Social Communication Among Primates,* Chicago: University of Chicago Press, 1967.

XIV. Observation and Experimentation with Living Primates and Carnivores

Altmann, Stuart A., "Sociobiology of Rhesus Monkeys. II: Stochastics of Social Communication," *Journal of Theoretical Biology,* Vol. 8, No. 3, 1965.

Estes, Richard D., "Predators and Scavengers," *Natural History,* February and March, 1967.

———, and Goddard, John, "Prey Selection and Hunting Behavior of the African Wild Dog," *Journal of Wildlife Management,* January, 1967.

Fox, M. W. "A Comparative Study of the Development of Facial Expressions in Canids; Wolf, Coyote and Foxes," *Behaviour,* Vol. 36, 1970, pp. 49–73.

———, "Socio-Ecological Implications of Individual Differences in Wolf Litters: A Developmental and Evolutionary Perspective," in press.

Gallup, Gordon G., Jr., "Chimpanzees: Self-Recognition," *Science,* January 2, 1970.

———, "Chimps and Self-Concept," *Psychology Today,* March, 1971.

Harlow, Harry F. and Margaret K., "Social Deprivation in Monkeys," *Scientific American,* November, 1962.

Harlow, Harry F. and Suomi, Stephen J., "Social Recovery by Isolation-Reared Monkeys," *Proceedings of the National Academy of Sciences,* July, 1971.

HARLOW, HARRY, and ZIMMERMANN, ROBERT R., "Affectional Responses in the Infant Monkey," *Science*, August, 1959.

HARLOW, M. K. and H. F., "Affection in Primates," *Discovery*, January, 1966.

HINDE, R. A., "Rhesus Monkey Aunts," in *Determinants of Infant Behavior*, Vol. III, New York: Wiley, 1965.

————, ROWELL, T. E., and SPENCER-BOOTH, Y., "Behaviour of Socially Living Rhesus Monkeys in Their First Six Months," *Proceedings of the Zoological Society of London*, Vol. 143, Part 4, 1964.

————, "Effects of Brief Separation from Mothers on Rhesus Monkeys," *Science*, July 9, 1971.

————, "The Study of Mother-Infant Interaction in Captive Group-Living Rhesus Monkeys," *Proceedings of the Royal Society*, B, Vol. 169, 1968.

KÜHME, WOLFDIETRICH, "Communal Food Distribution and Division of Labor in African Hunting Dogs," *Nature*, January 30, 1965.

SCHALLER, GEORGE B., *The Deer and the Tiger*, Chicago: University of Chicago Press, 1967.

————, *Serengeti—A Kingdom of Predators*, New York: Knopf, 1972.

————, *The Serengeti Lion*, Chicago: University of Chicago Press, 1972.

————, "The Tiger and Its Prey," *Natural History*, October, 1966.

SHANNON, CLAUDE E., and WEAVER, WARREN, *The Mathematical Theory of Communication*, Urbana: University of Illinois, 1949.

XV. Contemporary Hunter-Gatherers: Last Representatives of the Stone Age

ELKIN, A. D., *The Australian Aborigines*, New York: Doubleday, 1964.

GOULD, R. A., "The Archaeologist as Ethnographer: A Case from the Western Desert of Australia," *World Archaeology*, October, 1971.

————, "Chipping Stones in the Outback," *Natural History*, February, 1968.

————, "Living Archeology: The Ngatatjara of Western Australia," *Southwestern Journal of Anthropology*, Summer, 1968.

————, "Notes on Hunting, Butchering, and Sharing of Game Among the Ngatatjara and Their Neighbors in the West Australian Desert," *Kroeber Anthropological Society Papers*, No. 36, Spring, 1967.

————, *Yiwara: Foragers of the Australian Desert*, New York: Scribner, 1969.

JONES, RHYS, "The Demography of Hunters and Farmers in Tasmania," in *Aboriginal Man and Environment in Australia*, Canberra: Australian National University Press, 1971.

MULVANEY, D. J., "The Prehistory of the Australian Aborigine," *Scientific American*, March, 1966.

STREHLOW, T. G. H., *Aranda Traditions*, Melbourne: Melbourne University, 1947.

————, "Culture, Social Structure, and Environment in Aboriginal Central Australia," in *Aboriginal Man in Australia*, Sydney: Angus and Robertson, 1965.

WHITE, CARMEL, and PETERSON, NICOLAS, "Ethnographic Interpretations of the Prehistory of Western Arnhem Land," *Southwestern Journal of Anthropology*, Spring, 1969.

XVI. The Behavior of Primitive Peoples

BIRDSELL, JOSEPH B., "Some Environmental and Cultural Factors Influencing the Structuring of Australian Aboriginal Populations," *American Naturalist*, Supplement, May–June, 1953.

————, "Some Population Problems Involving Pleistocene Man," *Cold Spring Harbor Symposia on Quantitative Biology*, Vol. XXII, 1957.

————, "On Population Structure in Generalized Hunting and Collecting Populations," *Evolution*, June, 1958.

HEINE-GELDERN, ROBERT, "Vanishing Cultures," *Scientific American*, May, 1957.

HELM, JUNE, and LEACOCK, ELEANOR BURKE, "The Hunting Tribes of Subarctic Canada," in *North American Indians in Historical Perspective*, New York: Random House, 1971.

LEE, RICHARD B., "Subsistence Ecology of !Kung Bushmen," Ph.D. dissertation, University of California, Berkeley, 1965.

————, "Trance Cure of the !Kung Bushmen," *Natural History*, November, 1967.

————, and DEVORE, IRVEN (eds.), *Man the Hunter*, Chicago: Aldine, 1968.

MURDOCK, GEORGE P., personal communication to the author, December 20, 1967.

PFEIFFER, ANTHONY J., "A Cultural, Ecological View of Some Aspects of Pygmy Life," unpublished manuscript, 1972.

SERVICE, ELMAN R., *Primitive Social Organization*, New York: Random House, 1962.

THOMAS, ELIZABETH MARSHALL, *The Harmless People*, New York: Knopf, 1959.

WATANABE, HITOSHI, "The Ainu," *Journal of the Faculty of Science, University of Tokyo*, July 30, 1964.

XVII. Experimental Archeology

CHILCOTT, JOHN H., and DEETZ, JAMES J., "The Construction and Uses of a Laboratory Archeological Site," *American Antiquity*, January, 1964.

CRABTREE, DON E., "A Stoneworker's Approach to Analyzing and Replicating the Lindenmeier Folsom," *Tebiwa, the Journal of the Idaho State University Museum*, Vol. 9, No. 1, 1966.

————, "Notes on Experiments in Flintknapping," *Tebiwa, the Journal of the Idaho State University Museum*, Vol. 10, No. 1, 1967.

———, and BUTCHER, B. ROBERT, "Notes on Experiments in Flintknapping," *Tebiwa, the Journal of the Idaho State University Museum,* Vol. 7, No. 1, 1964.

———, and DAVIS, E. L., "Experimental Manufacture of Wooden Implements with Tools of Flaked Stone," *Science,* January 26, 1968.

GOULD, RICHARD A., KOSTER, DOROTHY A., and SONTZ, ANN H. L., "The Lithic Assemblage of the Western Desert Aborigines of Australia," *American Antiquity,* April, 1971.

HARLAN, JACK R., "A Wild Wheat Harvest in Turkey," *Archaeology,* June, 1967.

ISAAC, GLYNN, "The Diet of Early Man: Aspects of Archaeological Evidence from Lower and Middle Pleistocene Sites in Africa," *World Archaeology,* February, 1971.

JEWELL, P. A., "An Experiment in Field Archaeology," *Advancement of Science,* May, 1961.

PFEIFFER, JOHN E., "Dr. Leakey and His Olduvai Digs," *Think Magazine,* September, 1963.

SEMENOV, S. A., *Prehistoric Technology,* London: Cory, Adams and MacKay, 1964.

SWANSON, EARL H., "An Introduction to Crabtree's Experiments in Flintknapping," *Tebiwa, the Journal of the Idaho State University Museum,* Vol. 9, No. 1, 1966.

WITTHOFT, JOHN, "The Art of Flint Chipping," *Ohio Archeologist,* October, 1956–July, 1957.

XVIII. The Human Infant: A Study in Living Prehistory

AINSWORTH, MARY D., "Patterns of Attachment Behavior Shown by the Infant in Interaction with His Mother," *Merrill-Palmer Quarterly of Behavior and Development,* Vol. 10, No. 1, 1964.

———, *Infancy in Uganda,* Baltimore: Johns Hopkins, 1967.

———, BELL, SYLVIA M., and STAYTON, DONELDA J., "Individual Differences in the Development of Some Attachment Behaviors," *Merrill-Palmer Quarterly.*

———, and WITTIG, BARBARA A., "Attachment and Exploratory Behavior of One-Year-Olds in a Strange Situation," in *Determinants of Infant Behavior,* Vol. IV, New York: Wiley, 1968.

ALTMANN, STUART A., "Primate Social Signals," in *Animal Communication: Techniques of Study and Results of Research,* Bloomington: Indiana University, 1968.

ANDREW, R. J., "Evolution of Facial Expression," *Science,* November 22, 1963.

———, "The Origin and Evolution of the Calls and Facial Expressions of the Primates," *Behaviour,* Vol. XX, 1963.

———, "The Origins of Facial Expressions," *Scientific American*, October, 1965.

BEACH, FRANK A., and JAYNES, JULIAN, "Effects of Early Experience upon the Behavior of Animals," *Psychological Bulletin*, May, 1954.

BLURTON, JONES, N., "Comparative Aspects of Mother-Child Contact," in *Ethological Studies of Child Behavior*, New York: Cambridge University Press, 1972.

BOWLBY, JOHN, "An Ethological Approach to Research in Child Development," *British Journal of Medical Psychology*, Vol. XXX, Part 4, 1957.

———, "The Nature of the Child's Tie to His Mother," *International Journal of Psychoanalysis*, Vol. XXXIX, Part V, 1958.

———, "Ethology and the Development of Object Relations," *International Journal of Psychoanalysis*, Vol. XLI, Parts IV and V, 1960.

FREEDMAN, D. G. and NINA CHINN, "Behavioral Differences Between Chinese-American and European-American Newborns," *Nature*, December 20, 1969, p. 1227.

KAGAN, JEROME, "Do Infants Think?" *Scientific American*, March, 1972.

LETTVIN, J. E., *et al.*, "What the Frog's Eye Tells the Frog's Brain," *Proceedings of the Institute of Radio Engineers*, November, 1959.

PFEIFFER, JOHN E., "Vision in Frogs," *Natural History*, November, 1962.

PFEIFFER, TONY, "Some References to the Study of Human Ethology," *Man-Environment Systems*, May and September, 1971 (Published by the Association for the Study of Man-Environment Relationships, Box 57, Orangeburg, N.Y. 10962).

XIX. The Evolution of Language

ANDREW, R. J., "Evolution of Intelligence and Vocal Mimicking," *Science*, August 24, 1962.

BELLUGI, URSULA, and BROWN, ROGER, "The Acquisition of Language," *Monographs of the Society for Research in Child Development*, Vol. 29, No. 1, 1964.

BORDES, FRANÇOIS, "Physical Evolution and Technological Evolution in Man: A Parallelism," *World Archaeology*, June, 1971.

GARDNER, BEATRICE T. and R. ALLEN, "Two-Way Communication with an Infant Chimpanzee," in *Behavior of Nonhuman Primates*, New York: Academic Press, 1971.

GARDNER, R. ALLEN and BEATRICE T., "Teaching Sign Language to a Chimpanzee," *Science*, August 15, 1969.

GESCHWIND, NORMAN, "The Development of the Brain and the Evolution of Language," *Monograph Series of Languages and Linguistics*, No. 17, April, 1964.

GREENBERG, JOSEPH H., "Language Universals," in *Current Trends in Linguistics*, The Hague: Mouton, 1966.

HALDANE, J. B. S., "Animal Communication and the Origin of Language," *Science Progress*, Vol. 23, 1955.

HAYES, C., *The Ape in Our House,* New York: Harper, 1951.

HEWES, GORDON W., "Language Origins: A Bibliography," Boulder: Department of Anthropology, University of Colorado, 1971.

HOCKETT, CHARLES F., "The Origin of Speech," *Scientific American,* September, 1960.

——, "Comments on 'Current Trends in Linguistics,'" *Current Anthropology,* April–June, 1968.

——, and ASCHER, ROBERT, "The Human Revolution," *Current Anthropology,* June, 1964.

KELLOGG, WINTHROP N., "Communication and Language in the Home-Raised Chimpanzee," *Science,* October 25, 1968.

KEYSER, SAMUEL J., "Our Manner of Speaking," *Technology Review,* February, 1964.

LANCASTER, JANE B., "Primate Communication Systems and the Emergence of Human Language," in *Primates: Studies in Adaptation and Variability,* New York: Holt, Rinehart and Winston, 1968.

LENNEBERG, ERIC H., *Biological Foundations of Language,* New York: Wiley, 1967.

——, "The Biological Foundations of Language," *Hospital Practice,* December, 1967.

MACDONALD, CRITCHLEY, "The Evolution of Man's Capacity for Language," in *Evolution After Darwin,* Vol. 2, Chicago: University of Chicago, 1960.

——, "The Nature of Animal Communication and Its Relation to Language in Man," *Journal of the Mount Sinai Hospital,* May–June, 1961.

MCNEILL, DAVID, "Developmental Psycholinguistics," in *The Genesis of Language,* Cambridge: M.I.T., 1966.

——, "The Creation of Language," *Discovery,* July, 1966.

MILLER, GEORGE A., "Some Psychological Studies of Grammar," *American Psychologist,* November, 1962.

——, "Linguistic Communication as a Biological Process," in *Biology and the Human Sciences,* Oxford: Oxford University Press, 1972.

——, "The Psycholinguists," *Encounter,* July, 1964.

——, "Communication and the Structure of Behavior," in *Disorders of Communication,* Vol. XLII, Research Publications, Association for Research in Nervous and Mental Disease, 1964.

ORR, WILLIAM F., and CAPPANNARI, STEPHEN C., "The Emergence of Language," *American Anthropologist,* April, 1964.

PREMACK, DAVID, "The Education of Sarah," *Psychology Today,* September, 1970.

——, "A Functional Analysis of Language," *Journal of the Experimental Analysis of Behavior,* July, 1970.

——, "Language in Chimpanzee?" *Science,* May 1, 1971.

——, and SCHWARTZ, ARTHUR, "Preparations for Discussing Behaviorism with Chimpanzee," in *The Genesis of Language,* Cambridge: M.I.T., 1966.

SEBEOK, THOMAS A., "Discussion of Communication Processes," in *Social Communication Among Primates*, Chicago: University of Chicago, 1967.

XX. Study of Man: The Power of the Past, the Potential for Change

BRANNIGAN, CHRISTOPHER R., and HUMPHRIES, DAVID A., "Human Nonverbal Behavior, a Means of Communication," in *Ethological Studies of Child Behavior*, Cambridge University Press, 1972.

CHANCE, M. R. A., "A Biological Perspective on Convulsions," *Colloques Internationaux du Centre National de la Recherche Scientifique*, No. 112, 1963.

DEMENT, WILLIAM C., "Toward an Evolutionary Theory of Dreaming," *American Journal of Psychiatry*, August, 1966.

ESSER, A. H., "Interactional Hierarchy and Power Structure on a Psychiatric Ward," in *Behavior Studies in Psychiatry*, New York: Pergamon Press, 1970.

FOX, ROBIN, "Human Mating Patterns in Ethological Perspective," *Animals*, July, 1967.

———, "In the Beginning: Aspects of Hominid Behavioural Evolution," *Man*, September, 1967.

GEIST, VALERIUS, *Mountain Sheep—A Study in Behavior and Evolution*, University of Chicago Press, 1971.

GOOD, ROBERT A., "Disorders of the Immune System," *Hospital Practice*, January, 1967.

GRANT, EWAN C., "An Ethological Description of Some Schizophrenic Patterns of Behaviour," *Proceedings of the Leeds Symposium on Behavioural Disorders*, March, 1965.

———, "Human Facial Expression," *Man*, December, 1969.

HAMBURG, DAVID A., "The Relevance of Recent Evolutionary Changes to Human Stress Biology," in *Social Life of Early Man*, Chicago: Aldine, 1961.

HOLLOWAY, R. L., "Human Aggression," *Natural History*, December, 1967.

HUMPHRIES, D. C., HUMPHRIES, D. A., and DRIVER, P. M., "Erratic Display as a Device Against Predators," *Science*, June 30, 1967.

HUTT, CORINNE, "Exploration and Play in Children," *Symposia of the Zoological Society of London*, No. 18, 1966.

———, "Specific and Diversive Exploration," in *Advances in Child Development and Behavior*, Vol. 5, New York: Academic Press, 1970.

JONES, N. G. BLURTON, "An Ethological Study of Some Aspects of Social Behaviour of Children in Nursery School," in *Primate Ethology*, Chicago: Aldine, 1967.

———, "Emotional Behaviour in Children and Monkeys," *Animals*, November, 1966.

———, "Nonverbal Communication in Children," in *Nonverbal Communica-*

tion, Cambridge University Press, 1972.

——, "An Ethologist Looks at Socialisation and Nursery School," in *The Integration of the Child into a Social World,* Cambridge University Press, 1972.

——, and LEACH, GILL M., "Behaviour of Children and Their Mothers at Separation and Greeting," in *Ethological Studies of Child Behaviour,* Cambridge University Press, 1972.

MACKENZIE, NORMAN, "Sweating It Out With B-P," *New Statesman,* October 15, 1965.

McGREW, W. C., "Aspects of Social Development in Nursery School Children, with Emphasis on Introduction to the Group," in *Ethological Studies of Child Behavior,* Cambridge University Press, 1972.

PRICE, JOHN, "The Dominance Hierarchy and the Evolution of Mental Illness," *The Lancet,* July 29, 1967.

——, "Genetics of the Affective Illnesses," *Hospital Medicine,* July, 1968.

REYNOLDS, V., "Open Groups in Hominid Evolution," *Man,* December, 1966.

ROFFWARG, HOWARD P., *et al.,* "Ontogenetic Development of the Human Sleep-Dream Cycle," *Science,* April 29, 1966.

SCHNEIRLA, T. C., "Instinct and Aggression," *Natural History,* December, 1966.

SOUTHWICK, CHARLES L., "Rhesus Monkeys in North India," in *Primate Behavior,* New York: Holt, Rinehart and Winston, 1965.

TIGER, LIONEL, *Men in Groups,* New York: Random House, 1969.

——, and FOX, ROBIN, *The Imperial Animal,* New York: Holt, Rinehart and Winston, 1971.

——, "The Zoological Perspective in Social Science," *Man,* March, 1966.

TINBERGEN, N., "Aggression and Fear in the Normal Sexual Behavior of Some Animals," in *The Pathology and Treatment of Sexual Deviation,* New York: Oxford, 1964.

——, "On War and Peace in Animals and Man," *Science,* June 28, 1968.

WHITE, ROBERT W., "Motivation Reconsidered: The Concept of Competence," *Psychological Review,* September, 1959.

Epilogue: The Future of Man, an Ex-Hunter, in a World That Has No Place for Hunters

ALEXANDER, CHRISTOPHER, "The City as a Mechanism for Sustaining Human Contact," Institute of Urban and Regional Planning, University of California, Berkeley, *Working Paper No. 50,* October, 1966.

DILLON, WILTON S., *Gifts and Nations,* The Hague: Mouton, 1968.

GRAHAM, MICHAEL, "Crowds and the Like in Vertebrates," *Human Relations,* Vol. 17, No. 4, 1964.

JONGE, DERK DE, "Applied Hodology," *Landscape,* Winter, 1967–68.

MASCIONI, JOHN, *Report of Probes Conference on Government Office Buildings, 15–17 June 1967,* Institute for Applied Technology, National Bureau of Standards.

MORISON, ROBERT S., "Where Is Biology Taking Us?" *Science*, January 27, 1967.

PARR, A. E., "Urbanity and the Urban Scene," *Landscape*, Spring, 1967.

PFEIFFER, JOHN E., "Problems, Too, Have Problems," *Fortune*, October, 1961.

———, "Machines That Man Can Talk With," *Fortune*, May, 1964.

———, *New Look at Education: Systems Analysis in Our Schools and Colleges*, New York: Odyssey, 1968.

SAGAN, CARL, "Direct Contact Among Galactic Civilizations by Relativistic Interstellar Spaceflight," *Planetary and Space Science*, Vol. II, 1963.

———, SAGAN, LINDA SALZMAN, and DRAKE, FRANK, "A Message from Earth," *Science*, February 25, 1972.

TANNER, J. M., "Earlier Maturation in Man," *Scientific American*, January, 1968.

Index

Picture Credits

Environmental Science Services Administration, 22
Stuart A. Altmann, 27, 64, 288, 299, 302, 339, 479
Elwyn L. Simons, 33, 37
San Diego Zoo, 45
National Geographic Society, 59, 93, 94(top), 310, 311
Bryan Patterson & the Harvard News Office, 72
Phillip V. Tobias & Alun R. Hughes, 76, 77(center)
Phillip V. Tobias & Paul Keen, 77(top)
Zdenek Burian, 77(bottom), 108(bottom), 110, 185, 187, 190, 243
American Anthropological Association, 79
Charles Brain, 82
Revil Mason, 94(center)
American Museum of Natural History, 94(bottom), 108(top), 184, 196, 224,
     261, 262, 263, 271
Irven DeVore, 100, 101, 122, 286, 291, 292, 295, 298, 301, 384, 387, 392, 398
Henry DeLumley, 113, 142
George Schaller, 131
F. C. Howell, 136, 139
Zbigniew Rajchel and Wanda Steslicka-Mydlarska, Warsaw Univ., Poland, 175
Smithsonian Institute, 192
François Bordes, 201, 205
Don E. Crabtree, 226, 409, 410
Leslie Freeman, 235
Joe Ben Wheat, 247
French Government Tourist Office, 254, 255
University of Wisconsin Regional Primate Research Center, 324, 325, 328
Richard Wright, 333

About the Author

Research for *The Emergence of Man* began a decade ago when John Pfeiffer undertook to investigate the much neglected area of prehistory, convinced that despite all controversy and calculation, "we know very little about ourselves as a species and most of what we think we know is false." He concentrated first on archeology, with digs in the Rockies and at two French sites, "rather hair-raising" explorations of art caves in France and Spain, and three trips to Africa to visit the sites of the earliest known pre-men. He then began a related study of the behavior of living species—with adventures such as keeping watch over savanna baboons for a month to glean clues about man's own early savanna days.

Mr. Pfeiffer, who has recently joined the staff of Livingston College at Rutgers University as professor of anthropology, was science and medicine editor of *Newsweek* before his World War II service, then science director of CBS and an editorial board member of *Scientific American* until 1950. He has served as a consultant for the National Science Foundation, the Educational Development Center, UNESCO, and several universities, among them the University of Chicago and Princeton. Among his many awards are a Guggenheim Foundation grant, Fulbright Fellowship, Wenner-Gren Foundation for Anthropological Research grant, and a Carnegie Corporation grant which made possible the research for this book. He is a member and past president of the National Association of Science Writers. Among his other books are: *The Human Brain, From Galaxies to Man,* and *The Search for Early Man.*

74 75   10 9 8 7 6 5 4